Contemporary Debate

J. W. Patterson
University of Kentucky

David Zarefsky
Northwestern University

Houghton Mifflin Company   **Boston**
Dallas   Geneva, Illinois   Hopewell, New Jersey
Palo Alto   London

For our daughters—

Elizabeth Leigh Patterson

and

Beth Ellen Zarefsky

Library of Congress Catalog Card Number: 82-82020

ISBN: 0-395-33164-1

Contents

UNIT TWO
THEORY AND PRACTICE OF ACADEMIC DEBATE

UNIT THREE
THE CONTEXT OF ARGUMENTATION AND DEBATE

Preface

Contemporary Debate attempts to reflect and refine current theory and practice in argumentation and debate. It draws on our experience as researchers and teachers in this field, both for our theoretical formulations and for our suggestions about how students can learn to become more effective arguers.

Five basic principles have guided us in preparing this book. First, we believe that proficiency in argumentation and debate is both a skill and an art. It is a skill because it can be learned, practiced, and refined, and throughout the book we shall advise students on how to become better arguers and debaters. It is also an art because it is creative. While our advice may apply generally, each situation an advocate faces is unique. Effective arguments in one situation may be unsound in another. It is impossible, therefore, to prescribe any universally applicable rules or principles of argumentation. Rather, students need to develop the conceptual apparatus to apply general principles to specific occasions, modifying the principles as required by circumstance. Such patterns of creative and critical thought can be nurtured only if students clearly understand the underlying theories of the field. Hence, this book blends theoretical explanation and practical advice.

Second, we believe that debate is a subset of general argumentation. In order to become talented in debate, students must master the basic terms and theories common to all argumentation. For this reason we devote the first unit of the book to an understanding of general argumentation, the nature of arguments and arguing. A firm grasp of the principles of argumentation is necessary as a prelude to the more specific study of academic debate.

Third, while academic debate is a part of general argumentation, it involves highly specialized applications of general principles. Textbooks that focus exclusively on general argumentation are therefore of limited use to students of academic debate. Unit Two describes how the norms and conventions of academic debate adapt argumentation to a specialized forum and then it explores in detail the processes of analysis, case construction, attack and defense, communication, and evaluation within that specialized forum.

Fourth, we believe that, properly conceived, argumentation and debate are methods for testing the probable truth of hypotheses offered by advocates. When empirical questions are involved, the probable truth of a statement can be determined by direct observation. When the issue involves the uncertain and contingent, however, argumentation becomes the path to probable truth. An arguer puts forth a hypothesis that is subjected to rigorous challenge by another advocate. Hypotheses withstanding this test can be regarded as true and acted upon with a greater degree of confidence, particularly if the test occurred within the formal and carefully controlled context of debate. Since we regard debate as an exercise in testing hypotheses, we have explained theoretical and strategic notions from that point of view. At the same time, we have made clear those matters on which another point of view would lead to different advice and have explored the nature of those differences.

Fifth, although argumentation and debate are skills enjoyable to acquire for their own sake, we believe that they contribute to the development of individuals and to the resolution of society's disputes within the public forum. We therefore conclude the book with an exploration of our ultimate purpose in helping students learn to become more effective advocates.

In the preparation of this book, we have drawn not only on our own experiences but on valuable insight we have received from many others through the years, beginning with our own teachers and coaches of debate. We are especially indebted to the many intercollegiate debaters and students in our argumentation classes at Northwestern University and the University of Kentucky, on whom we have experimented with many of these ideas. Our thoughts about the theory and practice of academic debate have also been sharpened by interactions with our colleagues in other universities and by our annual involvement with the work of high school debaters at the National High School Institute in Speech at Northwestern University and the Kentucky High School Speech Institute at the University of Kentucky.

Although the final responsibility for this work is ours, it has benefited greatly from the careful attention of others. The entire manuscript was read by Bill Henderson, Director of Forensics, University of Northern Iowa; Thomas Kane, Department of Speech and Theatre Arts, University of Pittsburgh; Lucy M. Keele, Professor of Communications, California State University, Fullerton. In addition, major portions of the book were reviewed and critiqued by Erwin Chemerinsky, DePaul University; G. Thomas Goodnight, Northwestern University; David B. Hingstman, Northwestern University; Diana B. Prentice, Topeka Public Schools (Kansas); Richard B. Sodikow, Bronx High School of Science (New York).

The work would not have come to fruition without the dedicated services of several competent secretaries. Earlier versions of the manuscript were typed by Barbara Alt, Nancy Ames, Irene Klotz, and Mary Ralston. We are indebted to all of them and especially to Carol Mikkelsen who skillfully prepared the final manuscript on an exceedingly tight schedule.

Finally, we wish to thank all those at Houghton Mifflin who have worked on the development of this book since we first proposed to write a debate text a decade ago. This book is far different from what we would have written then. We have been encouraged to persevere in the project and to incorporate recent advances in debate theory and practice, in no small measure because of the continued support we received from the editors at Houghton Mifflin. We must confess that there were occasions when their faith in the potential of our ideas greatly exceeded our own.

J.W.P.   D.Z.
Lexington and Evanston

Unit One

Understanding General Argumentation

Chapter 1

Introducing Argumentation and Debate

Friends dispute the merits of a recent movie they have seen. To one, it is a vibrant, artistic statement about the human condition. The other finds it only mildly entertaining and lacking in artistic merit. In discussing the movie, they make clear their judgments and criticize each other's implicit standards of art.

The president of the United States appears before a joint session of Congress to plead for his economic program. He describes current inflation and unemployment and promises that his proposals will correct these evils. For the unconvinced, he also explains why things will get worse if his program is not adopted and current trends continue.

"Authorities" on television commercials promise that certain products will ease minor pains, provide a new source of recreation, or be useful to one's daily work. Demonstrations, statistics, and testimonials from satisfied customers are introduced to back up this promise.

Lawyers disagree about which of two competing principles should govern a case. One argues that the First Amendment's protection of freedom of speech should apply, whereas the other thinks that property rights are paramount. Each lawyer identifies the precedents and underlying assumptions supporting his or her position. A judge is asked to choose between the two.

This book is about interactions among people such as those in the examples above. Like presidents and lawyers, people disagree, try to change one another's belief or secure a favorable judgment from some other audience, and proceed by setting forth claims and offering reasons for them. More precisely, we can say that they are engaged in *argumentation*. Sometimes the occasions are formal and public, and the results affect an entire society. At other times the occasions may be extremely casual, the outcomes trivial, and no one affected other than the actual participants in dispute. But the basic activity is the same.

This book is about argumentation. Our approach is descriptive, explaining what happens when people disagree and try to change the minds of others. It is also normative, helping you develop skills as a participant in and evaluator of argumentation.

First you need to understand some key terms. Argumentation, as we have said, is setting forth claims and offering reasons for them in an attempt to influence the beliefs or behavior of other people. This enterprise may be examined from either of two points of view. One focuses on the activity in which people are engaged—*arguing;* the other refers to the discourse they produce—*arguments.*

We have also said that argumentation takes place in both informal and formal situations. When the situation is structured, when there are clear rules of procedure, and when the choice between advocates is made by a third party rather than by the participants themselves, then *debate* is taking place. Debate is a specialized form of argumentation.

In this chapter we shall explore the key terms of argumentation: *arguing, arguments,* and *debate.* Through these terms, we shall lay the foundation for the theory on which this book is based.

Arguing

Arguing as a Process

Arguing is a particular type of human behavior. Just as we think, hear, eat, and read, we constantly argue. We engage in this behavior in order to accomplish some goal, such as reassuring ourselves, making decisions, gratifying our egos, or altering others' beliefs.

Arguing occurs in interaction with others. People argue when they hold beliefs they think are incompatible and when they wish to achieve agreement by communicating about their differences. This definition makes it possible to distinguish arguing from other types of interaction. For example, if people have identical beliefs and merely state them, they do not argue. If people state their beliefs, discover that they are different, and then decide to go their separate ways (agreeing to disagree), they do not argue. Or if people do not ever state their beliefs but communicate with one another only to regulate their daily routines, they do not argue. The two factors, then, that distinguish arguing from other forms of human interaction are, first, that people hold what they think are incompatible beliefs and, second, that they wish to achieve agreement through verbal means.

Arguing can take place in almost any social situation. Family members argue about managing the household. Husbands and wives argue about how to meet their personal and career needs. Friends argue about issues that are important to their relationship. Citizens argue about matters of public policy. Theologians and philosophers argue about principles of value. Scientists and historians argue about what may be considered true.

Preconditions for Arguing

Whenever people argue, certain conditions are present. We shall discuss five preconditions.

The Existence of Controversy.   People do not dispute what is certain. If we know some fact beyond any possibility of doubt, there is no reason to argue about that fact. But we can be certain about few, if any, things. If we share the same thoughts or beliefs and are confident of them, however, we treat them as if they were certainties. Until something happens to cause the belief to be questioned, there is no reason to argue.

To explain this first condition another way, for every statement an arguer makes, an opposing arguer could make at least one counterstatement. Although arguing is an attempt to influence belief, it does not automatically command belief because arguing always permits the opportunity for response. In short, arguing occurs in situations in which there is controversy.

Whether a controversy is present is a matter for the people in the situation to determine. An external observer might think that there is no real disagreement between two people, but as long as those people think that there is, they will act accordingly.

Non-trivial Controversy.   In our daily lives, we are uncertain about many matters, yet we do not regard them as worth arguing about. For most people, questions about what to eat for breakfast, what path to take in walking to school, and how to spend leisure time are usually not regarded as momentous. They typically do not provoke the sorts of disagreements that give rise to arguing; people tend instead to reach agreement by chance, taking whichever choice presents itself first. In contrast, arguing takes effort. It involves the mind both in conceiving and expressing beliefs and in processing the responses from other persons. It involves the ego in a relationship with others. People avoid these efforts when the stakes are not worth it. So when people argue, we can conclude that they regard the controversy as non-trivial.

Participants' Desire for Agreement.   As we have noted, people can observe that a controversy exists and then simply retire from the situation, agreeing to disagree. They can show contempt for each other's point of view by dismissing it out of hand. They can be so indifferent to each other that neither cares what the other thinks. None of these responses leads to arguing. When people argue, it means that they care enough to want others to agree with their own beliefs. Sometimes the others are participants in the controversy; sometimes they are members of an audience observing the dispute.

Agreement Valued Only if Freely Given.   Arguing is a risky means of gaining another person's assent. Our efforts might fail, or worse yet, the other person might succeed in convincing us to discard our own belief and to adopt another. If agreement were our only objective, there would be more certain methods to obtain it, ranging from coercion and intimidation to bribery and subliminal stimulation. When people argue, it means that they value one another. An arguer wants the other person to agree, but only if the assent is freely given.

No Simpler Means of Resolving Disagreement.   Sometimes controversies can be settled by other methods. If the dispute concerns the current outdoor temperature, there is no reason to argue about it; both disputants will readily agree that a thermometer can answer the question. If the question is the margin by which Abraham Lincoln won the 1860 presidential election, reference works can be consulted to find the answer. Many controversies can be similarly settled by direct verification or by consulting accepted references.

Arguing, in contrast, occurs when the dispute cannot be settled by simpler means. And many disputes cannot—because they involve the future (which party is likely to win the next election?); matters of value (is individual freedom more important than the public good?); criteria for reaching a decision (should experience or a mathematical model be our guide?); or the accuracy of a given label used to describe a set of phenomena (should the state of the economy be described as a recession?).

When these five preconditions are satisfied, people argue. We should make clear that arguing does not imply contentiousness; people are not being impolite or uncivil when they argue with one another. Quite the contrary, they are indicating that they wish to reach agreement in a way that recognizes and respects the belief of the other person. The negative stereotypes that equate arguing with hostility or impoliteness are actually referring to a perversion of argument—a situation in which people repeatedly proclaim their own beliefs without much concern for whether, or how, others come to agree.

Procedural Norms of Arguing

We seldom articulate all our basic assumptions when we argue. Nevertheless, some basic assumptions are implicitly made when we choose this method to resolve disputes, reach decisions, or make choices.

Cooperativeness.   Perhaps the most fundamental assumption is that arguing is a *cooperative* enterprise. It may seem strange to talk about arguing as cooperation, since by popular belief the arguer is aggressive, hostile, and stubborn. But such a person actually has *every* reason not to argue, thinking it far better to maintain his or her own position and let the other person remain condemned to error. People argue because they think they know what is right, but they cannot be certain, and they want to make the best decision. So they agree to participate with other people in a procedure to test their belief.

If two people argue, they share the goal of achieving the best possible decision. Furthermore, they agree that, in order to reach that goal, each person's task is to make the strongest case possible for one of the competing positions. If our adversary's strongest case fails to shake our belief, then that belief—having withstood the test—is likely to be the stronger. On the other hand, if an adversary's case turns out to be stronger than our own, we know that our position is probably not the better of the two. We can then consider some other position and subject it to the same sort of scrutiny.

It is useful to think of arguing as roleplaying. In order to reach the best possible decision, people agree to play the roles of advocates committed to opposing views. Out of the argumentative interplay, the participants hope that the best choice will emerge. In many situations, people play roles in which they quite sincerely believe. But it is not uncommon to find people self-consciously assuming a role in order to provide a good test of another's claim. When someone plays the role of devil's advocate, he or she supports a position not out of personal belief but out of a desire to test another person's statements. A person who makes an assumption only for the sake of argument is doing much the same thing.

In short, cooperation is fundamental to arguing. The arguers share a common goal of making the best decision, and they share a commitment to reach that goal by pitting the strongest possible cases against one another.

Bilaterality.   A second underlying assumption is *bilaterality.* This term means that both parties to a dispute have opportunities to influence each other or a neutral observer. Neither physical strength nor social status nor any other external factor will determine the outcome; the outcome will depend only on the strength of the argument itself.

You can understand the significance of bilaterality by imagining its opposite. If one person were totally resistant to influence, it would make no difference how good were the reasons given by the other. The first person would still persevere in his or her belief or conduct, dismissing any challenges without giving them even the briefest consideration. In such a situation there would be no real incentive to argue because the result would make no difference. Influence would be felt in one direction only. From a parent's point of view, the classic case of unilaterality occurs when a small child repeats, "But I *want* to play in the street," even after the parent has explained all the reasons why such behavior is unsafe. From a child's point of view, unilaterality is epitomized by a parent's "because I said so" in the face of the child's seemingly irrefutable reasons to the contrary.

Significant corollaries follow from this assumption. First, bilaterality provides the incentive for each participant to marshal the most persuasive grounds for belief, rather than merely to accept the first ideas that come to mind. In an attempt to defeat us, our adversary will look for weak defenses. Realizing this fact, we need to be especially critical of our own arguing. We try to offer only those claims that we think will withstand scrutiny.

Second, bilaterality means that arguing involves risks. Just as we think we are right and wish to influence the thought or action of others, we recognize the equal possibility that others—also thinking themselves to be right—will succeed in influencing us instead. We would not willingly expose ourselves to the risk of being proved wrong if we did not wish to give our viewpoint the strongest possible test.

Reflective Judgment.   A final assumption made when people argue is that they want *reflective judgment*. When a man decides which tie to wear on a given day, he does not care to reconstruct the mental processes that led to that choice. The final decision itself is all that matters. On the other hand, when we argue about something, we want not only a decision but also a decision that can be explained to ourselves and to others. We therefore use a process that makes evident all the grounds for a decision; the justifications are laid out during the course of the controversy. Our reasoning processes as well as our conclusions are open for critical examination by others. A goal of arguing, then, is the testing and criticism of claims made by the parties to a dispute, so that the final decision will be carefully reached and hence made with greater confidence. In this sense we can say that arguing is an instrument of critical, rather than impulsive, choice.

Arguments

We have been describing arguing as a specific process of communication. The outcomes of this process are arguments. The arguing process itself is ephemeral—it ends when a dispute is settled. But the arguments outlast the specific controversy that gave them birth. They remain available for repetition, refutation, or analysis by other persons or at some other time.

Argument is a specific type of discourse. By *discourse* we mean words produced by one person in an attempt to generate an intended meaning in the mind of another. Discourse is the product of verbal interaction. The passage you are now reading is a sample of discourse—our attempt to cause the term *argument* to evoke the same meaning in your mind as it does in ours.

Under the broad heading of discourse, several different types can be identified. *Expository* discourse seeks to convey information or to explain what is difficult to understand; this chapter is an example of exposition. *Narrative* discourse tells what happened; it relates the details of events in an orderly progression. A chronicle of the steps leading to the last presidential election would be an example of narration. *Descriptive* discourse tries to evoke a certain mood or emotional reaction in the listener or reader. An account of conditions in the Catholic slums of Northern Ireland that attempted to create a certain mental picture in the reader's or listener's mind would be an example of description.

Argument is a category of discourse different from each of these three types. Whereas exposition aims for understanding, narration for sequential awareness, and description for emotion, argument aims for assent. An argument consists of a *claim* on the belief of a listener or reader, together with support for that claim. Discussions of these and the other components of argument follow.

Claim

The claim is the statement that the arguer wants the listener or audience to accept. If a listener were to ask, "What are you trying to prove?" or "What do you want me to believe?", the answer would be a claim. The claim is offered as a hypothesis, a proposal about what is probably true. The process of arguing tests this hypothesis in order to permit a judgment of whether it is probably true and hence worthy of belief.

Usually the claim is explicit. It is possible, however, for the claim to be implicit in the structure of argument. If, for instance, a speaker were to denounce foreign aid by saying, "Foreign aid has supported dictators in Iran, South Korea, and El Salvador," the speaker has not made any overt claim. He or she has merely recited factual statements. Still, it is clear that the speaker supports the implicit claim, "Foreign aid has been wrongly spent to prop up dictatorships." In Chapter 2 we shall explore the nature of claims in more detail and see how they relate to other elements of argument.

Evidence

The second element of argument is the supporting material, or evidence on which a claim depends. Evidence is the raw material of an argument, the data on which the argument is based. There is potentially no limit to the types of supporting evidence that can be drawn on in an argument. Examples of wasteful government programs would constitute evidence for the claim that the federal budget ought to be cut. Other forms of evidence for the same claim might include: statistical distribution of government funds to low-priority projects, citations from relevant statutes outlining the function of specific government agencies, and testimony or assertions of authorities. In short, any information drawn on to establish a claim falls under the heading of evidence. Chapter 3 will examine the nature of evidence in more detail.

Inference

The third element in a unit of argument is the *inference*, which links the supporting evidence and claim. An inference is a license that authorizes the arguer to make a certain claim on the basis of the evidence offered. This portion of the argument also indicates how the evidence truly does support the claim.

In our example of American foreign aid to dictatorships, the inference would be that "Iran, South Korea, and El Salvador are typical recipients of American military aid." This inference allows us to dismiss the possibility that the speaker selected the only three cases in which the United States had supported dictators. Believing that the examples are typical, we could conclude that the evidence did indeed lend support to the claim. If we had used a testimonial quotation instead of a series of examples as our form of supporting material, then the inference might be a statement such as "Senator X is a reliable authority on the subject of American foreign aid."

It is crucial to be able to identify the inference in a particular argument, for only by doing so can we know whether the reasoning process used in constructing the argument is valid. If the reasoning is invalid, the argument is unsound, even though the supporting evidence may be true. If there is no link between the evidence and the claim, then the claim could be false. Suppose that Iran, South Korea, and El Salvador had not been typical cases. Then, even if it were true that the United States had supported dictators in those countries, the general conclusion about the effects of our foreign aid might be false.

Identifying the inference is difficult because it is seldom stated explicitly. The supporting evidence is presented and the claim is usually stated; from these two parts of the argument the audience must often decide which inference has been employed. Among the more common inferences are: X is a sign of Y; X is a cause of Y; X, Y, and Z are representative of the total population Q; if X, Y, and Z are similar in all essential respects, then they are probably similar in the respect under discussion; and X is a reliable authority concerning Y. We shall examine these inferential patterns in detail in Chapter 4. For now, it is enough to note that each of these statements asserts a relationship between evidence and claim, entitling a person to make the claim on the basis of the evidence offered. Each form of inference has tests and rules to determine its validity, and we shall examine these in Chapter 4 as well.

Context

The fourth component of a unit of argument, its *context,* is often the most neglected. Context refers to the set of underlying assumptions or values on which the entire argument depends. These are almost never stated; sometimes they are not even realized by the advocate. Yet they are always present. No argument occurs in a vacuum; it is always based on some beliefs or axioms.

When President Lyndon Johnson claimed that the United States must stay in Vietnam because of commitments made by three earlier presidents, he based his argument on certain unstated assumptions. To recognize them, consider his argument with respect to the component parts we have discussed so far. Had Johnson offered specific evidence, it would have consisted of the actual statements of President Dwight D. Eisenhower, President John F. Kennedy, and himself. Since the claim is "Three Presidents have committed the United States to Vietnam," then the inference licensing this statement is, "Eisenhower's, Kennedy's, and Johnson's statements are signs of a national commitment" — as opposed to statements that are, say, purely symbolic reassurance for American allies or campaign oratory intended for domestic consumption.

So far the argument appears clear enough. The presidents did make the statements, and these statements do represent commitments of the United States government. Yet this argument was especially unsuccessful in convincing at least some segments of the population that President Johnson was right. The doubters questioned not the content of argument but its underlying assumptions: that historical consistency is inherently good and that reneging on one's commitments is always bad. The argument depends on these assumptions, which can be supported or attacked. Should someone be able to refute them, the argument fails. If it were established, for example, that a policy of blind adherence to the past is morally bankrupt, then President Johnson's argument would be undercut, even though its internal structure is sound. Every argument depends on some set of underlying assumptions, and we shall examine these in more detail in Chapter 4.

Summary: The Components of Argument

We have suggested that arguments are a form of discourse that has four major components. The claim is the statement that the arguer wants to induce the audience to believe. Supporting evidence provides the raw materials, the grounds for accepting the claim. The inference links the supporting materials to the claim, giving the audience a warrant to conclude that the claim is true on the basis of the evidence. And the context consists of the underlying assumptions on which the argument depends.

We have visually represented the components of argument in Figure 1.1. Notice that the evidence supports the claim and that the inference authorizes this relationship. The context of the argument surrounds the internal structure so that we can say that the argument is embedded in a context.

Figure 1.1

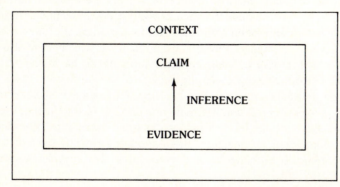

Arguments encountered in discourse are seldom laid out with the neatness and precision that this discussion may imply. Some parts may simply be assumed; other parts may need to be pieced together from different aspects of a conversation. There may have been interruptions, questions, or tangential discussion during the course of an argument's development. But the discourse can always be recast into the form of arguments, and doing so permits us to understand its internal structure.

Debate

Debate as Formalized Argumentation

When argumentation occurs in a formal setting, the result is usually debate. In this category of argumentation, speaking opportunities are formalized. Rather than speaking for varying lengths, interrupting one another, and taking turns as in ordinary conversations, participants speak at assigned times and for designated amounts of time. Likewise, the specific subject in dispute is usually, though not always, formally stated.

Perhaps the most important feature of debate is that the advocates do not attempt to convince each other but appeal to a presumably neutral third party. The third party may be an impartial arbitrator, a specific group, or the public at large. In any case, the decision is made by outsiders who choose among the participants, rather than by the participants who reach some compromise or consensus among themselves.

Debate, then, is a specific situation in which the procedure of argumentation is employed to reach decisions. It is an arena in which the general principles of argumentation can be applied. An understanding of how people argue and what an argument is should be helpful to anyone planning to participate in debate. Debate and argumentation relate to each other as part to whole.

Varieties and Formats of Debate

Many varieties of debate can be found in our society. Perhaps the most prominent is political debate. In Congress or a state legislature, consideration of proposed laws takes place in a system laden with rules that fix the amount of time available, the way the time is to be divided, the circumstances under which discussion will cease, and the advocate's duty to make remarks germane to the matter at hand. The specific bill or resolution becomes the subject of debate.

During political campaigns, another type of debate can be observed. Candidates for a given office frequently debate one another face to face or answer questions submitted to them by a panel of experts. There is no specifically stated subject—except whether one candidate or another should be elected—but arguing occurs according to formal rules and procedures. These typically concern such matters as the number and type of formal statements, the length of the question periods, and the order of speaking. The presidential debates of 1960, 1976, and 1980 have undoubtedly encouraged candidates in primary elections and in lesser campaigns to submit their differences to the voters in this format.

Legal debate is another common type. In the courtroom, attorneys debate one another in an attempt to make the strongest possible cases for their clients. In a criminal case, the subject at issue is the defendant's guilt or innocence. In a civil case, it is whether the plaintiff is entitled to relief under the rules of the law. Arguing, once again, takes place according to carefully structured rules concerning such matters as the standards of evidence, the burden of proof, the pertinence of questions, and the nature of cross-examination.

Scholarly debate is yet another variety. Scientists, philosophers, historians, and critics debate in professional organizations and publications. They argue according to procedures that are accepted by their disciplines, and they try to convince the broader scholarly community that their position is right.

In public debate, the subject concerns a specific matter of public policy, and opposing advocates argue in an attempt to convince the general public. During the 1970s the television program "The Advocates" offered public debates. Pro and con newspaper articles, in which writers take opposing positions on some question, are another example of public debate.

One of the most popular forms of debate is academic debate—that is, the use of debate as an educational exercise. The outcome of academic debate is not a particular policy decision or scientific judgment. Rather, debate is a means of improving the argumentative skills of the participants. Thousands of high school and college students participate each year in academic debate. Unit Two will apply general principles of argumentation to the specific context of academic debate.

Even within academic debate, however, there are numerous variations in format and approach. The most typical format has these features: (1) the debate is concerned with a specific issue of public policy that is identified and formally stated in advance; (2) two teams of two advocates each support and oppose the statement of the issue; and (3) the final decision is based not on the judge's view of the subject but on the judge's comparative estimate of the skills of the debaters.

Recently, however, innovations in format and approach have gained popularity. One innovation involves the use of questions that do not relate to public policy but that typically raise conflicts between values. The Cross-Examination Debate Association (CEDA) features this format. Arguments tend to be concerned with the relative ordering of values or the desirability of a particular value, rather than the question of what action ought to be taken. Another recent innovation is a one-on-one exchange patterned after the Lincoln-Douglas debates. In this format, each speaker presents a constructive position, questions the opponent, replies to questions, refutes the opponent's position, and defends his or her own position. Debates in this format may also employ subjects other than matters of policy choice.

Different formats emphasize the cultivation of different skills. In any case, academic debate represents the application of general theories and principles of argumentation to a specific laboratory setting. The practice of formal debate both applies and modifies many theoretical beliefs about argumentation.

Summary

Arguing is a particular type of human interaction that occurs when people hold what they think are incompatible beliefs and when they desire to secure agreement by communicating about their differences. It takes place in a variety of situations, ranging from the most casual and informal to the most highly structured and formal. Arguing occurs when there is a controversy that is nontrivial, when the participants care about one another and seek one another's free assent, and when there are no simpler means available for resolving the dispute. Although arguers seldom acknowledge it, their activity is guided by certain procedural norms, including cooperativeness, bilaterality, and reflective judgment.

The products of arguing are arguments, samples of discourse. These products outlast the original controversies in which they were created and become available for inspection or use by other people and at other times. As a unit of discourse, an argument has four basic components. The claim is the statement of belief that the audience is asked to accept. Evidence consists of the raw material, the data, on which the claim is based. An inference is a link between the evidence and the claim; it authorizes the claim on the basis of the data. Finally, the context of an argument consists of those unstated but basic assumptions on which the entire structure depends. Seldom will you find actual arguments laid out with all these components in everyday discourse, but you should be able to recast everyday discourse into argumentative form.

Debate is formalized argumentation, characterized by procedural guidelines and by decisions that are made by a third party rather than by the disputants themselves. Debate takes place in a variety of formats and forums, including politics, law, and education.

The next several chapters will enable you to understand in more detail the components of argument. Then we shall turn our attention more closely to how these arguments are put together in the process of arguing.

Questions for Discussion

1. Under what conditions might people choose not to argue but instead to resolve their differences by other means?
2. We have described arguing as a cooperative activity. Why is it frequently regarded as a hostile activity?

3. How would a weakness in claim, evidence, inference, or context undermine the argument of which it is a part?
4. What are the strengths and weaknesses of debate, as opposed to less formalized argumentation?
5. Which varieties of debate are the most common? Which are most influential? In which have you been a participant or a member of the audience?

Chapter 2

Claims

A person who makes an argument hopes to convince an audience to agree to the claim. Since it is the claim for which assent is sought, the claim is usually the most prominent feature of the argument. This chapter discusses the nature of claims and how they fit together to make structures of argument. We shall begin by examining the types of claims and then discuss the related concepts of resolutions, issues, burdens of proof, and presumption.

Types of Claims

Claims can be divided into four major types. *Claims of fact* involve the truth or falsity of reports about the world; they are descriptive. *Claims of meaning* concern how a given situation or set of data is to be defined or viewed; they are interpretive. *Claims of value* express degrees of preference and judge whether something is right or wrong; they are evaluative. Finally, *claims of policy* suggest that a proposed course of action should or should not be undertaken; they are advisory. Depending on the context of an argument, a given claim may fall into more than one of these categories, but the distinctions call attention to the different types of work that claims do.

Claims of Fact

A claim of fact describes a view of reality. In deciding whether to believe a claim of fact, a listener or reader will ask, "Is it accurate?" The purpose of the argument is to establish whether the stated description is correct.

In the last chapter we suggested that people do not argue about matters that can be resolved empirically. It might seem strange, then, to think of factual claims as parts of arguments. If someone asserted, "The rate of inflation is slowing this year," you might think it possible to test this claim without recourse to argument. But a more careful inspection of the claim will suggest otherwise. What is "the rate of inflation"? Which of several measurements is to be used? What is meant by "inflation," anyway? What constitutes "slowing down" — a month-to-month fluc-

16

tuation or a long-term trend? What is "this year"—the calendar year, the fiscal year, the most recent twelve-month period, or what? None of these questions can be answered empirically; in each case, the answer requires agreement on a certain set of data. Such agreement is the result of arguing about the seemingly direct factual claim. The questions posed in our example may seem overly specific, but the answers can significantly affect whether or not the rate of inflation is judged to be slowing.

Of course, some factual claims can be settled without argument. Suppose the statement about inflation read, "The consumer price index rose 7.2 percent during this January, as opposed to 8.6 percent last January." This claim could be verified without argument merely by looking up the two consumer price index figures. But not all factual claims are of this type, and so they frequently become the subjects for argument.

Factual claims may be offered with respect to the past, present, or future. Claims of past fact typify legal procedure. A jury serves as a trier of fact and determines what took place in a disputed situation. Historical arguments also contain claims of past fact. "Advertising was a more significant force in American life in 1920 than it is today" is an example. Claims of present fact, such as our example about the inflation rate, refer to the situation at the time the claim is made. Claims of future fact are predictions. "The Republican party will become the majority political party in the United States by the year 2000" is a claim of future fact.

Just because we have referred to this type of claim as a claim of fact, you should not assume that the statements contained in the claims are necessarily true. Were that the case, there would be no need to argue about them. The very purpose of arguing about factual claims is to determine whether they are probably true.

Claims of Meaning

In discussing claims of fact, we noted that it is sometimes necessary to specify what key terms in the claim mean before we can test the claim. But in a claim of meaning, interpretation or definition itself is the primary function. Much of reality is ambiguous, and determining how it is to be viewed is a major task. The purpose of a claim of meaning is to place facts in one or another category and thereby to influence how an audience will perceive and respond to those facts.

Recent controversy over affirmative action programs illustrates the way claims of meaning work. These programs involve special efforts to recruit previously underrepresented minorities for higher education and employment. A supporter of affirmative action might view such programs as reparations, the just compensation for years of discriminatory treatment. Another person, who also favored affirmative action, might object to this view of the matter. For this person, affirmative action is a pragmatic scheme to produce a wider range of role models in key professions or occupations. A third person might object to affirmative action programs and define them as "reverse discrimination" because they give preferential treatment to minorities.

Were any two of these three people to engage in argumentation, the focal question would be how affirmative action is to be categorized. If the claim were "Affirmative action is reverse discrimination," only the third person would support the claim. If it were "Affirmative action programs are an obligatory form of reparations," only the first person would support it. At issue in this situation is precisely what *affirmative action* means, how it should be interpreted.

Our example of affirmative action is not atypical. Many times in public discussion the heart of a controversy is how to categorize or view an ambiguous situation. Whether the signing of the Panama Canal treaties in 1978 was a just act or a giveaway depends on the question of what sovereignty over the canal means. Whether the 1980 election results reflected a new conservative momentum or the rejection of a particular incumbent is a similar question. So is the question of whether the fetus is a person, a central issue in the dispute about abortion. In such situations, advocates make and respond to claims of meaning.

Claims of Value

When people judge a situation, object, or person, they make claims of value. By *value* we mean, broadly speaking, a notion of what has positive or negative worth. A claim of value indicates to what degree the object measures up to a standard. The standard can be either absolute or relative.

An absolute claim of value judges an object according to some fixed standard. If a person asserts, "Capital punishment is morally wrong," he or she is making an absolute claim. The person is suggesting there is some moral principle that capital punishment always violates, regardless of what its actual effects are or whether other alternatives are available. Likewise, a speaker who alleges, "We have a moral duty to protect the environment for future generations," is making an absolute claim.

In contrast, a relative claim asserts that the object is to be preferred over something else. The statement "Segregation is better than busing" does not evaluate either term according to an absolute standard. Rather, it suggests that in a hierarchy of values one is preferred over the other. Similarly, the statement "A compassionate government is better than an efficient one" illustrates a relative claim.

Both types of value claims are common, but relative claims tend to predominate because few of us see most values as absolute. We recognize that choices must often be made between values both of which may be desirable or undesirable in the abstract. On the other hand, for each of us there are beliefs, objects, or persons we value in an absolute sense.

Claims of Policy

Claims of policy advocate some course of action. Sometimes they propose the achievement of a policy objective but do not specify in detail how the goal is to be met. "The rate of inflation should be slowed down" and "The power of labor unions and major corporations should be curtailed" are examples of this sort of claim. At other times the policy claim may prescribe specific actions. A claim such as "The federal government should adopt wage and price controls" recommends a means of slowing inflation or of achieving another end that the advocate may propose. Similarly, the claim "The defense budget should be increased by 5 percent above the rate of inflation" is a claim about specific measures.

Policy claims may also advise an audience against taking an action. The claim "Social security benefits should not be changed" is every bit as much a policy claim as is the statement "Social security benefits should be modified." Any claim that offers advice regarding some possible action is a claim of policy.

Policy and value claims often overlap. When we support a policy, we do so because it is valuable in itself or because it is a means to some valuable objective. When we judge a value to be desirable, we imply that we should act to obtain or increase the value. Arguing about value claims differs from arguing about policy claims only in emphasis — the former focuses on evaluation; the latter, on action.

Summary: Types of Claims

We have examined four basic types of claims, each of which performs a distinct function. Claims of fact are descriptive; claims of meaning are interpretive; claims of value are judgmental; and claims of policy are advisory.

This classification is important for two reasons. First, knowing the type of claim presented in a controversy enables us to say precisely what the listener is requested to believe. Is the listener asked to accept that certain conditions are facts? to assent to a particular perspective on a subject? to share a judgment? to endorse an action? The listener may be willing to grant one kind of belief but not another. For instance, a person might accept a characterization of affirmative action as "reverse discrimination" without agreeing that such a practice is wrong. It would be vital for this listener to know whether a claim of meaning or a claim of value was at issue. Or a person might agree with the claim "Inflation is greater this year than last" while rejecting the claim "Federal policies should make controlling inflation the top priority."

The other reason why it is valuable to distinguish among types of claims is that different questions are raised in seeking to prove or disprove different types of claims. To see this, you need to understand how claims relate to *resolutions* and *issues*.

Claims, Resolutions, and Issues

The Resolution

Each argument, no matter how simple, contains its own claim. Often, however, a group of arguments is used together to establish a more complex claim. There may be several steps in the reasoning pattern or several different reasons why the complex chain is true. In this section we shall examine these complex claims, which are called *resolutions.*

An advocate who wished to support the claim "United States defense spending should be increased" would need to develop several subsidiary arguments, each with its own claim. Examples of such subsidiary arguments might include the claims that the symbolic value of higher defense spending is important, that Soviet defenses have been strengthened relative to those of the United States, that potential instability in the Middle East requires additional American defense spending, or that the success of the volunteer army requires increased spending on military personnel. Each of these statements is itself a claim established by supporting evidence and inferences. But each also functions as support for the more complex claim that defense spending should be increased.

This more complex claim is the resolution, the ultimate claim that an advocate tries to establish in a given dispute. Here the advocate is resolved that American defense spending should be increased and seeks to convince an adversary or an audience of the merits of this position. The other claims are subsidiary to the resolution. (Sometimes the terms *proposition* and *topic* are used as synonyms for *resolution.* We believe that our explanation will be clearer if we use *resolution* throughout.)

Just as we can describe four types of claims in general, so we can say that there are resolutions of fact, meaning, value, and policy. Each type of resolution makes a different request for the listener's belief and presents unique proof requirements. The resolution is not always stated explicitly, but an observer or analyst should be able to infer it from the context of the dispute. The resolution should be clearly worded, preferably in a single, simple sentence. It should be free of question-begging terms that assert as true what the resolution itself is trying to establish. The resolution should be free of negative or ambiguous language that makes it difficult to know what support or opposition really means. An example of a resolution that meets these tests is "Resolved: That the governor of this state should be reelected."

In short, the resolution is the top of an argumentative pyramid. It is the ultimate claim that the advocate wishes to establish, and the subsidiary claims work together to support it. Now we are ready to explore in more detail the relationship between a resolution and its subsidiary claims.

The Nature of Issues

In order to affirm the resolution "Wage and price controls should be imposed," we need to answer several subsidiary questions: Is the goal of wage and price controls appropriate? Does it conflict with more important goals? When imposed in the past, were wage and price controls effective in achieving their goal? Are there other methods that might be more effective? Were past controls accompanied by any serious problems? Are there ways to avoid these problems?

These subsidiary questions are called *issues.* In ordinary usage, we often talk about an issue as any point in controversy, as when we say, "Don't make an issue of it." But a more specific definition for this term is needed. Issues are the subsidiary questions inherent in a resolution — that is, they grow naturally out of a pattern of thinking about the resolution. As soon as we think about how to prove or disprove the resolution, we think of the issues. Issues are also vital to the success of the resolution because we cannot assert that it is true unless we can answer all the issues satisfactorily. For example, we might establish that wage and price controls have the appropriate goal of reducing inflation and that there is no other way to achieve that goal. Even so, if it could be shown that wage and price controls would introduce a problem more serious than inflation, then the resolution to adopt them would fail.

A caution is necessary at this point. When we speak of issues as certain questions that naturally develop from the resolution, we presuppose a style of thought characteristic of Western culture. Clearly, there are other cultures whose patterns of reasoning are quite different from our own. For example, in certain Eastern cultures, reasoning processes do not give great weight to internal consistency or the avoidance of self-contradiction. If we lived in such a culture, then questions different from the ones we have described would come to mind. In other words, argumentation operates within the codes of reasoning and values that are sanctioned by a particular culture. But even though the context of the issues will vary from culture to culture, they will still arise naturally from the resolution.

Thought Patterns for Discovering Issues

We have said that a person may discover the issues in a resolution by applying a certain way of thinking about the resolution. Here we shall illustrate five different thought patterns from which issues naturally grow. Some are more useful with respect to one type of claim than another, but all are commonly used.

Cost-Benefit Analysis.   Influenced by the utilitarian philosophers, we frequently make decisions in an attempt to maximize pleasure and minimize pain, hoping to provide "the greatest good for the greatest number." Accordingly, we may ask of a resolution: What will be the benefits if we assume that the resolution is true? What will be the costs? How do alternative resolutions compare in costs and benefits? The answers to these questions enable us to assign a weight of value to each cost and each benefit. If the value of the benefits minus the value of the costs is greater for the resolution than for any alternative, we assert that the resolution is probably true; otherwise, we refrain from doing so. According to this pattern, the issues are discovered by searching for the resolution's benefits, costs, and alternatives.

Effectiveness of Programs.   Policies are adopted to achieve certain goals; they are continued or abandoned depending on their effectiveness in meeting these goals. As a result, we frequently examine a current policy by asking how many people it has been able to help, how significant its impact has been, and whether, as a result of its existence, we are substantially closer to the goal for which we adopted the policy in the first place. These questions represent the issues. If the answers to these questions are affirmative, we are likely to perpetuate the existing program; if they are negative, we are likely to search for new ones.

Although this pattern of thought is most easily applied to resolutions of policy, it is adaptable to other types of resolutions as well. Educators might ask what the results have been of defining *academic success* in a certain way. If this definition has led to positive results, they are likely to continue using it; if not, they may seek a new definition. In the face of declining student scores on the Scholastic Aptitude Test, for example, some educators have argued that SAT scores are no longer an appropriate predictor of academic success. This example illustrates how thinking about effectiveness can suggest issues for a resolution of meaning. Likewise, we might examine resolutions of fact or value by considering whether our current assumptions about the resolution lead to effective results.

Determination of Priorities.   We live in a world of scarce resources. Neither individuals nor societies can have everything they desire, and pursuing one objective invariably involves trade-offs or sacrifices of other objectives. Therefore, we must make decisions regarding the relative urgency of competing claims. We must ask, for instance, whether it is more important for us to get a job or to read a textbook, whether a gain in freedom of information is worth a loss in government secrecy, or whether pollution control is justified to avert a low-level environmental risk that has serious potential consequences. Asking these questions about priorities establishes the issues. Good arguments can usually be made on both sides of such questions, but only by asking them can we force ourselves to order our values and goals along a scale.

Historical Continuities.   Seldom do our choices make sharp, overt breaks from the past. Instead, we usually try to make our choices consistent with tradition. Radical arguments are often justified on the grounds that they are really conservative. This practice was used by some of the most effective propagandists during the American Revolution. They talked about merely restoring the situation that had existed in the colonies prior to 1763, although the means by which they proposed to reach that objective were new and untried. In light of our traditionalist orientation, a relevant question to ask about choices we consider is: Is this choice consistent with other facts, meanings, values, or actions that we regard as justified or appropriate? This question and its variations will determine the issues.

Interpretation of Data.   We have already noted that the methods of scientific research are not well suited to answering questions of value or policy, to telling us what is right or what we ought to do. They are, of course, well suited to supplying factual data, but the interpretation of those data then becomes a matter for argument. During the 1960s it was difficult to interpret empirical data related to the war in Vietnam. Did the allegation that more explosives were being dropped over North Vietnam than had been dropped during all of World War II mean that the United States was winning the war and undermining its enemy's will to resist? Or did that statement mean that the United States was confronting an implacable foe whom it could not bomb into submission and so should have realized the folly of its effort and quit?

Questions of this sort relate to our interpretation of the data. The question of how to interpret data poses an issue, which is then answered by imagining various possible interpretations and finding reasons to favor one point of view over the others. This pattern for discovering issues is especially useful for resolutions of meaning, but interpretive questions frequently arise with other types of resolutions as well.

Issues and Claims

We are now ready to specify relationships among the terms we have examined. We have said that the resolution suggests subsidiary questions, known as issues. These issues are answered by arguments consisting of the claim and its support. An individual claim, then, is a statement of position on an issue, answering the issue in such a way as to affirm or deny the resolution.

For example, the resolution that defense spending should be reduced would give rise to subsidiary questions such as "What is our current level of spending?" "How serious is the danger to our national security?" and "Are there more pressing needs for the funds?" Each of these questions would be answered with a claim, and the claims, taken together, would affirm or deny the resolution.

Figure 2.1 shows the relationship among the resolution, issues, and claims. It also illustrates our earlier statement that the resolution may be seen as the top of an argumentative pyramid.

Stock Issues

Different subjects and types of statements give rise to their own issues, and so no two resolutions will produce exactly the same issues. Yet there are recurrent patterns, and resolutions of the same type will suggest similar issues. These issues fall into categories of questions that a reasonable person would naturally ask when confronting a resolution of a given type. These categories of issues that repeatedly arise are called *stock issues*.

Stock issues should function as aids to analysis. Rather than having to examine the substance of each resolution we encounter in argument, we can identify the type of resolution and then decide what sorts of issues are appropriate. Once we know that we are considering a resolution of value, for instance, we can determine what kinds of issues we must address in order to affirm the resolution. (We cannot determine the specific issues through this method, since they will remain unique to each particular resolution. But we can determine the patterns that these

Figure 2.1

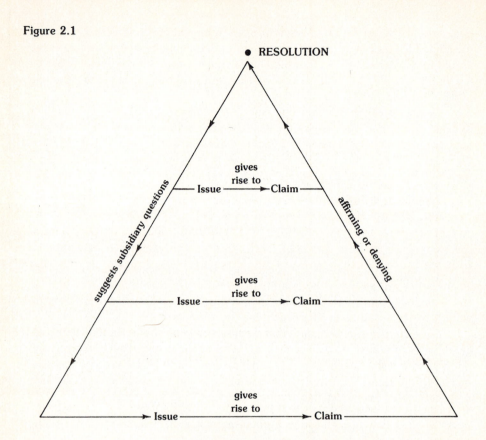

issues are likely to take.) The usefulness of stock issues will be clearer if we consider some examples.

On Resolutions of Fact

One stock issue on a resolution of fact is the criterion used for assessing the truth of the resolution. If we wish to determine whether today is the hottest day of the year, do we rely on objective data or our own impressions? Do we take temperature readings in the sun or in the shade? at our home or at the official weather reporting station? For any resolution of fact, there will be an issue in the general form of "What criterion is appropriate?"

The other major stock issue on a resolution of fact is whether the accepted criterion has demonstrated the truth or falsity of the resolution. In our example, does the criterion of temperature we have chosen to use show that today is hotter than other days of the year? This sort of issue may be resolved quickly if the empirical evidence exists and is clear-cut, but there may often be contradictory data, or it may not be clear whether the data satisfy the stipulated criterion.

On Resolutions of Meaning

When the resolution states that a set of facts is to be viewed in a certain way, different types of issues typically arise. For example, one stock issue would be "Is the proposed interpretation relevant to our purpose?" Since any categorization is in some sense arbitrary, it is always important to know what purpose is served by one perspective rather than another. During the period shortly after the Second World War, the question of whether an agreement to divide political control of Europe should be regarded as *appeasement* was very relevant. Prior to the Munich Agreement of 1938, however, appeasement did not carry a negative connotation when it was used to classify a diplomatic action.

Another stock issue would be "Is the interpretation fair?"—that is, does it give us an equal chance to affirm or deny the resolution? An interpretation that is loaded or that prejudges the truth or falsity of the resolution is unlikely to be acceptable. For example, if we must decide whether abortion is murder or manslaughter, we have prejudged the question of whether the fetus is a person. What *fairness* means in any specific dispute over meaning will depend, of course, on the particular context, but the stock issue of fairness will emerge repeatedly in resolutions of meaning.

A third stock issue is "What principle should govern the choice among competing meanings?" It is always possible to see the same event or fact through different lenses. In a resolution about abortion, this stock issue would ask, "How should we choose among these different interpretations of what *abortion* means?" We might choose to follow common usage, the usage of experts in the particular field being discussed, the rule that the simplest interpretation is to be preferred, or some other standard. But some principle for choice is needed, and the question of what it should be is a stock issue.

On Resolutions of Value

If the dispute involves value judgments, one stock issue is "Is the value truly good—or bad—as alleged?" For instance, an advocate who believes that abortion is wrong because it is murder would first need to establish that murder is wrong. Although this example is obvious, advocates often find themselves advocating a value position without addressing the question of whether the value itself really is good. Economic growth and additional leisure time are examples of values that are often assumed to be good but about which there might be serious question.

A second stock issue in resolutions of value is "Which among competing values is to be preferred?" Seldom are we confronted with choices between absolute good and absolute evil; when we are, we can make those choices without argument. More typically, we must choose between desirable but incompatible values, or we must determine which is the lesser of two evils. Inexpensive energy and clean air are regarded positively; yet we may have to choose between them. Higher taxes and increased unemployment are regarded negatively; yet we may have to put up with at least one of them. In such situations, advocates seek criteria by which one value can be placed above the other. Perhaps one value is necessary for the existence of the other; perhaps one enhances some third value more than the other; or perhaps one satisfies a basic human need better than the other. We must decide whether these criteria have been properly employed so that the appropriate choice can be made.

A final stock issue asks, "Has the value been properly applied to the specific situation?" There are always overriding situations in which the ordinary choice among values does not hold. Life is widely regarded as an almost supreme value, and yet society permits loss of life by constructing highways or by permitting citizens to possess firearms. Moreover, in wartime, society voluntarily sacrifices life for what it believes to be a higher value. To note these exceptions is not to deny society's reverence for life; it is merely to observe that for any value position there are over-riding cases. This stock issue asks whether the case at hand should override the general value.

On Resolutions of Policy

Resolutions of policy deal with proposals for action. When action is considered, the first stock issue is whether there is a problem that calls for action. If things are generally satisfactory, there may not be. But if there is some clear evil present or if we are forgoing some benefit that we could obtain, then the prospect of elim-inating the evil or obtaining the benefit would be a reason to take the action stated in the resolution. To illustrate, there would be no reason to discuss proposals to modify the social security system unless it could be established either that the cur-rent operation is producing problems threatening the future of social security or that some alternative to the system might produce greater social benefits, such as encouraging early retirement.

But a policy resolution not only evaluates the existing state of affairs, it also seeks to determine responsibility for those conditions. Therefore, a second stock issue involves the question of where credit or blame is due. Unless we can answer this question, we do not know if the proposal being advanced addresses the true source of the problem. The financial crisis of social security may be caused by in-dexing of social security benefits for inflation, a trend toward early retirement, the escalation of medical care costs, the greater longevity of Americans, or all of these causes together. Until we know which causes are most important, we cannot consider a proposal with any confidence that it might resolve the problem.

The third stock issue involves whether the proposal will overcome the problem or obtain the benefits. Here, we would inquire, for example, whether a proposal to delay the social security retirement age or to recompute the cost of living would really take care of the problem in the social security system. The prob-lem might be significant, but unless the proposal will solve it, we have no reason to consider the proposal seriously.

The last stock issue addresses the effects of the proposal, apart from whether or not it will cure the problem. There may be unanticipated effects or hidden costs of a proposed change. Perhaps modifying social security would lead people to question the soundness of the whole system and withdraw from it, thereby precipitating the collapse of the system—precisely what everyone wanted to avoid. If a proposal introduces evils greater than those that it might correct, it would be foolhardy to accept the proposal. On the other hand, if a proposal has beneficial by-products in addition to solving the problem to which it is addressed, the by-products would provide extra reasons to consider the proposal seriously.

The four stock issues on a resolution of policy are sometimes abbreviated as ill, blame, cure, and cost. Each represents a pattern of issues that grow naturally out of a policy resolution and that are vital to the resolution's success.

Claims and Burdens

When an advocate asserts a claim, he or she assumes a certain burden. We refer to this burden as the *burden of proving assertions*—simply stated, "one who asserts must prove." In the course of a controversy, this burden is borne by all participants. Were you to offer an assertion but make no attempt to back it up, another advocate could simply dismiss the assertion out of hand. Whereas the burden of proving assertions applies at the level of individual arguments, the other burdens that we shall discuss involve the relationship between individual claims and the ultimate claim or resolution.

Burden of the Resolution

The *burden of the resolution* is the responsibility to demonstrate that the resolution is probably true; it is the burden of proving assertions applied to the ultimate claim that is in dispute. Just as someone who offers an assertion has the burden of proving that assertion, so the advocate who asserts the resolution has the responsibility to demonstrate that it is probably true. At the end of the dispute, the audience must ask whether the supporters of the resolution have established that truth is probably on their side. If so, the supporters are victorious; if not, they lose. The question is asked about affirmative arguments, because the burden is on the advocate who favors the resolution. Opponents of the resolution can prevail merely by casting enough doubt on the affirmative arguments, without establishing definitely that the resolution is false.

Presumption

The presumption is the opposite of the burden of the resolution. Therefore, an arguer who opposes the resolution enjoys presumption. This term indicates which side will be presumed correct in the absence of argument to the contrary. The following discussion explains why presumption rests against the resolution.

The resolution, like any claim, is a hypothesis to be tested. If we confirm the hypothesis, then we commit ourselves to the probable truth of the statement; if we reject the hypothesis, we leave open a wide range of alternatives. There is risk in committing ourselves to a hypothesis that turns out to be false. Therefore, we want to be sure that the hypothesis is tested rigorously enough so that if we affirm a resolution, we can do so with confidence. In argumentation, we guarantee a rigorous test by saying that there is a presumption against the resolution. In other words, if there were no argument in favor of the resolution, it would be rejected—not because it is necessarily wrong but because no good case has been made for it.

Since presumption rests against the resolution, the proponent of the resolution must initiate the dispute. The side enjoying presumption has no incentive to do so because it will prevail in the absence of controversy. If at the end of the dispute the two sides are argumentatively equal (a rare situation), then the victor is the opponent of the resolution—again, not necessarily because the resolution was flawed but because the proponents did not have an argument strong enough to overcome the contrary argument of the negative side. In such a case, the principle of presumption would dictate a finding against the resolution.

There are two key implications of this discussion about presumption. First, to say that presumption weighs against the resolution is not to say that the arguments against the resolution are compelling. Indeed, presumption is assigned even before knowing what those arguments are. Assignment of presumption merely describes the situation at the outset of controversy and indicates which participant must present the first case.

Second, we have located presumption against the resolution because that is where it ideally belongs. In actual arguments, however, it is not uncommon to find both supporters and opponents of the resolution claiming that they enjoy presumption. Supporters might insist that the resolution enhances freedom and that there is a presumption favoring freedom over restriction. Opponents might respond that the resolution requires a change and that there is a presumption favoring the status quo. Here, the question is which of the two competing presumptions should govern. Since it is strategically valuable to have presumption on one's side, it is not surprising to find arguers jockeying for presumption. Nevertheless, as a normative principle, the fundamental presumption ought to rest against the resolution in order to assure that the resolution receives a thorough and rigorous test.

Ideally, neither the presumption nor the burden of the resolution shifts from one side to the other in a dispute. The participant who supports the resolution should shoulder the burden of the resolution throughout the dispute, and the party opposing the resolution should enjoy presumption throughout. In contrast, the burden of proving assertions moves back and forth between advocates, as does the final burden we need to consider.

Burden of Rejoinder

We must remember that presumption describes the situation only at the outset of a controversy. Once a supporter of the resolution has presented reasons for affirming it, he or she has dislodged the presumption. It then will not do for an opponent to say, "Well, we do not like your arguments, and remember that we have presumption." Instead, the obligation now is on the opponent to demonstrate to the audience's satisfaction that the affirmative arguments do not in fact represent good reasons for affirming the resolution.

In other words, the opponent of the resolution now assumes the *burden of rejoinder*. This is the responsibility to produce additional arguments to sustain the controversy, and it falls alternately on each party to the dispute. After the opponent has responded to the initial arguments in favor of the resolution, the responsibility for going forward with the dispute now rests with the supporter of the resolution. A supporter can neither ignore the opponent's remarks nor merely repeat the original statements in the resolution's behalf. It is necessary to come to grips with what the opponent has said — by arguing that it is not applicable, that it is not correct, or that it does not dislodge the original arguments.

Two points about the burden of rejoinder should be made explicit. First, it requires each advocate to respond to the arguments that his or her adversary has made, in order that the controversy can proceed. Second, it requires that the statements made by each advocate be truly responsive to the other's position. It does not do to repeat one's own arguments, to dismiss cavalierly those of the opponent, or to ask questions as a substitute for making constructive argument. The obligation imposed by the burden of rejoinder is to carry arguments forward once one's adversary has dealt with them.

Summary

The claim is an assertion that serves as the basis for controversy; it is a request for an audience's assent. There are four major types of claims: claims of fact, meaning, value, and policy. Claims of fact describe what exists, has existed, or will exist. Claims of meaning categorize in order to determine how something will be interpreted. Claims of value concern whether something is to be preferred. Claims of policy involve action that may be undertaken. Being able to identify claims by type is important so that you can determine what sort of request for assent is being made and which proof requirements must be satisfied.

Claims are parts of individual arguments, but they are typically arranged in a structure to support larger arguments. The ultimate claim in a controversy is the resolution. Like any claim, a resolution can be classified as one of fact, meaning, value, or policy. The resolution generates subsidiary questions that must be answered satisfactorily in order to affirm it. These subsidiary questions are issues, which are inherent in the resolution and vital to its success. They are answered by the claims of individual arguments. Issues are generated naturally as a result of characteristic styles of thought; these styles, however, are constrained by culture.

Although each resolution contains unique issues, there are recurrent patterns of issues that arise in considering resolutions of a given type. These recurrent patterns are called stock issues, which are different for each of the major types of resolutions. Stock issues function as an analytical shortcut. Once someone knows what the stock issues are, he or she can immediately proceed to find out how the pattern of stock issues is expressed in the specific resolution at hand.

When a person offers an assertion, he or she assumes the burden of proving it; this burden shifts back and forth among the disputants in a controversy. The supporter of the resolution has the burden of the resolution; this burden is the responsibility to show that the claim embodied in the resolution is probably true. This burden does not shift but remains with the affirmative side. The opponent of the resolution likewise enjoys presumption, which is set against the resolution in order to assure that it undergoes a thorough test. Once either party has introduced an argument, however, the obligation is on the other party to come to grips with it. This responsibility to keep the controversy moving, which requires that arguments be extended rather than repeated or ignored, is referred to as the burden of rejoinder.

Questions for Discussion

1. How do the four types of claims overlap? How do they differ?
2. How would arguing about a resolution be affected if issues had not been identified fully or accurately?
3. What are the dangers, if any, of using thought patterns such as cost-benefit analysis or historical continuities to determine issues?
4. We have stated that the presumption and the burden of the resolution do not shift between advocates. How would arguing be different if they did?
5. In addition to our example of a presumption favoring freedom, what are some other common presumptions?

Chapter 3

Evidence

Evidence is the supporting material that justifies the acceptance or rejection of a claim. It consists of statements about reality that are presented as facts or as opinions about facts. By *fact* we mean verifiable observations. By *opinion* we mean judgments about reality. In this chapter we shall describe types and tests of evidence, sources of evidence, and methods of presenting evidence.

Types and Tests of Evidence

Any statement from which a claim may be inferred can be considered evidence. These statements can be grouped into several forms, and each form has its own test of accuracy. Statements of fact may be reported in any of the forms described below, but statements of opinion are reported only in the form of *testimony*.

The first three forms of evidence can be expressed as examples or statistics. If we assert that union members elect their own officers, we have cited a specific example. If we claim that 90 percent of union members in America elect their officers, compared with 50 percent of union members in foreign countries, we have used a statistic.

Direct Observation

All evidence originates from observations of perceived reality. *Direct observation* means experiencing a situation for ourselves, using one or more of our senses to gather the information. For example, if you wanted first-hand information on the effects of strip mining on the land, you would go to areas where such mining is done and observe the actual effects. In making an argument against strip mining, you might say, "I observed strip mining in Bell County, and here is how the land looked before and after the mining." Or if you observed several cases, you might say, "I observed strip mining in ten counties and found that in nine out of the ten cases the land was left in the following condition." The first observation illustrates how to report a specific example; the second, how to report statistical evidence.

Three questions constitute the main tests for direct observations used in supporting claims: (1) Is the person qualified to analyze what he or she observed? (2) Was the person in a position to see accurately what he or she observed? (3) Did the person accurately describe what he or she observed?

Inference from Indirect Observation

It is often unnecessary and, in fact, sometimes impossible to observe all the events and behavior we use as evidence for arguments. Instead, we must frequently use *indirect observations* based on the findings of others. In some cases we report what others said they observed as eyewitnesses. More often, however, we report generalizations others have drawn from surveys they have conducted, because we do not have the time or the expertise to do the sampling ourselves.

Usually, a listener is more receptive to a claim based on a survey of all the members of a group than to one based on a survey of a selected portion. For example, suppose you were claiming that many Americans do not think they receive adequate medical care. Ideally, either you or a more-qualified person would conduct a survey of all the American people. Such a survey would be more convincing than interviews with, say, five thousand people. In practice, however, it is rarely feasible or desirable to question the total population. In many instances the findings would be obsolete by the time they could be ascertained. Instead, pollsters often gather the opinions of a portion of the population. We then take the generalizations of the surveys and cite them to support our claims. This procedure is widely used in both the social and physical sciences. Conclusions drawn from fragments of the total group are generally very reliable and require considerably less effort than do surveys of the entire population. For example, we might use the findings of a national survey of a portion of the American people to show that a majority of Americans either approve or disapprove of the legalization of marijuana. The argument can be made that in an ideal world all Americans would be asked to register their opinions. Experience, however, indicates that such practices are rarely feasible and certainly not necessary to arrive at valid generalizations.

The following questions should be asked about the generalizations drawn by surveys or polls: (1) Did the person conducting the survey possess the skills necessary to conduct social research, such as the ability to phrase questions clearly, and to compile the findings according to the norms of statistical analysis? (2) Was the sample representative? In other words, did the people excluded from the survey differ in any significant way from those surveyed? (3) Was the sample truly random—that is, did each member of the population being surveyed have an equal chance of being included in the sample? (4) Was the sample large enough to be considered statistically accurate?

The last question is usually dependent on both the size of the total population and the diversity within that population as measured by certain key indicators. Groups that are homogeneous are similar in age, educational background, geographical location, occupation, income, lifestyle, and other factors. Groups that are heterogeneous may differ on several of these variables. In highly heterogeneous groups, a larger sample size may be needed in order to control for the possible effects of the intervening variables. For example, a study concerning occupational safety and health might need to control for variables such as industrial characteristics, occupation, union membership, and past health of employees. A larger sample may be needed in order to accommodate all of these controls.

In addition, when two groups of equal size are surveyed, a heterogeneous group requires a larger sample than does a homogeneous one in order to yield the same degree of accuracy. To illustrate, a study concerning the ravages of unemployment might control for factors such as age, duration of unemployment, and psychological stability of the participants in the sample, while at the same time surveying thousands of people across the country for years. This combination of high heterogeneity and large sample size would probably yield accurate results. Conversely, in a group with little or no heterogeneity, a very small sample will usually yield accurate results. If the subjects are alike in most respects, their responses should also be similar.

Experimental Data

Specific examples and statistical information often grow out of the results of experimental findings. *Experiments* are controlled tests of the effect of one variable on another. Findings from laboratory and field experiments are often cited to defend claims. In a laboratory experiment, the researcher examines the impact of one variable on another in a tightly controlled setting. In a field experiment, the impact is examined in the real world. Both types attempt to demonstrate either a causal or a correlative relationship between two or more variables.

In an ideal world, the experimenter would control all factors that might affect the outcome. Since such conditions rarely occur, the most the experimenter can hope for is to compare the outcomes of two situations which are essentially similar, except that a factor is present in one and absent in the other. For example, in a study of the effects of exercise on blood pressure, one group of people would engage in an exercise program, and a comparable control group would not. Naturally, the more similarities there were between the groups in all other respects that might affect blood pressure, the more faith we would have in the results. However, it would be impossible to find two totally identical groups and to observe each group member twenty-four hours a day. Thus, the experimenter would have to settle for results of a test in which the largest number of variables could be controlled. In the study of factors influencing blood pressure, other controlled variables might include body weight and the use of cigarettes. The evidence of such an experience would not be conclusive, but it could enable us to make some useful generalizations about the effects of exercise on blood pressure.

When making claims based on experimental data, we should be aware of how the experiments were conducted. A laboratory experiment usually has tighter controls over the factors affecting the outcome than does a field experiment. Suppose you claimed that saccharin was unsafe because laboratory studies proved that rats fed saccharin had a higher rate of cancer than did rats that received no saccharin. You could probably show that the experimenter was able to control most of the variables that could have affected the outcome, such as the amount of saccharin fed each rat, and other factors in the experiment.

On the other hand, there are several reasons why experiments are conducted wholly, or in part, outside the laboratory. Many argue that findings from laboratory experiments on animals are not truly applicable to human beings. Furthermore, many of the data we want cannot be obtained in the laboratory. For example, researchers who want to know how cigarette smoking affects humans probably could not confine their studies to controlled groups who live entirely in laboratories. Instead, they might have to conduct their studies entirely outside the laboratory. They might select one group of people who smoke and a group of similar people who do not and then study the instances of lung cancer occurring in each group. Of course, the researchers would try to control as many factors as possible, but many things in the environment, such as exposure to certain types of pollution, might be impossible to hold constant. Thus, at best, they could claim a correlation, but rarely complete causality, since factors beyond their control could have caused any difference in the results. It is possible, however, to calculate the probability that the experimental results were obtained merely by chance.

As an arguer, you will frequently make claims based on experimental data. Some key questions to ask about such data are (1) Were the variables in the situation sufficiently controlled to warrant the findings? (2) Was the environment in which the experiment was conducted too artificial to warrant calling the outcome a true representation of reality?

Common Knowledge

Many argumentative claims we make, particularly those of fact, are based on knowledge generally accepted by most people as true. For example, if you claimed that millions of Americans watch television each day, the claim would probably be accepted without evidence. Nor would you need to cite opinions or survey results to get most people to accept the statement that millions of people smoke cigarettes. Basing a claim on common knowledge is probably the easiest method of securing belief in an idea because an audience will accept it without further challenge. Of course, what is considered to be common-knowledge will vary over time. But at any given time there is a fund of common-knowledge beliefs to which audiences subscribe.

Although most controversial claims hinge on disputed facts and opinions, in any argumentative discourse you will usually employ many common-knowledge statements. Since you, in effect, are asking your audience to accept the accuracy of a statement without evidence, you should ask yourself two questions when using such information: (1) Even though the information is commonly accepted as true, could it be, in fact, a myth? If the information is untrue, you are misleading your audience by playing on their ignorance of reality. (2) Will the audience agree with you that the information truly is common knowledge? For example, you may think everyone agrees that cigarette smoking causes lung cancer when, in fact, many of your listeners may have doubts about the validity of this conclusion. If such is the case, your statement may need further verification or support.

Primary Documents

Another means of accumulating specific examples and statistical information is through the use of *primary documents.* These are accounts of events and behavior compiled by people at the scene, as opposed to secondary documents, which are compiled by people who merely talked with eyewitnesses or read accounts written by people at the scene. The Declaration of Independence is a primary document; a historical document of the writing of the declaration would be a secondary document.

Primary documents are available from several sources: the mass media, such as newspapers, periodicals, magazines, and books; the government, which keeps records of congressional sessions, committee hearings, treaties, negotiations, and other events; business organizations, labor groups, and professional associations—all of which also keep records; and individuals who have kept diaries and written letters, autobiographies, and memoirs.

The advantage of using primary documents is the access it gives us to events or behavior that we cannot observe directly. Even if the event is happening now, we obviously cannot be in all places at all times. If the event happened in the past, primary documents may be the closest we can come to re-creating the event. We thereby avoid the danger of bias or misinterpretation by others.

Two considerations, however, should guide you in your use of primary documents: (1) Is the content of the document valid? Often there is a large lapse of time between the event and the recording of it. Does the document appear to be genuine? Although such matters are difficult to verify, many internal checks, such as consistency of style, can sometimes help you determine if more than one writer produced the document. If the author has written other materials, compare their style of composition with that of the document in question. (2) Is the document an accurate record of the event it seeks to explain? Again, compare the document under consideration with something else written by the same author. In addition, whenever possible, compare one author's account with an account of the same event prepared by another author. This comparison is usually *easy* to make when dealing with records of current events, since the mass media employ several analysts to cover the same event.

Testimony

In the types of evidence described above, we have dealt with information that we can gather through firsthand experience, although more often our sources will be secondary. Testimony, however, is always secondary—an opinion of reality as stated by another person or information recorded by another.

Opinion Testimony.   One type of testimony is the recorded opinion of another person. Usually, such opinions are presented as a means of showing that someone who has expertise or who has been in a better position to know than we were has reached a certain conclusion. If you were arguing about an issue before the United Nations, for example, you might give the opinion of the American ambassador. Your objective would be to show that a qualified person much closer to the situation than you agrees with your claim. If, in another situation, you were arguing that Americans should adopt a policy of free trade, you might cite the opinion of a noted professor of international trade who agrees with your claim. In this case, you would be saying, in effect, "Don't just take my opinion that free trade is a good idea; rather, take the opinion of an expert." Your hope is that your audience will be more willing to accept claims based on testimony from people perceived to be more competent and less biased than you.

Factual Testimony.   In many situations we support our claims by citing facts others have gathered. Such testimony could be an Associated Press account of what happened in West Germany on a given day, or it could be a reference to a record of events made by someone with expertise in a given area. For example, you might cite information collected by a professor of preventive medicine on the health of Americans in order to support your claim that certain people do not have adequate medical care.

Tests for Testimony.   When citing the opinion and factual testimony of others, you are implicitly asserting that your claim is warranted because of the witness's testimony. Whether the testimony is yours or another's, it should be subjected to the following tests: (1) The person giving the testimony must have been in a position to make an accurate record of what happened or to observe the facts necessary for a reasoned opinion. Even the most talented and renowned economist in the world may not be able to give a good opinion of the state of the economy if he or she does not have access to the data that determine economic indicators. (2) The person giving the testimony must have the expertise to form an intelligent opinion or to record accurately the observable data. Albert Einstein was obviously an expert on certain aspects of physics, but this expertise did not necessarily qualify him as an expert in international relations. A talented actor may possess nothing more than a layperson's view of nuclear energy. As an arguer, unless you are reasonably sure that your listeners regard your witness as an expert, you should establish the credentials qualifying the expert to give the opinion or data you cite. (3) The person giving the testimony must not hold a special bias. Even though the president of the American Federation of Labor might be an expert on labor relations, his testimony on any matter adversely affecting labor would probably be viewed with suspicion. If an expert stands to gain from the consequences of his or her testimony, it does not follow that the expert is wrong. But when self-interest and expertise are mixed, it is hard to know in what proportions each contributes to the final statement. Therefore, if you think your witness's testimony will be perceived as biased, you will need to compensate for that bias. Otherwise, if the acceptance of your claim hinges on that witness's testimony, your claim is likely to be rejected.

These guides may help in evaluating expert testimony. But even when all these standards are met satisfactorily, expert witnesses may still disagree. The listener may be left in a quandary as to which expert's advice to accept. Although there is no absolutely reliable method of choosing, you can help your case by offering your listener some general guidelines. First, indicate where the consensus of expert opinion lies. It is always possible that the one dissenting expert may turn out to be right, but you might argue that, other things being equal, it seems more sensible to place confidence in the judgment of a body of experts. Second, persuade listeners to accept your expert's opinion by drawing on other evidence that supports your expert's testimony. Statistics or documents used to support one expert and challenge another, are valuable additional forms of evidence. Third, examine the expert's "track record." If there is disagreement among experts, and one of them has been inclined in the past to offer claims that turn out to be incorrect, then that expert's subsequent claims might be taken somewhat less seriously.

Sources of Evidence

In describing the various types of evidence, we alluded to certain sources where they can be found. More specific recommendations for places to find information follow. In general, your best sources of information will be written material, interviews, and direct observation of events and behaviors.

Written Sources

The library is likely to be the most valuable storehouse of written sources. A large university library is more likely to have diverse sources of information than a small city library. You also should not overlook specialized libraries. Many organizations, such as the Council on State Governments, have their own special collections. When you consult a library for information, you should consider at least some of the following sources.

Books.   Both general and specific books on your topic can be valuable sources. The card catalogue is usually a good place to begin to find them. First look under general headings. If you are preparing a speech calling for federal control of labor unions, you probably would first look in the card catalogue under unions. A quick examination of these books would probably lead you to headings like trade associations, collective bargaining, trade unions, public sector unions, strikes, and organized labor. You may also wish to consult such sources as Winchell's *Guide to Reference Books* and Shore's *Basic Reference Books.*

Periodicals.   Another rich source of information is periodicals. Begin by consulting the librarian in charge of reference material. Following this, you can use the several indexes to periodical articles. Among them is the *Reader's Guide to Periodical Literature,* which indexes articles appearing in popular magazines. But unless you are in a very small library, you probably will find specialized indexes more useful. These indexes, usually arranged in the same format as the *Reader's Guide,* list journals with more limited circulations. The specialized indexes include the *Social Sciences Index,* the *Business Periodicals Index,* the *International Index to Periodicals,* and the *Bulletin of the Public Affairs Information Service.*

Government Documents.   Government documents are often useful as well. These resources include bulletins, reports, studies, and special publications of state and national governments. Many libraries also have foreign government documents and publications from the United Nations.

The American federal government publications are published by the United States Government Printing Office. Indexes to government publications include the *Monthly Catalog of U.S. Government Publications, Congressional Information Service Index, Congressional Record Index, American Statistics Index, Index to U.S. Government Periodicals,* and many specific studies prepared by the Congressional Reference Service. Each state has certain libraries designated as government depositories, which means that they receive all government documents. You can get a list of these depositories by writing to the United States Government Printing Office, Washington, D.C. 20402.

Many people using government documents for the first time are discouraged by what first appears to be a very complicated process of locating sources. Actually, with the help of your librarian and the usual printed directions, you can learn the process rather quickly.

A brief description of how to use the *Monthly Catalog* should help you find your desired information. This publication is perhaps the most comprehensive index to U.S. government publications. You can find indexes by author, title, subject, series and/or report number, and the Superintendent of Documents number. Publications are arranged alphabetically by the agency that publishes them. If you were using this publication for information on tobacco, you would probably look first at the subject index in the back of each monthly issue or in one of the cumulative indexes. Under the subject heading are the titles of the publications. Along with the title is an entry number to help you locate more complete information on the document, including the call number and the Superintendent of Documents number.

A brief description of how to locate materials in the *Congressional Information Service* should also help you use government documents. This service is an index to the papers of the United States Congress and contains such information as testimonies before congressional committees, reprints from national journals and newspapers, and even many unpublished reports. This is a monthly publication appearing as an index issue and an abstract issue. The indexes are arranged by name, title, subject, and congressional bill number. There also are cumulative indexes covering certain years. To use these indexes, first look under your subject. Usually you can find numerous publications listed with each entry number, which in turn you can use to find other information in the abstract volume.

Newspapers.   Although your daily newspaper can offer much information, you may also wish to consult those newspapers that give a more comprehensive coverage of current events and opinions. Many of these have their own special indexes, including the *New York Times,* the *Christian Science Monitor,* the *Wall Street Journal,* the *Washington Post,* the *Chicago Tribune* and the *Los Angeles Times.* The value of these newspapers goes far beyond their comprehensive coverage of events, as most of them also contain well-written interpretations and evaluations of current affairs.

Scholarly Journals.   Most academic disciplines publish their own journals. Examples are *Psychological Abstracts, Journal of the American Medical Association, American Bar Association Journal, Journal of the American Academy of Political Science, Political Science Quarterly,* and *Journal of the American Forensic Association.* Most libraries have a list of the journals they carry, and the reference librarian can direct you to them. In these sources you can find the results of experiments, surveys, and historical and critical analyses compiled by experts in various fields. Many of these journals are listed in specialized periodical indexes. For example, legal journals are listed in *Index to Legal Periodicals;* medical journals, in *Index Medicus.* In addition, most academic disciplines publish abstracts, or short summaries, of articles in the journals of that discipline. At a major library, the reference librarian can direct you to these abstracts, which should save you considerable time in determining which journal articles are worth reading.

Interviews

Another valuable source of information is interviews with eyewitnesses to events or with experts with firsthand knowledge. For example, if you want to know about the management of a national forest, you might consult a forest manager. If you want to know about international trade, you might interview a professor of economics who specializes in international economics. If you do use interviews, prepare for them, as advance study will enable you to ask more relevant questions. In addition, specialists usually can direct you to other sources of information and other specialists.

Direct Observation

Another source of evidence is your own observations. If, for example, you are arguing for improved dormitories on your campus, you may wish to observe firsthand the actual living conditions in several housing units. This would enable you to say to your adversary, "I went to several dormitories and looked at the living conditions. Here is what I found." This information can be valuable if your audience accepts that you made a thorough observation, that you were capable of observing what you saw, and that your report is accurate. In some cases, an audience is very impressed with firsthand reports.

Presentation of Evidence

The believability of your claim often hinges on the accuracy of your information. Likewise, it may often hinge on how you present your evidence. Since argumentation is a means of testing the truth of a disputed issue, you should consider several items in presenting your data.

You often may need to explain your evidence. Facts do not necessarily speak for themselves. For example, what are the implications of the fact that personal income rose 3 percent last year? In order for the evidence to have the impact you desire, you may need to show how this affects the whole economy and ultimately the well-being of your listeners. Or, what are the implications of the statement that a given country spends only 15 percent of its total income on education? If you are trying to show that more money is needed to offer quality education, you may need to show why 15 percent of a country's total income is inadequate. Evidence by itself does not make up an argument; explanations will also be needed to link the evidence to the claim.

It is also important to be as specific as possible in presenting your evidence. In identifying your sources, rather than refer to "some experts," you should name them. Also, be specific about what the expert said. For example, if you are paraphrasing a witness, rather than saying, "Professor Jones says that it is undemocratic to restrict those who can speak on campus", it is better to say, "Professor Jones says that restraining speakers from speaking on campus distorts the democratic process because it denies people access to information and new ideas—concepts that are fundamental to a free society." Such precision is more likely to give your evidence the impact it merits.

For argumentation to serve as a truth-testing device, it is essential that certain standards be observed by those presenting the evidence. For example, information that can affect the outcome of your claim should not be withheld from your audience even if it weakens your position. To do so makes it much less likely that the truth will emerge.

It is also important that quoted material contains the exact words of those cited. Obviously, the omission of words such as *not* in a statement like "The president of the United States says that we should not send wheat to the Russians" can change its entire meaning. Unintentional omissions are the result of carelessness; avoid them by checking your evidence against the original source.

Keep your evidence in context. For example, you might quote the governor of your state to the effect that strip mining is economically helpful and use this information to support your claim that the state should adopt a policy of strip mining. But if the governor concluded that despite these desirable consequences, we should not have strip mining, then you are quoting the governor out of context and are giving his statement undue support for your claim.

Finally, never falsify your evidence. Creating facts or changing the conditions under which a statement was made distorts the validity of your claim and, in some cases, leads your listeners to believe that something is true when, in fact, it is false. Such practices make critical decision making through the use of argumentation virtually impossible.

Summary

Evidence, claim, and inference are the three major components of a unit of proof. Evidence is the raw material from which claims are made through the use of inferences.

The types of evidence include direct observation, inferences from indirect observation, experimental data, primary documents, and testimony. Each has certain tests that help determine the strength of the evidence.

The sources of evidence include books, periodicals, government documents, newspapers, and scholarly journals. In addition to written sources, interviews with witnesses and specialists can provide information, as can your own observations.

In presenting evidence, you should be aware of certain factors that can affect the strength of your claims. You should explain your evidence and be as specific as possible. Do not withhold information that could affect the outcome of your claim, and try to be accurate in presenting your information and keeping your evidence in context.

Questions for Discussion

1. In what ways does the quality of evidence affect its reliability?
2. When choosing different types of evidence, what principles should guide your selection?
3. Which types of evidence are the most susceptible to a biased viewpoint?
4. How does the nature of a situation determine the strongest evidence to use?
5. What are the relative merits of supporting claims with different types of evidence and supporting claims with only one type?
6. Does evidence derived from experimental research have elements of opinion and value? Why or why not?
7. What are the ethical implications of misrepresenting evidence?

Chapter 4

Inferences

An argument consists of claims made on the basis of evidence. But the claim is never identical with the evidence, and it always goes beyond the specific information provided as evidence. How can we get from the evidence to the claim? Why is the evidence a good reason for believing the claim? What does it mean to say that the claim follows from the evidence? This chapter will attempt to answer these questions.

Evidence and claim are connected by a mental operation called an *inference*. An inference is a license, or warrant, for drawing a conclusion. It is like a ticket enabling us to travel from one place — the evidence — to another — the claim. Sometimes inferences are referred to as the links between the evidence and the claim. Since the claim draws on the evidence but establishes a position not contained in the evidence, an advocate must make a mental leap from the evidence to the claim. Inferences justify or permit these mental leaps.

But sometimes inferences may ticket us to the wrong destination. We may be led from the evidence to a claim that is not supported by or grounded in the evidence. It is important to consider what a good inference is. We shall approach this topic both as a general matter and in its application to specific patterns of inference.

The Standard of Reasonableness

Precisely because the claim always goes beyond the evidence, we can never be absolutely certain of the claim, even if we are sure of the evidence. It is always possible that the evidence may be true, but the claim may be false. For this reason, arguments in ordinary usage must meet a standard of validity different from that of formal logic. We can never be sure that acknowledging the truth of the evidence requires us to acknowledge the truth of the claim. Yet formal logic provides no other standard for distinguishing a strong inference—which we can make with confidence despite the mental leap involved—from a weak inference—about which we have serious doubts.

The standard of *reasonableness* addresses this problem. Generally, an infer-ence is reasonable if it would be made by most people when exercising their critical judgment. This standard is more stringent than is *logical possibility,* or the absence of self-contradiction. Just because an inference does not deny itself, there is no assurance that anyone will take the inference seriously. But reaonableness is a less stringent standard than is *formal validity* which requires that claims follow from the evidence with absolute certainty.

Reasonableness depends on the audience's judgment. It is determined not by any intrinsic features of the inference but by how people generally react to the inference when they are thinking critically. Reasonableness also depends on his-tory. Because in the past a certain pattern of inference usually led to satisfactory results, audiences in the present are prepared to make that inference confidently. Experience, rather than abstract logic, decides which inferences people will judge to be sound. In sum, making an inference always means taking a gamble, since our ticket cannot guarantee safe passage from evidence to claim. But subjecting inferences to the standard of reasonableness permits an intelligent gamble sup-ported by the weight of experience.

But the standard of reasonableness will be of little use unless we can specify what sorts of inferences people are likely to accept. Generally, an inference is reasonable if (1) the underlying assumptions of the argument are shared by the audience and (2) the form of the inference is correct. The first condition is *substan-tive,* as it relates to the content of the argument, and the second condition is *formal,* as it relates to the argument's structure.

Congruence of Underlying Assumptions

In Chapter 2 we discussed the context of an argument, noting that every argument is grounded in a context of basic, but usually unstated, assumptions. No argument is made in a vacuum; it is always embedded in a context of underlying assump-tions. The reason that these assumptions are seldom stated—indeed, the advocate may not even realize them—is that they are widely shared among the community of people to whom the argument is addressed. They may be said to constitute a part of that community's social knowledge. Since these assumptions are accepted as knowledge, they can be compared with statements whose probable truth is in dispute. An inference that conflicts with these underlying assumptions probably will be rejected as unreasonable.

A few examples should illustrate the importance of an advocate's being con-sistent with the audience's underlying assumptions. Suppose that President Ronald Reagan argues that we should abandon the approach of solving problems through major government programs and regulations because that approach has been tried and failed. His evidence consists of examples of past unsuccessful programs, and he attempts to generalize from these cases to a broader claim. Underlying his argu-ment is the assumption that history is relevant to policy choices, that there is some continuity between the present and the past.

If Reagan's audiences share that assumption (as most people do), then his inference may seem reasonable. On the other hand, suppose that an audience believes that history has nothing to teach us, that the present is totally unlike the past, and that situations never repeat themselves. Such an audience is likely to find the president's appeal to history to be irrelevant and to deny that experience forms the basis of an argument. To this audience, Reagan's inference is unreasonable.

In another example, advocates often call for the centralization and coordination of government programs. When considering the feasibility of establishing a national data center, many arguers point to the federal government's vast yet fragmented storehouse of information on social policies. Information on urban poverty, for instance, is scattered among several dozen government departments, bureaus, agencies, and offices. It seems desirable to collate and coordinate this information so that the government can more systematically attack the problem of urban poverty.

This argument, too, depends on underlying assumptions. In this case an audience must believe that there is some relationship between the quality of information and the ability to design and execute successful programs. This assumption is at the foundation of policy research and planning theories, and it too is accepted by most people. But suppose that an audience denies it. If the listeners do not believe that better information will produce better decisions, they will dismiss the argument for a national data center as being unreasonable, even though an advocate may be able to demonstrate fragmentation in current data gathering or the opportunities for improved coordination. The argument is simply incompatible with the basic beliefs that this audience regards as knowledge.

Our final example should explain the importance of underlying assumptions. Throughout the history of the United States, advocates have championed economic policies that are supposed to promote growth and increase individual income and wealth. There has been wide disagreement about what policies can achieve these ends, but the ends themselves have not been subject to much dispute.

These arguments have also rested on underlying assumptions. In this example, the assumption involves a hierarchy of values, that most people regard greater income and wealth as desirable. Again, suppose that an audience does not share these assumptions. If they believe that individual wealth conflicts with other, more important values such as environmental protection, they will dismiss the advocate's argument as unreasonable, even if the advocate can demonstrate that a particular policy would achieve greater wealth.

These examples have illustrated three different types of underlying assumptions — about history, causality, and values — but there are many other types of assumptions, as well. We often assume, for instance, that politicians are motivated primarily by the prospect of reelection. We assume that an organization's chief executive officer is responsible for its policy choices. We assume that our friends should have the benefit of the doubt when they have acted in a way that we find hard to explain. We assume that actions are taken with the knowledge of their consequences. Because underlying assumptions are content-specific, it is impossible to list all the forms that they might take. But it is essential that an argument agree with them if the inference is to be taken as reasonable. Thus it is valuable for arguers to practice examining their own arguments from a distance, in order to be able to identify their underlying assumptions. It also is valuable to analyze the audience in order to determine which underlying assumptions are likely to be shared by the listeners. Often this analysis cannot be precise, but if the listeners are seen as representing a larger community, educated guesses about their underlying assumptions can be made.

One more point needs to be made with respect to underlying assumptions. In suggesting that they are the bench marks against which inferences are tested, we may seem to be implying that underlying assumptions never change. But obviously, they do, as arguments are products of their time. People today reject many assumptions that were accepted by people in earlier times, and there is no reason to doubt that the revision of underlying assumptions will continue. But change is gradual, resulting from the repeated inability to square underlying assumptions with actual experience. Eventually the range of events that challenge an assumption may be so great that it causes the assumption to fall from the weight of all its exceptions. But seldom does a single claim, or a succession of claims by a single advocate, have this effect. Since arguments typically occur in a much shorter time span than does the change in underlying assumptions, it still makes sense to say that consistency with underlying assumptions is a basic condition of reasonableness.

Form of the Inference

The second condition for reasonableness is the form of the inference. Again, whether the form of an inference is correct does not really depend on the form's intrinsic features. Rather, certain forms of inference usually produce acceptable results.

Four general tests can be applied to any inference. First, does the claim have anything to do with the evidence? If not, the argument is said to be a *non sequitur*, meaning that the claim does not follow from the evidence. Such an inference can be dismissed as unreasonable. For example, if someone asserted, "Senator Smith is a poor politician; he wears a bow tie," the argument probably would be dismissed as a non sequitur. Most audiences do not believe that wearing a bow tie has anything to do with being a good or bad politician.

Second, does the claim really go beyond what is said in the evidence? If the claim merely restates in other words what is contained in the evidence, then the argument may be said to be *begging the question*. The argument "Freedom of speech is for the common good because the unrestrained expression of opinion is in the best interest of all" is an example of begging the question. The argument asserts to be true what it is setting out to prove to be true. The evidence that supposedly proves the claim is actually just a restatement of the claim. So the argument proceeds in a circle: no real inference is involved. An argument that begs the question generally is dismissed as unreasonable.

Third, does the claim respond to the subject at hand? When an arguer's inference leads to an irrelevant conclusion or when a person develops an inference so as to divert attention away from the subject at hand, he or she is *ignoring the question*. In discussing the artistic merit of a book or film, if an arguer uses an inference from one of its artistic features to judge its financial success or failure, then the arguer has ignored the question. Arguments of this type are sometimes referred to as *red herrings*. They prove something that is not pertinent to the situation. These inferences are regarded as unreasonable.

Fourth, is the language equivocal? Arguments are cast in language, and words are capable of many meanings. If the same words are used in the same argument, but with different meanings, then *equivocation* has been practiced, and we can conclude that the inference is unreasonable. A humorous example may help illustrate this problem. An advocate reasons as follows: "I love you; therefore I am a lover; all the world loves a lover; you are all the world to me; therefore you love me." In this argument several key terms change their meaning during the course of the same argument. The terms *lover* and *all the world* mean different things in the two statements in which they appear. A more common example is the politician who campaigns for office on a platform of "no tax increases." After having been elected, the politician explains that "increase" refers to the imposition of new taxes, not to raising the rates of existing taxes. When equivocation has been committed, the claim of the argument may refer to something quite different from that suggested by the evidence, even though the same words are used.

Arguments that fail to satisfy these general tests can be regarded as unreasonable; the inferences are not in the proper form. Other tests of the form of an inference are more specific. To understand these tests, we must know something about the general patterns of inference. In subsequent sections of this chapter, we shall discuss the five most common categories of inference: example, analogy, sign, cause, and authority.

Inferences from Example

The Nature of Example

The first type of inference occurs when we relate particular events or occurrences to more general claims. A motorist in an unfamiliar city observes three cases of reckless driving and concludes, "They sure are crazy drivers in this town." A citizen believes that political candidates typically give long and dull speeches and predicts that the candidate due to visit her town will do so as well. A defense attorney loses three cases and concludes that juries are generally disposed to favor the prosecution. A researcher determines that 75 percent of the people on a certain block believe that inflation has hurt them personally and thus concludes that about 75 percent of the entire population probably shares this belief. In each of these cases, the arguer has brought together in an argument particular situations and general claims, illustrating inferences based on example.

Inferences can proceed in either direction. Often the particular cases represent the evidence, and the advocate cites them in order to arrive at the more general claim. Sometimes, however, the generalization itself represents the evidence, and the argument illustrates the generalization by applying it to a particular case. The claim is that the generalization applies to the case at hand. Our example above of the citizen who expects politicians to give dull speeches is an example of illustrating a general statement by applying it to a specific situation.

Whether the argument proceeds from the specific to the general or from the general to the specific, the basic inference is the same. The particular instances being discussed are representative of the more general category. If the particulars are atypical or aberrant, then we can have no confidence in a statement that what is true of the particulars is true of the generalization, and vice versa. We can never be completely sure that the examples are representative, but we can select the examples so as to remove all known sources of distortion or bias.

Uses of Inference from Example

Inferences based on example are used in several types of argument. One such type is the statistical generalization, exemplified by the researcher surveying beliefs about inflation. In this sort of argument, a small sample is drawn from a larger population. The perception that inflation is personally harmful is found to apply to a certain portion of the sample, and it is claimed that the same characteristic will apply to about the same percentage of the entire population. If the sample is representative of the larger population, then what is true of the part should be true of the whole.

Rather than making a statistical generalization, we sometimes identify several particulars and then draw a general conclusion. Deriving general claims by enumerating examples is probably the most common use of inference based on example. From an accumulation of details we can infer a more general claim. After observing that traffic is congested in five big cities, we may conclude that it is generally congested in all big cities. One question that often arises is how many examples must be presented in order to establish the generalization. In one sense, the more the better: several examples taken from different times and places add to the force of the generalization. But a complete enumeration is usually impossible, and an audience is likely to become bored once enough examples have been given to show the link between the general and the particular. A small number — usually three to five — of carefully chosen examples may be sufficient. If, however, the arguer offered only a single example, as in the above case of the motorist and the defense attorney, we would treat the example as isolated and atypical unless the arguer could convince us that it was the most representative case, or prototype, of the generalization.

The third major type of argument containing an inference from example is the application of a general principle to particular circumstances. This type is demonstrated in the case of the citizen who believes that politicians always kiss babies and therefore expects a specific politician to do so. The effect of the application is to make the general principle more salient by showing how it is displayed in a specific situation. Again, the inference is that the particular situation identified in the claim is truly representative of the general category described in the evidence.

Tests for Inferences from Example

Example-based inferences cannot be established absolutely. There always is room to question whether the particulars are representative. Even if they are, they may not share all the features of the whole.

Inferences from example are regarded as reasonable if there is no cause to doubt them. Doubt might result if the number of instances is very small, particularly for a statistical generalization. A small sample increases the risk that the generalization will not apply. Or there may be room for doubt if the instances are ambiguous. If the same particulars can support quite different generalizations, it may be unsafe to assume that they count as clear support for the general claim that a specific arguer wants to establish.

Two other problems with inferences based on example are the *fallacy of composition* and the *fallacy of division*. Both fallacies can be committed by an arguer who assumes that the whole is always equal to the sum of its parts. For instance, no family can survive long if it is always in debt. But it does not follow that the nation is equally unable to remain in debt. The individual's debt is to another party, but the nation's debt, being all-inclusive, is a debt to itself. What is true of the part is not always true of the whole.

Similarly, it does not automatically follow from the statement "My university has a distinguished faculty" that "Every faculty member is a distinguished scholar." The first statement may be a generalization about the group as a whole, a statement that recognizes the existence of exceptions to the rule. What is true of the whole is not always true of each part. An arguer needs to be sure that the shift from the part to the whole is not a difference in kind as well as degree.

Inferences from Analogy

Often arguments compare something not very well known to something with which we are far more familiar. The inference in these arguments is called *analogy*.

The Nature of Analogy

We could say that the leadership struggles in a professional society are just like big-city machine politics. Or we could say that state and local governments are attracted to federal grants-in-aid just as bees are attracted to a pot of honey. In each case we have taken the object of our argument (professional society politics or the search for federal funds) and said something about it by comparing it to something else with which the listener should be more familiar (big-city machines or the attraction of bees to honey).

Sometimes the comparison is quite direct, being between the objects or events themselves. For instance, Chicago is a major northern urban center that has a declining population and industrial base. Pittsburgh, we observe, is also a major northern urban center, and so we conclude that it, too, probably has a declining population and tax base. In this example we have made a direct comparison between the cities of Chicago and Pittsburgh; our implicit inference is that the two cities are essentially similar. When our comparison is direct, the analogy is said to be *literal,* and the above comparison between professional society politics and big-city machines is thus a literal analogy.

Sometimes, though, the comparison is indirect. Rather than finding like-nesses in the objects or events we discuss, we discover similarities in the relation-ships among them. If an arguer says, "Our governor is just like the moon, whereas the president is the sun," no direct comparison is made between the governor and the moon. The point is not that the governor has deserts and valleys like the moon or that the governor is made of green cheese. Rather, the inference is that the rela-tionship between the governor and the president is like the relationship between the moon and the sun. Just as, say, the moon reflects light from the sun without having any light source of its own, so the governor mirrors the president's ideas and wishes without ever exercising independent initiative.

In this example, we have made a claim about the object of the argument (the relationship between the governor and the president) by comparing it with another relationship (that between the sun and the moon). Analogies that compare relation-ships rather than objects or events themselves are referred to as *figurative* analogies. Our above reference to the bees and the honey pot is an example of a figurative analogy.

Analogies figure prominently in argumentation because the easiest way for a person to come to terms with the unknown is to compare it to something else with which he or she is more familiar. Analogies, however, cannot be absolutely valid. The objects, events, or relationships being compared are never identical. They are similar, but there also are respects in which they are different. Whether the analogy is reasonable will turn on the question of whether the essential similarities outweigh the essential differences.

Tests for Analogy

To determine whether the essential similarities outweigh the essential differences, two basic tests are applied. First, are there key differences between the items com-pared? To change our example about big cities, suppose that an advocate has asserted that New York City and Chicago are alike in most important respects: both are northern metropolitan areas, both have very high population densities, both are ringed by suburbs that have taken away much of the city's tax base, and so on. The advocate asserts, on the basis of these similarities, that the two cities will probably have the same problems of government. But another arguer could observe that there is a crucial difference between the cities: for many years New York has been influenced by reform-minded political organizations, whereas Chicago has been subject to the influences of "machine politics." Identifying the key differences between the items compared is the first step in casting doubt on analogy.

The second test is also imperative: Do the important differences really matter? Do they outweigh the essential similarities? To call an analogy into question, it is not enough merely to find differences between the items compared; these differences must also be shown to make a difference. In our example, it is quite likely that the differences between reform organizations and political machines would determine whether New York and Chicago have the same problems, even if the two cities were alike in other respects. On the other hand, suppose that most of the political power were wielded by a small, nonpartisan social elite. Then the difference in political orangizations might not matter. Despite these differences, the two cities would be essentially alike and would be expected to have similar problems of government. Hence the user of an analogy will emphasize the essential similarities between the items being compared, whereas the challenger of an analogy will search for their essential differences.

Inferences from Signs

A sign is something that stands for something else. If a sign is present, we can predict the presence of the object that it symbolizes. Often this object is an abstraction: we cannot directly observe or know it, but we can infer its existence from the presence of something tangible that we regard as a sign.

The Nature of Signs

The formula of an argument containing a sign inference is "X exists (evidence); X is a sign of Y (inference); therefore, Y probably exists (claim)." The sign inference, then, enables us to conclude that there is a predictable relationship between two variables, but it does not explain the linkage. We may know that two things tend to occur together, but a sign inference does not enable us to explain why.

Theoretically, anything can function as a sign for anything else. In most arguments with sign inferences, however, one of three basic types of signs is used. Often we use *statistical indexes* as signs. For example, the concept of economic health is an abstraction; we cannot know directly whether the economy is in good or bad shape. But various statistics are taken as signs of economic health. Among them are the gross national product, the prime interest rate, the Dow-Jones Industrial Average, and the consumer price index (CPI). If we were to state, "The consumer price index is up by five points, and so the economy must be in bad shape," we would be saying that a CPI increase of that magnitude is a sign of a weak economy.

Sometimes *physical observation* furnishes the basis for sign inferences. If we awake to the sound of the alarm clock, look out our window, and see a bright sun, we probably will conclude that morning has arrived. We say, in effect, that the sun is a sign of morning. Knowing that the sun is there, we can infer that morning has come. Or we observe a crowded parking lot next to a concert hall and conclude that the concert in progress is popular. Here our reasoning is that a crowded parking lot is a sign of a popular concert. In each case we make an inference about something we do not know directly, by referring to something else that we take as a sign.

A third type of sign is an *institutionalized regularity*, that is, a pattern that occurs as a result of a norm or convention. If a newspaper reporter finds a pattern of frequent, unscheduled meetings among top-level executives, the reporter might interpret the frequency of the meetings as a sign that the organization is undergoing some crisis. For many employees, payday comes at the end of the month, and receiving a check is a sign that it is the last working day of the month. Artificial conventions, rather than natural ones, form these regularities.

But the sign does not always stand for the thing signified. If it did, the sign would be infallible, but there are few, if any, infallible signs. A decline in the gross national product usually is seen as a sign of economic trouble; but it could be a good sign if it resulted from a deliberate decision to limit growth in order to maintain economic balance. The crowded parking lot usually indicates a popular concert, but it could be that all illegally parked cars in the city are towed to this lot. Election campaigning normally is a sign of an impending election, but it could be a style adopted year-round in order to publicize the candidate's name. Since these exceptions can always be present, we must be careful in asserting that a sign relationship exists between two variables. We cannot stop using sign inferences, but we can subject our inferences to careful tests.

Tests for Sign Inferences

We want to know, first, whether it is reasonable in the case at hand to interpret a particular thing as a sign of something else. Is an alternative explanation of the relationship perhaps more plausible? In 1977, when newly inaugurated President Jimmy Carter left his limousine and walked down Pennsylvania Avenue, his decision to walk was widely taken to be a sign of his desire to identify with the people. It is possible, however, that his parade car had become disabled and that it was necessary for him to walk in order to reach his destination. Although in this example the alternative interpretation is highly unlikely, in other circumstances there may be a quite reasonable alternative to the alleged sign.

A second question is whether the alleged sign was observed when the thing for which it stands was not also present. If so, the sign relationship can be called into question. If, for instance, energy prices increased on several occasions without a drop in fuel supplies, we could question the statement that increasing prices are a sign of declining fuel supplies.

Finally, we should ask whether the sign is recurrent or an aberration. If a single politician kisses a baby, we may think nothing of it; but if we repeatedly observe politicians kissing babies, we may conclude that kissing babies is a sign of being a politician.

Even if we can be fairly confident that we have a reasonable sign inference, we must always remember that sign reasoning shows only that there is some predictable relationship between things. It does not explain the relationship. Being a politician does not necessarily cause one to kiss babies. That is the major difference between sign and causal inferences.

Inferences from Cause

Shortly after the federal government ended price controls on gasoline, the price of gasoline at service stations rose by about fifteen cents per gallon. We may notice these two events and see nothing more than coincidence. On the other hand, the advocate who asserted, "Price controls were ended; therefore, prices rose," would have something more in mind. This advocate would be suggesting that something about the ending of price controls caused gasoline prices to rise. The implied inference would be "Ending price controls caused prices to go up."

The Nature of Causality

Like signs, causal inferences posit a relationship between objects or events. But whereas sign inferences merely identify such a relationship, causal inferences seek to explain it by noting the influence of one event or object on the other. We need, then, to be more precise about what we mean in saying that one object or event "influences" another.

The concept of influence is elusive. Three guides are commonly used, either together or separately, to determine what constitutes influence.

Human Activity. Influence is often associated with human activity. According to this approach, only human beings can be conscious of their actions. In other beings, regularities may be observed and described, but they are not seen as cases of causal influence, since no other elements in nature act with conscious purpose. In contrast, human beings have the capacity to intervene in the natural order and to be aware of doing so.

From this point of view, it would be a mistake to say, for example, that a crop failure caused famine in the Third World. Rather, the causes of famine would be found in the ways that people reacted to a natural occurrence or pattern—whether they shifted to other kinds of food, brought in food from other lands, decided that the situation was hopeless, and so on. There is much to recommend this view, and—particularly in the social and policy sciences—we do typically think of people as the causal agents. At the same time, however, this view has limitations. We often wish to inquire into the causes of purely natural events, such as what caused the 1980 explosion of Mount Saint Helens. On these occasions the rule that influence requires human action is not very useful.

Deviation from the Norm.   Second, influence is typically found in deviation from the normal course of events. When we investigate the cause of a particular event, we are asking, in part, what makes it different from other events. We tend to distinguish between the ever-present circumstances and the factors uniquely present in the case at hand. We refer to the latter as *causes.*

    Suppose that we wished to explain a person's particularly bad disposition on a certain morning. We could not find the cause in the poor quality of the mattress on which he slept the night before if the person always used the same mattress and yet usually awoke cheerfully. The cause would not be the early rising hour if the person habitually awoke at the same time. It would not be the absence of morning coffee if the person never drank coffee. But if the person normally fell asleep quickly but had had insomnia the previous evening, then we would be likely to identify insomnia as the cause of his bad temper. The idea here is that when we seek causal explanations, we usually wish to account for an aberrant situation, one that departs from some basic pattern. We do so by referring to those elements of the situation that themselves are departures from the norm.

Sufficient Conditions.   Third, we frequently explain causal influence by trying to identify *sufficient conditions* for the object or event being explained. A sufficient condition is one whose presence assures the presence of the effect. If drinking whiskey is a sufficient condition for a headache, then a person who drinks whiskey should always get a headache.

    In practice there is usually no single sufficient condition; many conditions typically precede any effect. From these conditions we may select the one that comes last in time, the one that appears to be most conspicuous, or the one that seems intuitively to be the "last straw" and designate it as the sufficient condition. Although the procedure may seem lacking in rigor, there is an easy test of its accuracy: if we can find cases in which the alleged cause was present but the effect did not ensue, then—by definition—we have not identified a sufficient condition.

The Uses of Causal Arguments

Which of these concepts of causal influence should be used depends on the purpose for which the argument is being advanced. Causal arguments sometimes explain changes in the natural or material world by predicting what leads to what. An arguer who contended, "Depletion of fossil fuels will cause an energy shortage," would be making an argument of this type. It depends primarily on a view of causation as sufficient condition, although each of the other two views may also sometimes be appropriate. In this example, depletion is clearly something that people do (hence also satisfying the first approach to definition), but it is not a departure from the norm (hence the second sense of influence would not be appropriate to this argument).

Another use of causal arguments is to assign responsibility, whether praise or blame, for the course of events. Since responsibility presumes avoidability — we do not praise or blame things that are inevitable — it implies a self-consciousness of choice that, to the best of our knowledge, is a distinctly human trait. For this reason, the concept of causal influence as human action is most prominent in this usage, although the other views may also be employed. An advocate who maintained, "Greed of the oil companies is the cause of the energy shortage," clearly would be using the concept of causal influence in this second sense. In this example, although greed probably is also seen as a sufficient condition (the third sense of influence), it may or may not be viewed as departure from the norm. The key idea is that it assumes the existence of motives in human beings who have the capacity for choice.

Sometimes causal inferences are used to explain actions that otherwise do not seem to make sense. An apparent paradox, such as "Why would the most energy-rich nation on earth have an energy shortage?" illustrates the sort of phenomenon needing explanation. Here a sense of causation as a departure from the norm is prominent. In response to the question, an advocate will need to find some unexpected and usually obscure factor in the situation that can explain the seeming paradox. Perhaps a sudden and unanticipated growth in demand for energy may be the reason. This reason may also be a sufficient condition, and it may be a case of human action, but it need not be either.

A fourth common use of causal influence is relating means to ends. A person who says, "To end the energy shortage, step up the development of solar power," is implicitly relying on the warrant that the use of solar energy will cause the shortage to disappear. The cause is then a means to the desired end or effect. Reasoning in this way enables us to relate problems to solutions, by claiming that a proposed solution is a means by which to resolve the problem. For this usage, the most appropriate sense of causation is sufficient condition, since we are searching for factors whose presence will assure the desired effect.

These four examples certainly do not exhaust the uses of causal inferences, but they should indicate that the appropriate view of influence depends on the use for which the argument is made. Arguers whose concept of causal influence does not fit their purpose may have great difficulty establishing their claims.

Tests for Causal Inferences

Like signs, causal inferences never are absolutely valid: there always may be grounds to doubt whether a true cause has been identified. The question therefore is whether the causal inference is reasonable. If any of several errors in inference are present, then the audiences will be far less likely to view the inference as reasonable.

One common error is *confusing sign and cause.* Particularly when the data are statistical, it may be hard to distinguish between sign and causal relationships. Frequently, the statistical evidence refers to the correlation between two variables. A correlation is a measure of a sign relationship's strength. If the correlation is positive or negative, then the relationship between the variables is patterned and predictable. If the correlation is tenuous, then the relationship is largely unpatterned and random. But no measure of correlation permits an inference concerning causation. One could establish, for example, that students in wealthy school districts continually scored much higher on standardized tests than did students from impoverished school districts. Such a proof would establish that school districts' wealth was a sign of the students' educational performance, but not necessarily that the two were causally related.

A second common deficiency is the *fallacy of common cause.* It occurs when one factor is alleged to be the cause of another, whereas in reality both factors are the effects of some other cause. In the example above, the school district may be wealthy because its population includes many affluent families, who, because they can afford leisure, spend more time on activities that might be classified as informal education—reading, discussions, television and movies, travel, and so on—and the students' test performances are high for the same reason. If this conclusion were correct, then it would not be wise to infuse additional money into poorer schools in the belief that doing so would end the disparity in test performances, as the reason for the disparity might instead be influences in the family.

A third weakness in causal reasoning is referred to as the *post hoc fallacy.* The name comes from the Latin phrase *post hoc, ergo propter hoc,* which means "after this, therefore because of this." This fallacy is committed when an advocate assumes that an earlier event caused a later event. This fallacy is committed frequently in political discourse. The Democrats observe that recessions occur after the Republicans have been elected to office and thus blame the Republicans for recession. But the Republicans observe that wars occur after the Democrats have been elected and thus blame the Democrats for war. Unless they can demonstrate that the first event exerts some sort of control on the second, they should not assume that the first is a cause and the second is an effect.

Another deficiency frequently committed in causal reasoning is overlooking the existence of important multiple causes or effects. For instance, the high costs of medical care may be caused by an inefficient geographical distribution of doctors. But the small total number of doctors, cost increases in medical technology, wage increases for auxiliary health personnel, and the persistence of a fee-for-service system of payment also may be important causes of the high costs of care. If this were correct, a redistribution of doctors by itself would not necessarily lower medical care prices. If the other factors still were sufficient conditions, then geographical redistribution would be futile. Similarly, if a single cause were responsible for the production of multiple effects, we could not eliminate a single effect without eliminating them all.

Finally, advocates may overlook the existence of intervening causes that block the causal inferences. They may argue, for example, that the concentration of power in the hands of big business or big labor causes them to determine the levels of wages and prices independently of the market mechanism. If, however, the causal force of business and labor is offset by government pressures, ranging from the sale of stockpiles to the establishment of wage and price controls, it does not follow that controls on business and labor are necessary. By ignoring the existence of possible intervening causes, we may exaggerate the strength of an actual causal relationship.

Inferences from Authority

As we saw in Chapter 3, evidence often takes the form of statements by authorities. When the claim involves a complex subject about which most people lack direct knowledge or experience, we tend to rely on the judgment of experts or specialists. Few of us are competent, for example, to assess whether the stock market will do better in the coming months, and so we defer to the judgment of a broker whom we trust. The expert or specialist probably has reasoned by using one of the inferential patterns already described. As far as we are concerned, however, the authority's conclusion is the basis for our acceptance of the claim. Accordingly, we reason using the formula "Claim X is true because authority Y says so."

When we infer a claim from an authority's statement, the basis for our inference is the belief that the authority is reliable with respect to the subject of the claim. If we accept the judgment of a distinguished jurist, nuclear physicist, or economist, we are assuming that these individuals are reliable authorities in their fields.

The tests for inferences from authority are therefore different from those of the other patterns we have examined. It is not so much the inference that is tested; rather, it is whether or not the authority can be regarded as reliable. The tests for an authority's reliability were discussed in Chapter 3. To review, we should ask (1) whether the person has the necessary training in the field of specialization, (2) whether the person is speaking in his or her field of expertise, (3) whether the expert has a vested interest in the outcome of what he or she says, and (4) whether there is a clear basis for judgment regarding the issue at hand. When the authorities disagree, we ask where the consensus lies, whether there is another form of evidence that might corroborate the expert, and what the expert's previous record is of making judgments that were validated by experience.

Summary

Inferences are mental operations that enable us to link evidence and claims. They are like tickets authorizing us to travel from the evidence to the claim. Since the claim always goes beyond the stated evidence, we can never be certain that the inference is reliable. We will be on safer ground if we insist that the inference be reasonable. A reasonable inference is one that would be made by most people when thinking critically. Reasonableness depends on two basic conditions: that the underlying assumptions of the argument are shared by the audience and that the form of the inference is correct.

Assumptions are substantive in nature and specific to a given argument. They represent the basic beliefs or social knowledge of the listeners to whom an argument is addressed. Their function is to serve as standards for comparison with the other claims being examined by the listeners. If an argument's assumptions are incompatible with those of the audience, the argument is likely to be rejected as irrelevant, even if the statements are true and well supported.

Four general tests can be applied to the form of any inference: (1) does the claim have anything to do with the evidence? (2) does the claim really go beyond what is said in the evidence? (3) does the claim respond to the subject at hand? and (4) is the language equivocal? If the answer to any of the first three questions is no or if the answer to the fourth question is yes, then the reasonableness of the inference should be questioned.

Other tests of reasonableness apply to the specific patterns of inference, of which the five basic forms are example, analogy, sign, cause, and authority. Arguments from example relate parts to wholes; arguments from analogy involve comparisons; sign arguments describe a relationship between variables; causal arguments describe and account for such a relationship; and arguments from authority rely on the judgment of experts.

For arguments from example, the standards of reasonableness are the size and representativeness of the sample and whether the parts and the wholes are different in kind. For analogies, we want to know whether the essential similarities outweigh the essential differences. For sign arguments, we ask whether an alternative explanation is plausible, whether the sign appears without the thing signified, and whether the sign is recurrent. For causal arguments, the key tests are whether sign has been confused with cause, whether there is a common cause, whether temporal order has been confused with cause, and whether there are multiple causes or effects. Finally, arguments from authority are tested by asking whether the authority is reliable.

We have considered the major parts of an argument—claims, evidence, and inferences—and now are ready to turn our attention to how individual arguments are put together in the process of arguing.

Questions for Discussion

1. Why must a claim always go beyond the stated evidence, necessitating an inference?
2. How do audiences acquire the basic assumptions that they use to decide whether an argument is reasonable?

3. We have identified four general tests for the form of an inference. Can you find arguments that fail to meet one or more of these tests?

4. What are the primary differences between inferences from sign and inferences from cause?

5. Under what circumstances is each of the five basic patterns of inference preferred? Are any stronger or weaker than the rest?

Chapter 5

Constructing a Case

Few resolutions can be advanced or attacked successfully by a single argument. Most subjects about which people argue are complex enough that several claims and their supporting evidence must be joined to support or oppose the resolution. Individual arguments that affirm or deny the resolution are chosen from a much larger pool of potentially available arguments.

The process of arguing consists of selecting, arranging, and presenting constructive arguments on behalf of the resolution. It also examines the arguments of one's adversary, determining how and which arguments should be attacked and developing these attacks. Finally, arguing includes analyzing the attack that has been made on your own position and extending that position by resubstantiating your arguments.

Whether you are making an initial argument, attacking another person's argument, or defending your own argument, the structure of arguments actually presented is known as the *case*. From among all the possible arguments in support of an advocate's position, he or she chooses a body of arguments that will finally be offered. This body of arguments is the advocate's case.

In this and the next chapter, we shall be concerned with the process of arguing. We shall begin by examining the process by which cases are initially composed. Then we shall examine the attack and defense of arguments after their initial presentation.

Selecting the Case

The first step in constructing a case is to determine which arguments are available for inclusion. Then you can decide, from among the available arguments, which ones finally to use.

Identifying Potential Arguments

Generating a pool of potential arguments requires analysis of the resolution, reflection on your own experience, and research and study in the specific subject area. If the resolution is formally stated, then an analysis of its terms and their relationship to one another will suggest what must be proved to affirm the resolution. From a knowledge of the proof requirements, you can identify possible ways in which they might be satisfied. If no explicit resolution is stated, then the analysis must begin with a formulation of the resolution that is implicit in the interaction between the arguers. This step is crucial for the many varieties of informal debate.

When the resolution involves a subject about which you have had personal experience, use of that experience can be an additional source of possible arguments. From what you have learned through your own involvement or from your feelings about a subject, arguments can be formed. Finally, if the subject is not one on which you have personal expertise, further research and study will be needed. This research may be as simple as talking to a friend who is better informed about the subject, or it may require consultation with experts or extensive library research.

Choosing Among Arguments

Analysis, reflection on experience, and research can be expected to yield far more arguments to support a claim than can actually be used. Many of these arguments overlap, and so the arguer must decide which claims to advance in support of his or her position. The goal is to select the strongest possible arguments. But what is the strength of argument, and how can you decide what the strongest possible arguments are?

The Meaning of Strength.   The strength of an argument depends on two factors. First, how likely is it that the audience will accept the evidence as true and the inference as reasonable? An argument that people are likely to view as sound —as both true and reasonable—is a strong argument. If they believe in the foundation of the claim, people can then be induced more easily to accept the claim itself. In contrast, an argument about which people harbor strong doubts regarding its evidence or inference is less strong, because more effort is required to predispose them in the argument's favor. The first criterion of strength, then, is the ease with which the claim can be established—which in turn depends on the intensity of the audience's adherence to the claim's premises.

The second factor affecting strength is how relevant the argument is to the resolution. A certain claim may be easy to establish, but doing so may progress only a short way toward verifying the resolution. This would happen only if the claim were fairly obvious to start with, if it related only tangentially to the resolution, or if it were only a small step toward the goal of supporting the resolution.

Criteria for Strength. Strong arguments are those that build on premises that the listeners are likely to accept and that support the resolution. In trying to decide whether one argument is stronger than another, the advocate should consider the following four criteria:

1. What degree of probability is involved in the proofs? An argument that relies on empirical evidence usually is preferable to one that is inherently speculative, since the amount of needed guesswork and intuition is smaller in the former situation than in the latter. For example, the argument that consumer spending is declining, based on actual data on the volume of spending, is preferable to a similar argument based on statements regarding how people expect to modify their spending patterns in order to cope with inflation. In the former case, the data are empirical; in the latter, they are speculative and hence far less certain.

2. What is the time frame of the argument? A claim whose manifestations are immediate is generally preferred over one whose soundness can be determined only in the distant future. If one were to choose between two arguments concerning the consequences of unemployment — that it leads to civil disorder and that it reduces achievement levels among children of the unemployed—the former argument would be preferable if the other factors were equal. The reason is not that the consequences of civil disorder are worse than the effects of reduced achievement levels but that they are more immediate. We would need to wait a generation to determine whether reduced achievement levels would result and, if so, what they would imply for a policy to respond to unemployment.

3. How credible are the sources of the two arguments? Other things being equal, an argument supported by a more credible source will be easier to establish. Whether a source is credible is determined by the tests of evidence described in Chapter 3.

4. Is the argument strong in this particular situation or context? It is impossible to say in the abstract that one particular type of argument will always be stronger than another. The specific resolution, the historical background of the controversy, the values and motives of the arguers, and the course of the controversy itself will affect the criteria of strength. What we have attempted to do here is to offer general guidelines and to explain that strength is the criterion by which advocates select arguments from the available pool.

Number of Arguments. A closely related question is how many arguments to include. Time constraints and the patience of your audience will limit the number of arguments to be used. Moreover, an advocate may wish to present fewer arguments than the maximum possible. Competing considerations are involved, and tradeoffs must be weighed.

One reason for presenting multiple arguments involves audience analysis. Often, the members of an audience will represent a variety of backgrounds and interests. An argument with which one person can easily empathize may be meaningless to another. By combining a variety of strong arguments, therefore, the arguer ensures that the total case will include arguments palatable to the audience's diverse interests. In addition, the inconclusiveness of individual arguments may prompt a speaker to include multiple arguments, especially when the issues themselves are complex.

At the same time, there are risks in including multiple arguments in a case. These risks represent arguments for parsimony—for including the smallest possible number of arguments necessary for the case to prevail. For example, the audience may not share the advocate's judgment that all of the arguments presented are strong. If the listeners judge one claim to be weak, that unfavorable judgment often will adversely affect, as well, their view of the other claims. The entire structure of arguments may be perceived as weaker than it really is because the negative reaction to one claim contaminates judgments of the rest. Including many arguments also may cause the listeners to become bored or confused. Furthermore, although the speaker undoubtedly will regard all the arguments as being compatible, a listener might regard some of them as being inconsistent with the others. Although logic does not require it, many listeners respond to a perceived inconsistency by rejecting all of the seemingly incompatible arguments. The speaker thus could be in a worse position than if he or she had presented only one of the arguments.

It may be possible to avoid this danger by making some arguments conditional on the others. For instance, an advocate could say, "I don't favor having the federal government spend more on education, but if they are going to do it, the best way is through a voucher system that lets individual families decide which educational opportunities are best." The audience might think it inconsistent to present arguments both favoring and opposing increased federal spending. But by making the argument for vouchers conditional (or hypothetical) and stressing that the primary position is the absence of a need for any increased federal funding, the advocate avoids this possibility.

Through analysis of the resolution, study of the subject area, and reflection on personal experience, an advocate can generate a large pool of potential arguments. Evaluating the strength of arguments will narrow the pool to those that can reasonably be included in the case. Then the speaker must evaluate the comparative merits of presenting many and few arguments in order to determine how many of the available arguments to use.

Arranging the Arguments

The next consideration in constructing a case is how to organize the arguments that are finally selected for inclusion. Questions of arrangement can be applied to the case as a whole (macro-organization) and also to individual arguments in the case (micro-organization).

Macrolevel Organization

Two general choices are available at the macrolevel: *logical order* and *topical order*. In logical order, each argument depends on the others. But in a case arranged by topical order, each argument contributes to the resolution independently of the others.

For example, you could develop quite different cases for the resolution that the federal government should establish a universal system of voter registration. On the one hand, you could maintain that confusing and disparate registration procedures lead people to conclude that becoming politically informed is not worth the effort, that this belief in turn promotes political apathy, that apathy discourages registration, that low registration rates are manifested in a low turnout of voters, and that a low turnout threatens democracy. In this example, the arguments are like links in a chain. Each step in the causal claim depends on those that have preceded it. Consequently, each step in the argument must be sustained if the final claim is to be advanced successfully. Put another way, the chain is only as strong as its weakest link. This example illustrates the features of logical order.

On the other hand, you could advocate the same resolution on quite different grounds. For instance, you could claim that universal voter registration is desirable because it would increase turnout, increase the voters' feeling of identification with the political system, be easier to administer than separate state registration systems would be, and eliminate any local inequities that might result from treating differently people whose situations are essentially similar. Each of these reasons offers independent support for the resolution; that is, the strength of any particular argument does not depend on the strength of any of the others. This second example illustrates the principles of topical order. Figure 5.1 should help make clear the difference between logical and topical order.

Which organizational principle is preferable? As with the other choices we have examined, there are merits and drawbacks to both possibilities. Topical order may seem preferable because it is more flexible; it enables the advocate to lose one step in an argument without losing the entire case. Indeed, this flexibility is probably the strongest benefit of topical order. But if it is fairly easy to establish the first step in a logical progression that then moves through subsequent steps, then logical order may be preferable. For example, suppose that you could show that restricting the money supply would cause interest rates to rise and that the links between high interest rates and a recession were clear-cut. Then logical order would be the better way to arrange a case arguing that restricting the money supply leads to recession. In other words, if the focus of argument is on the first step and this step—if used—sets off the rest of the chain, then one will accomplish more through logical order than through topical order, in which each separate argument must be proved independently.

It also is possible to combine the principles of logical and topical order. For instance, you can argue for universal voter registration, as in the second example above, using topical structure for the major arguments. Each of these arguments,

Figure 5.1

MACRO-ORGANIZATIONAL PRINCIPLES

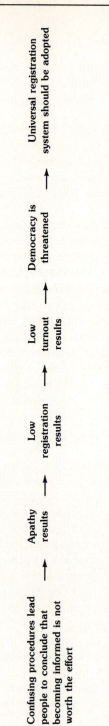

Confusing procedures lead people to conclude that becoming informed is not worth the effort → Apathy results → Low registration results → Low turnout results → Democracy is threatened → Universal registration system should be adopted

Logical Order

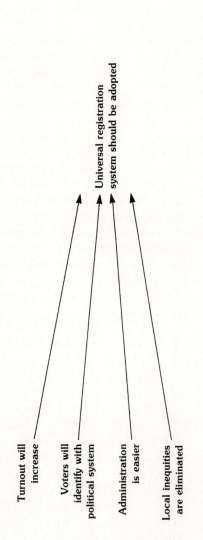

Turnout will increase

Voters will identify with political system

Administration is easier

Local inequities are eliminated

Universal registration system should be adopted

Topical Order

however, can be developed in a logical order in which the argument's subpoints are the links in a chain leading to the claim.

Microlevel Organization

Ordering of Arguments.   If you choose to follow logical order, then the microlevel organization will be dictated by the steps in the logical progression. With a topical order, however, you must choose the order in which to array the arguments that independently strengthen a claim. Logically, it makes no difference, but for other reasons it can make a great difference. Here such considerations as clarity, emphasis, and strategic advantage come into play. For example, if the audience — whether an adversary or a group of disinterested listeners — does not appear particularly knowledgeable or concerned about a subject, it may make sense to present first a startling or unexpected argument in order to gain attention. If the final impression is more important, then it may be wise to present last the most graphic or emotionally powerful argument. Because such factors as subject, the audience's predisposition, and the speaker's credibility can affect this choice, empirical research does not consistently support either initial or final impressions. There is general agreement, though, that the psychologically weakest argument should be placed in the middle of a sequence, since both the initial and the final impression are stronger than that of the middle position.

Anticipatory Refutation.   Another organizational question at the microlevel is whether advocates should present only arguments that support their own position or whether they should acknowledge opposing arguments, anticipating and preempting possible refutation. The classic study on this question, conducted during World War II, concluded that the two-sided message — one that includes preemptive treatment of opposing arguments — is more persuasive, either if the listeners are highly educated or if they are strongly predisposed against the speaker's position. Otherwise, the one-sided message, which contains only supportive arguments, is more persuasive. This finding is not difficult to explain. A highly educated audience presumably is able to think critically and thus will raise questions about a speaker's claims. Such mental activity might interfere with their comprehension of the speech. But if the speaker acknowledges these questions and doubts, not only will the danger of distraction be minimized, but also the speaker will appear to be more fair-minded and impartial because he or she has acknowledged the opposing view. Likewise, people with strong predispositions against the speaker are likely to approach the situation skeptically at best. The speaker who at least acknowledges the possibility of counterarguments is more likely to be given a fair hearing.

Structural Devices.   Another organizational choice at the microlevel is the cues to structure that the advocate chooses to include. Messages that appear to be well organized are more likely to be reviewed favorably. For this reason, structural devices such as previewing the major headings, numbering the headings and subheadings, and offering summaries and clear transitions, help clarify and strengthen the structure of the message.

The Case Outline

A valuable aid to organizing arguments is the *case outline*. By outlining the structure of the case, advocates can clarify the relations among the arguments. The notational system in the outline (roman numerals, capital letters, arabic numerals, and so forth) serves this purpose if it properly reflects coordination and subordination. In other words, all of the elements in the outline listed as roman numerals should be of the same order of importance: all of these elements are coordinate. Elements identified by, say, the capital letters A, B, and C under roman numeral I not only should be coordinate with one another but together should support the idea developed in roman numeral I. The major arguments to be included in the case—usually between two and five in number, aside from introductory and concluding remarks—are designated by roman numerals. The subordinate arguments are identified with capital letters, and if any of these arguments needs to be divided further, the substructure should be designated by arabic numerals. Division beyond the third level generally should be avoided, as the resulting argument is less likely to be clear. Once the structure of claims is complete, then the supporting evidence can be included under those claims to which it relates.

Some additional hints may be useful in constructing a case outline:

1. Include as much detail as possible. Avoid the tendency to develop just a brief "key-word" outline. Although a short outline may be helpful when you are about to give an extemporaneous speech, it is not a very useful way to construct a case. The outline should include a complete and exact statement of the major arguments.

2. Devise a useful notational system. In order to include as much detail as possible, you will need to devise a system of symbols and abbreviations. There is no one standard system; you should devise one that simplifies your outlining as much as possible. Of course, avoid using abbreviations and symbols whose meaning you will not remember later!

3. Be careful not to be overcomplex. If your outline has seven or eight different orders of magnitude, you probably have mistakenly analyzed the relationships among your arguments, and you should reexamine the case to see if you can discern simpler relationships.

4. Ask someone to examine the outline to see if it makes sense. Like any other skill, proficiency at outlining improves with practice. For this reason, besides outlining your own case, you may find it helpful to practice outlining the cases implicit in newspaper editorials, opinion magazines, and tape recordings of speeches. After you have completed each outline, check it against the suggestions

described here in order to make sure that you have the best possible record of the arguments and the relationships among them.

Presenting the Case

The final set of choices related to case construction is the way in which the case will be presented. These choices concern matters of language, since most arguments are embodied in language.

For example, a variety of *connotations* can be used to convey different images of the same referent, or denotation. A fairly neutral verb, such as *said,* can be given a positive connotation by using a synonym such as *exclaimed,* or it can be given a negative connotation if replaced by a synonym such as *confessed.* Language is not neutral; the words in which arguments are expressed exert great influence over audiences' reactions to the arguments. In constructing a case, therefore, advocates should consider whether positive, negative, or neutral connotations are the most desirable and should word their arguments accordingly.

A second linguistic variable is *precision.* Arguments can be stated precisely, or they may be relatively ambiguous. It sometimes is assumed that all arguments should be precise. But a degree of vagueness may be desirable. Vagueness may offer the opportunity for a more thorough consideration later, or it may permit people with different interests to agree on a common goal, even though they may do so for different reasons. Vagueness also can reduce the total number of arguments necessary. But the arguments should not be less precise than is appropriate for the arguer's purposes. Explanation, careful definition, and analogy are ways in which speakers can reduce the vagueness in their arguments.

Intensity is a third linguistic variable. Essentially the same argument can be presented with varying intensity. At one extreme, a speaker may use irony, deliberately stating the opposite of what he or she really means. At the other extreme, the advocate can use hyperbole, considerably overstating his or her claims. An audience unfamiliar with the subject may need some degree of overstatement in order to become concerned. But an audience that easily understands the subject and is familiar with the arguments may be more susceptible to understatement, since it implies that the listeners are able to figure out the speaker's true meaning. Either extreme, however, is likely to backfire: hyperbole may be so intense as to alienate the listener, and irony can be easily mistaken for sarcasm.

The final linguistic choice we shall discuss is *style.* Should the arguments be presented in straightforward prose or indirectly through figures of speech? Figures of speech are often treated as merely ornamental stylistic devices, but they can have important argumentative uses as well. They may make an idea more salient to the listener by evoking a vivid mental picture. Analogy, simile, and metaphor can be especially useful in this regard. A statement such as "Using the Justice

Department to expose official corruption is like leaving a fox in charge of the chicken coop" makes one idea clearer and more vivid in the minds of the audience by comparing it to another with which they are more familiar. When arguments involve abstract or complex concepts, the use of such figures may be particularly helpful.

Although we have examined only four presentational choices, there are others as well. For example, phrasing arguments in statements using the same basic structure may help clarify the organization and enable the listeners to anticipate the form. Using carefully chosen nouns and verbs, rather than adjectives and adverbs, may help convey arguments more clearly and efficiently. Using value terms when the audience holds the value in high regard will make the case more persuasive. The basic idea underlying all presentational choices is that language is not a neutral instrument, a vehicle in which the contents of argument are conveyed. Rather, language is an inseparable part of the argument itself and one that exerts great influence on how listeners perceive and react to the case.

Summary

In this chapter we examined the process of arguing. The first step in that process is the construction of a case, the structure of the arguments that will be used to support or to oppose a resolution. Case construction requires choices regarding the selection, arrangement, and presentation of arguments.

Since more arguments are available than can be used, advocates must be selective. They should choose the strongest arguments, with strength being a function of the listeners' predispositions and of the relevance of the argument to the advocates' purposes. The evidence's degree of probability, the argument's time frame, and the evidence's credibility all may affect the argument's strength. Selection also involves how many arguments to present. Multiple arguments may enable advocates to appeal to different segments of the audience and to hedge their bets, but they may jeopardize the advocates' credibility if any of the arguments appear weak.

There are questions of arrangement at both the macrolevel and the microlevel. At the former, the main choice is between logical order, in which each argument depends on the others, and topical order, in which each argument contributes independently to the resolution. Which is preferable depends on the given situation or context. If topical order is chosen, then there are a number of microlevel choices. Among them are the order in which to present logically independent arguments, the issue of whether opposing arguments should be mentioned and discussed, and the cues to structure that should be included. A valuable aid to organizing arguments is the case outline, which should reflect the proper coordination and subordination of the arguments.

Presentational choices involve the use of language. Such choices include the selection of desired connotation, the degree of precision desired, the appropriate level of linguistic intensity, and the use of figures of speech and other linguistic devices. Basic to these choices is the belief that language is not a neutral vehicle for conveying arguments but is an inseparable part of the arguments themselves.

Questions for Discussion

1. Find an example of argument in a newspaper. Identify arguments that might have been made but were not. Based on the criteria discussed in this chapter, were the strongest arguments chosen?
2. If you decide to present a relatively small number of arguments, how can you select the arguments so that they will have the greatest impact?
3. We have said that the choice between logical and topical order depends on the specific situation. What are some of the relevant factors?
4. Why is language not a neutral vehicle for conveying arguments? What happens when arguers assume that it is?

Chapter 6

Refuting and Rebuilding the Case

Many arguers painstakingly develop the arguments that they will initiate, leaving no detail untouched. The structure of the argument is carefully prepared: the supporting material is judiciously chosen, and the explanatory material is clearly and interestingly worded. It is surprising, therefore, that arguers often give so little consideration to the processes of attack and defense. They may attack arguments at random, rather than making the strongest possible counter to the original argument. Their defenses may be little more than a repetition of their initial view, as if the intervening attack had not occurred.

If argumentation is to test the probable truth of a position, then the constructive arguments must be tested against the strongest possible attacks, and it is highly unlikely that these positions of strength will appear intuitively or at random. At the very least, hoping for such a result is entrusting much of one's fate to luck. Similarly, the strategic advantages of the individual arguer are unlikely to be maximized if whimsy and chance become the guiding lights. For these reasons, therefore, conscious, careful crafting of attacks and defenses is crucial. This point cannot be overstressed; indeed, all of this chapter is an elaboration of this theme. The topic will be subdivided into (1) the procedure of attack and defense, (2) kinds of attack and defense, (3) strategic decisions in attack and defense, and (4) advanced planning for attack and defense. Attacks enable an arguer to refute an opponent's case; defenses, to rebuild one's own.

The Process of Attack and Defense

Attacks are the criticisms you launch against your opponent's constructive arguments. The major objective of an attack is to refute your adversary's argument.

70

Defenses are the responses you make to your adversary's attacks on your constructive positions. The major objective of defense is to rebuild your arguments once an attack has been launched against them. The process of refuting or rebuilding a case is normally executed in four steps:

1. *Presenting the argument you intend to attack or defend.* If you are defending, you should first state the argument that is being challenged, followed by a statement of the opposing attack. If attacking, you should first state the opposing argument. In both instances, you should state both your own argument and the opposing attack in the same words in which they were originally presented.

2. *Presenting the attack or defense being advanced against or in support of the argument.* In other words, you should state concisely the claim that you are advancing as an attack or defense. If necessary, you should explain in more detail what this claim means and how it refutes or rebuilds the original argument.

3. *Supporting your attack or defense.* In some instances, your argument attacking or defending an original argument may require evidence only to substantiate your claim, but often it will include subsidiary claims and a more complex structure.

4. *Explaining how your attack or defense either weakens or strengthens the probable truth of the resolution.* As explained in Chapter 2, the ultimate claim in a dispute is the resolution. Advocates hope to establish that the resolution is either probably true or probably false. All other claims in the dispute are subsidiary to the resolution. Unless this relationship is kept in mind, attacks and defenses may do little or nothing to enhance the larger goal of proving the resolution probably true or false. You therefore should explain how your exposure of a false claim or your support for a sound one either diminishes or strengthens the probable truth of the resolution.

Illustration of the Four Steps

The following example shows how this four-step process can be used for a resolution calling for federal gun control. If you are defending the resolution, you could claim that gun control is needed to prevent unnecessary deaths resulting from the easy access to handguns. In refuting this claim, your opposition could argue that people who kill with handguns will substitute long arms if denied access to handguns. In defense you could say: "I argue that federal control of handguns is needed to curtail deaths resulting from easy access to handguns. My opponent claims that fewer deaths would not result from eliminating handguns because those wishing to kill with handguns will kill with long arms. I disagree because long arms are not as easily concealed or as prone to accidental firing. I support my claim with evidence from countries that have abolished the sale of handguns. In such countries, deaths from handguns have decreased. Thus, the opposing claim is untrue. My original argument stands. The sale of handguns results in unnecessary deaths, and this supports my main contention that the sale of handguns should be abolished in order to stop these unnecessary deaths."

If you are opposing the resolution on handgun control, you could argue: "My opponent claims that we should have the federal government halt the sale of handguns because the easy access to these instruments results in thousands of unnecessary deaths. I contend that this is untrue. Many of those who wish to kill will simply use long guns instead of handguns. I offer examples from several cities in which this has been the case. I ask you to conclude, therefore, that prohibiting the sale of handguns will not result in decreasing unnecessary deaths and to reject the proposition that the federal government should stop the sale of handguns." (In this example we assumed that the two arguers were speaking to a third party. Obviously, if they were addressing each other, the conversation would be more informal.)

Extending Arguments

When people argue, they usually do not merely restate their original claims. In response to attacks and defenses, they amplify their initial claims and may introduce new ones. This process of elaborating the original claim is called *extending the arguments,* and it is a vital part of refuting or rebuilding a case.

One way to extend an argument is to use *counterevidence.* Suppose that you are supporting the resolution that the federal government should act to increase the energy independence of the United States. Your major supporting claim is that reliance on foreign fuel sources hampers American economic development, and you propose an increased reliance on domestic coal to alleviate this problem. Under your proposal, reliance on foreign oil would be gradually phased out as the federal government provided the necessary financial and technical incentives to increase coal production. In attacking your reason for supporting the resolution for energy independence, suppose that your opponent claims that greater coal production would pose an immediate danger to the environment and that nonfederal efforts to increase nuclear power should be encouraged instead. You could extend with counterevidence that indicates that the long-term environmental dangers of nuclear energy are much greater than the risks associated with coal.

Another way of extending your arguments is to present *counterarguments.* These are claims that dispute the opposition's claims. The relation between the opponent's evidence and claim is not in dispute, but the claim itself is directly challenged. Suppose that you support the resolution that the president of the United States should be elected by the direct vote of the people. Your major supporting claim is that the direct vote method for choosing a president is more democratic. Your rationale is that many voters are denied a voice in the outcome because each state is assigned a set number of votes based on its population and that the candidate with the most popular votes in each state receives all of the electoral votes. Under your proposal, in order to determine the winner, all votes would be totaled nationally, and the choice of each voter in each state would be included in the final count. In attacking your reason for supporting the resolution for direct election, suppose that your opponent claims that your proposal would be less democratic because a direct election would allow people living in the heavily populated states to dominate those living in sparsely populated states. As a supporter of direct popular vote, you can present counterarguments claiming that the electoral college method is even less democratic for people in the smaller states. Your rationale can be that the electoral college permits the candidates with the most votes in each state to claim all of the electoral votes, allowing the losing candidates no votes from that state.

Finally, you can sometimes extend your arguments by *turning the opposing argument*. In this case, you can try to show that your adversary's line of reasoning actually supports your position. The above arguments for the direct election of the president resolution illustrate this method. If your opponent alleges that direct election is undemocratic because it permits the big states to dominate the small states, you can try to show that this argument actually supports your position. For example, you can claim that it equalizes the votes of all people in all states, that it assumes that a voter in a heavily populated state, such as New York, should have an influence equal to that of a voter in a sparsely populated state, such as Wyoming. Each vote cast would be one vote counted in determining the final outcome of the election.

As an advocate, you may also turn your opponent's argument to go beyond the support of your original position and develop additional benefits associated with your proposal. For example, suppose that your opponent claims that increasing the democratic nature of elections by equalizing the votes of all people and increasing direct representation are a mistake, since the general populace is politically uninformed and does not have the political interest and expertise possessed by members of the electoral college. You not only can refute but also can turn this argument by claiming that the political knowledge and interest of the general public would be greatly enhanced as a result of the publicity surrounding a change to direct election, thereby enhancing the democratic decision-making process. This strategy can be employed by any advocate in the dispute, and several methods can be used to refute or rebuild arguments.

Kinds of Attack and Defense

Exposing Deficiencies in the Opposition's Argument

As we explained, an argument consists of claims based on evidence, and inference is necessary to get from evidence to claim. One of the principal ways to attack or defend an argument is to question the soundness of one or more of these elements — evidence, inference, or claim. For example, you can often expose a deficiency in your opponent's use of evidence; that is, the evidence may not pass one or more of the evidence tests discussed in Chapter 3, with the result that it may be incomplete, inaccurate, or nonexistent.

Another way to expose a proof deficiency is to subject the opponent's claim to the general tests of inferences suggested in Chapter 4. Remember that inferences enable you to connect evidence with claims, and you should insist that the inferences be reasonable. You can usually show that an inference is unreasonable if you can demonstrate that the claim has nothing to do with the evidence and, thus, does not follow from the data. You can also sometimes expose a faulty inference by showing that the claim merely repeats the evidence and, in effect, actually asserts as true what must be proved to be true. You can assert in this case that the argument begs the question. Third, you can sometimes show that the claim resulting from the evidence acutally ignores the question, because the conclusion is irrelevant. On occasion, you can also show that the opponent has used equivocal language; that his or her claim actually relates to something other than that suggested by the evidence. This may be the case even when the words used are the same.

Finally, you can often expose a proof deficiency by exposing critical assumptions or by showing that the opponent's inferences do not withstand the tests of formal correctness that we suggested in Chapter 4. You should examine carefully the form of the five most common categories of inference: sign, cause, example, analogy, and authority. Claims are never identical with the evidence but always require a mental leap. Sometimes this mental leap results in a claim not justified by the evidence. When this happens, you should demonstrate that the inference does not justify the mental leap.

Turning the Evidence

Sometimes you can show that your opponent's evidence actually proves your position. When using this method to attack or defend, you usually do not criticize the evidence, inference, or the claim. Instead, you show that the entire unit of proof supports your side of the resolution. In effect, you present a new interpretation of the proof. For example, if you were defending a resolution advocating decreased power for labor unions, your opponent could claim that such action would destroy the labor movement. It is conceivable that you could turn this argument in your favor by showing that decreasing the power of the unions in one area might solidify union membership behind other union concerns and, in the long run, result in a stronger association.

If your opponents have properly developed their position, avoiding deficiencies of proof and analysis, then this may be the best strategy to use to attack your opponent's arguments. It is here that an advocate's use of superior evidence and more extensive or analytical reasoning can be used to full advantage.

Reducing to Absurdity

Traditionally, the method of *reducing to absurdity* is identified by its Latin name, *reductio ad absurdum*. When using this method, you do not quarrel directly with the evidence, the inference, or even the claim. Instead, you show that the logic of making a decision based on such claims would lead to absurd behavior. For example, if you are advocating increased employment, your opponent may argue that with more jobs, people will increase their consumption of beef and other high cholesterol foods, resulting in more deaths from heart attacks. In defense, you can argue that if people followed this reasoning, they would eliminate all jobs so that very few could earn enough money to spend on such food.

Using Counterarguments

When you use counterarguments, you do not necessarily expose insufficiencies in the opposition's proof. Instead, you show that arguments and evidence not presented by your adversary point to a different and more probable conclusion. For example, if your opponent's claim rests on the testimony of an authority, you may be able to show that other, more reliable authorities have looked at the same evidence and reached different conclusions.

In other instances, you may be able to use counterarguments to expose the opposition's faulty inferences. For example, they may misuse inferences from sign. They may argue that the president's canceling of a news conference was a sign that he was unprepared to face the nation regarding a specific problem. You can counter that it also may be a sign that he had other problems to which he attached a higher priority. The counterargument can also sometimes be used to refute inferences from cause. Your opponent, for example, may argue that "we stopped giving foreign aid to country X, and they switched their allegiance to the Soviet Union." You may be able to show that the cause for the new allegiance resulted from an internal change in political ideology rather than from the foreign aid issue.

Attacking Inconsistencies

Arguers will sometimes make claims that result in inconsistent positions, and you should expose such errors. Inconsistencies can both weaken the logic of the argument and undermine the listener's confidence in the arguer. Inconsistencies often appear in different sections of your adversary's case. In one argument, an opponent may contend that we do not need new programs to send food to those starving abroad; that we, in effect, are feeding these people today. In another argument of the same case, the opponent may argue that we do not have enough food to feed the "have-nots", and so the resolution calling for increased food aid for foreign countries is doomed. The two arguments are inconsistent: if we do not have enough food to feed the have-nots, then how can we be feeding them today?

Using Dilemmas

The term *dilemma* is used to describe a situation in which all recognizable alternatives are inadequate or undesirable. If you use this attack, you must be sure that you have described all of the possible alternatives and shown them to be unsatisfactory. Obviously, your opponent may evade the dilemma by uncovering a new alternative. For example, suppose that your opponent advocates a proposal to send more food to the less-developed nations. You can allege that the proposal will not work because the food cannot be transported to where the food is needed. You can argue that we do not have the facilities to deliver the food and that the recipients do not have the technical ability to transport it, either. No other means of transportation is available. You can probably prove that your opponent's proposal will not work if your options are all-inclusive and if you offer proof that, without proper transportation, the food will not reach its intended destination. Obviously, if your opponent presents another method of delivering the food, he or she will probably overcome your dilemma unless, of course, you can prove that the new option is also doomed to failure.

Strategic Decisions in Attack and Defense

In attacking your opponent's case and defending your position, several strategic decisions must be made before you begin your arguments. Your failure to do so can result in two potentially damaging outcomes. First, it may lower the credibility and clarity of your own arguments. Second, it will leave your arguments highly vulnerable to attack by opponents who employ strategic considerations in building their position. Deciding which arguments to refute or rebuild, which parts of arguments to refute or rebuild, and which type of attack and defense to launch is essential to the development of strategically sound argumentation.

Which Arguments to Refute or Rebuild?

Not all disputed claims are equally important to the probable truth or falsity of the resolution. Novice arguers often mistakenly believe that it is necessary to attack *every* constructive argument that the opposition presents, in order not to lose their tactical advantage. Moreover, beginners sometimes believe that the most effective attack on an argument is direct denial. Thus, for each argument that "X is true" the adversary must respond with "X is false." This view of attack is naive, and if you use it, you will involve yourself in tenuous and time-wasting disputes that divert the audience's attention from the significant questions. But it is more likely that you may be perceived as unreasonable, interested only in argument for argument's sake, and aiming to accumulate debating points rather than to deliberate intelligently. It is even possible that in your quest for attacks, you may take positions that are internally inconsistent, thereby casting doubt on the credibility of your entire presentation.

For each constructive argument, you have three options. You may ignore the argument, saying nothing about it. You may admit it, conceding its essential truth. Or you may attack it, choosing to develop and present a refutation.

There may be several situations in which ignoring or admitting an argument may be advisable. For example, there is no gain in contesting the obvious. Little will be accomplished by the advocate who attempts to deny that inflation sometimes exists in the United States or that international conflict exists between the United States and the Soviet Union. Although theoretically it is possible to dispute each of these claims (one could, for instance, adopt an exotic definition of inflation according to which there is none), they are such widely accepted matters that a challenge is unlikely to succeed. Nor, for that matter, is challenge needed. It is not necessary to deny the existence of inflation, for example, in order to oppose the elimination of all welfare programs.

In like manner, arguments that are incidental to the outcome, though not obviously so, may not be worth an attack or defense. In seeking to defend uniform national levels of spending for education, arguers frequently begin with the observation that our nation is dedicated to the principal of equal protection under its laws. That this is the case is by no means clear: one probably could find enough examples of unequal treatment of citizens in similar circumstances to cast doubt on the reality of our dedication to this principle. But to do so may not be productive, especially if the constructive argument will stand or fall for reasons entirely independent of the observation. If the opponent can lose this observation and still win the main argument, it probably will not be profitable for you to expend your energies attacking the observation. (It should not be assumed, incidentally, that an equal protection observation always is incidental: it may represent the "guts" of the constructive argument. Decisions about the importance of arguments must be made with reference to each situation in which people argue.)

In addition to obvious and incidental arguments, two other types may be considered as unworthy of attack or defense. First, your opponent may sometimes present several arguments leading to the same end. In terms of the function they perform, these arguments are duplicative, and it may not be necessary for you to respond to them all. If, for instance, three separate arguments are made that the use of quotas in employment discriminates against certain groups of people, then a blanket justification for, or denial of, such discrimination makes it unnecessary to attack the arguments individually. In short, *functionally duplicative* arguments may not require attack.

Finally, arguments that are developed with several different types of evidence may not require separate attacks or defenses of each type. Suppose that you defend the argument that American military preparedness is inadequate, by using generalizations contained in expert testimony and Defense Department statistics regarding specific military programs. If the attacker can defend each of the examples against each of the statistical demonstrations, he or she may not need to attack the generalization as well. By implication, it will have been exposed as having been predicated on faulty data. (But if the specific examples represent a small sample of all programs, you will want to contest the generalization too; otherwise, all of the remaining programs could still be deficient.) Similarly, if you successfully counter the generalized expert testimony, you will not need to dispute each of the examples. They will have been exposed, by implication, as unusual or atypical cases, even if true. With respect to different levels of generalization or abstraction, then, *multilevel arguments* may not require attack at each level.

Obvious, incidental, functionally duplicative, and multilevel arguments all are examples of arguments that may be ignored or admitted without hazard. The decision as to which arguments not to consider is the first strategic judgment to be made in preparing an attack or defense. This decision enables the arguer to clear away the underbrush and focus on the crucial targets in refuting or rebuilding the case.

Which Parts of the Argument to Refute or Rebuild?

Since each component of an argument—claim, evidence, and inference—is essential to the success of the argument, the attacker who undermines any of the steps will undermine the argument. In any argument, the attacker can deny the truth of the evidence on which it is based, dispute the conclusion drawn from the evidence, or quarrel with the inference authorizing the conclusion. (The attacker can also use several of these steps in combination.) Since so many points of attack are available, it is necessary that the attacker carefully select those that will be the strongest.

It is impossible to stipulate which component will be the strongest in all cases, as their strength will vary from argument to argument and from debate to debate. As a general guideline, you should follow a *minimax principle:* you should minimize the effort required to lodge the attack and maximize your adversary's difficulty in reconstructing the attack.

Consider a case for American aid to Western Europe. Both military and economic aid have been justified on political grounds for the purpose of strengthening our alliance and on humanitarian grounds to compensate for the devastation of World War II. These ties arose in the context of a traditional, indeed ancestral, relationship between Western Europe and the United States.

Suppose that a speaker justifies American aid to Western Europe by referring to the original commitments of President Harry S. Truman. You can attack this argument by claiming that President Truman never intended or made a commitment of the scope of that of succeeding presidents. If you choose this argument, you will be disputing the truth of the evidence on which the original argument was based. Seemingly, this attack involves minimal effort. But the reconstruction of the argument can also be easily accomplished. The original speaker may choose to concede the point as far as subsequent presidents are concerned. After all, nothing is magic about the number of presidents involved. American commitments presumably are just as sacrosanct if only one president has articulated them. (Conceivably, one might also argue that a commitment should be honored on the strength of only one president.) In other words, it probably is unwise to attack this argument at the level of evidence. As easily as the attack may be made, the argument may be defended just as easily.

Suppose, in contrast, that the attacker chooses not to consider the evidence, even though it may be open to dispute, and to lodge the attack, instead, at the underlying assumptions of the inference. The attacker may argue that historical continuity is not an inherent good, that blind adherence to precedent may lead to calamity, and that willingness to admit errors and make changes is a mark of maturity among nations, just as it is among people. The burden on the original advocate now is considerably increased. It will not suffice merely to read a piece of testimonial evidence; certainly it will not suffice to concede the point to the attacker! Instead, the first speaker now must construct a new argument, the purpose of which is to justify the assumptions of the original argument. Unless the context of this second, justificatory argument is admitted by the attacker, it too can be questioned, and it is possible that the first advocate can be kept perpetually on the defensive, his or her underlying presuppositions never having been granted.

It may be tempting to infer from the above example that the minimax principle is better served if you always attack the inference than if you attack evidence or claim. Indeed, for many arguments this is the case, but it cannot be stated as a universal rule. There are many arguments whose underlying assumptions are granted by most reasonable people. For such arguments, the minimax principle is served by granting the assumptions of the argument and then attacking the argument within the framework of those assumptions, by questioning the evidence, inference, or claim.

Although we have so far considered a situation in which only one attack is made on an argument, it certainly is possible to lodge multiple attacks at different levels of the argument. In the above example, one can both question the open-endedness of President Truman's commitment and dispute the underlying assumptions of the argument. At first glance, it may seem that the more attacks that are brought against an argument, the better; for more options are left open to the attacker. But the development of multiple attacks may easily reach a point of diminishing returns. Arguers who wish to develop multiple attacks should apply the test of the minimax principle to each attack: does it maximize their gains (in terms of the effort required of their opponent to reestablish the argument) and minimize their costs (in terms of the effort required to develop and launch the attack)?

The preceding paragraphs have focused on selecting the part of the argument to attack. Choices of the defense are far more limited. Generally, you must defend an argument at the points at which it is attacked. The only exceptions are a circumstance in which the attack, even if successful, does not impair the argument, or a situation in which you can lose the individual argument and still prevail on the overall case.

What Type of Attack or Defense to Launch?

As an attacker, your preliminary work is not finished when you have decided which arguments to attack and at which points to attack them. It is also important that you decide what sort of attack you wish to make. Here we shall consider three major types of attack.

Questions.   The question is usually not designed for clarification, but for challenging your adversary to raise additional points, on which the success of the argument supposedly depends. If the original advocate asserted, for instance, that respect for human life was at its ebb throughout the nation, and supported this positional statement by referring to increases in the homicide rate in Atlanta, the attacker might question whether the example was typical. Similarly, if a controversial point were established by the testimony of only one person, the attacker might ask whether this person's view represented a lone voice or whether this view commanded substantial support by experts.

These examples show the strength of asking questions: they permit an attack to be developed easily, and they establish a burden on the original advocate. But they also illustrate a weakness of this device: they can be answered easily. If the original speaker provides the information that was requested, the attacker will be left with nothing to show for his or her effort. Much like apartment renters who build no equity in their homes and have nothing to show for their rent payments when they move, attackers who rely on asking questions build no equity in their argument if the original advocate can satisfactorily answer the questions. As a general rule, therefore, it is wise not to rely heavily on questions.

To avoid both having your attack evaporate and having its importance ignored, if you confine your attacks or defense of an argument to raising questions, you should (1) be reasonably certain that the answer to the question is not immediately available to the opponent, (2) be very careful that when you raise the question you explain why the question is important and why the opponent's argument depends on his or her ability to answer the question successfully, and (3) ascertain that an answer places an opponent in a difficult position with respect to other strategy situations developing in the course of a dispute.

Identification of Internal Deficiencies.   Deficiencies result from the failure of the evidence or inference to meet the tests described in Chapter 3, in which we identified common deficiencies in each of the four types of evidence we discussed.

Empirical Data. The results of direct or indirect observation are empirical data. As such, they ultimately depend on human perception with all its frailties. Often, therefore, the data will be the product of observers who see what they wish to see. Specific cases or illustrations may be aberrant instances, rather than representative examples, of a phenomenon. The data may be accounted for in ways other than by reference to the factors they supposedly exemplify. What one advocate presents as a specific example of bureaucratic bungling in Washington may instead be an example of local error in applying government funds to solve a specific problem. Or the data may be insufficient in quantity or detail. The speaker may not provide enough information about the data to enable the listener to determine their accuracy.

These three deficiencies may plague any form of empirical data, whether it is the direct observation and reporting of an example or statistical summary and generalization. In addition, statistical reports may be based on a sample insufficient to permit meaningful results. It is not always helpful, for example, to refer to a change from one unit to two units of some social good as a 100 percent increase. Or the statistics may depend on an inappropriate measure of central tendency or summation, or on the failure to apply the necessary tests of statistical significance. Finally, the units used in the statistical summation may be ambiguous or inconsistent. For example, statistics that portray America as having made major strides in reducing poverty over the last several decades are complicated by the fact that there has been a corresponding increase in expectations and in the standard of living, and so a higher income is required to escape what we now call poverty than would have been the case a generation ago.

Experimental Research Studies. You may find deficiencies in experimental research studies if these studies have departed from the ideal of experimental design, which is to take two groups of people, in which any one has an identical chance of being placed; to treat these two groups alike in all respects except that one receives experimental treatment and the other does not; and then to compare the results. Only by using such a rigorous design can you say with any degree of confidence that the results were obtained for the reason that you hypothesized, rather than as the result of accident or chance.

There often are two problems in using experimental data in public policy. First, many experiments are *post facto* studies. This means that the experiment begins after, rather than before, the experimental variable has been induced. For example, if you compare the data of accident fatalities and the effects of mandatory seat belt usage on accident deaths, you may find little measurable effect from the added crash protection. The findings do not necessarily mean that the seat belts were ineffective in protecting crash occupants but, rather, may mean that the drivers of the equipped cars overcompensated for the new safety devices (because of a false sense of security) in such a way as to be involved in more accidents. Since this study would have been conducted *post facto,* it would be impossible to test directly either of these explanations. Consequently, the questions cannot be answered meaningfully.

A second common deficiency of experimental data is the failure of the experimental design to hold all other factors constant. If you compare the relatively low cost of pilot programs in prepaid group medical practice and the higher costs of individual practice, you may conclude that group practice is effective in reducing medical costs. But unless all members of the population have an equal chance of receiving either group or individual treatment, it is possible that the supposed advantage of group practice may really be attributable to the fact that only middle- and upper-income groups, consisting (on the average) of healthier people, were able to join the group practice plan. In short, to the degree that the experiment fails to keep constant all of the important factors, save one, the results of the research may be faulty, since alternate explanations cannot account equally well for the same data.

Documents and Historical Records. Documents and historical records are subject, first, to textual corruptions and inaccuracies in transcription. You should be careful not to ignore the social context of documents. References to such concepts as national security in documentary materials may well have been intended to suggest meanings other than those pertinent to the current patterns of diplomacy and military technology. Other temporal errors may be made when using information compiled in the past. You also cannot assume that people's motives are faithfully reflected in the texts of their documents. The fact that Congress in 1946 committed the nation to full employment should not be taken to prove the existence of nationwide sentiment favoring the government as an employer of last resort. People's motives should always be checked against their acts.

Testimony. The last type of evidence we considered was testimony. Testimonial conclusions depend for their success solely on the willingness to rely on the wisdom of the authority. Few individuals do, or should, command that degree of blind respect. Even testimony that contains an underlying rationale should be examined carefully. Authorities may not be experts in the specific subject on which they are quoted. But even if they are, they may not be in a position to make the specific statement that has been quoted. Finally, an authority may disagree with most of the other authorities in the field. It is conceivable, of course, that a minority of one may be in the right. But the views of an expert whose colleagues almost unanimously reject him or her should be examined with more than the usual degree of care.

Regarding the weaknesses of conclusionary statements, little need be said. These are statements such as "Organized labor is on the brink of disaster." These statements are bereft of even a hint as to how the authors reached their conclusions. In both attacking and defending you should insist on examining the data on which such statements are based.

Counterarguments.   The third type of attack is to develop a counterargument. To review, a counterargument does not challenge the evidence or inference of the original argument but develops an opposing constructive argument that denies the original claim.

Once again, choices in rebuilding an argument are limited by the way in which the argument has been refuted. If the refutation is based on a misconception of the original position, repetition with further explanation should suffice. If questions have been the focus of the attack, then a direct response to the questions should rebuild the argument. In response to an attack based on internal deficiencies, an advocate needs to justify the original evidence, inference, or claim and provide additional supporting materials as necessary. Finally, if the attack has developed counterarguments, you will need to rebuild the case by refuting them or explaining why they do not apply.

Preparation for Attack and Defense

The major preparations for effective attack and defense include both planning before the argument and planning during the dispute.

Advance Planning

Planning before the argument begins with thorough research on the issues surrounding the resolution. Sometimes this research is a review of your own experience, but at other times it may require consulting with others or examining printed literature. If you are defending the resolution, you must not only be familiar with your own case, but you must also anticipate the major arguments that your opponent could launch against you. If you are attacking the resolution, you must both anticipate the various approaches to the resolution that your opponent may advance and have an inexhaustive list of arguments with which you can oppose the resolution. Being adequately prepared thus demands exhaustive research, analysis, and imagination in the planning and construction of arguments.

Planning During the Dispute

Effective attack and defense during a dispute usually hinge on your argument selection and accuracy in recording the progress of the arguments. Deciding which arguments to attack and which kinds of attacks to use is crucial. Seldom will it be appropriate, or will you have the time, to present all of the arguments you have accumulated for or against the resolution. You must choose those that seem to hold the most promise for proving the resolution true or false, depending on the side of the resolution you are arguing.

Equally important to argument selection is accurately recording the progress of attack and defense. Rare indeed is the arguer who can remember all of the arguments and the evidence used in attacking and defending a resolution. If you are participating in a spontaneous or informal argument, your notes will have to be mental. But if you are participating in a panel discussion, writing a letter to the editor, composing an argumentative essay, or appearing at a formal hearing, you should outline the progress of the dispute on paper. Likewise, if you are observing other people arguing, written notes are best. Chapter 5 listed techniques for organizing arguments into a case outline and suggested a notational system that should enable you to clarify the relationship among arguments. We recommend the following plan for recording the progress of a dispute:

1. Take a large sheet of paper, perhaps 8½ by 14 inches, and turn it sideways, thus giving you the maximum amount of horizontal writing space.
2. Divide the sheet into as many columns as you think there will be participants in the argument.
3. In the far left column, outline the first speech as it was presented. This outline should follow the procedures discussed in Chapter 5.
4. In each subsequent speech, record the arguments, not necessarily in the order in which they are presented, but parallel to the arguments that they attack or defend. It is important to record both what your opponent says about a given argument and your extension.

As we indicated in Chapter 5, your skill in outlining the progress of arguments will usually improve with practice. You can speed your progress by listening to tapes of speeches or by listening to others argue and outlining the flow of their arguments.

Figure 6.1 shows the record of an argument.

Figure 6.1

First Speech	Second Speech	Third Speech	Fourth Speech	Fifth Speech	Sixth Speech

I.
  A.
    1.
    2.
    3.
  B.
    1.
    2.
II.					

Summary

Constructive arguments should be tested against the strongest possible attacks. Then rigorous defenses of these positions should be advanced. These are the processes by which advocates refute their opponents' cases and rebuild their own.

Attack and defense have four steps: (1) presenting the argument that you plan to attack or defend, (2) presenting your position on the attack or the defense, (3) presenting evidence or reasons to support your attack or defense, and (4) explaining how your attack or defense either weakens or strengthens the probable truth of the resolution.

An exhaustive confrontation on any given resolution usually includes numerous attacks and defenses of specific subsidiary arguments. These additional responses are called extensions. Three ways to extend are using counterevidence and counterarguments and turning the opposing argument.

Several methods can be employed to defend and attack arguments. These include exposing deficiencies in the adversary's arguments, turning the evidence, reducing the argument to an absurdity, using counterarguments, attacking inconsistencies, and using dilemmas.

The effective use of argument also calls for a number of strategic decisions in attack and defense: (1) which arguments to attack or defend, (2) which steps of an argument to attack or defend, and (3) which types of attacks or defenses to launch.

Effective preparation for an attack or defense includes careful planning before and during a dispute. Thorough research on the substance of the resolution is necessary in planning arguments to defend your position or to attack the position of your opponent. Systematically outlining the progress of the argument as it proceeds is necessary for most arguers in order to recall the order of the arguments and for the listeners or readers to relate the attack and defense to the original positions.

Questions for Discussion

1. What are the primary differences among the various kinds of attack and defense? How does each refute an opponent's claim?
2. How can the economic principle of maximum return for minimal expenditures be applied when making strategic decisions in regard to attacking and defending arguments?
3. How does extending an argument differ from repeating an argument?
4. What are the implications of the statement that the advocate who wins the most arguments should be declared the winner of the dispute?
5. When is it more desirable to attack your opponent's strong arguments than to attack his or her weak arguments? When is the reverse true?

Unit Two

Theory and Practice of Academic Debate

Chapter 7

The Conventions of Academic Debate

Argumentation is a communication process in which people make, attack, and defend claims in order to gain the assent of others or to justify their own beliefs and acts. This process can take place in many different settings, ranging from an informal conversation around the dinner table to a highly structured formal proceeding in the courtroom. The basic principles we have studied so far are applicable to the process of argumentation in all settings.

Each specialized forum for argumentation has its own specific procedures and principles. In this unit, we shall examine academic debate. This activity attracts thousands of intelligent and articulate students, who participate in classroom, intramural, and interscholastic debates as a way to improve their skills in argumentation.

We must stress that the forum of academic debate is not only specialized but somewhat artificial. Its format and procedures do not totally resemble any situation in which argumentation occurs in daily or public life. Rather, these norms are created and maintained in order to enhance the educational potential of academic debate as a means of training students in the skills of analysis and advocacy.

In this chapter we shall discuss some of the basic conventions of academic debate before examining its specific theories and techniques.

The Debate Resolution

As we saw in Chapter 2, the resolution is the central claim that is in dispute when people argue. Other claims and evidence are offered to support or oppose this central claim. In most informal disputes, the resolution is not explicitly stated but is implicitly recognized by all of the participants in the dispute.

In academic debate, the resolution is formulated in a different way. Students debate not because they have personal disagreements but because they wish to improve their argumentative skills. Consequently, the resolution cannot grow out of the circumstances of the disagreements, but it is decided before the debate begins. At both the high school and college levels, there are elaborate procedures for soliciting suggestions, composing a ballot, and conducting a national referendum to select the national debate resolution. Other resolutions are sometimes used, but they too are decided in advance.

Resolutions Have Policy Implications

For many years, national debate resolutions were exclusively resolutions of policy. But since policy resolutions involve subsidiary claims of fact, definition, and value, using policy resolutions offers students the opportunity to practice advancing and attacking all types of claims.

In recent years, however, the use of nonpolicy resolutions has grown rapidly. The introduction of the Lincoln-Douglas debate format at the high school level and the growing popularity of the Cross-Examination Debate Association at the college level are two developments that have encouraged the use of nonpolicy resolutions. Unlike the more traditional resolutions, these do not ask debaters to support or oppose a specific action.

But even nonpolicy resolutions frequently have policy implications. "Resolved: That American television has sacrificed quality for entertainment" is a resolution of fact, but it is hard to imagine an advocate affirming the resolution without at least implying that some changes should be made in television content. Similarly, "Resolved: That inflation is a greater evil than unemployment" is a resolution of value, but to affirm or deny this resolution is to imply that another approach to monetary and fiscal policies ought to be pursued. Nonpolicy resolutions do not ignore the question of what action should be taken, but they clearly do subordinate it to other inquiries. Determining the effects of different specific proposals does not assume so large a role.

There are two important implications of the fact that academic debate resolutions have policy implications. First, many of the same processes of analysis and case construction apply equally to policy and nonpolicy resolutions. There will be differences in some of the specific details and in the mechanics of presentation, but for the most part the discussion in the following chapters will apply equally to policy and nonpolicy resolutions. In either case, the goal is a decision about whether or not the resolution is probably true.

Second, the statement that resolutions have policy implications is sometimes misunderstood. Although they talk about questions of policy, debaters and judges do not actually make policy. Like all advocates, they must acknowledge that argumentation occurs in the world of words and is at least one step removed from action. If argumentation supports a tax cut, for example, the act of cutting taxes is not itself part of the argumentative process. Debaters, like any advocates who talk about policy, do not do anything but, rather, attempt to find out whether the statement embodied in the policy resolution is probably true.

Resolutions Are Worded Broadly

A second characteristic of the debate resolution is that it is selected for an entire year. The resolution is chosen, usually in late spring or early summer, for the following academic year. To sustain a year's worth of debating, a resolution is often worded fairly broadly. Rather than calling for the deployment of a specific missile system, for example, the resolution probably would propose something like a "significant strengthening of American military commitments."

This breadth of wording is both a virtue and a vice. The virtue is that meaningful study and discussion are permitted on a wide range of related subject areas. With a more limited wording, it is likely that the major ideas and arguments will have been thoroughly researched and practiced well before the end of the year. Breadth of wording helps assure freshness in analysis and advocacy.

The vice is that a broadly worded resolution may embrace many disparate subjects. "Strengthening military commitments," for instance, can encompass subjects ranging from labor recruitment, to the development of weapons systems, to arms-limitation agreements, to international treaty commitments. Each subject has an entirely different set of questions. Although this diversity may encourage freshness of thought, it may also deter some students from participating in debate because of the amount of work required. And it complicates the task of analyzing the resolution. Of course, some resolutions are broader than others, and so the virtues and vices are found in different proportions each year.

Resolutions Propose Actions Unlikely to Be Taken Soon

Suppose that the resolution were "Resolved: That the president should be given the power to impose wage and price controls." If, midway through the debate season, Congress gave the president just such powers, the debate process would seem to be rendered moot. And in one sense it would be moot: why talk about whether we ought to do something that already has been done?

But in another sense, it would make no difference whether or not the action specified in the resolution were actually taken. Since the dispute is over what should be done, it is appropriate for advocates defending Congress's action to maintain that it is entirely proper and for advocates opposing the resolution to deny the merits of the action, even though it has already been taken. In practice, however, most resolutions are drafted so as to avoid the possibility that they will be enacted.

How can this possibility be prevented? There are two commonly used methods. One is to word the resolution so that it calls for a more drastic action than is likely to be taken. Whereas public discussion may focus on the need for government incentives to encourage the development of new forms of energy, a debate resolution may propose nationalization of all energy resources. When the resolution proposes more drastic action, however, debaters may have difficulty in finding evidence bearing directly on the resolution, since it is not the focus of public attention. Moreover, if the resolution proposes an action that is known to be politically infeasible, it may be hard to devise a plan of action that can ever be implemented.

The other method is to word the resolution so that it calls not for a specific action but for a direction of change. This effect is achieved through the use of terms such as *significantly strengthen, substantially curtail,* or *greatly increase.* Whatever actions may be taken during the year, the resolution will still call for something different. The drawback of this approach is that events are always in flux. Since the resolution is not evaluated against a fixed base line but against a constantly changing one, it always is possible to quibble about whether the specific change being discussed in a given debate is significant, substantial, or great. The direction of change also may not be as obvious as it appears. One means of strengthening defenses may be to add weapons, but another may be to abandon obsolete weapons so that those remaining will be stronger. But the latter option can also be interpreted as weakening rather than strengthening. If it is unclear whether a change falls under the resolution or its opposite, the chances of confusion are increased. Such confusion is heightened by the inclusion in the resolution of terms such as *significant* when it is not clear against what base line the significance of a change is to be determined. Is a change significant if it has significant effects or only if it greatly changes the procedure?

Meaning Is Not Self-Evident

The final implication of selecting resolutions is that they are selected before the debate and by persons other than the debaters. Therefore, the meaning of the resolution is not self-evident from the context in which it arose. Instead, one of the central tasks in analyzing the resolution (to be considered in Chapter 8) is to determine its meaning. The applications of this analysis and the methods for conducting it will be discussed below. Here we wish to note only that it is a convention peculiar to academic debate — the fact that resolutions are developed externally — that makes this stage of analysis necessary.

Sides and Duties

The two sides in a debate are the *affirmative* and *negative.* Each side's primary duty is dictated by the resolution.

Fundamental Duties

The job of the affirmative is to support the resolution. In other words, the affirmative must advance arguments that, taken together, will establish that the resolution is probably true. Conversely, the job of the negative is to oppose the resolution, to offer arguments that establish that it has not been shown to be probably true. The negative need not prove that the resolution is probably false (though it often may be wise to do so) but must cast substantial doubt on the resolution's probable truth as argued by the affirmative.

It is sometimes argued that the basic duties of the affirmative and negative go beyond the requirements mentioned here. For instance, it is often said that the affirmative must advocate a change from the existing system. But this requirement holds only when the wording of the policy resolution itself calls for a change. The fact that most resolutions do call for change may have confused matters. It is the wording of the resolution, not an externally imposed burden, that determines whether the affirmative must propose a change. If the resolution were "Resolved: That current arms sales policies should be maintained," the affirmative obviously would not need to propose a change.

Likewise, it is sometimes said that the affirmative must present a plan, a specific program to take the action contemplated by the resolution. But here again, the wording of the resolution is the crucial consideration. If the resolution is specific enough that the nature of a plan is self-evident, nothing more may be required. For example, in the early 1960s, colleges debated the resolution that the United States should extend diplomatic recognition to the People's Republic of China. This resolution probably does not require a specific plan. The action to be taken is stated in the resolution itself. But if the resolution is vague, and yet a knowledge of specific means of implementation is essential, then considerably more detail may be needed. The resolution that the United States should increase its military commitments is an example in which a specific plan would be quite useful.

Similarly, some may insist that the negative is obliged to defend the present system. Negatives frequently do offer such a defense, and it certainly is one means to oppose the resolution, but it is not the only one. To require that the negative defend the present system is to substitute one of several means to an end for the end itself. The same error is made by stating that the negative must show the disadvantages of the plan. Again, such a statement takes one way in which the negative might oppose the resolution and makes it the necessary way to go about the task.

Since misconceptions about the duties of each side may interfere with analysis and creativity, it is good at this point to keep the requirements quite simple. The basic job of the affirmative is to support the resolution, and that of the negative, to oppose it. In subsequent chapters we shall consider the means to fulfill these requirements.

Debating Both Sides

Which side should you defend, affirmative or negative? One of the conventions of academic debate is that the choice is usually not up to you. In some areas of the country, students participate on four-person teams and debate only one side of the resolution. But the most common procedure is for students to debate both sides, either in alternation or as determined by the toss of a coin. This practice sometimes is criticized by people who think it improper to require that a person advocate a position that opposes his or her own beliefs. But debate assumes that neither side of a controversy can be proved to be absolutely true. Resolutions force the discussion of topics for which strong arguments can be made on both sides. Debating both sides assures that students will examine competing arguments in deciding what they believe. Moreover, for the students who have not taken sides on the resolution, arguing both sides can be a helpful way of arriving at a position as a result of reflective judgment. And for those who already have taken a position, the practice of arguing out the other side of the case enables the constant testing and checking of their beliefs, strengthening them and not permitting them to harden into blind prejudices.

The fact that students usually debate both sides of a resolution has an important implication for their role as advocates. People are most likely to assess accurately the probable truth of a resolution when the strongest arguments that can be made in its behalf are confronted by the strongest arguments that can be made against it. From this point of view, it follows that academic debaters must play the role of committed advocates for or against a resolution. For example, they must act as if their own beliefs support the resolution, for it is this assumption that provides the incentive to marshal the strongest possible arguments. Arguments with which we agree are often stronger because we give them the force of conviction. Advocates who do not feel that their personal position is at stake are less inclined to insist on the strongest possible arguments. Likewise, when debaters are assigned to oppose the resolution, they must act as if its affirmation would be very harmful to their own beliefs. Outside academic debates, role playing is seldom used: people usually argue precisely because their personal beliefs have been challenged. But since academic debate represents a contrived rather than a natural controversy, it is necessary for debaters to play the role of committed advocates. (The fact that debate is basically a role-playing activity reduces the possible drawbacks of debating both sides. Although arguing against one's own beliefs may affect these beliefs, the effect is reduced by the absence of public commitment. Debaters are not asked to repudiate their own values in a public forum.)

The Debate Format

In informal situations, argumentation is relatively unstructured. People argue whenever they recognize that they disagree and that each desires the agreement of the other. Each arguer speaks in turn, and the argument continues until there is a natural termination. One arguer concedes to the other, one withdraws from the controversy, or they determine that they cannot resolve the matter and agree to disagree. Disputes in families and discussions with friends usually proceed in this unstructured fashion.

Formal situations are much more structured, and argumentation occurs within the conventions dictated by the format. In academic debate, the format has a clear structure.

Time Limits

Perhaps the most obvious element in the format of a formal debate is its time limit. A finite amount of time—usually sixty to seventy-two minutes—is allowed for argument. The controversy ends when the clock runs out, not when it has reached its natural termination. As we shall see, this convention imposes its own requirements on the dynamics of the dispute.

The speaking time is divided equally between the affirmative and the negative sides of the resolution. This convention, which is designed to assure fairness, follows naturally from the limit on the total speaking time. If only sixty or seventy-two minutes are available, it is reasonable that within that constraint, each side has an equal opportunity to make its case.

The time is also divided between the advocates on each side. Although the number has varied from time to time, currently each debate team consists of two people. The format is arranged so that each member has an equal amount of speaking time. For example, if there are sixty minutes of total speaking time, each team will be assigned thirty minutes, which is divided equally between the two speakers.

Types of Speeches

A debate includes both *constructive* speeches and *rebuttal* speeches. These labels may be misleading. The constructive speeches include quite a bit of refutation, and the rebuttal speeches are not limited to attacks on the opponent's arguments. As in any argumentation, attack and defense are related, but there is a functional division between the two types of speeches. All arguments in the debate are initiated in the constructive speeches so as to permit maximum development and testing of the arguments. It is in these speeches that the basic position of each side is laid out and supported. The development of constructive arguments does not proceed in a vacuum, but rather, the arguments of one side are examined in the course of developing the other. The rebuttal speeches develop the arguments initiated in the constructives and summarize the grounds for a favorable decision. These tasks, too, answer the opposition's arguments in the course of advancing the advocate's side.

Typically, the debate format provides for one constructive and one rebuttal speech by each participant. The debater on each side who gives the first constructive speech often will give the first rebuttal speech as well, although it is sometimes permissible to reverse the order when on the affirmative—for the first constructive speaker to give the second rebuttal. Although it is not required, the constructive speeches tend to be twice as long as the rebuttals. The two most common formats feature eight-minute constructives and four-minute rebuttals or ten-minute constructives and five-minute rebuttals.

Time is usually provided for cross-examination, as well. Cross-examination permits the debater who has just spoken to be questioned by one member of the opposing team, in order to clarify ambiguous points or to elicit information for use in subsequent speeches. Again, formats vary, but the most common practice is for a three-minute cross-examination period to follow each constructive speech. Usually it is up to the debaters to decide which member of the opposing team will conduct the questioning—the first affirmative constructive speaker, for instance, may be questioned by either the first or the second negative—provided that each debater conducts one questioning period. In this way, each of the four debaters gives one constructive speech and one rebuttal speech and questions once and answers once.

Not all debates include cross-examination, and so this element of the format may be regarded as optional. However, it has been in wide use in high school debate since the mid-1950s and in college debate since the mid-1970s, and it is clearly the predominant style of debate today. The principles and techniques of cross-examination are examined in Chapter 17.

The order of the speeches in a debate is arranged to reflect the placement of presumption and the burden of proof. Since the affirmative shoulders the burden of proof, it must initiate the controversy. As a compensation for the burden of proof, the affirmative also is given the privilege of speaking last—so that both the opening and the closing speeches are affirmative. To achieve this, the negative has two successive speeches in the middle of the debate, with only a cross-examination period between them. These speeches, the second negative constructive and the first negative rebuttal, are referred to jointly as the *negative block*.

Finally, it is increasingly common for each team to be assigned a certain amount of preparation time—usually five or ten minutes. This time can be divided between the speakers on a team as they wish. The preparation time is taken between the speeches and the cross-examination periods and is charged to the team speaking or questioning next.

The Format in Summary

We now can summarize the basic features of the academic debate format. There is a fixed total amount of speaking time, which is divided equally between the sides and equally between the debaters on each side. The debate includes both constructive and rebuttal speeches, and a cross-examination period typically follows each constructive speech. The affirmative speaks both first and last, and the negative has two consecutive speeches in the middle of the debate. Notice that all of these features are included in the following outline of the two most common debate formats:

Debate Elements	60-Minute Total	72-Minute Total
First affirmative constructive speech	8	10
Cross-examination of first affirmative	3	3
First negative constructive speech	8	10
Cross-examination of first negative	3	3
Second affirmative constructive speech	8	10
Cross-examination of second affirmative	3	3
Second negative constructive speech	8	10
Cross-examination of second negative	3	3
First negative rebuttal speech	4	5
First affirmative rebuttal speech	4	5
Second negative rebuttal speech	4	5
Second affirmative rebuttal speech	4	5

There can be numerous variations in the format. Some formats include only one rebuttal per side. Some feature only one cross-examination period per side, with the cross-examination occurring after all four constructive speeches have been completed. Some formats omit cross-examination, and some vary the time limits of particular speeches or even the number of debaters per side. The Lincoln-Douglas format does not have teams of debaters but pits one person against another. Nevertheless, most debates in which you will participate are likely to use one of the two formats listed above.

Duties of the Speakers

Another convention in academic debate is the assumption of specific duties by each of the speakers. It is important to stress that the duties are assigned to specific speeches only by convention; there is no logical or strategic reason for their being assigned in this way. Indeed, there are many possibilities for creative experimentation in debate simply by departing from the conventional assignments. Before considering any variations, however, you should understand the conventional division of labor, since it is the pattern that characterizes most debates and is therefore recommended for beginners.

First Affirmative Constructive

The first affirmative constructive speech presents the basic affirmative case—the collection of arguments that constitutes a reason to affirm the resolution. Not all constructive arguments must be presented in the first speech, but the first speaker does introduce the basic arguments that comprise the affirmative case. Specifically, this speaker will usually begin by demonstrating the existence of a problem that is serious enough to warrant action. The problem may be a current, undesirable state of affairs—for example, people die needlessly as a result of air pollution. Or the problem may be stated as an opportunity to improve conditions by making a change—for example, a new system of trade policies could enhance the economic growth of the Third World. It is not enough for the first affirmative speaker to identify a problem; the problem must also be shown to be serious enough to warrant attention. These duties often are referred to as *harm* (identifying the problem) and *significance* (showing its seriousness).

The first affirmative speaker also tries to demonstrate that the action envisioned by the resolution is necessary in order to solve the problem. Measures short of, or different from, the stated action will be shown to be inadequate. In the examples above, the speakers sought to demonstrate that only federal controls of air pollution or only a new system of trade policies could resolve the problems addressed. If not, one would not need to commit oneself to the probable truth of the resolution. This duty is referred to as *inherency.*

Finally, the first affirmative speaker attempts to prove that the action stated in the resolution is sufficient to overcome the problem. To accomplish this goal, the speaker usually presents the specific policy proposal (the plan) that the affirmative advocates as a means of implementing the resolution and explains why the implementation of this plan can overcome the problem. This duty is referred to as *efficacy.* Each of these duties — harm, significance, inherency, and efficacy — will be discussed further in later chapters.

The first affirmative speaker need not present all of the arguments that the affirmative will advance in fulfilling any of these duties. The second affirmative may add more significance arguments, more explanations of inherency, or a further defense of efficacy. But the initial presentation of arguments under each of these headings usually is found in the first affirmative speech.

First Negative Constructive

The first negative constructive speech, by convention, has two separate, though related, duties: to introduce and develop the negative position and to initiate responses to the case arguments advanced by the affirmative. The negative position is the overall stance taken by the negative with respect to the affirmative case. Any affirmative case or argument permits several possible stances by the negative. For example, suppose that the affirmative argues that the current American defense policy weakens the United States in regard to the Soviet Union. This argument can be answered in several ways: the argument is not true; the argument is true, but the benefit to the Soviet Union is slight; the argument is true, but the benefit can be offset in other ways; the argument is true, and it is desirable to help the Soviet Union. The negative selects a stance to take in response to the affirmative case and defends it. Sometimes this may be done by briefly stating the negative approach at the beginning of the speech and then discussing the specific affirmative arguments. But at other times the negative position will involve matters not touched on by the affirmative. In such circumstances the negative will need to present additional constructive arguments of its own.

The other major duty of the first negative speaker is to respond to the case arguments of the affirmative. By convention the first negative speaker usually deals with the harm, significance, and inherency arguments, leaving the arguments about the plan for his or her colleague to consider. (There are exceptions to this pattern, of course.) If the negative disputes the way in which the affirmative has interpreted the resolution, this dispute also will usually be initiated in the first negative constructive. In responding to the affirmative's case arguments, the first negative may demonstrate deficiencies in the affirmative's evidence and reasoning, may present counterarguments that reply to the claims of the affirmative, or may use a combination of these two approaches. Since the second negative constructive speech usually is reserved for discussion of the affirmative plan, the first negative will try to introduce all of the arguments to be made against the affirmative case itself—although, of course, these arguments will be extended by the negative during the rebuttal speeches.

Second Affirmative Constructive

The second affirmative constructive speech has the major responsibility of rebuilding the affirmative case after the initial negative attack. Depending on the nature of the attack, there are several ways in which the second affirmative can proceed. Elements of the affirmative case that escaped attack can be noted, or if the negative attack has focused mostly on the evidence, additional evidence may be cited to support the initial affirmative arguments. If the reasoning process of the affirmative has been questioned, the original reasoning can be defended and new arguments added to support the original position. If the negative has presented constructive arguments of its own, the second affirmative will respond to these. The overall goal for the second affirmative is not merely to repair the damage inflicted by the first negative but also to resubstantiate and advance the affirmative position so that the case is as strong as possible at the end of the constructive speeches.

If the first affirmative speaker has neglected to present any portion of the affirmative case, the missing element must be provided by the second affirmative. Although it is uncommon to do so, the affirmative speakers may choose to defer the presentation of the plan until the second speech; sometimes they will choose to defer part of their significance, inherency, or efficacy arguments. Deferring parts of the case is seldom advised, however, because it does not permit adequate examination of the issues. Audiences usually prefer that the entire second affirmative speech be available for attacking negative arguments and rebuilding the affirmative position.

Second Negative Constructive

The second negative constructive speech customarily pertains to the affirmative plan. In some respects, this speech is analogous to the first affirmative. The first affirmative speaker identifies problems in the absence of the action stated in the resolution, and the second negative identifies problems in the light of such action.

The problems are typically of two types. The negative may argue that the plan cannot succeed in resolving the problem to which it is addressed. The plan's own design may make it inadequate for the task, or the actions of other people may frustrate its effectiveness. In either case, the negative is arguing that the plan lacks efficacy. For example, if the affirmative proposes that an international commission be established to inspect nuclear power plants, the negative may argue that international commissions cannot overcome national sovereignty (the plan's design is inadequate) or that terrorists will thwart its effectiveness (other actors frustrate the plan).

The other type of problem in the affirmative plan relates to the consequences that will result from the proposed action. Here the negative maintains that the affirmative plan will lead to problems that will be far more serious than those that it is intended to correct. It is not enough for the negative to prove that the plan has problems; the problems must also be shown to outweigh the benefits. Federal controls on hospital costs, for example, may result in lowering the quality of medical care, in decreased innovation, and in the continued use of obsolete facilities and equipment—problems that the negative believes would be far worse than the problem of inflation, which was the affirmative's reason for supporting cost controls. These consequences of the plan are referred to as *disadvantages,* and the aim of the second negative constructive speaker is to establish that the plan as a whole is disadvantageous.

First Negative Rebuttal

The first negative rebuttal speech extends the case arguments initiated in the first constructive speech. Extension is the process of developing arguments beyond their initial presentation. It may respond to the answers offered by the second affirmative; it may present additional evidence to support the first negative arguments; or it may focus on the original arguments and explain why the affirmative responses are inadequate. Usually the first negative rebuttalist employs all of these techniques. Always, however, the focus is on extending the original arguments rather than presenting new ones, as new arguments probably would not receive sufficient attention in the brief time remaining. This is one difference between the constructive and rebuttal speeches. In extending arguments, the first negative rebuttalist also should avoid repeating the arguments made by the second negative constructive that the affirmative has not yet been able to answer.

Not all case arguments are extended. Some may have been introduced through misjudgment and are better dropped. Others may have been fully answered by the second affirmative. And the negative may decide that some arguments are not worth the effort, that they will do the negative little strategic good, even if they are won. The first negative rebuttalist must be selective, deciding on what to include before giving the speech. One function of this speech is to explain why certain arguments have been chosen for extension and why those extensions will cause the negative side to prevail.

First Affirmative Rebuttal

The first affirmative rebuttal speech faces a substantial problem. Since the preceding two speeches have been from the negative, the affirmative must answer twelve (or fifteen) minutes of negative argumentation in only four (or five) minutes. This speaker must decide which arguments to discuss and which points in a given argument merit attention and synthesize those arguments. The affirmative team should do much preliminary planning and use the preparation time to make these decisions.

The initial responsibility of the first affirmative rebuttal speaker is to respond to the arguments introduced by the second negative, which are usually plan objections. These objections must be answered in this speech, since the negative would otherwise have no opportunity to extend them. The affirmative need not analyze each detail of every objection but, rather, should argue (with supporting reasons and evidence if necessary) that the objection will not come about, that it may come about but can be dealt with by the affirmative plan, that it may be less likely to occur with the affirmative plan than without it, or that it may come about but would be a good thing. For instance, if the negative argues that wage and price controls will increase the risk of strikes, the affirmative need not examine every step of the reasoning that led to this conclusion. But the affirmative should argue that the risk will not be increased enough to matter, that the increased risk can be managed within the affirmative plan, that strikes are more likely without the affirmative plan, or that strikes may be a good thing. The first affirmative rebuttalist should answer both the efficacy arguments and the disadvantages presented by the negative.

The first affirmative rebuttalist then should extend as much of the case argument as possible, by replying to the specific extensions of the first negative rebuttalist or by showing why the position developed in the affirmative constructive speeches is still valid. Again, the speaker needs to be selective, focusing on those arguments that will do the affirmative the most good if they are extended.

Second Negative Rebuttal

The second negative rebuttal speech offers the final presentation of the negative position. It has two main functions: to complete any necessary extensions and to highlight the decision rules, the criteria for judgment that warrant a negative decision. The first of these tasks involves processes similar to those we have already examined. The speaker rebuilds the plan objections after they have been answered

by the affirmative and clarifies, as necessary, the case arguments. The task of formulating decision rules is more complex, as it requires weighing and balancing the
competing arguments in the debate; indicating the crucial issues in the dispute; and
explaining why, on those issues, the negative position is preferable to the affirmative. For example, if the affirmative plan saves lives but threatens freedom, the
negative will want to explain why freedom determines the quality of life and why
that is more important than the number of people who live. The argument that
quality is preferable to quantity (for some stated reason) is a decision rule. If the
task of highlighting these rules is handled well, the debaters will be able to influence
the judge's action by arguing the reasons for it. If it is handled poorly, the debate
will end in a muddle, and the decision-making process is likely to be confused.

Second Affirmative Rebuttal

The second affirmative rebuttal speech is the mirror image of the second negative.
It has the same tasks of completing any necessary extensions and formulating the
decision rules, though, of course, the perspective is that of the affirmative.

Cross-Examination

The cross-examination periods after each constructive speech are designed to clarify vague points in the preceding speech, force the opposition to take a stand on
a specific argument, and probe potential weaknesses in the opposition's stance.
The questioner controls the time during the cross-examination. The results obtained in questioning should be utilized in subsequent speeches.

Two Caveats

Before leaving this discussion of the speakers' duties, we shall make two observations. First, it is important to remember that these conventions are not rules.
Although they describe the normal pattern of a debate, there is considerable room
for variation. For example, the choices of which arguments are presented in which
speeches are matters of strategy rather than rule. Second, we described the speeches
briefly here so that you can understand both the dynamics of a debate—its development and progression of arguments—and its format. The theory and technique
related to the construction of the affirmative and negative cases, to the specific
speeches, and to cross-examination will be considered in detail in Chapters 9
through 17.

Paradigms of Debate

In describing the process of arguing, we noted that it contains certain implicit
assumptions. If one asked, "What are people really doing when they argue?" we
could reply that they are cooperating in a search for the best choice of decision,

that they are attempting to influence one another in a way that makes them equally vulnerable to influence from the others, and that they are explaining their justifications because they desire reflective judgment rather than impulsive action. These key assumptions together represent an outlook on the process of arguing, a *paradigm,* or model, of arguing.

In the same way, we can talk about a paradigm of debate, referring to the fundamental outlook that characterizes this formal version of argumentation. For many years one could have said that the paradigm of debate is a model in which citizens actively make decisions on public issues that affect them, in the manner of grassroots democracy. Or one could have said that the paradigm of debate is a criminal trial, in which the defender of an existing system is put on trial and the other advocate tries to show that the system is guilty. Both of these views, however, have receded during the past generation. The attempt to model debate on the criminal trial has suffered because the analogy becomes strained. The attempt to model debate on grassroots democratic theory has been weakened by the growing specialization of society and the increasing tendency for specific policy decisions to be made by elites.

But the decline of the older models does not mean that debate takes place in a vacuum, that people have no basic assumptions about what is happening when they choose to participate. During the past decade, other possible paradigms or models have been proposed, and we shall examine the two most influential.

Debate as Policy Making

The policy-making model of debate assumes that people live in a world of constant change. Since change is inevitable, it is pointless to debate whether or not to change. The only questions are how much and which change. Participants in the debate cannot evade this choice. Not to choose is to choose—it is to accept the rate and type of change now under way. The most intelligent way to decide about change is to imagine competing courses of action—competing policy proposals or systems—and to test them. Let the strongest possible case be made for each, and let the judge or audience choose between the two.

The question to be decided at the end of the debate is which of the two proposed approaches to change is better. All of the arguing is guided by this definition, and the goal is always to select the better policy, and so it is necessary to consider the competing proposals comparatively. The point of arguing that one approach is undesirable, for instance, is not to make an absolute judgment but to establish that the other approach is comparatively better. Finally, the chooser of policy proposals (be it an audience or judge) is assumed to be prepared to act on the choice. Although the audience or judge does not actually enact a policy, all of the participants must assume that the effect of the decision is the adoption and implementation of the preferred proposal.

This model of debate has commanded considerable support during the past decade. It appeals to the urge for action, to the belief that competing policies rather than competing principles are at issue, to the belief that judgments must be made in a comparative rather than an absolute sense, and to the conviction that one cannot evade his or her responsibility to choose. To the degree that one questions any or all of these beliefs, the model is, of course, much less suitable.

Debate as Hypothesis Testing

Quite a different model of debate results if different values or beliefs are paramount. The major competitor of the policy-making paradigm of debate is a view of debate as an activity in which people test hypotheses for their probable truth, as the critical philosopher or scientist does. According to this point of view, the purpose of an inquiry is to determine whether the statements presented are probably true. But only factual statements can be tested empirically for their probable truth. Statements regarding values, policy, predictions, or meaning must be tested in some other way. Debate is the method for testing these statements. Although a debate is not a laboratory, it attempts to serve the same purpose as empirical science does—the careful and critical determination of probable truth.

In performing this test, debaters function as advocates for the truth or falsity of a given statement that serves as a hypothesis. Should the statement be determined to be probably true, the debaters will commit themselves to it and be prepared to act on it as if it were true. Should its probable truth be in doubt, the statement will be set aside. But unlike the policy making model, the decision to reject one statement does not necessarily commit the debaters to accept any other alternative. They have the option, in other words, not to choose. They choose which arguments are worthy of belief, not which action to take. Therefore, their rejection of one statement may leave them uncommitted to any particular alternative.

According to the hypothesis-testing model, argument itself never ends in action but remains in the world of words. Hence a decision that a statement is probably true, or is probably not true, does not by itself produce any action. When action does ensue, that result goes beyond the process of debate.

The hypothesis-testing model of debate appeals to many of the values and beliefs that conflict with those of the policy-making model. For example, it favors contemplation and care over action. It appeals to the belief that decisions are made more among competing values and general principles of conduct than among specific actions. It reflects a belief that judgments may be made in an absolute sense—that a given statement may be accepted or rejected on its own merit without implying an alternative. And it maintains that, in the sense that choice implies commitment, one can certainly elect not to choose.

Because this set of views agrees with our own, we reflect the hypothesis-testing model throughout our discussions of debate. We will often recommend the same argumentative behavior as would adherents of the policy-making model, but on the basis of a different theoretical grounding. At other times we will urge a different course of action and will try to explain where the policy-making model diverges from our suggestions. Finally, we have selected the hypothesis-testing model in the belief that it produces clearer, more consistent, and more generalizable theory and practice than the alternatives do.

Other Possible Paradigms

Policy making and hypothesis testing are by no means the only two possible paradigms of debate. Debate theory is in a state of flux, with much self-conscious discussion of just what it is that we do when we engage in debate. This self-examination is healthy, but it means that the accepted paradigms of debate may change more rapidly. But even though the content of paradigms may change, their basic function remains the same—explicating the implicit assumptions that underlie the activity of debate, making clear its general outlook, and answering the question, "Just what are we doing when we debate?" And, as we shall see, our answers to most of the questions about debate theory and practice can be derived from our choice of a basic paradigm.

The Nature of Judgment

The final convention we shall consider involves the role of the judge. In most argumentative situations, disputes are decided in one of two ways. The participants themselves may be the judges, or they may agree in advance to submit their dispute to a third party and to abide by the outcome. The first approach characterizes an informal dispute among friends, and the second characterizes a political campaign or a court. In either case, judges are asked to decide on the substantive merits of the question in dispute. They draw on their prior background and beliefs, as well as on the specific contents of the argumentative exchange. Their judgment represents, in effect, a personal commitment in regard to the probable truth or falsity of the resolution.

The Judge's Role in Academic Debate

In academic debate, the situation is somewhat different. Just as the debaters play the role of committed advocates, so the judge plays the role of arbiter. Like the political campaign, the academic debate entrusts the decision to a third party. But unlike the campaign, the debate judge decides not on the substantive merits of the resolution but on the argumentative skills of the debaters. As a result, the judges frequently find themselves voting for positions that they do not personally endorse. The seeming paradox of a judge who votes half of the time in favor of a resolution and half of the time against the same resolution can be understood when we realize that the judge is not expressing a personal view of the resolution but is deciding whether or not it is probably true based only on the arguments made by the debaters.

This position is sometimes misunderstood, however. To say that a judge judges argumentative skills is not to say that he or she disregards the content of the debate. A judge does not ignore the development of argument and focus only on proper documentation of evidence, incisive refutation, effective word choice, engaging delivery, and other artistic skills. Although those skills are important, their importance is demonstrated through the development of argument. That is, the judge deliberately suspends his or her own beliefs regarding the resolution and votes only on the basis of those arguments presented and developed in a given debate. A judge who votes affirmatively is saying, in effect, "Based solely on the arguments in this debate, I believe that the resolution probably is true"; a judge who votes negatively is saying the opposite. The effect of suspending one's prior beliefs about the resolution is to focus the decision on the argumentative skills exhibited in the debate.

Implications of the Role

At least two implications of this convention are worthy of note. First, at least in theory, it assures any argument a fair hearing before any judge. The fact that a debater is assigned to defend national health insurance before a judge who is known to oppose it does not mean that the decision in the debate is predetermined. Instead, since both the debaters and the judges are playing roles, they can detach their personal beliefs from the demands of their role. Hence, in a given debate, the arguments can be evaluated on the strength with which they are presented.

For the same reason, appealing to the audience's predispositions will not necessarily enhance the prospects for victory. In normal argumentative situations, speakers may present incomplete arguments, suggesting premises that the listeners can supply on the basis of their own experience and beliefs. But in academic debate, the judges try to set aside their beliefs and personal experience. Consequently, the full development of an argument is necessary even if the judge is known to be predisposed in its favor.

This convention of suspending personal belief in regard to the resolution is an ideal. It is impossible for people to suspend all their predispositions, as they are not always even conscious of them. But it is an ideal toward which judges aspire and one that experienced and conscientious judges approach. And it is an ideal on which academic debate is based.

Summary

Like any specialized forum, academic debate has the features of general argumentation that we examined in the first unit of this book. But specialized forums also have unique conventions. In academic debate, several conventions are important. The resolution is selected by a process outside the debaters' realm, and so its meaning must be determined by analysis. It is usually selected for a full year, and so its wording tends to be fairly broad in scope, and it tends to propose a more drastic action than is being considered in the public press. The resolution defines the sides in the debate and their essential duties: the job of the affirmative is to support the resolution, and that of the negative is to oppose it.

The debate format also is the result of convention. Particularly important is the time limitation: the division of time between sides, among speakers, and between constructive and rebuttal speeches; the inclusion of time for cross-examination; and the arrangement of speeches so that the affirmative speaks both first and last and the negative has two successive speeches in the middle. Each of the eight speeches in the debate has certain conventionally assigned responsibilities. Depending on the speech, these duties include presentation of constructive arguments, response to arguments of the opposition, extension of arguments, and formulation of decision rules.

As is true of more general arguing, certain basic assumptions are reflected in debate, but there is less agreement about what those assumptions are. One of the two most influential contemporary paradigms of debate views it as essentially an activity of policy making, and the other views it as essentially an activity of testing hypotheses for their probable truth. The latter perspective is employed throughout this book.

Finally, since judges decide debates on the basis of argumentative skills rather than on their personal beliefs regarding the resolution, the strength of an argument is determined anew each time it is presented.

With this understanding of the conventions of academic debate, you should now be prepared to learn the theories and techniques of argumentation within this specialized forum.

Questions for Discussion

1. How would the conventions of academic debate be affected if there were no formally stated resolution?
2. Why do resolutions generally favor change?
3. All things considered, does the conventional debate format promote or impede fairness?
4. Under what conditions should the conventional duties of the individual speakers be modified?
5. In what ways does your selection of a debate paradigm reflect your assumptions about the nature of the activity? Why does this selection influence other theoretical choices?

Chapter 8

Analyzing the Resolution

The first step in preparing to debate is to analyze the resolution. Analysis will make clear what functions the resolution serves, which arguments can be advanced by the affirmative and which by the negative, what the key terms and the resolution as a whole mean, and what the underlying issues and potential case areas are. With this information, both the affirmative and the negative will be able to formulate the collection of arguments that they will use.

Dividing the Universe of Argument

The affirmative will try to establish that the resolution is probably true, and the negative will try to cast doubt on its truth. Although the affirmative and negative have opposite goals, they cooperate in testing the same resolution. From among all the arguments that possibly could be advanced on a multitude of subjects, they limit themselves to those that are germane to the resolution.

The Composition of the Universe

The arguments pertinent to the resolution may be thought of as the *universe of potential arguments*. Ordinarily the composition of this universe may be inferred from the subject matter of the resolution. If, for example, the resolution is that law enforcement agencies should be given greater freedom in investigating crime, you may assume that the universe of potential arguments will come from the field of law enforcement. You must be careful, however, not to construe the universe of potential arguments too narrowly. Sometimes a resolution is advocated as a means to achieve some objective in a different field. Greater freedom for law enforcement agencies, for instance, can be a means either to establish new crimes or to eliminate old ones. Similarly, a resolution may be opposed because it prevents some more desirable activity in another field. Greater freedom for law enforcement agencies can be opposed on the grounds that law enforcement budgets instead should be spent on something else. Likewise, controls on oil imports can be discussed from the standpoint of their diplomatic as well as energy consequences.

Boundaries and Territories

A major purpose of the resolution is to determine which arguments from the universe may be advanced by the affirmative and which ones are open to the negative. Simply put, those arguments that represent reasons that the resolution is true are available to the affirmative, and those that cast doubt on its truth can be used by the negative. In addition, there is a large pool of arguments that by themselves establish neither the truth nor the falsity of the resolution but that can be used together with other arguments to do so. All of these possibilities are illustrated in Figure 8.1.

The universe of possible arguments may be thought of as a large territory. The resolution is a boundary line dividing the territory into two parts, which we have labeled *affirmative land* and *negative land*. The small letters *a* represent arguments that affirm the resolution, and those that negate it are designated *n*. The arguments identified *x* are not automatically either affirmative or negative but can be combined with *a* or *n* arguments as the debaters choose.

An example may help clarify the nature of *a, n,* and *x* arguments. For the resolution that public education should be financed exclusively by the federal government, the argument that states and localities have exhausted their financial resources would lie in affirmative land. It would be an *a* argument because it tends to affirm the resolution; it is unlikely to be useful to the negative. For similar reasons, the argument that states can utilize new sources of revenue would be an

Figure 8.1

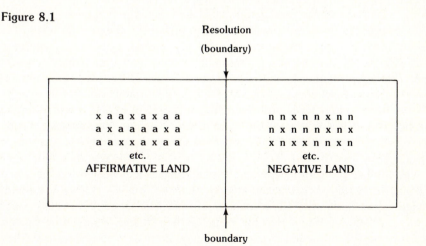

n argument, located in negative land. But the argument that school enrollments will continue to decline for the next five years is an example of an *x* argument. By itself, it neither favors nor opposes the resolution. It can be found, therefore, in either affirmative land or negative land and can be used with either *a* or *n* arguments to achieve either side's purpose.

The primary function of each team in the debate is to defend its assigned territory. The affirmative will describe a problem that can be solved only by embracing the resolution and thus figuratively residing in affirmative land. The negative will argue that, above all else, affirmative land ought not to be chosen as the figurative home.

We shall pursue this territorial analogy in our discussion of the affirmative and negative cases. For the present, two points should be remembered. First, each side's land is composed of those arguments that are available to it and, by implication, not available to its opponent. Even the *x* arguments may be used in combination with *a* arguments only by the affirmative and can be joined with those designated *n* only by the negative. Were either side to present an argument lying in the other's land, it would be undermining its own purpose. The affirmative would be casting doubt on the resolution's truth, and the negative would be upholding the resolution.

The other point is that it is solely the resolution that determines which arguments lie in affirmative land and which are in negative land. This point is sometimes misunderstood. Some debate theorists maintain that the affirmative must advocate a change from present policies and therefore that any argument that defends the current system lies in negative land. They assume that the two lands represent change and stability and that the facts of the current situation will determine where an argument belongs. This position, however, confuses convenience with necessity. It is true that most resolutions are written so that they propose a change, because such a wording offers a convenient assignment of presumption and burden of proof. But a resolution need not favor change. Debaters could consider the resolution that the president of the United States be empowered to ration gasoline even if the president already has such power. Or they could defend the resolution that the United States develop the MX missile, even if the country is already doing so. More generally, the resolution that the nation continue its present policies is an appropriate resolution for debate if one wishes to place presumption in favor of change. Whenever a policy results in death and suffering, it may be wise to reassess it periodically, presuming that it should be changed and requiring that it be justified if it is to continue. The rationale behind "sunset laws," which abolish government agencies if their existence cannot be periodically justified, is similar.

Yet another problem in equating the affirmative and negative respectively with change and stability is that the affirmative never upholds change in general but defends specifically what the resolution requires. Consequently, stability is not the only alternative position that the negative may defend. (Indeed, it can be argued that we live in a world of constant change, in which the notion of stability is an illusion.) The negative may defend any change other than that stipulated in the resolution. Likewise, defending "the current system" will not always work to the negative's benefit. If the resolution is worded so that arguments favoring the status quo lie in affirmative land, then the negative would be advocating the resolution by defending them. It would abandon its primary task of opposing the resolution. The point is that whether an argument is in affirmative land or negative land is determined not by the factual state of affairs but by the specific wording of the resolution.

Jurisdictional Questions

In dividing the universe of arguments, the resolution determines which side has *jurisdiction* over any potential argument—which side can be said to "own" the argument. Sometimes there will be a dispute over where the jurisdiction lies. When there is, the jurisdictional question must be settled before the substantive issues can be resolved. If the affirmative, for instance, presents arguments over which it lacks jurisdiction, the substance of those arguments will not matter. They do not lie in affirmative land and hence are not available to the affirmative. In academic debate, there are three similar, yet distinct, jurisdictional issues that may arise, involving the questions of topicality, justification, and extratopicality.

Topicality

Topicality pertains to the relationship between the resolution and the action implied by the affirmative arguments. This action must be within the scope identified by the resolution. We shall discuss topicality from the standpoint of both the negative and the affirmative.

Topicality and the Affirmative. The first question is whether the affirmative actually advocates the resolution, whether it proposes that the action specified in the resolution be taken. Topicality is determined by examining the action supported by the affirmative to see whether it matches the action referred to in the resolution. If the affirmative presents a specific plan, then the question is whether the plan proposes to implement all of the key terms of the resolution. If the affirmative does not advocate a specific plan, then the topicality question is whether the affirmative arguments in fact support the statement embodied in the resolution.

Under what circumstances could the affirmative fail to be topical? Three possibilities come to mind. First, the affirmative may be in error as to crucial facts. For instance, suppose that the resolution called for a significant reduction in the powers of the president of the United States. The affirmative argued for the curtailment of a power that did not in fact reside with the president, but with Congress or the judiciary. If the president did not have the power in question, then curtailing that power would not significantly reduce the president's powers. By inattention to the relevant facts, the affirmative would fail to be topical.

A second, and far more common, peril for the affirmative arises from ambiguous wording in the resolution itself. Consider the resolution that law enforcement agencies should be given greater freedom in investigating and prosecuting crime. Political philosophers have identified two different senses of the term *freedom*. One kind of freedom, often called *freedom to*, is a license to perform some particular act. The other, *freedom from*, refers to the removal of constraints on individual choice and the exercise of discretion. These two notions can have contradictory results.

For example, an affirmative that argued that police departments should be required to report suspected child abuse cases could maintain that it wished to give law enforcement agencies greater freedom (in the sense of *freedom to* report cases). But the negative could insist that the case was not only nontopical but also antitopical, since the affirmative proposed to restrict freedom (in the sense of *freedom from* outside directives). Such a clash cannot be resolved in advance, as its outcome will depend on the supporting claims for each view of the term freedom.

Third, the affirmative could fail to advocate all the key terms in the resolution. Sometimes the resolution will impose multiple requirements on the affirmative in order to limit the number of possible affirmative arguments (to affect the boundaries of affirmative land). The clearest example occurred several years ago when high school students debated the resolution that the federal government establish, finance, and administer programs to control air and water pollution in the United States. The affirmative had to advocate that the federal government establish and finance and administer programs to control both air and water pollution. If the affirmative advocated some lesser action, it would not be topical, since it would fail to support all of the key terms of the resolution. The language of the resolution, in short, would make the affirmative nontopical.

If the affirmative were to lose topicality, it would lose the debate. Topicality, in other words, is the most basic requirement that it must satisfy. Sometimes one may think that the purpose of the resolution is merely to facilitate a good discussion and that if such a discussion results, it does not matter whether the affirmative is topical. But this line of reasoning surely puts the cart before the horse, for the purpose of having a good discussion is to test the resolution's probable truth. If the affirmative is not truly supporting the resolution—which would be the case if it loses topicality—then there is nothing to test. Since topicality is such an important consideration and since it seldom is a clear-cut case but instead is settled by evaluating the competing arguments, it is not surprising that negative teams frequently raise the challenge.

Topicality and the Negative.   So far, we have been discussing topicality as if it were solely an affirmative obligation. But it is just as important for the negative team to be certain that it is not topical—that it does not inadvertently affirm the resolution. The reason is similar to the one stated above: if the resolution is affirmed by default, then it has not received the test that the debate was to provide.

The negative, if it is not careful, may unintentionally become topical. For instance, it could support a course of action whose natural effect would be to achieve the conditions stated in the resolution. For a resolution that the United States should significantly increase its energy independence, suppose that the affirmative argues for the increased use of nuclear power. If the negative replies by supporting conservation, it would be topical if the effect of energy conservation were to increase significantly the United States' energy independence.

Another way in which the negative may blunder into topicality is by supporting an outcome for which the affirmation of the resolution is a prerequisite. For the resolution that the United States significantly change its foreign trade policies, the negative could propose instead that all industrialized nations together devise trade policies. But such a proposal would require a significant change on the part of the United States (as one of the industrialized nations) and therefore would fall victim to the charge of topicality.

The negative can also become topical by blindly supporting the present system and its evolution. Sometimes this stance will be strong for the negative. But if defending the present systems also affirms the resolution, then the negative will have supported a topical action. Suppose that the resolution is that the United States ration the use of gasoline. The negative supports the present system, which includes the president's power to ration. In an emergency, the negative argues, this power could be used. But by supporting the exercise of this power, the negative has supported the resolution, even though the present system has not been abandoned. When the negative makes this mistake, the reason is usually that it has confused topicality with another concept, inherency, which we shall examine in Chapter 9. It must be remembered that the resolution, not the present system, determines whether an argument resides in affirmative land or negative land.

Since nontopicality is a minimum requirement for the negative, affirmative teams frequently argue that the negative actually supports the resolution.

Clarifications.   Several clarifications are necessary at this point. First, we have been considering topicality as if it were an all-or-nothing matter. We have been assuming that either all of the action supported by the affirmative is topical or else that none of it is. Similarly, we have been assuming that if the negative ever affirms the resolution, then all of its argument will fall. Often these assumptions are correct. But either the affirmative or the negative can develop a complex case. One part of the affirmative case, for instance, may be clearly topical although another part is not. How should you treat a situation involving partial topicality? The answer is that anything in the affirmative case that is not topical, or anything in the negative that is, is usually dismissed from further consideration. If one part of the affirmative's case is topical and another is not, then the test of the resolution is made on the basis of the topical portion alone. It therefore is a waste of time for either team knowingly to develop arguments that do not lie within its jurisdiction.

It should also be clear that topicality is a minimal requirement. The affirmative may go beyond the resolution as long as it does affirm the resolution and it affirms nothing incompatible with the resolution. This is another way of saying that the affirmative can support any action implied by the x arguments as long as it supports some action implied by the a arguments. But if the x argument can be located equally well in affirmative land or negative land, then by itself it represents no real grounds for affirming the resolution. For this reason, affirmatives often argue that an action identified by an a argument is a necessary condition for x. In other words, x cannot exist by itself but only in combination with a, and the combination of a plus x can exist only in affirmative land.

For the resolution that the federal government should provide a comprehensive program of medical care, the control of general price inflation is an action that can be justified by either affirmative or negative arguments. Hence, claims on its behalf are x arguments. This situation makes the control of general price inflation an irrelevant reason to affirm the resolution. To avert this possibility, the affirmative could argue that the only way to control general price inflation is to change monetary and fiscal policy and also to control medical care costs, because medical care costs make up a very large percentage of total inflation. The affirmative is arguing for the combination of an a and an x argument, and that combination can exist only in affirmative land. According to this reasoning, the affirmative may be able to claim that supporting x does constitute affirmation of the resolution, since x cannot be obtained except in conjunction with the resolution. This argument would establish the topicality of x by showing that a was necessary for it. The discussion then would proceed to the merits of the case. The affirmative then would need to show that a is a sufficient condition for the desired result, so that x will follow a.

Finally, it should be stressed that topicality is a subject to be decided by the arguments in the debate. It is not for a judge to determine, based on personal opinion, what is topical; it is an argument that the judge should evaluate objectively. To return to the above example, freedom can be decided by the same judges sometimes to mean freedom from and sometimes freedom to. Since the judge's standards depend on the argumentation, it is necessary for the debater to be skilled in arguing about the meaning of key terms. We shall return to this problem shortly.

Justification

The concept of justification is related to topicality, but its function is different. With topicality, the key question is whether the affirmative really endorses all of the key terms in the resolution. Justification refers to whether the affirmative has given reason to endorse them all. Justification arguments often arise when the affirmative does support all the key terms but discusses only certain terms as the source of its desired outcome, ignoring the rest of the resolution. Suppose that the resolution calls for the federal government to liberalize welfare payments. If the affirmative speaks exclusively about the benefits of liberalizing welfare payments, without mentioning the agent for liberalizing them, the negative can respond that the key term, federal government, has not been defended and hence that the resolution taken as a whole has not been justified.

What is the function of justification arguments? You should remember that the goal of debate is to test the probable truth of the resolution. What the justification argument says, in effect, is "Even if we take the affirmative arguments at face value, they will not add up to support of the particular resolution being discussed." The reason is that an alternative resolution (in our example, liberalizing welfare benefits regardless of the level of government involved) would respond equally well to the situation discussed. Since presumption is placed against the resolution, as we saw in Chapter 2, the negative would profit from the argument that an alternative is equally good. This argument establishes that there is no unique merit to the resolution and hence that that presumption has not been overturned. If the affirmative arguments, even taken at face value, do not justify the resolution, then there is no need to consider the substantive merit of the individual arguments. Justification, like topicality, is a basic affirmative requirement.

Some theorists and critics object to using the justification arguments, and they reason along the following lines: The affirmative must affirm the resolution (either generally or by reference to a specific illustration of its principles). Likewise, the negative must support a specific position, for reasons that we shall consider in Chapter 12. Consequently, the key question in the debate is a comparison of the two positions' merits. But justification arguments, the reasoning goes, do not refer to the comparative merits of the negative position. Rather, they concern hypothetical other alternatives that are not defended by either team in the debate. Therefore they are moot points, and the justification argument is irrelevant.

This criticism of justification arguments, though popular, seems to be based on a significant confusion. Although the affirmative indeed is required to support the resolution, the advocacy of a specific negative position is a strategic choice and is not required by the negative's fundamental duty to oppose the resolution. It is possible to object to the resolution on the grounds that it is bad, without having any other alternative in mind. One reason that the resolution may be bad is that the arguments offered to support it can be used equally well to support alternatives to it. Hence the presumption against the resolution has yet to be overturned, since there is no unique merit to the resolution.

It is possible for the justification arguments (like any form of argument) to be poorly used. The thorough testing of the resolution is ill served by a scenario in which the negative mindlessly asks, "Why the federal government?" "Why all citizens?" "Why in the United States?" These undeveloped questions usually can be answered satisfactorily in an equally skimpy way. But to note the potential for abuse is not to argue against the validity of the justification arguments. It is to say that here, as elsewhere, a question that is not developed into an argument will not accomplish much.

Justification, like topicality, is often not a clear-cut matter. It may not be immediately obvious whether the affirmative has given a reason for all of the resolution's key terms. Justifications seldom are organized separately but, rather, are implicit in the substantive arguments. When the negative raises the argument, a jurisdictional issue is raised that takes precedence over the substantive issues. If after hearing arguments from both teams about the link between the affirmative arguments and the resolution, the judge finds the resolution to be justified, then the question will turn to the actual merit of the resolution. On the other hand, if the resolution is found not to be justified, then the negative will win without further consideration of the merits, since the affirmative's arguments have been rendered moot.

Extratopicality

The final jurisdictional concern is the question of extratopicality. Topicality pertains to the question of whether the affirmative actually supports the resolution, and justification is a matter of whether the affirmative's arguments, taken at face value, give reason for supporting that particular resolution. In comparison, *extratopicality* is a question of whether the resolution is the true source of the affirmative's advantages. An argument is extratopical if it stems not from the affirmation of the resolution but from some other source.

A simple example will illustrate this concept. For the resolution that scarce world resources should be controlled by an international organization, suppose that the affirmative also argues for the mandatory domestic conservation of energy. The affirmative would be exercising its right to advocate more than the resolution requires. One of the affirmative's supporting arguments is that conservation will reduce air pollution. In this case, the source of this benefit is the proposal for domestic conservation — not the control of resources by an international organization. Indeed, domestic conservation could occur whether or not the resolution were affirmed. Since the basis for the argument is not grounded in the resolution, the argument does not represent a good reason to support the resolution. Instead, the benefit of controlling air pollution is extratopical. It can be obtained equally well by supporting some alternative to the resolution.

Sources of Extratopicality.   There are two situations in which the affirmative can fall victim to extratopical arguments. One is illustrated in the above example: the affirmative proposes more than the resolution requires, and the additional elements turn out to be the true grounds for its claim that it can solve a problem or derive a benefit.

The other situation leading to extratopicality results when affirming the resolution is a necessary, but perhaps not a sufficient, condition for the affirmative's argument. For example, for the resolution that the United States should renounce the use of nuclear weapons, the affirmative could claim that enhancing world peace would be one of the benefits. If so, the negative probably would be quick to observe that whether or not world peace is the consequence depends on how other nations respond to United States renunciation. They could view it as a challenge to them to follow suit, or they could regard it as a sign of weakness to be exploited by means of a preemptive nuclear attack. In other words, the American renunciation of nuclear weapons could be a precondition for the advantage of world peace, but whether the advantage actually will result cannot be determined by the action of the United States alone. Consequently, the benefit of world peace is extratopical, since affirming the resolution is not a sufficient condition for attainment.

The Meaning of Sufficient Condition.   It is important, however, to qualify the statement that the resolution must be a sufficient condition. In a literal sense, no resolution can be a sufficient condition for any outcome. No result can come about without a seemingly infinite number of conditions that are not stated in a resolution. Among the necessary conditions for world peace, for instance, are the existence of life, the existence of the universe, and the existence of human beings. The statement of the resolution refers to none of these, but each in a sense is a basis for the affirmative advantage. On these grounds, if one declared the affirmative argument to be extratopical, then the affirmative always would be extratopical. There is no way that all the necessary conditions can be stated in any resolution.

The way out of the problem is to focus more sharply the definition of sufficient condition. If affirming the resolution is a sufficient condition for solving a problem, then no action should be required except for (1) the resolution, (2) the necessary conditions for all resolutions, or (3) the outcomes that can reasonably be expected to follow the affirmation of the resolution. According to this standard, the affirmative cannot be deemed extratopical on the basis that solving a problem requires the existence of people but that the resolution says nothing about people. Likewise, in our example above, world peace would not be an extratopical argument if the affirmative could establish that the likely result of the United States' renunciation of nuclear weapons would be similar action by other nations. Under those circumstances, although it is true that world peace depends on something in addition to the United States' action, that "something else" would be forthcoming as an effect of the American action. Hence the benefit of world peace could be a valid argument for a unilateral decision by the United States.

The Impact of Extratopicality.   If an affirmative argument is found to be extratopical, the effect is to moot consideration of that argument, since it is irrelevant to the merits of the resolution. Extratopicality is not necessarily an absolute issue; the affirmative still may win the debate by defeating the negative on the remaining arguments. As long as the affirmative remains with some problems solved or advantage gained and as long as the action implied by the resolution is the true source of that benefit, the resolution can be tested on the basis of the arguments regarding that problem or advantage. Only if *every* reason given by the affirmative to support the resolution were found to be extratopical, would extratopicality lead to a negative decision without consideration of the resolution's substantive merits.

Defining the Terms

Whenever there is a jurisdictional dispute of any of these three types, its outcome will likely depend on arguments regarding what the resolution means. One meaning may render the affirmative topical, but another may not. One meaning may show the terms in the resolution to be synonymous and therefore not needing individual justification, but another may find the resolution not to have been justified. Consequently, defining the terms of the resolution is extremely important—particularly since virtually any term can have many definitions.

Means of Definition

The initial choice of definitions is the prerogative of the affirmative, in order to offset the facts that the affirmative shoulders the burden of proof. Affirmatives typically approach the task of definition in any of three ways. They can *stipulate a meaning for each of the key terms.* For the resolution that the federal government should provide comprehensive medical care for all citizens, the affirmative could begin by explaining its definitions of *provide, comprehensive, medical care,* and *citizens.* This term-by-term approach to stipulating definitions used to be the most common, but in recent years it has been supplanted by the other approaches.

A second means of defining the terms is to *stipulate a meaning for the resolution as a whole,* usually by expressing it in a synonymous sentence. For example, the medical care resolution mentioned above could be defined as meaning that the federal government should make a wide range of medical services available to all United States citizens without imposing user fees. In this method of definition, each of the key terms is explained specifically or implicitly. "Make . . . available . . . without imposing user fees" is an explanation of *provide,* for example.

The third method of definition is *operational.* The resolution is given meaning by specifying the actions that would be taken if it is affirmed. Operational definition is one function of the affirmative plan, as we shall see in Chapter 10. The team that uses this method of definition is suggesting that the resolution means a particular set of actions. Of course, affirming the resolution does not mean that the actions are actually taken. Rather, the affirmative plan is a hypothetical illustration of how the resolution's central principles might be put into effect. Nor does the use of an operational definition imply that the resolution has been defined exhaustively. Other operational definitions may also be possible, even though they are not the focus of a given debate.

The Reasonableness of Definitions

Whichever method of definition the affirmative employs, its prerogative to interpret the resolution is constrained by the requirement that it must be reasonable. An unreasonable interpretation would thwart the function of giving the resolution a thorough test, since it would draw the boundary between affirmative land and negative land so as to deny the negative an ample supply of arguments against the resolution.

Sometimes reasonableness has been viewed as a minimal requirement, and any definition that did not contradict itself was presumed to be reasonable. More recently, however, the practice has been to label as reasonable only the better definition advanced in the debate. This better-definition rule obviously increases the affirmative's burden to prove that its interpretation is reasonable.

Not surprisingly, disputes about the resolution's meaning frequently begin by the negative's charging that the affirmative is unreasonable. There is no objective standard of reasonableness, however, and so whether the affirmative interpretation is legitimate is a matter to be settled by argument. But there are several things that can be said about the conduct of this argument.

We shall begin by identifying some common misconceptions about definitional arguments. First, reasonableness is not something to be determined by the judge's personal beliefs or prejudices apart from the arguments made by the debaters. It would be unfair, for example, for the judge to decide that "emergency medical services" is an unreasonable interpretation of "comprehensive medical care" because he or she does not like it, even though the affirmative's arguments that it is reasonable have not been refuted in the debate. To do otherwise would be to usurp the debater's responsibility to analyze the resolution and would violate the principle that disputes should be settled by argument rather than dictum.

Second, the fact that the negative may offer an alternative definition of the resolution does not mean that the affirmative's definition is unreasonable. There may be many reasonable interpretations, and the affirmative's assignment is not to find the only possible definition but rather to find a reasonable one. Even under the better-definitions rule, the affirmative need only show that its interpretation is more reasonable than the negative's—not that it is the only reasonable position.

Third, consulting a dictionary to obtain definitions of the individual terms in the resolution is not necessarily a reliable way to determine what the resolution means. Dictionaries define terms, not resolutions. Combining several dictionary definitions into a sentence will often result in nonsense, suggesting that there is a meaning to the resolution as a whole that may be lost in a word-by-word division. Besides, dictionaries reflect general usage, whereas the terms in the resolution may have more precise meanings in the particular fields being discussed. And usage changes over time; so the dictionary definitions may no longer reflect current practice. Moreover, a comprehensive dictionary will list several meanings for most terms. Some of these meanings may be incompatible, and there is no way to determine which are the most reasonable. Consulting a dictionary as a way of defining the resolution may offer us no clearer idea of what it reasonably means than when we began.

Fourth, consulting an authority is not always a reliable guide to interpretation. Debaters sometimes refer to the "spirit of the resolution," presumably referring to the meaning intended by those who wrote the resolution. But the framers' intentions usually cannot be known; they are a matter of speculation. And even if they could be known, to say that the resolution means only what its framers intended it to mean would be to deny the truism that meaning is bestowed by the receivers of communication at least as much as it is supplied by the senders. For the same reasons that the spirit of the resolution is an unreliable guide to meaning, so are statements by people who purport to explain what the resolution means. Such statements are valuable in that they suggest ideas and possible arguments about meaning, but it must be remembered that the resolution's meaning is ultimately to be ascertained by the arguers.

It should be evident from the foregoing discussion of misconceptions that the only way to determine whether an interpretation of the resolution is reasonable is by referring to *context*. Several contexts can be used, and arguments can be offered for each.

1. You can claim an interpretation to be unreasonable because it violates common usage, arguing that debate is a public activity and therefore that common public usage should prevail.

2. You can appeal to the specialized usage of the term in a particular field, maintaining that the standards should be derived from the field that is being discussed. For example, economic terms should be defined as they are by economists.

3. You can hold that since we debate policy resolutions, the relevant context for determining reasonableness is the policy makers' and analysts' usage of the terms.

4. You can appeal to a functional context, stating that the functions of any resolution are to identify the specific universe of possible arguments and the boundaries between affirmative and negative territory and then protesting that the affirmative's interpretation makes it impossible for the resolution to achieve these functions.

5. You can even appeal to grammar or syntax, asserting that an interpretation is unreasonable because it does not consider which terms have been modified by which other terms or because it violates the general norm of avoiding redundancy in sentence construction.

6. Finally, you can appeal to any stipulated context that is officially provided with the resolution. At the high school level, the national resolution is given a context by the statement of a problem area to which it responds. At the collegiate level, a brief interpretive statement of substantive parameters

accompanies the resolution. Although this statement is not binding, it does offer a valuable context to which arguments regarding reasonableness can refer.

To be sure, replies can be made to each of the above definitional arguments. The affirmative can defend its interpretation by showing its fidelity to the context established by the negative or by arguing that the negative's suggested context is not appropriate. Furthermore, there may be many other contexts to appeal to, besides those stated here. The important point is that questions about reasonableness of interpretation can be settled only by argument regarding the applicability of context. Once the matter of context is settled, however, a relatively limited number of possible interpretations of the terms will emerge as reasonable.

Determining the Issues

The final step in analyzing the resolution is to determine the central points likely to be in dispute. We noted in Chapter 2 that the issues are those questions inherent in the resolution and vital to its success. Locating the issues enables the debater to find out what questions must be investigated through research and what responsibilities must be discharged in constructing a case. Usually, several processes are used simultaneously to determine the issues.

Through Reflection

One process is to study the historical background and current controversy in the subject area. This study will inform the debater of the disputes that have dominated the public press and decision-making bodies and that may be responsible for the current interest in the resolution. For example, for the resolution that the federal government should significantly increase the regulation of the mass media, a study of historical background and current controversy would inform the debater about such subjects as media influence on attitudes and behavior, whether there is a right of access to the media, monopoly control of media, cable television, and the like. Each of these subjects represents a possible area for an affirmative case and negative argumentation. You can use research to investigate the arguments regarding these topics and to find out the essential points of controversy.

Another process for locating the issues is brainstorming. This technique, usually employed in small groups, is an attempt to generate as many ideas as possible. Without evaluating their ideas, participants draw on their own experience, knowledge, and imagination to suggest as many subject areas as possible that might apply to the resolution. It is not uncommon for a group of four or five people to formulate one hundred or more subject areas during a fairly short discussion. Then, having recorded all the ideas, the group can eliminate those that are not likely to be productive and can determine which of the remainder merit further investigation and research.

Both of the first two approaches determine the issues inductively, by examining the specific subject matter of the resolution.

A third process for locating the issues on a particular resolution is to apply the stock issues. As we saw in Chapter 2, stock issues are types of issues that recur regularly in regard to resolutions of a given type. Resolutions of fact will recurrently have certain issues, as will resolutions of value or of policy. The stock issues of policy are of special concern to us here and will be considered at length in Chapter 9. These stock issues represent analytical categories that can be used to examine any particular resolution. For example, one stock issue is the question of whether there is a significant problem. So, for the specific policy resolution, the debater would ask, "What are the significant problems?" The same procedure then could be used for other stock issues. You should remember that the stock issues are aids to the analysis of particular resolutions. Significant problems will not take exactly the same form from one resolution to another. But as an aid, a stock-issues analysis can be valuable in identifying the central points of dispute.

Through Research

Having identified the issues and the major subject areas in the resolution, debaters should be prepared to begin intensive research. In general, research for academic debate follows the same general principles for research that we outlined in Chapter 3. A few special matters deserve mention, however.

First, library research is by far the most common mode. Few debaters are themselves experts in the subjects they debate, and few are able to interview experts in the field.

Second, debate research often requires using specialized or technical materials. The general indexes to the various forms of literature, which we described in Chapter 3, are less useful to the academic debate participant than to arguers in general. The reason is that these indexes usually do not list specialized or technical publications. Instead, it is usually necessary to consult other indexes. Many of these have formats similar to those of the general indexes. With others, you will need to ask the reference librarian for help. A few of the specialized indexes are described here.

In researching books, the card catalogue of your local library will be an insufficient index, and so it will be necessary to work in a major research library or to become familiar with the interlibrary loan system and the *Library of Congress Catalogue*. With respect to periodicals, the *Reader's Guide* will be of limited use. You will want to use the *Bulletin of the Public Affairs Information Service*, the *Social Sciences Index,* and the numerous indexes and abstracts in particular subject fields. The *Social Science Citation Index* is a particularly useful reference. In researching government publications, do not neglect the *Monthly Catalog of U.S.*

Government Publications or the *Congressional Information Service Index.* For newspapers, remember that there are indexes to such major papers as the *New York Times, Wall Street Journal,* and *Washington Post.*

Third, the mechanics of recording evidence warrant special attention. Although some debaters photocopy the original source, the most common practice is to keep records on note cards. It is important to place on the card the complete documentation for the evidence, including—at minimum—the following items:

1. The name of the person being quoted.
2. His or her qualifications.
3. The title of the publication.
4. The date.
5. The page number.

This information will enable you to assess the strength of the source as well as to retrieve the quotation at a later date. The quoted matter should be copied onto the card with an absolute minimum of editing. Generally, the only editing needed is the insertion (in brackets) of referents for otherwise unclear words, such as a pronoun whose antecedent is not included in the quotation. At both the high school and college levels, debaters often must be able to supply the exact wording of the quotation as it appears in the original source.

Fourth, it is important to devise a system of filing evidence so that it can be easily located and so that it may be reorganized as changes in the analysis of the resolution require. Filing systems are ultimately a matter of individual convenience. Most debaters find it useful to divide their evidence by subject area, into relatively small divisions, with related subjects filed in close proximity and with the subject (typically the specific argument) indicated at the top of the card, in order to permit refiling and retrieval without rereading the evidence.

Finally, debate research is a continuing process. It occurs when the resolution is first determined and the preliminary analysis is completed. But unless the resolution is debated only a single time, the research should continue. It is necessary to stay abreast of changes and developments in the topic and to examine further those arguments that have already been used.

Summary

The subject matter of the debate resolution establishes a universe of possible arguments for discussion, and the wording of the resolution divides that universe into those arguments available to the affirmative and those available to the negative. We referred to this division by an analogy to a territory divided between affirmative land and negative land. Some arguments may be available to either the affirmative or the negative, depending on the other arguments with which they are combined. The primary duty of each side is to defend its figurative territory, the affirmative by showing that the resolution is probably true and the negative by casting doubt on its probable truth.

The resolution also determines which side will have jurisdiction over any particular argument. Three types of jurisdictional questions may arise in a debate. Topicality involves the question of whether the affirmative actually advocates the resolution and whether the negative actually avoids doing so. Justification is a matter of whether the affirmative arguments, taken at face value, warrant the precise resolution that is in dispute. Extratopicality deals with the possibility that the basis for the arguments on which the affirmative advocates the resolution might be some external factor rather than the resolution itself. These jurisdictional questions preempt the substantive issues, meaning that if the negative can defeat the resolution on jurisdictional grounds, it usually will not need to consider the resolution's merits.

The affirmative has the prerogative to define the resolution, provided that it is defined in a reasonable way. Stipulations of individual terms, restatement of the resolution in synonymous language, and operational definitions are the methods most commonly employed. When the reasonableness of the affirmative's interpretation is in dispute, it can be settled only by reference to context and by argument about what context is appropriate.

Finally, analysis of the resolution includes locating the issues so as to guide research and case construction. Studying the historical background and current controversy on the resolution, brainstorming possible case areas, and applying the stock issues to the particular resolution all are valuable methods for this stage of analysis. Following this preliminary analysis, intensive research begins. Debate research is like any other, except that it relies more heavily on published evidence, it is more specialized, it depends on precise documentation, and it is ongoing.

Questions for Discussion

1. Must the areas of affirmative land and negative land be equal? What are the implications for a debate if one side's territory is substantially larger than the other's?

2. For the resolution that the federal government should adopt wage and price controls, what is an example of an x argument? How can it be used by both the affirmative and the negative?

3. What are the major differences between topicality and extratopicality? Between topicality and justification?

4. We have said that jurisdictional questions preempt the substantive issues. Why is this so?

5. What are the comparative merits of requiring the affirmative to provide *a* reasonable interpretation and *the most* reasonable interpretation of the resolution?
6. How are stock issues used to analyze the issues in a specific debate resolution? Are there any drawbacks to this approach?

Chapter 9

Affirmative Case Construction: Requirements

In this chapter we shall examine the stock issues of a resolution dealing with policy. (Many elements, though, will also apply to nonpolicy resolutions.) Since they are issues, we know that the affirmative must sustain its position on each of them in order to be able to affirm the resolution. The stock issues therefore are also regarded as the proof requirements of the affirmative. Consequently, affirmative debaters should construct their arguments with an eye to these stock issues, to be sure that the affirmative case—the total structure of argument—responds to them.

There are many different ways in which to classify the stock issues, and the number of stock issues identified will vary with the method of classification. We shall discuss the affirmative proof requirements under four stock issues. The affirmative must prove the existence of a significant problem, the inherency of this problem, the efficacy of the proposed solution, and the solution's favorable ratio of benefits to disadvantages.

Significance of the Problem

The stock issue of significance requires that the affirmative prove that it is addressing an important problem. We shall first examine the reasons for this requirement and then consider how the affirmative provides the needed proof.

The Concept of Risk

As we have seen, to affirm a resolution is to entail risks. First, there is the risk that we will commit ourselves prematurely to a position. As long as we withhold assent to a resolution, we can keep our options open, but once we commit ourselves to the truth of a resolution, we stop examining other alternatives. For example, we may be uncertain about the proper response to energy shortages, and so we are prepared to consider all proposals. But once we determine that we should adopt a policy to develop synthetic fuels, we have committed ourselves to that option and stop searching for others. When we affirm a resolution, there always is the risk that we may be making this commitment prematurely on the basis of inadequate information.

In addition to the risk of premature commitment, there is the risk of error. There always is the chance of being proved wrong: we can be just as mistaken in rejecting a resolution as we can be in affirming it. But the consequences are less severe if we err in rejecting a resolution, since negating it leaves all options open for reexamination—including the resolution itself, in the light of new information or ideas. By contrast, affirming a resolution means that we are prepared to act on the assumption that it is true.

Finally, there is the risk of having to modify our belief system in order to take new information into account. Unless one is a committed supporter of the resolution in the first place, affirming the resolution may challenge one's fundamental beliefs. The more basic these beliefs are, the more resistant they are to change, and the more likely it is that change will have far-reaching consequences. Since these consequences often cannot be predicted, the act of affirming a resolution entails this third type of risk as well.

It is worth remembering that the affirmative constructs its case with an eye on these risks; they represent the reasons that presumption always is placed against the resolution. The affirmative case must provide reasons to convince an audience that affirming the resolution is important enough to be worth confronting the risks. The first step in this reasoning is to establish that the resolution will respond to a problem significant enough to justify running the risks.

Proving That a Problem Exists

The requirement that the affirmative prove the existence of a significant problem has two separate, though closely related, parts. In the first place, there must be a problem. Otherwise it would make little sense to affirm the resolution; one does not, after all, run risks for no reason. To establish the existence of a problem, the affirmative needs to demonstrate that there is a situation that violates a value judgment shared by the debaters and the audience. For example, if life and health were regarded as positive values, then proof of death and suffering would establish the existence of a problem. If efficiency were valued, waste would be a problem. If individual freedom were considered valuable, then regulation or government control would be a problem.

Sometimes the value judgment is unanimous and virtually uncontested—hardly anyone denies the value of life, for instance—and so the affirmative need only demonstrate that the value is being violated. In other circumstances, the value judgment may not be so nearly universal. Efficiency, for instance, may be valuable in that it cuts costs and conserves scarce resources, but not valuable in that it may destroy jobs, require the standardization of products, or not give enough weight to individual differences. In such a case, demonstrating the existence of a problem would involve two steps: justifying the value judgment itself, and then showing that the value is being violated. Since it seems easier to assume than to prove a value judgment, debaters sometimes tend to limit their consideration of problems to those that violate universal values. Some may even argue that death and suffering are the only legitimate problems for discussion. But there are many other values for which a strong defense may be easily constructed, such as equality of opportunity, personal security, and education. And even the seemingly universal values may need to be defended if the negative should choose to contest them. For this reason, it is never wise to assume that a value judgment will be shared by all.

We have been discussing a problem as though it refers only to some existing condition that people find unacceptable. It can, of course, refer to such a condition. But the absence of a benefit may also be called a problem: benefit and problem are opposite sides of the same coin. If, for example, a new agricultural policy could increase crop yields and preserve the quality of the soil, then the fact that we are not now achieving those advantages would constitute a problem. In short, a problem can refer either to an undesirable state of affairs that exists now or to the absence of a desirable set of conditions that could be obtained in the future.

Proving That the Problem Is Significant

It is not enough, however, to show that there is a problem. There always will be problems and missed opportunities, no matter what resolutions we may choose to affirm. It therefore is the task of the affirmative to establish that the problem is *significant* enough to warrant concern. Significance involves the questions of (1) how important the value at issue is and (2) how seriously the value is violated. The first of these is a question of justification; the second, a question of measurement.

Justifying the Value.   An example will illustrate the need for the affirmative to show the importance of the value. Many people believe that a balanced federal government budget is desirable. Accordingly, an affirmative could show that a value is being violated, by proving that government fiscal policies unbalance the budget. But how important is this problem? In times of recession, a budget deficit may be economically necessary, whereas in times of rampant inflation, a large deficit may pose serious risks. No value is equally important under all circumstances. Likewise, at any given time, not all values will weigh equally. Violations of some values may be necessary in order to enhance others. Therefore, the affirmative must establish that the value being violated is important. It can do so by exploring the consequences of violating the value, by showing that the value is necessary to achieve some other value on which both sides agree, by appealing to historical precedents or examples when the value has been proclaimed and preserved, by appealing to authorities who speak to the importance of the value, and so on.

Measuring the Violation.   It is also necessary to know the extent of the violation, since minor problems may not be worth the risks of affirming the resolution. The affirmative will want to show that the problem is widespread, and there are several possible ways in which it can do so. It can measure the absolute numerical dimensions of the problem — for example, that trade barriers add, say, 10 percent to the price of all goods. It can identify the number of people affected by the problem — for instance, the thousands of deaths and serious injuries attributable to air pollution. It can enumerate the probability of some future calamity—such as the odds of a serious accident at a nuclear power plant. Each of these examples illustrates a quantitative method for determining the extensiveness of a problem. If these methods are employed, significance becomes a matter of multiplying the probability of a given occurrence (which would be 1.0 for events that actually had occurred in the past and a number smaller than 1.0 for anticipated future events) by the extensiveness of the occurrence and then multiplying the total by some number reflecting the importance of the value that has been violated. In reality, these multiplications are seldom as exact as we have suggested here. The probability, extensiveness, and value of most events cannot be specified with this degree of precision. The multiplication that usually occurs is more conceptual than mathematical.

Not all forms of significance lend themselves readily to measurement, moreover, and it is a mistake to assume that what cannot be quantified is necessarily unimportant. Sometimes the degree to which a value is violated can only be approximated. When we talk in such loose terms as a "very serious problem," an "urgent matter," or a "fundamental task," we are indicating that significance can be known only in a quasi-numerical way; it can be approximated but not specified. Sometimes the violation of a value is absolute—that is, any abridgment of the value is necessarily a serious one. Defenders of the Bill of Rights, for example, maintain that the First Amendment cannot be breached at all without undermining the basic freedoms of speech, press, religion and assembly. The argument is that if any exceptions to these basic rights are permitted, then the rights are not secure. The logic that permits one exception today could well lead to other exceptions in the future (for the sake of consistency), and the exceptions would undermine the value. Partly for this reason, civil libertarians often insist that the guarantees in the Bill of Rights must be preserved intact, lest the guarantees come unraveled under the pressure for exceptions.

So far we have seen that the requirement of the affirmative to describe a significant problem gives the affirmative the means to overcome the risks of affirming the resolution. The requirement is documenting the existence of a situation that violates a value shared by the affirmative debaters and the judge. It also is necessary to show how much the value is violated and how important the value is.

How Much Is Enough?

Perhaps the most difficult question to answer is, "How much significance must the affirmative demonstrate?" After having shown the importance of the values, how much inflation or how much risk of war must the affirmative establish in order to be assured that it has described a significant problem? This question cannot be answered in the abstract, and it should be fairly easy to see why. At the end of the debate, the affirmative must have enough significance so that, even considering the objections raised by the negative and any residual risks in the minds of the audience, there still will be reasons for affirming the resolution. But at the outset of the debate, when the affirmative makes its claim of significance, it is not possible to know just what objections the negative may sustain or what residual risks may lurk in the listeners' minds.

Since significance must be proved even without this information, debaters often are advised to make their initial significance claim as large as possible. In this way, even after significance has been whittled down by the negative, they will have an amply significant problem remaining.

But this approach often is misguided. A very large significance claim simply may not be credible—if, for instance, the affirmative claims a monetary harm larger than the gross national product. Or a significance claim may be so large that the problem appears to be insoluble. Or the affirmative may invite negative arguments based on the upsetting effects of a change that would need to be very drastic in order to solve such a huge problem. For these reasons, it is wise not to inflate the significance claim beyond the bounds of the reasonable. It also is wise, however, to try to anticipate arguments that the negative reasonably may make, in order to select significance claims that will outweigh those disadvantages at the end of the debate. In case the audience envisions additional risk not developed in the disadvantages, the margin of advantage over disadvantage should not be trivial.

Inherency

Having established that there is a problem significant enough to warrant attention, the affirmative is now prepared to confront the question of *inherency*. This proof requirement is complex and often misunderstood, and so it deserves our careful attention.

The Basic Question

Inherency is a causal relationship between the absence of the resolution and the continuation of the problem cited. It asks why the problem will continue as long as we fail to affirm the resolution, or—to state the same thing in other words

— why affirming the resolution is a necessary condition for the solution of the problem. More specifically, the affirmative will satisfy the inherency requirement by answering the question, without the action stated in the resolution, why will the problem continue? If the resolution calls, say, for handgun control, the inherency question will ask, without handgun control, why will accidental deaths continue?

What Inherency Is Not

It is important at the outset to recognize what the inherency question does not ask. First, it does not ask what brought the problem into existence in the first place. Discovering the original cause of a problem is often impossible and may be irrelevant to the current discussion. For a resolution calling for free trade, for example, the affirmative that seeks the original cause of protectionist sentiment will need to go back to the arguments, concerning the relative importance of industry and agriculture, between Alexander Hamilton and Thomas Jefferson during the 1790s. Few will maintain that those disputes are pertinent to contemporary American trade policy. Rather than inquiring about the original cause of a problem, then, we are asking why we permit a problem to continue.

Second, the inherency question does not ask why the affirmative's plan has yet to be adopted. This comment, which often is misunderstood even by experienced debaters, warrants an explanation. If the resolution calls for a program of guaranteed jobs in order to combat unemployment, the responsibility of the affirmative is not to explain why we have not yet adopted a guaranteed-job program. Attempting such a task would lead only to a circular argument — we do not have a program because we have never adopted one. Moreover, attempting such a task would shift the focus of discussion away from the merits of the resolution and toward the less important question of whether the resolution will actually be adopted. It would lead to the absurd result of arguing that a proposal ought to be passed precisely on the grounds that it will not! It is to avoid such problems that resolutions contain the term *should*. Instead, the inherency question asks us to consider why we cannot solve the problems of unemployment *without* adopting a program of guaranteed jobs. The issue, in short, is not why we have not yet affirmed the resolution. Rather, the issue focuses on the question of why we must affirm the resolution in order to be able to solve the problem.

Why Inherency Is Necessary

To answer the inherency question, then, is to resolve a paradox — people's toleration of a condition acknowledged to be a problem. Before we examine how to satisfy the requirement of inherency, it is important to consider why the requirement is imposed on the affirmative in the first place.

Suppose that we proved only that there was a significant problem — for example, thousands of people dying needlessly. This fact is susceptible to many different interpretations:

1. It might mean that people are unaware of the problem but that if they knew about it, they could solve it without the risks implicit in the affirmation of the resolution.

2. Or it might mean that people only recently have become aware of the problem and have taken steps to deal with it but that the results are not yet apparent because of their recency.

3. Or it might mean that people are aware of the problem but have determined that any possible solution would introduce even worse problems.

4. It might mean that people have determined that there is simply no way in which the problem can be solved.

5. Finally, it might mean that there is some force that is blocking solution of the problem, but that can be overcome if the resolution were affirmed.

Now, to say that the affirmative is not required to establish inherency is to say that the fifth interpretation is the correct one. But in advance of analysis, there is no more reason to assume that this one is the correct interpretation than there is to assume the truth of any of the alternatives. To grant this last interpretation such a privileged status would be to assume that alternatives to the resolution could not be effective, merely on the basis that a problem exists. And it would be to assume that the affirmative could solve the problem simply because it supports a proposal. Comparing the resolution as a theoretical ideal with alternatives to the resolution as they actually exist is a flawed comparison that is biased in favor of the affirmative. Proceeding in such a biased fashion is effectively to shift presumption to the affirmative and the burden of the resolution to the negative as soon as the affirmative has shown that a problem exists. Such a shift would ignore the reasons set forth in Chapter 2 for placing presumption against the resolution.

To avoid this situation and to make sure that the resolution is tested rigorously, the affirmative is obliged to answer the inherency question. By doing so, the affirmative presents reasons to believe that the problem is not just one of misperception, that it is not already on the way to solution, and yet that it is not insoluble. These reasons explain why the problem is unlikely to be solved as long as we refrain from affirming the resolution.

How to Prove Inherency

How, then, does the affirmative establish inherency? Two basic steps are involved: identification of the essential elements of negative land (as we described that territory in Chapter 8) and a causal link between these essential elements and the problem discussed.

Identifying the Essential Elements of Negative Land.   As we know, the world never remains static; evolution and change are the order of the day. Nevertheless, certain elements of negative land remain relatively constant throughout this evolution, and these elements represent negative land's *essence,* or *core.* In Chapter 8 we explained that negative land includes both *n* and *x* arguments. The core consists exclusively of the *n* arguments. Figure 9.1 makes clear which elements of negative land are its core features and which are peripheral.

It is usually easy to get a general idea of what these core elements are simply from the wording of the resolution. If the resolution calls for self-sufficiency in energy, for example, then a core element of negative land will be dependence on foreign nations for energy. Similarly, if the resolution calls for a system of national health insurance, then the absence of such a system will characterize the essence of negative land. It must be remembered that it is the wording of the resolution, not the state of things at any particular time, that determines the boundary between affirmative land and negative land.

The first step in the analysis of inherency, then, is to locate and identify the core of negative land. Sometimes it may consist of laws; sometimes, administrative arrangements; sometimes, economic or philosophical principles; and sometimes, all these things. But they all presumably exist for some reason, because they fulfill some function. If so, then even more central to negative land than any of these entities are the people who are impelled by motives. The first step in analyzing inherency therefore is to identify the core motives that buttress and defend negative land.

This identification will be difficult, because motives cannot be observed but must be inferred from statements and behavior. At times, these approaches may be satisfactory. The Employment Act of 1946, for example, established that the true motive of the United States is to maximize employment, growth, and purchasing power — the goals stated in the act. But, alternatively, these goals could be ritualistic or symbolic expressions that no one takes seriously — as some critics of the United States' economic policy have suggested.

Figure 9.1

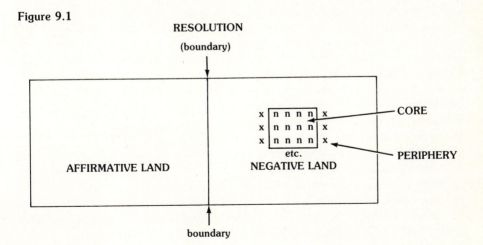

But if statements are not always reliable guides of motive, neither are actions. The American citizen who takes a lengthy foreign vacation is not necessarily showing disdain for the goal of reducing the deficit in the American balance of payments. It may be that the person simply has compartmentalized judgment, treating questions of individual benefits and questions of national interest in different "parts" of his or her mind. Neither statements of interest nor overt behavior is always a reliable guide to the core motives of negative land. Probably the best advice is to search for consistent patterns of words and deeds, extending to many different agents over a sustained period of time.

Compounding the problem is the need to distinguish among motives that characterize an individual person and motives that affect any occupant of a given role. It is one thing to say that President X will succumb to pressures from labor unions to relax wage and price guidelines, but it is quite another to say that virtually any president, regardless of previous background or commitments, will succumb to the same pressures. In the first case, the problem can be solved just by electing a different person as president. Negative land need not be abandoned; it need only be composed of different people. In the second case, it is the system itself that needs to be changed. As long as we remain in negative land, no matter who occupies the territory, the problem will continue. The affirmative wants to identify motives affecting the entire system of negative land, since only they will provide a reason that negative land itself must be abandoned.

These difficulties in identifying core motives mean that we will never be able absolutely to know what they are, that they will always be subject to argument. Indeed, much of the argument over inherency in debate involves the question of whether the alleged core is truly the core of negative land. But the impossibility of knowing core motives with absolute certainty is not a reason to avoid trying to find them. It means only that the identity of the core is always subject to dispute and that both sides in the debate must search for good reasons to support their version of the core.

Several examples illustrate the kinds of motives that can constitute the core of negative land. One core motive may be self-interest, real or perceived. For example, the motive for the oil industry's opposition to a windfall-profits tax on oil may be the belief that the tax will reduce needed investment funds. Another example of a core motive may result from role definition. Government regulators, according to this view, are likely to see problems as calling for regulation, since that is their role. Or, caught in a conflict between researching and promoting alternate energy sources, government agencies may incline toward promotion because that is their primary role. A third example of core motives is conflict in value hierarchies. The values that warrant action to remedy the problems are less important to decision makers than are competing values that perpetuate the problems. For instance, in investigating the distribution of U.S. foreign aid to other nations, the debater could decide that aid is given both for humanitarian motives and for economic interest but that economic interest predominates. If our choices of what sort of aid to offer had the effect of distorting the development priorities of other nations, this distortion could be explained by the predominance of economic over humanitarian motives.

These three examples certainly do not exhaust the possible types of core motives. Rather, they illustrate the kind of answer that we are trying to find to the question of why the resolution must be affirmed in order to overcome the problem. Now we are ready to consider the second step in determining that answer.

Explaining a Causal Relationship Between the Core of Negative Land and the Problem.   Once the core of negative land—agents with motives—has been identified, it must be shown to be sufficient to perpetuate the problem. Therefore, the only way to solve the problem is to change the core elements of negative land. But since it is these core elements that distinguish the negative from the affirmative, to change the core of negative land will require affirming the resolution.

How can this causal relationship be demonstrated? First, it must be shown to be plausible. That is, some means must be available by which the agents of negative land can express their motives. The means may be an explicit mandate for them to act in a certain way—for example, the requirement that the Food and Drug Administration ban the sale of products suspected of causing cancer. The means may be found in a grant of discretion, enabling the agents to act in a certain way if they are so inclined. The Federal Reserve Board, for instance, has control over the money supply and consequently can cause the interest rate to be set as high or low as they choose. Another means that may be available stems from the impossibility of detecting abuse; it was this means that enabled the Central Intelligence Agency to engage in covert operations to undermine foreign governments. There may, of course, be other types of possible means. The point is simply that if there is no way for the core motives of negative land to be expressed, they cannot possibly cause the perpetuation of a problem.

But having established that a causal relationship between the core and the problem is plausible, the affirmative debater must go on to show why such a relationship is probable. Here the search is for reasons to believe that the particular combination of agents, motives, and means does explain the continued existence of a problem. For example, the affirmative may argue that only the political influence of the Organization of Petroleum Exporting Countries can explain why oil prices remain high regardless of market forces. The reasons establish that as long as we keep negative land basically as it is, we will be stuck with the problem. Since the core of negative land is defined by its contrast with the resolution, the only way it can be changed and the problem solved is by affirming the resolution.

Perhaps we should consider why the causal link must be drawn to the core of negative land rather than to its peripheral features. The reason is simple. The peripheral features do lie in negative land, but only accidentally so; they do not define its fundamental nature. They illustrate what we referred to in the last chapter as *x* features. They happen to be in negative land, but they do not need to be. They can just as easily be in affirmative land or outside the universe of potential arguments being considered. Since these peripheral features do not define the essential nature of negative land, they can be altered without making negative land basically different from what it now is. They are not reasons to affirm or to reject the resolution. Therefore, if a problem is shown to be caused by the peripheral elements, we will have a reason to change those particular elements, but not to change the core of negative land and hence not to affirm the resolution.

Typically the peripheral elements are (1) specific administrative structures, such as whether an agency is equipped to deal with a problem without backlog; (2) sources of revenue, such as whether an income tax or a sales tax is most often used; (3) decisions about how to implement a settled policy, such as what specific regulations to issue in order to implement an act of Congress; and (4) matters of similarly peripheral scope.

We may summarize the discussion so far by remembering that inherency is an attempt to answer the question of why affirming the resolution is necessary to solve a problem. Deriving the answer is a two-step process. First, negative land — the universe of alternatives to the resolution — is analyzed to determine its core features, which ultimately will be people with motives to act. Second, a causal relationship is established between this core and the continuation of a recognized problem. Not only must such a relationship be plausible, but there also must be reasons to believe that the core of negative land actually is a sufficient condition for the survival of the problem.

Inherency in the Debate

The two steps in the analysis of inherency should suggest the questions to be considered in appraising an inherency claim in the debate.

Is the Alleged Core Truly the Core of Negative Land?   If it turns out to be only a peripheral feature instead, then the problems can be solved without affirming the resolution. So we should consider whether the agents named are really the primary decision makers. Do they have the power to make choices affecting the persistence or solution of the problem? Likewise, we should consider whether the motives are only as claimed or whether there are also countermotives that can lead the agents of negative land to solve the problem. We should also consider whether the agents are even able to perpetuate the problem and whether other agents, also in negative land, can control it. The answers to questions such as these should indicate whether there is some aspect of negative land that is more fundamental than what the affirmative has identified.

Is the Causal Relationship Posited by the Affirmative Valid?   Since the affirmative has claimed that the core of negative land is a sufficient condition for sustaining the problem, the tests of sufficient condition should be used. Are there examples in which the problem has been solved without altering the core? Is it reasonable to expect that there may be such examples? If so, then again the problem could be solved without affirming the resolution.

Although the analytical process of deriving and testing inherency may seem complex, the concept itself is quite simple. Basically, what is sought is a reason to believe that the affirmation of the resolution is necessary in order to solve the problem.

Efficacy of the Solution

A related responsibility of the affirmative is to demonstrate that affirming the resolution will permit us to solve the problem. It is not enough to know that we cannot solve the problem without affirming the resolution; the question here is whether we can do so by affirming the resolution. If an originally insoluble problem remains insoluble, then we are no better off by affirming the resolution than we were before. Therefore, the resolution must be shown to be efficacious. Acting on it must produce the results on which solving the problem depends.

Like the issue of inherency, the question of efficacy requires causal arguments. Whereas inherency dealt with the antecedents of the resolution, efficacy deals with its consequences. The debater must identify the agents of the resolution and show that they do not have the same motives and means that prevent the problem from being solved in negative land. At least one of the three elements — agents, motives, and means — must somehow have been changed.

Changing the Core

The core can be changed by changing the agents responsible for dealing with the problem. Shifts in jurisdiction from the private to the public sector, from the states to the federal government, or from the State Department to the Defense Department, illustrate this change. Of course, it cannot be assumed that the new agents, once put in charge of the problem, will not have the same motives that now characterize negative land. It will do little good, for example, to maintain that the federal government should assume responsibility for a problem that the states have ignored, if the federal government is equally disposed to ignore the problem. Even stipulating that the new agents be "imbued with the affirmative philosophy" may not be a sufficient protection, especially if role definition, self-interest, or some other motive comes to outweigh philosophical commitment. Instead, the affirmative must prove that the new agents will not be tainted by the harmful motives that currently characterize negative land.

The complex of agent, motive, and means also can be changed by revising the motive structure. One way to do this is through incentives that create counter-motives. For example, people have been conditioned to waste energy, as a result of the traditional abundance of cheap energy. Raising the prices of electricity and gasoline, however, could create incentives for energy conservation — the desire to save money would form a countermotive. Or, if the problem is one of conflict in roles, it may be possible to rearrange institutions in order to separate the roles that are in conflict. Dividing one agency that has both advocacy and regulatory responsibilities into two agencies, each with only one of the roles, is an example of this approach, which was used in the split of the old Atomic Energy Commission into two different agencies.

Besides changing the agents or the motives, affirming the resolution may change the means currently available to the agents of negative land. If, for example, the means for domestic spying is at the broad discretion of the Central Intelligence Agency, then discretion could be replaced with specific legislative or administrative mandates. Or, if a specific mandate leads the agents to perpetuate the problem, that mandate could be revised or withdrawn.

Whether it is the agent, the motive, or the means that is changed, the question to examine is whether affirming the resolution will produce a situation substantially different from the core of negative land. If the core is not fundamentally changed, then affirming the resolution will not solve the problem.

Proving That the Change Makes a Difference

It is not enough to show that the core is changed. The affirmative must also demonstrate that the new combination of agent, motives, and means will resolve the problem. What is required here is a step similar to one we encountered in analyzing inherency. There, we wished to determine that the core of negative land was sufficient to sustain the problem. Now, we want to be sure that affirming the resolution will be sufficient to solve the problem.

Efficacy in the Debate

Mirroring the inherency issue, the causal analysis of the question of efficacy suggests the two focal points that are likely to be at issue in a debate. First, has the original complex of agent, motive, and means really been altered? A challenger might try to establish that the current agents still have adequate motives and means to circumvent the solution. Or it could be argued that the new agents, far from being disposed to solve the problem, actually have the motives and means that will enable them to block effective action.

The second question is whether the alteration of agent, motive, or means really will solve the problem. In order to examine the sufficient condition alleged by the affirmative, one should consider whether there are reasons to believe that the problem would persist despite the change. For example, the scope of action stated in the resolution may simply be inadequate for the magnitude of the problem. Or the resolution may omit some necessary element of jurisdiction or power. Or perhaps there are additional agents, motives, or means not addressed by the proposed action that will remain powerful enough to perpetuate the problem, despite the best efforts of the intended solution. If any of these challenges proves to be correct, it will establish that — even though the affirmative called for fundamentally changing the core of negative land — the change will not accomplish its intended goals and consequently will not effectively resolve the problem.

Avoidance of Greater Disadvantages

It is possible to imagine a situation in which a change in the core of negative land indeed solves the problem to which it is addressed, but only at the price of introducing problems more serious than the one originally considered. No sensible person will affirm a resolution if doing so will leave him or her worse off than before. To avoid such a situation, the affirmative is required to prove that affirming the resolution avoids greater disadvantages.

It is important to stress that this requirement involves an on-balance judgment. No resolution will be completely free of defects, and it would be foolish to reject a resolution simply because it is not perfect. Rather, the affirmative's responsibility is to show that the disadvantages of the resolution are outweighed enough by its advantages to make affirming the resolution worthwhile. Fulfilling this responsibility completes the weighing of benefits and costs to which we alluded when discussing significance.

It is not always recognized that this burden rests with the affirmative, since it is the negative who initially presents and proves the disadvantages. The affirmative is not expected to anticipate every possible disadvantage to the resolution and refute it in advance. But once the initial proof of the disadvantages has been presented, it is the affirmative's duty to show that the evils are outweighed by the benefits of the resolution. For strategic reasons, the negative also will attempt to make on-balance judgments, but the ultimate responsibility belongs to the affirmative.

In meeting this requirement, the affirmative typically will try to minimize the scope of the disadvantages, showing that they have less significance than the negative claims they do. Then the affirmative will argue that this reduced significance is exceeded by the significance of the advantages.

Sometimes the affirmative will be able not only to minimize the disadvantages but also to eliminate them, showing that they have no force against the resolution. Such a situation exists when the disadvantage is not applicable to the resolution or when crucial causal links are not supplied.

Sometimes the affirmative may be even luckier. It may be able to argue that the alleged disadvantages not only are not reasons to reject the resolution but also are additional arguments in its favor. Disadvantages may be "turned around" in either of two ways. The affirmative can grant that the disadvantage really is an evil but argue that the same evil will be present to greater degree if the resolution is not affirmed — hence providing an on-balance argument in favor of the resolution. Or the affirmative can argue that the alleged evil really is a benefit and hence an additional reason to support the resolution. Being able to demonstrate that a disadvantage is turned around into an additional benefit of the resolution is the most desirable way to demonstrate that the resolution is relatively free of disadvantage. The nature of the turn around will be considered at length in Chapter 16.

But the affirmative need not wait for the presentation of the disadvantages in order to begin thinking about how to meet this proof requirement. In constructing its case, the affirmative should think about disadvantages that are likely to be argued and preempt them where possible. Sometimes disadvantages can be preempted by affirmative constructive arguments, and sometimes they can be avoided through the formulation of the affirmative plan. The affirmative also should try to determine, before the actual debate, what the most effective responses to disadvantages will be once they are introduced by the negative.

Summary

In this chapter we examined the stock issues of a policy resolution, which represent the proof requirements imposed on the affirmative. First, the affirmative must demonstrate the existence of a significant problem, a situation that violates, to a widespread degree, an important value. Then, it must show that the problem is inherent, that it will continue unless the resolution is affirmed. In other words, affirming the resolution must be shown to be a necessary condition for solving the problem. Third, the affirmative must establish that the resolution is efficacious, that the action envisioned by the resolution will be sufficient to solve the problem. Finally, the resolution should be shown to avoid, on balance, greater disadvantages; the evils should be outweighed by the benefits of the resolution.

In constructing its case, the affirmative should be certain that these four proof requirements are satisfied. In addition to these requirements that derive from the resolution, there also are considerations that derive from the specific affirmative plan. We shall explore those considerations next.

Questions for Discussion

1. Why should the affirmative lose the debate if it fails to establish all four of the stock issues discussed in this chapter?
2. How can one establish that an affirmative that proposes to remove billboards from all highways is addressing a significant problem?
3. In response to an affirmative, the negative argues, "You must prove that the present system will not adopt the resolution." Is this a correct interpretation of inherency? Why or why not?
4. Under what circumstances is each of the possible changes — agent, motive, and means — most likely to ensure the efficacy of the solution?
5. In what ways can the affirmative prove that the disadvantages are outweighed by the benefits of the resolution?

Chapter 10

Affirmative
Case Construction:
The Plan

In the last chapter, we reviewed the basic proof requirements of the affirmative. If the affirmative is able to sustain its position on each of these stock issues in the face of negative refutation, then the affirmative should win the debate. We did not include among the proof requirements that the affirmative must present a specific plan of action, outlining what it will do to implement the resolution. This omission reflects our belief that the resolution, not a specific plan, should be the focus of attention. The objective of the debate, after all, is to determine whether or not the resolution is probably true. The outcome of the debate involves belief and stops short of action; the details of possible action that the resolution might suggest are not the central focus. Consequently, there is nothing in the logic of debate theory that requires the affirmative to present a specific plan.

Nevertheless, the presentation of a plan is almost always to the affirmative's advantage. Few, indeed, are the debates on resolutions of policy that do not have an affirmative plan. Consequently, it is important to understand the theory and mechanics of plan construction — the objectives of this chapter. We shall begin by discussing the functions served by the presentation of a plan, proceed to a review of the structural features of plans, and conclude by considering problems in plan argumentation. We include a sample plan on page 151, but you may wish to examine it now to have a sense of what a plan is like before we proceed further.

Functions of the Plan

Two of the stock issues relate to the efficacy of the resolution and its freedom from disadvantages. If the resolution is relatively specific, it may be possible to discuss these issues without a specific plan. For example, for the resolution that the airline industry should be deregulated, it may be possible to examine the efficacy of deregulation in the abstract and to consider its costs and benefits without having a specific timetable or set of administrative procedures. Similarly, the resolution that the president of the United States should be elected by direct popular vote is straightforward enough that the nature of action to be taken is clear without a more specific plan. But resolutions are seldom this specific. As we noted, they are deliberately general in order to withstand a year's debating.

This generality, however, makes it difficult to address the issues of efficacy and disadvantages merely from the statement of the resolution itself. Not long ago, high school students debated the resolution that the United States should significantly change its foreign trade policies. This resolution permitted a host of possible changes, some of which were clearly incompatible with others. Moves toward free trade and moves to increase protectionism fit equally well in the scope of the resolution. Under the circumstances, it was nearly impossible to know in the abstract whether change would be efficacious or desirable, because there were few circumstances in which the affirmative could claim that the current situation was so bad that any change would be an improvement. Rather, the questions of efficacy and advantage turned on what specific change the affirmative had in mind.

What Plans Do

The preceding discussion should suggest the first and most significant of three functions of the affirmative plan: to narrow the scope of a general resolution in order to permit meaningful discussion. Without such narrowing, it is difficult for the affirmative and the negative debaters to focus on the same aspects of the resolution. The result is a lack of argumentative clash and a failure to subject arguments to a rigorous test. Rigor is lacking because the debaters present separate and unrelated arguments, without coming to grips with their opponents' ideas. The affirmative that chooses to present a plan is saying, in effect, that it wishes for the truth of the resolution to be determined by considering a specific example of action that might be taken pursuant to it. In this sense, it provides an operational definition of the resolution, explaining what the resolution means by indicating some of the specific actions that could be taken once it has been affirmed. The operational definition is narrower in scope than the resolution itself is.

The notion of an operational definition is sometimes misunderstood, however. In presenting a plan, the affirmative is not maintaining that the plan and the resolution are one and the same; neither is it implying that because one interpretation of the resolution is desirable, all are. Nor does the affirmative yield to the negative the privilege of advocating anything it wishes, other than the specific plan, without the fear of being topical. The reason is that there always are many other operational definitions of the resolution, even though the affirmative does not choose to use them in the particular debate. When a plan is presented, the affirmative asks for the probable truth of the resolution to be determined on the basis of a more precise specification of what it could mean. For instance, the merit of significantly changing foreign trade policies could be determined on the assumption that the change being referred to is the extension of trade preferences to the less-developed nations, the subsidization of American exports, or a freeze on the imports of crude oil. The first function of the plan, then, is to narrow the scope of a very general resolution.

Closely related is the second major function: to illustrate the central principles of the resolution. Sometimes it may be inconvenient to examine the basic ideas behind a resolution without having some specific form in which to embody them. For example, it may be easier to evaluate the merit of a governmental guarantee of jobs for all citizens by examining how that guarantee might be implemented, rather than as an abstract proposition. Terms such as *guarantee, protect, regulate,* or *control* may be overly vague and not specify the form that the guarantee, protection, regulation, or control could take. For example, regulation could mean standard setting, day-by-day administration, or periodic review. Since such abstract verbs appear frequently in the wording of debate resolutions, it is not surprising that affirmative plans frequently are presented in order to illustrate what is meant. Productive discussion is more likely if abstract concepts have been clarified, and the presentation of a plan serves this purpose by illustration.

A third purpose of the affirmative plan is to demonstrate the affirmative's skills at craftsmanship. According to this view, developing the plan is a strategic act that enables the affirmative to place the resolution in its most favorable context by proposing the plan most likely to achieve the desired advantages. This privilege serves to equalize the affirmative's burden of proving the resolution to be probably true. According to this theory, the affirmative is allowed to devise a plan that puts the resolution as much in its favor as possible but then will be held rigorously to whatever plan it devises.

Plans Do Not Implement the Resolution

Other functions sometimes claimed for the affirmative plan include providing an analogy to a piece of legislation. Underlying these notions of the plan is the basic assumption that the plan exists to implement the resolution—that it represents the specific action that will be taken if the affirmative team is victorious in the debate. But we find this assumption to be mistaken. Rare, indeed, is the plan that can be specific enough to resemble a piece of legislation — which for major subjects of public importance is likely to be several hundred pages in length. More fundamentally, it seems unrealistic to assume that the outcome of a debate is the taking of some action.

In academic debate, of course, the decision makers lack the power to act. But even when real-world decision makers choose to hold a debate, its outcome is always one step removed from actually taking action. For example, during the Cuban missile crisis of 1962, President John F. Kennedy's advisers engaged in intense debate over the relative merits of a blockade and an air strike in response to the installment of Soviet missiles in Cuba. The outcome of the debate favored the blockade. But the president's decision that a blockade was the best option was not the same thing as the specific instructions he issued to put the blockade into effect. The initial decision — a matter of belief — was the result of the debate, whereas the orders — a matter of action — went beyond the process of debate.

If debaters decide that the plan really does implement action, their decision will have important consequences for the actual structure of the plan. It will be necessary to include many details, such as financing, administrative structure, and enforcement, to be sure that the powers granted in the plan are sufficient for its implementation. The omission of these details would be as serious to the affirmative as would be a badly written piece of legislation to the member of Congress who proposed it. Many of the typical provisions of affirmative plans reflect this assumption that the plan is a set of actions that will definitely be taken if the resolution is affirmed.

Even though plans do not implement action, however, the inclusion of some of the details may be equally important. By specifying such matters as how a proposal can be financed and endorsed, the affirmative may be able to remove finance and enforcement from dispute and thereby focus the debate on the central question of whether affirming the resolution is the best response to a problem. The affirmative may be able to prevent bickering over peripheral questions by specifying these matters in the hope that they will be waived from further argument.

Structural Elements of the Plan

Whether or not one believes that the function of the plan is to implement action, it may be useful to design the plan carefully.

The Agents

The first feature of most affirmative plans is identifying the agents who will administer the plan. Failure to specify an agent indicates that the affirmative is indifferent to the choice and hence is prepared to leave the selection of agents to the ordinary executive and legislative processes. Whether it is necessary to specify the agent depends on the affirmative's inherency arguments. If the problem persists because of the motives of a particular agency, for example, it is important to be sure that the same agency is not left in charge of the affirmative plan. Similarly, if the affirmative has found something intrinsic in the state level of government as the source of the inherency position, it should be sure that the operation of the plan is shifted away from the state level. Otherwise, it will be very easy for the negative to draw on the affirmative's own arguments and to establish that the effectiveness of the plan will be thwarted.

In recent years, it has become common for affirmative teams to locate the source of their inherency not in any one particular agent but in the political process as a whole. For example, in urging a long-term program of research and development of alternate energy sources, affirmatives often claim that the entire American political process is oriented to short-term crises and is systematically unprepared to deal with long-term needs. Likewise, affirmatives arguing for the creation of a consumer protection agency frequently charge that Congress, beholden to corporate contributors, favors industry rather than the consumer and will intervene to prevent any executive agency from doing otherwise. In such situations, overcoming the source of inherency may require the affirmative to specify an agent outside the normal boundaries of the political system. The usual means of accomplishing this goal is for the affirmative to create an independent agency with guaranteed funding, isolated from political considerations, with members appointed initially by the affirmative team itself, and with appointees naming their own successors. This combination of features is often summed up as "an affirmatively appointed, munificently salaried, independent, self-perpetuating board."

At first glance, it may seem that naming this sort of agent would overcome virtually any problems of motive that the affirmative might cite in its discussion of inherency. But this approach may introduce two problems of its own. First, if the members of a board serve as long as they wish, they may remain so long that their judgment and effectiveness become impaired. On the other hand, if the plan provides for a mandatory retirement age lower than what the law now requires, it will be open to the charge of age discrimination. Second, board members will be accountable to no one and therefore may be very dangerous. And, given a broad mandate, they can enjoy virtually unlimited power without the checks and balances that characterize American democracy. Each of these problems may give rise to negative plan objections based on the structure rather than on the substance of the affirmative plan. To reduce the risk of such "structural" plan objections, affirmatives that create an independent agency typically limit its discretion. Among the means to assert control over an independent, self-perpetuating board are (1) the specification of a fixed term of office, (2) very narrowly drawn mandates to limit the exercise of discretion, (3) a court review of the plan's provisions, and (4) an automatic termination or reconsideration date for the plan as a whole.

Some critics of debate have charged that the very idea of a self-perpetuating board, imbued with the affirmative's philosophical commitments and immune from the political process, is so unrealistic as to defeat the purposes of constructing a plan in the first place. To be sure, very few programs are, in fact, entrusted to agencies of this type, and legislators who attempt to create such an agency would find their actions subject to legal and constitutional tests.

But two replies may be made to this criticism by those who would defend the creation of independent authorities for the plan. First, such authorities combine several elements that are found in the actual political system. For example, some regulatory agencies are deliberately biased in favor of a certain philosophical position. Corporate boards of directors may be self-perpetuating. Judges generally serve an indefinite term of office and are thought to be insulated from politics. And in times of war or national emergency, blue-ribbon boards may be created with the authority to bypass or supersede conflicting statutory requirements.

Second, defenders of the self-perpetuating board could reply that the critics misunderstand the true function of the affirmative plan. Rather than being modeled on a piece of legislation that Congress may actually pass, the plan serves only to outline the kind of structure that would be appropriate in light of the affirmative case. The purpose is to improve the quality of the discussion of the resolution's merits, not to implement a specific measure. (Of course, one could not make this reply unless one rejected the analogy between the plan and a piece of legislation.)

However the affirmative chooses to identify the agents of its plan, it always is worth checking the fit between the affirmative's inherency and its plan. Does the affirmative rely on the same agents that the inherency analysis has indicted? If the agents are different, can one be sure that the agents of the plan are not tainted by the same motives described in the inherency arguments? These two questions should be kept in mind, not only while examining affirmative plans during the course of the debate, but also during the initial activity of constructing the plan.

Mandates

Having identified who will be administering the plan, the affirmative needs next to specify what the agents will do. This step indicates the powers, or mandates, of the plan. Generally, there are two basic approaches to this task. One is the formulation of specific mandates; the other, general guidelines along with criteria for the exercise of discretion.

Specific Mandates.   The affirmative that outlines specific mandates signifies that it not only understands what is to be accomplished but also wants to reach the goal by a particular method. For example, a board is directed to institute public employment programs in the inner-city neighborhoods of the fifty largest metropolitan areas. Such a mandate suggests not only that the affirmative wants to reduce ghetto unemployment but that it wants to do it in a specific way. It is likely that the affirmative problem cannot be solved, or the advantages cannot be gained, unless this method is used. Or the affirmative may not fully trust the judgment of the agents or may believe that the agents will be subject to adverse pressures and temptations if the mandate is not stated specifically.

The more precise the mandate is, the less room there is for errors of judgment or for intentional circumvention of the plan. By the same token, however, the plan is less adaptable to changing circumstances. A plan that mandates public employment, for example, must be put into effect, regardless of whether or not the economy remains conducive to it.

General Guidelines.   The other approach is to specify a goal to be achieved but to give the plan's agents considerable latitude in choosing how to go about it. For instance, rather than stipulate a public employment program, the affirmative could direct its board to achieve a national unemployment rate of 4 percent within the next three years. The board could use tax cuts, public employment, subsidies to private enterprise, incentives for increased training and job mobility, or any combination of these and any other measures that it devised.

The team that constructs its plan in this way signifies that it is less important to name the specific means to be used than it is to select good people and empower them to deal with the problem as they think best. Limiting the mandate to a general guideline also recognizes that external conditions affecting the plan will change and that not all possible changes can be foreseen. Therefore, it is thought prudent to trust experts in a given field to cope with inevitable changes over the life of the plan. On the other hand, a general mandate leaves in the hands of the agents greater discretion and, with it, greater risks of abuse of the mandate's intent.

Especially if the mandate of the plan is general, the affirmative should indicate criteria for the agents to use in selecting among alternative possibilities. Including such criteria usually will increase the affirmative's confidence that its advantages will be gained or its problems solved. In the case of the 4 percent unemployment target, the affirmative could indicate that its goal is to be met with maximum reliance on the private sector, by the quickest possible method, or with the least adverse impact on the international position of the dollar. Criteria such as these offer guidance to the plan's agents and enhance the probability that the agents will actually achieve the desired advantages.

One popular criterion in affirmative plans is *cost-benefit analysis*. This term refers to a mathematical procedure by which the merits and the drawbacks of proposed courses of action are measured, and then that action is selected that has the most favorable ratio of benefits to costs.

As used in debate, however, cost-benefit analysis often is a term that sounds precise but really offers little in the way of guidance. Before cost-benefit ratios can be calculated, someone must decide which effects count as costs, which count as benefits, and which weights to give to the various effects. Unless the affirmative is able to specify them, the words cost-benefit analysis hardly limit the discretion of its agents. Moreover, some values — such as aesthetics or the importance of leisure and recreation—may be virtually impossible to state in mathematical terms. The affirmative that proposes to apply cost-benefit analysis to such outcomes may be calling for the impossible. Rather than specifying criteria, it is using a phrase that sounds specific but really specifies little.

Limiting the Scope of the Mandate.   Whether the affirmative chooses a specific or a general mandate, it is important to be sure that the scope of the mandate does not go beyond the affirmative's intended area of concern. For example, an affirmative case is concerned with the dangers of pollution generated by fossil-fuel plants and wants to meet future increases in the demand for energy with nuclear power. A well-constructed plan could mandate a moratorium on the future construction of fossil fuel plants and their replacement with nuclear power. But a carelessly drawn plan could mandate only an end to fossil fuel plants. Although the affirmative no doubt intends otherwise, the plan would require the shutdown of most of the current sources of energy without considering the possibility of immediate replacement — an action that may invite a few plan objections from the negative!

To cite another example, many critics believe that Congress erred in mandating the Food and Drug Administration (FDA) to ban the use of any product that could cause cancer. Since almost anything could cause cancer in someone under certain conditions, the critics said, the FDA mandate ignored dimensions of reasonableness and possible offsetting benefits and led to the needless exclusion of products from the market. The scope of the plan mandate needs to be considered carefully, lest the affirmative render itself vulnerable to technical, but nevertheless serious, objections. These objections are important to people who see the plan as analogous to a piece of legislation, since they show that the bill was badly drafted.

The affirmative also should consider a time frame for the plan mandates. The time frame could indicate a period of years over which the plan will be phased in, in order to avoid, in the short run, excessive disruption of the adjustment costs. It could specify a target date for the achievement of the mandate so that the affirmative will be able to claim that its problem will be solved or its advantages gained within a definite period of time. Or it could identify a date for review and reconsideration of the whole plan in the face of changing circumstances. Failure to specify any time frame signifies that the affirmative is willing to see its plan fully implemented at once and to remain in force in perpetuity.

Aids to Effectiveness

The heart of the plan is the delegation of agents and the specification of their mandates. Often, however, the affirmative will wish to include in the plan various aids that will make the plan more effective, such as specific funding and enforcement planks. Omission of these planks does not mean that the plan is without funding or enforcement; common sense suggests that to pass a law is usually to imply that the law should be enforced or that to adopt a new program is to imply that necessary funds should be provided. Rather, omitting these details from the plan means merely that the affirmative is indifferent to the specific mechanisms to be used and presumes that these decisions will be made in the normal way by the political system. It is when the affirmative wishes to control these decisions, rather than leaving them up to the normal political process, that aids to effectiveness are mentioned in the plan. We shall briefly describe five of the common aids.

Funding.   The affirmative may wish to specify the funding mechanism. It would choose to do so if (1) it wished to avoid the consequences of drawing on general revenues and increasing the federal budget deficit, or if (2) congressional budgetary norms otherwise would work to undercut the plan's effectiveness. In response to the first concern, the affirmative could propose specific tax increases, call for closing specified tax loopholes, or earmark funds to be saved as a result of the plan. In response to the second concern, the affirmative could establish a trust fund (modeled after the highway trust fund or the social security trust fund) to be sure that the revenues intended for the plan could not be diverted to other uses by a budget-conscious Congress. Of course, the affirmative wishing to specify a funding mechanism risks plan objections to its particular provisions. There may be objections to a tax increase, to closing a loophole, or to an off-budget trust fund.

Enforcement Machinery.   The affirmative may wish to stipulate enforcement machinery for the plan. Such a stipulation would be particularly important if the affirmative inherency arguments indicted existing enforcement agencies. For example, if the inherency argument is that the Federal Bureau of Investigation (FBI) avoids taking on difficult cases in order to keep its record of success unblemished, it probably would be unwise to rely on the FBI to enforce the plan. Likewise, if the Antitrust Division of the Justice Department is claimed to be beholden to corporate lobbyists, then the affirmative would want to stipulate some other enforcement procedure. In the aftermath of Watergate and the discovery that the executive branch of the government concealed damaging information, many affirmative plans have provided for the appointment of special prosecutors. Or, in the wake of studies suggesting that heavy penalties may be counterproductive, some affirmative plans have stipulated that certain offenses will be treated as civil rather than criminal matters or as misdemeanors rather than felonies. As with the stipulation of funding, however, specifying enforcement machinery runs a risk for the affirmative. In its concern to find a way to overcome its inherency and to have an efficacious plan, the affirmative may invite plan objections that it disregards due process, violates civil liberties, or otherwise impairs legal and constitutional protections.

Research and Development.   The affirmative plan can provide for ongoing research and development. The absence of such a provision, of course, does not mean that no research will be done, but its presence ensures continued research simultaneously with action. Research and developmment planks will be particularly useful to the affirmative if the case pertains to a subject about which there is insufficient information but on which action is nevertheless imperative. The danger that fluorocarbons will deplete the ozone layer is an example of such a subject. The risk of acting hastily or making unwise choices is lessened by the plan's provision for research and development, the results of which could modify the specific steps taken as time passes.

Calling for more study of problems seems innocuous, and increasing numbers of affirmative plans contain a research plank. There are dangers in such a plank, however, particularly if the same agency is given responsibilities for both day-to-day operations and long-term research. In such a situation, the research can be systematically distorted to serve the operational needs with the result that policy decisions are made on the basis of inferior information. But this problem can be substantially offset by relying on different agencies for research and for operations.

Education.   Plans may include provisions for public awareness and education. Especially in plans that require significant changes in individual values, attitudes, or lifestyles, it may be useful for the affirmative to include provisions for mass public information and educational campaigns. The affirmative's intent in including such a provision is probably to increase the likelihood of voluntary compliance with the plan's provisions, thus reducing the need for coercive measures that might reduce individual freedoms.

The main difficulty that the affirmative faces in such a stipulation is that the efficacy of public information campaigns is unclear. For every study suggesting that such campaigns reach their intended audience and are successful in generating the desired attitudes, there is another study suggesting that campaigns attract the attention only of those who were interested in the subject in the first place. This conflict in the literature probably means that not all the possible methods of public information campaigns are alike and, consequently, that the affirmative wishing to enhance its chances through this sort of plan plank should indicate more precisely what form of public information campaign it wishes to use—interpersonal, broadcast, or print media—and in what combinations, what specific appeals to use, what audience to identify as the target for the campaign, and so on.

Review and Oversight.   The affirmative may wish to specify procedures for the review and oversight of the plan's operations. This goal is often accomplished through plan provisions calling for court review. Although it is reasonable to assume that court review will take place even without any specification, the affirmative that stipulates a review procedure signifies that no agent of the plan—not even the new authorities that have been created—supersedes the notions of justice and individual protection embodied in the judicial system. It must be realized, though, that court review serves as a limited check on the actions of administrative agencies. Courts review only to ensure that the agency is acting within the scope of its authority, that its actions are constitutional, and that its decisions are not arbitrary or capricious.

A related specification often found in plans is the stipulation that courts, in conducting their review, will defer to the legislative history of the plan as embodied in the affirmative speeches. *Legislative history* is a guideline for resolving otherwise insoluble problems regarding the plan's meaning and intended range of application. It reflects the belief that it is unnecessary and probably impossible to include all of these details in the plan itself. But it is often abused. Legislative history is not a cloak under which the affirmative may respond to negative objections with reference to the intent that may be in its mind but that is not argued in the debate. One should not appeal to legislative history as a way to say, "Well, that may be what we argued, but it's not what we really meant." Courts rely on legislative history only when the meaning of a law is not clear from the text itself. Likewise, arguments have a life of their own; legislative history may help resolve argumentative disputes, but it is not a way to avoid them.

These five examples do not exhaust the possible aids that can make the plan more effective. Rather, they illustrate the kinds of options that permit the plan to operate more smoothly and effectively. Each obtains an argumentative benefit for the affirmative (or else there would be no point in using it), but at the price of a possible plan objection based on the details of the specification.

A Model Plan

It may be useful to see how agents, mandates, and aids to effectiveness are incorporated within a specific plan. Here is an example of a plan for the resolution that the federal government should guarantee comprehensive medical care for all citizens of the United States:

1. The Department of Health, Education and Welfare will be instructed to carry out the following objectives: [*Agents*]

   A. All United States citizens will be guaranteed comprehensive medical care as a legal right. All medical care, except for nonreconstructive cosmetic surgery, will be provided free of charge.   [*Mandates*]

   B. Doctors wishing to practice medicine in the United States must practice solely under this plan. All doctors will be exclusively salaried, initially 10 percent above their present salaries and adjusted for inflation. Doctors will be required to work at least a specified minimum number of hours.

   C. When necessary, financial incentives to encourage the distribution of medical personnel will be provided.

2. Funding will be obtained from the best combination of: [*Aids to Effectiveness: Funding*]

   A. Independent trust funds based on the income tax.

   B. Diversion of funds from medical care programs no longer needed because of affirmative proposal.

   C. Cost controls when needed.

3. Federal support for medical research will be increased by 10 percent.   [*Aids: Research*]

4. Violators of the letter or intent of the proposal will be punished by loss of license, loss of salary, fines, and/or imprisonment.   [*Aids: Enforcement*]

5. Affirmative speeches will serve as legislative history for purposes of interpreting the plan.   [*Aids: Legislative History*]

In this example, notice that the agents, mandates, and aids to effectiveness all are combined in a coherent outline that specifies the focus that the affirmative wishes to give to the resolution.

Problems in Plan Argumentation

In constructing its plan, the affirmative should also be aware of the problems it may encounter in subsequent argumentation. Each of these problems has a controversial point of theory or practice on which debaters and their teachers do not always agree. In discussing each problem, we shall try to indicate the basis of the competing viewpoints and why we favor the position that we do. Two problems will especially concern us here: the legitimacy of plan spikes and the nature of a fiat.

Plan Spikes

Sometimes the affirmative plan will be constructed not just to operate smoothly but also to prevent disadvantages that it otherwise might invite. For example, suppose that a plan proposes to spend many billions of dollars to research and develop synthetic fuels. Fearful that the normal response to such an increase in the federal budget will be to cut military spending, the affirmative adds to its plan a provision that military spending be maintained at least on current levels. Such a plan provision is referred to as a *spike,* and its function is to *spike out,* or preclude, a disadvantage.

Plan spikes are distinguished by two features. First, they go beyond the terms and requirements of the resolution. They are compatible with the resolution, but they are not required by it. A resolution calling for energy independence, as in the example above, normally would be silent on the matter of military spending. A plan containing spikes, then, envisions doing more than the resolution requires. The second distinguishing feature of the spike is that it makes the plan immune to one or more disadvantages that otherwise might be presented. In the energy example, disadvantages to weakening our national defense could be argued against the plan, were it not for the spike that forbids cuts in military spending.

Whether plan spikes are legitimate is a controversial question. Theorists who oppose their use reason in the following way: they state that the need, or advantage, of the affirmative case is determined only at the end of the debate. The net benefit of the affirmative is obtained by subtracting the negative disadvantages from the affirmative significance. If the plan will solve a problem that results in, say, one thousand deaths per year but risks a disadvantage that will involve five hundred deaths each year, then the net advantage of the affirmative case is five hundred rather than the originally claimed one thousand deaths. The plan spike, by preventing the negative from arguing the disadvantage, artificially inflates the affirmative's net benefit, making it seem five hundred lives greater than it really is. This difference of five hundred lives is not a true advantage of the affirmative plan, since the plan must be topical (must lie in affirmative land), and yet the spike clearly goes beyond the requirements of the resolution. Consequently, it is argued, by eliminating a disadvantage, the plan spike gives the affirmative an extratopical advantage, rather than one that derives directly from the affirmative plan.

In our view, this criticism is mistaken. It must be remembered that the affirmative plan is not the central focus of our attention; we are interested in determining the probable truth of the resolution. Accordingly, what the plan spike establishes is that the disadvantage that it prevents is not intrinsic to the resolution in the first place. In other words, it is possible to take the action envisioned by the resolution without necessarily having to confront the disadvantage. In choosing to spend on energy research and development, for instance, we are not obliged to reduce the military budget. We could choose to increase taxes or to cut programs of lower priority than the military is. What the spike stipulates, in effect, is that the prospect of cuts in military spending is not a reason to oppose energy research and development, because that prospect can be avoided if we choose to do so. In this way, the plan spike permits concentration on the central issues regarding problem and solution and discourages diverting attention to side issues.

Nor can we agree with the opinion that the plan spike gains an extratopical advantage for the affirmative. To be sure, insulating the military budget from cuts (in our example) does not require that we affirm the resolution. The contents of the spike, in other words, may be located in either negative land (since the resolution is not essential to the cuts) or affirmative land (since they are not incompatible with the resolution). The spikes are what we earlier called x arguments, meaning that they can be either affirmative or negative. But the combination of the other plan features and the spike may be found only in affirmative land. So, if that combination is found to be desirable, there is a reason to affirm the resolution. In our example above, the only way that the benefits of energy research can be gained without cuts in the military budget is by supporting the total plan, including the spike. But the total plan can exist only in affirmative land, and so its benefits — rather than being extratopical — represent legitimate reasons to affirm the resolution.

Were we to decide otherwise, we would find it difficult to distinguish between plan spikes and the aids to effectiveness discussed above. In a sense, the specification of a particular finance mechanism also goes beyond the requirements of the resolution. It may be that a plan will be advantageous if funded through progressive income taxes, but far less advantageous if the funds come from a regressive sales tax or from cuts in other programs. By this reasoning, the affirmative that stipulates a means of financing, enforcement, or public education is artificially inflating its advantage in just the same way that it would be in presenting a plan including spikes. We think it is more reasonable to hold that—just as is true for spikes—the combination of the plan's other features with the specific method of enforcement or finance can be found only in affirmative land. Rather than constituting an extratopical advantage, the total plan (including the specific aids to its effectiveness) gives reason to affirm the resolution.

Having concluded that plan spikes are legitimate, we do not, however, advise that they be used automatically or unthinkingly. The spike, since it adds detail to the affirmative plan, may invite a plan objection based on its particulars that would not be presented in its absence. It is possible, for instance, that the effect of preventing defense spending from ever falling below current levels may be worse than the effects of spending on energy research and development without including the spike. The well-prepared negative team, at the same time that it develops its disadvantages against the affirmative, will search for other disadvantages that could be presented based on the spikes that the affirmative might include. Rather than placing spikes in its plan, the affirmative may try to anticipate and refute the negative disadvantages in the course of the case arguments. Or the affirmative may be able to turn around the disadvantages so that they become additional reasons for the resolution. These alternatives to the spike, as well as the possibility of including spikes, should be considered carefully by the affirmative, and the choice should be made in the initial process of affirmative case construction based on the merits of all the possible options.

The Nature of Fiat

The other major controversy regarding plan argumentation has do to with a frequently misunderstood term. Most of the plans presented in debates are not normally adopted. The reason usually is provided by the affirmative in its analysis of inherency: influential people and groups oppose the objectives of the plan and may oppose the plan's specific provisions as well. Hence, it is pointless to discuss the question of whether the plan will be adopted. Recognizing this situation, the writers of debate resolutions always use the term *should,* which focuses the debate on the question of what ought to be done, not necessarily what will be done. One way to explain this convention is to say that it is assumed that for purposes of testing the resolution, all participants in the debate stipulate that the plan is in effect. This stipulation, often referred to as fiat, makes it possible to waive from dispute the likelihood of the plan's adoption and thereby directs the discussion to the question of what ought to be done — to the merits of the resolution.

It needs to be remembered that fiat is not a real power granted to the affirmative. In debate, no plan actually is adopted by fiat; indeed, as we have explained, nothing is adopted. Rather than being a real power, fiat is merely a way of expressing the assumption, shared by all participants, that if the resolution were shown to be desirable, then a plan to implement it would be adopted by the agent named in the resolution. Abuses of the notion of fiat usually result from failing to remember that fiat is only a convention and thereby treating the power as if it were real. Even more abuse will result if debaters assume that fiat is a magical power that can be used to transcend the normal limits of politics and automatically change people's attitudes or values.

For example, suppose that the resolution being debated is "Resolved: That the federal government should increase welfare payments." The affirmative argues that at present there is no way to know that payments will go up; we can only hope so. In contrast, the affirmative promises, the affirmative can guarantee the increase. Now the basis for this guarantee is unlikely to be anything related to the federal government itself. In fact, in discussing inherency, the affirmative is likely to have proved that there is something preventing the goals of higher payments. Rather, the source of the guarantee is likely to be that the affirmative claims to be able to implement its plan by fiat.

This example illustrates a misuse of fiat. The affirmative is saying, in effect, "We should win because we are affirmative." The basis for decision is not the merits of the resolution but this mystical power possessed by one team. The affirmative assumes that the team (rather than the agent named in the resolution, the federal government) possesses fiat and that it is a real power.

Were these assumptions correct, there would be little need to debate the merits of any specific resolution. The affirmative need only identify some problem, wave a magic wand, and solve the problem by fiat. Ironically, it is in order to avoid such problems as this that the notion of fiat is introduced. It is a way to focus attention away from the questions of what actually will be done and toward consideration of the resolution's merits. In short, then, it is not legitimate for the affirmative to solve its problem or gain its advantages through the exercise of fiat rather than through the substance of the resolution.

Equally, it is a misuse of the concept for the negative to offer disadvantages grounded not in the resolution itself but in the fact that the affirmative presumably implements the resolution by fiat. For instance, imagine the following situation: against a proposal that the federal government increase welfare payments, the negative argues the disadvantage that the plan is undemocratic because it is adopted by fiat and not by legislation and, hence, that it violates basic values in our system of government. Now, there is nothing about increasing welfare payments per se that produces this disadvantage. Rather, the argument is that the affirmative has taken over the taxing and spending functions that belong to the Congress as elected representatives of the people.

But based on our analysis above, we should realize that the plan does no such thing. The affirmative debaters are not assigning to themselves the responsibility for the federal budget, nor are they saying that welfare payments will actually be increased. All they are saying is that if the resolution is found to be desirable, they assume that the agents named will act to implement it. They themselves do not adopt anything, and certainly not by fiat.

Of course, if the affirmative has abused the nature of fiat, claiming that some advantage results from it, it is only fair that the negative be permitted to ground its disadvantages in the same cause. But our point is that these affirmative and negative approaches both misconstrue the nature of fiat, treating a simple convention as if it were a real power.

Yet a third misconception of fiat rests on the assumption that it is a magical power that the affirmative uses to suspend reality for a moment in order to set its plan in place amidst a sea of hostile forces. Then, the adversaries are left with the same attitudes they had before, and presumably with the ability to terminate the affirmative plan. Accordingly, the negative argues, although the affirmative may implement its plan by fiat today, Congress will repeal it tomorrow. Again the errors are the same. It is not the affirmative who possesses fiat but, rather, the agent of the resolution. And it is not something that is actually exercised but a convention intended to focus discussion. Just as we assume that a plan to implement the resolution would be implemented if the resolution were probably true, we also assume that the plan would remain in force for the same reason.

The simplest way to avoid these three errors is to remember that the fiat power itself cannot be the basis of any arguments, whether advantages, disadvantages, workability arguments, or whatever. Fiat is not a real power but only a figure of speech that expresses an assumption shared by all debate participants. It is this assumption that permits them to focus their efforts and energies on the question of what should be done.

In closing, there are three additional comments about fiat that deserve mention. First, although the debate does not focus on what actually will be done, fiat does not excuse the debaters from limiting themselves to what could be done. It is idle to consider whether we should attempt to colonize Jupiter, for example, since (so far as we know) it cannot be done. Hence, in saying that fiat represents the assumption that the agents of the resolution would act if the resolution were found to be desirable, we assume that it is possible for them to do so.

Second, in suggesting that fiat is not a legitimate source of advantages or disadvantages, we assume that our remarks apply equally to both sides in the debate. Should one side attempt to claim an advantage or disadvantage from fiat, the other side legitimately can insist in the name of fairness that it be allowed to do the same. Fairness would be achieved at the expense of muddling the theoretical issues, however, and so we prefer to advise both teams to remember that fiat is only a convention.

Third, although we have discussed fiat in the context of the affirmative plan, the negative also may use fiat in certain circumstances. Possible uses of fiat by the negative will be considered in subsequent chapters.

Summary

Although the presentation of a plan is not strictly required by debate theory, rare will be the situation in which it is not in the affirmative's strategic interest to offer a plan. The plan serves to narrow a very general resolution to meaningful limits and to illustrate abstract terms or principles in the wording of the resolution. The plan also may be thought of as a tactical exercise in which the affirmative is helped to present its arguments in the strongest light. Other views of the affirmative plan, which we do not share, see it as analogous to a congressional resolution, congressional statute, or Constitutional amendment.

The major structural features of the plan are the identification of agents and the mandates that they are to achieve. The affirmative may utilize existing agents or create new ones; each of these approaches has both opportunities and risks. Mandates can be stated very specifically so that the discretion of the agents is narrowly circumscribed, or they can be stated as general goals, with wide latitude given to the agents as to the means for achieving the goals. In addition to these two basic features, plans often specify other matters as aids to effectiveness. Chief among these aids are stipulated funding methods, enforcement machinery, research and development, public information campaigns, and oversight and review.

Two basic controversies related to plan argumentation were considered. One is the question of whether the affirmative can legitimately spike its plan by including provisions intended to prevent disadvantages. The other issue is the nature of fiat and the confusions that result from the assumption that it is a real power possessed by the debaters, rather than an assumption made in order to focus discussion on the merits of the resolution.

Questions for Discussion

1. Under what circumstances, if any, can the affirmative choose not to present a specific plan?
2. What are the benefits and risks of relying on existing agents rather than stating new ones?
3. Is it better to define the plan's mandates broadly or narrowly?
4. Which of the aids to effectiveness are most desirable as components of a plan?
5. What are the strongest arguments against our view that spikes are legitimate parts of a plan?
6. Why is it improper to claim that one's advantages or disadvantages come about because a plan has been adopted by fiat?

Chapter 11

Affirmative Case Construction: Structures

In return for the requirements that the affirmative must shoulder, there are significant options that it may exercise. Essentially, as long as the affirmative satisfies the conditions imposed by the analysis of the resolution and the logic of debate theory, it may select whatever arguments it wishes to use, and it may arrange those arguments in virtually any manner it chooses. In this chapter we shall examine the commonly chosen options of selection and arrangement. Then we shall describe the process by which those options are exercised — the actual writing of the affirmative case.

Selecting the Case Area

On any resolution, there are far more affirmative arguments than can be presented in a single debate. For example, for the resolution that the United States should decrease its military commitments, the affirmative could argue about the strategic or diplomatic interest served by American policy anywhere in the world. It could argue about the economic effects of military versus nonmilitary spending, competing domestic priorities, or even issues of law and morals. Moreover, some of the available affirmative arguments will be inconsistent with one another. On the military commitments resolution, for example, the affirmative could propose to retreat from world leadership or — by relying more heavily on nonmilitary means—to enhance world leadership. Consequently, the affirmative must be selective. To form its case, it must choose from among the available affirmative arguments — the collection of arguments that it will actually use to try to convince the audience that the resolution is probably true.

Criteria for Choosing a Case

How should this choice be made? First, the debaters should research widely in the subject area of the resolution before choosing a specific area for the case. In this way, they will gain a good preliminary sense of what the available arguments are and how strongly they will be supported in the literature. Moreover, they will be likely to understand and anticipate a wide range of arguments that may be used against them. Debaters who select a case area before widely researching the resolution are exhibiting tunnel vision. Not only do they commit themselves to a case area on the basis of hasty judgments that the literature may not support, but since their selection of case area dictates their subsequent affirmative research, they may overlook even stronger evidence or arguments. It is better to begin by reading overviews and general works on the debate topic, then reading works on more specific aspects of the topic, and finally, selecting a case area only when convinced that a broad range of possible case areas can be identified and their strengths and weaknesses appraised. Proceeding in this manner, debaters are less likely to waste time in preparing cases for which crucial arguments are missing, and they are less likely to be surprised by arguments against the case which the negative side has discovered by thorough research.

A second criterion to use in choosing among case areas is that the debaters should be comfortable with the case. They will spend at least half of their debate rounds presenting and discussing the case, so it should be a topic of interest to them. If possible, the case should be consistent with the personal convictions of the debaters, since it is much easier to argue effectively for a position in which one believes. At the very least, it is wise to select a case area in which the fundamental value judgments do not conflict directly with the views of the debaters. At the subconscious level, if not the conscious, this discrepancy between private belief and public statement may prevent the affirmative from giving its case the strongest possible advocacy.

The third main consideration in selecting a case is that the affirmative should pick the strongest arguments possible. This piece of advice is not as obvious as it may sound, for the strongest arguments are those that will withstand the negative attacks and retain the greatest portion of the original affirmative argument. Consequently, arguments that seem strong when first presented may not always be best for the affirmative, because they may invite such a devastating negative response that there is little of the argument left. Similarly, arguments to which the negative has little to say may not always be the strongest arguments; they may just not be very potent in the first place. For instance, in an affirmative case dealing with education, the negative could say little against the argument that school enrollments are declining. But the argument, by itself, is not strong enough to support the claim that the federal government should assume all responsibility for education.

A final consideration is that the affirmative should try to control the number of arguments that can be advanced against the case. For example, a case with a strong central premise that can be used to answer many negative arguments is preferable to one that does not. The affirmative with the strong central premise can dispose of the negative arguments more efficiently. Likewise, a case against which there are few known disadvantages is preferable to one that will invite many disadvantages. And if the problem to which the case is addressed is regarded almost universally as a problem, the affirmative will be in a better position than if it must defend its basic value judgments against a strong negative attack.

Stock Cases or Squirrels?

There are differing views as to what makes the strongest case. One approach emphasizes those cases that are discussed most prominently in the literature. These, apparently, involve arguments that experts in the subject area consider to be the strongest and that have the greatest amount of evidence available to support them. Cases composed of these sorts of arguments are often referred to as *stock cases* and are referred to as lying *in the center of the topic* or reflecting *the spirit of the resolution*. Sometimes arguments of this type truly are the strongest, and a team may be able to use such a case throughout the entire year because they are familiar with the arguments and keep up to date on the issues. Moreover, the case area they chose may be dynamic enough to allow for expansion and new lines of defense, even though the negative knows the area very well. Sometimes, however, arguments that figure prominently in the literature may not be the strongest. For one thing, their very prominence in the literature ensures that the resolution's opponents will consider them and attempt to defeat them. Consequently there is likely to be a large volume of both negative and affirmative arguments and evidence. Though the affirmative arguments may initially seem strong, they may not be able to survive the negative attack. Hence they may not be true.

Another approach suggests that the strongest arguments may be those that initially seem peripheral rather than central to the resolution. They are not widely discussed in the literature and do not immediately come to mind when the resolution is mentioned. There may be important affirmative arguments in these areas, even though they have not been the focal point of controversy. Cases of this type often are referred to as *squirrels*.

Squirrel cases usually involve either a very narrow portion of a far more general resolution or an unusual interpretation of the meaning of one or more key terms in the resolution. An example of a narrow view is a case that, for a resolution calling for significant change in United States foreign trade policies, proposes to alter the regulations affecting the export of one particular product. An unusual interpretation of meaning is illustrated by the case that, for a resolution calling for a guaranteed minimum annual income for all citizens, defines *minimum* as "the smallest possible amount" and then offers reasons that people should not have cash in their possession.

Squirrel cases have been severely criticized by those who believe that they are intended to exploit the unpreparedness of the negative, that they depend for their success on surprise rather than their own merits, that they promote trickery rather than analysis, and that they discourage rather than encourage thorough public discussion. But we prefer a different interpretation of the decision to use a squirrel case. We think it is a mistake to assume that the motives of debaters using such a case are suspect, particularly when we cannot know what those motives are. Rather than assuming sinister intent, we prefer to believe that the team selecting a peripheral case area has determined, contrary to first impressions, that the strongest arguments for the resolution are to be found there. Presumably the debaters are as interested in careful analysis and discussion as are those who select a more central case area.

But we strongly caution affirmative debaters against yielding to temptation. Just because there may not be a wealth of negative evidence does not mean that the affirmative arguments necessarily are strong. On the contrary, they may be so weak that the negative is able to defeat them with little or no evidence, whether by arguing that they are not topical, by exposing their analytical flaws, or by other approaches. Moreover, some debate judges dislike squirrel cases because they are thought to weaken the clash of arguments in the debate. Anticipating the possibility of such resistance from the judge, debaters should consider whether the squirrel case really is their best option.

There is a third possibility that merits mention: a case that lies in the center of the topic yet that is argued unconventionally in one or more respects. Debaters sometimes refer to such a case as a *stock case with twists*. For example, for the resolution that the federal government should guarantee employment opportunities for all United States citizens, a stock central case could argue for the individual and social benefits of reducing unemployment. But such a case risks disadvantages: decreased unemployment may trigger an increased demand for goods and services, leading to inflation and unwise economic growth. In contrast, a stock case with twists may be able to argue for the benefits of lowering unemployment without the disadvantages. The affirmative could have the best of both worlds by advocating reduction in the workweek — in order to spread existing unemployment across the entire labor force rather than to increase aggregate demand. Such a case involves the affirmative in making the same arguments that figure prominently in the literature, while taking advantage of the relative scarcity of negative evidence and arguments concerning the particular twists it includes.

The point is that the selection of a stock case, a squirrel case, or a stock case with twists should be made on the basis of the debaters' interest in the subject and their assessment of the strengths of the alternative case, rather than on the basis of a priori judgments of the case's legitimacy.

Selecting the Case Format

A second choice that the affirmative must make is the format in which to present its case. The term *format* refers to the basic structure of the case—the way in which the major arguments will be organized and the order in which they will come.

Whatever format the affirmative selects, it must be able to meet the requirements that we discussed in previous chapters. Theoretically, the affirmative can select whatever format it wishes in order to maximize the clarity and effectiveness of its presentation and gain a strategic advantage. Nevertheless, although the range of formats is infinite, certain choices tend to be made so regularly that they constitute recognized case forms. We shall consider several of the more common case forms.

The Traditional Case

For many years, the format that we label *traditional* was virtually the only case form in existence. Sometimes referred to as the *need-plan* case, it organizes the affirmative arguments around the stock issues. Typically it begins with a contention, or major argument, establishing the problem's significance. Then a separate contention addresses the issue of inherency, explaining the causes for the problem's persistence. Usually at this point the affirmative plan is presented, followed by brief arguments that the plan will solve the problem and is relatively free from disadvantages.

The following outline illustrates the structure of the traditional case, for the resolution that the federal government should guarantee comprehensive medical care for all U.S. citizens.

I. Present health care policies result in needless death and suffering.
   A. Millions have no insurance coverage.
   B. Therefore, they delay seeking care or forgo it altogether.
   C. Unnecessary death and suffering result.

II. The problem is inherent.
   A. Medical care is a scarce resource.
   B. Increasing coverage under existing programs would increase the demand for care.
   C. Higher demand means higher cost, leaving even more people without needed care.

III. A nationwide program of health insurance organizations would solve these problems.
   [Presentation of the plan]
   A. Coverage would automatically be available to all.
   B. Incentives to delay or forgo care would be eliminated.
   C. Reorganization of medical care would increase efficiency.

IV. The plan is relatively free of defects.
   A. It would cost less than private insurance.
   B. It would provide the strongest incentive for efficiency.
   C. It would provide adequate, high-quality care to all.

The traditional case structure has two major features. First, the stock issues are clearly identified and correspond to the major divisions of the case. And, second, this case focuses directly on the resolution's antecedents. If the affirmative case area is characterized by glaring evidence of a serious problem, it may be wise to select the traditional format. Over half the case is usually devoted to existing problems and the reasons that they will continue unless something is done.

The traditional case sometimes is criticized by those who believe that the plan must totally solve the problem. If even a small part of the problem remains, the remnant will be sign evidence that the plan has not been effective in solving the problem. In our view, however, this belief is mistaken. If harms can be shown that are caused by the resolution's absence, a complete solution is not required. Rather, to whatever degree the plan diminishes the harms, that degree would represent a reason to affirm its probable truth. Just because one cannot eliminate all international tensions, for instance, does not mean that an arms limitation treaty cannot solve the problem of excessive armaments that create a tension of their own. The distinctive features of the traditional case, then, are its focus on the antecedent conditions of the resolution and its arrangement according to the stock issues.

The Comparative Advantage Case

In the early 1960s, a second case format came into wide use, and its popularity remains to this day. The comparative advantage case focuses less on the resolution's antecedents than on its consequences—the benefits it would bring. A comparison of the benefits that could be achieved with and without the resolution gave rise to the format's label, *comparative advantage.*

For nearly a decade after its widespread use, the comparative advantage case was the subject of strong controversy among debaters and judges. The point at issue was whether this format provided easier burdens for the affirmative than did the traditional case. Indeed, some championed the use of the comparative advantage case precisely in order to ease these burdens. For instance, they claimed that the comparative advantage case absolved the affirmative of the need to prove inherency and that therefore the case was useful for resolutions on which things were conceded to be working reasonably well without a compelling reason to change. Others suggested that the comparative advantage case be used when there were no clear-cut present evils, in order to reduce the affirmative's burden to prove significance. And still others suggested that comparative advantage cases were more realistic and pragmatic, approaching the grounds on which real-world decisions actually were made.

Basic to these three positions is the assumption that some resolutions may put the affirmative into a situation in which it would be impossible to satisfy the proof requirements of the traditional case and that in such situations one should seek to minimize one's burdens in order to improve the chance of eventual victory. Meanwhile, critics of the comparative advantage case opposed its legitimacy because they believed that the case eased the affirmative's burdens and that it was illogical and unfair to do so.

The assumptions underlying these positions have not fared well in recent years. With respect to inherency, it has been generally established that the phrase *inherent need* does not have to refer only to visible evils at the present time, but to any argument that establishes that there is good reason to affirm the resolution. Moreover, inherency actually is present in the comparative advantage case. The advantages must flow naturally from the resolution — they must inhere within it. And the advantages must be incapable of attainment without affirming the resolution. The affirmative must show why, in the absence of the resolution, the advantages will not be attained. With respect to significance, the same conclusion holds true. Minor changes are not worth arguing about, and insignificant effects may not be worth the risks of taking action, whether to solve problems or to obtain benefits. Of course, if the logical requirements of traditional and comparative advantage cases are the same, the question of which is the more realistic may be moot, since either case form may be translated into the other.

Over the past fifteen years, then, there has been a growing recognition that the comparative advantage case uses a different structure to satisfy the same requirements as does the traditional case. As this realization has spread, the use of the comparative advantage case has increased to the point that it is currently the most prevalent form. Here is an illustration of the comparative advantage structure for the resolution that the development of scarce world resources be controlled by an international organization:

> Presentation of the Affirmative Plan: International Control of Minerals in the Deep-Sea Bed, with a Mandate for Immediate Exploration.

I. Advantage of the plan: International control protects the developing nations.
   A. Mining of the deep-sea bed is inevitable.
   B. Unregulated mining threatens the developing nations.
      1. Wealthy nations can afford to mine the sea.
      2. They will price minerals artificially low so as to undersell the mineral-producing developing countries.
      3. Mineral-producing developing countries depend on exports.
      4. Therefore the developing countries will collapse.
   C. Regulated mining would protect the developing nations.
      1. It would limit how much can be mined.
      2. It would subsidize the mineral-producing nations for their losses.

A quick glance at this outline should reveal the key differences between the traditional and the comparative advantage case structures. For one thing, virtually the entire comparative advantage case is oriented to what will occur in the future. The comparative advantage case justifies the resolution on the basis not of its antecedent conditions but on the results that will follow if the resolution is affirmed and acted upon.

The other major difference is that although the stock issues are addressed by the comparative advantage case, the references to them are often less explicit, and the organization for addressing them is less direct. The stock issues are not singled out one at a time but usually are addressed in the course of arguments developing the affirmative advantage. In the example above, inherency is addressed in steps I-B-1 and I-B-2. These arguments establish that without affirming the resolution, unregulated mining will occur and that market forces will cause the mining to be done in an undesirable way. Steps I-B-3 and I-B-4 delineate the affirmative significance by describing the harm that unregulated mining will pose to the economies of mineral-producing nations and to the health of people all over the world. Efficacy is addressed in the presentation of the plan and in step I-C, which argues that the plan would overcome the forces now causing the problem to persist. Step I-A is an observation that undergirds the analysis. The one issue not directly addressed in this example is freedom from disadvantages. As we mentioned in discussing that issue, however, it is often left implicit. Presumably, the affirmative in this case has constructed its plan in order to reduce the risk of disadvantages and is prepared to respond to most of the disadvantages that the negative may present.

In light of these differences between the case forms, how can we decide whether to structure the affirmative case in the traditional or the comparative advantage format? It is a question largely of whether the subject matter of the case lends itself more naturally to a discussion of antecedents or consequences of affirming the resolution. And it is a question of whether the affirmative believes that its proof requirements on the stock issues can be met more easily by addressing them as separate actions of the case or in the internal structure of an advantage. The choice is a strategic and presentational one; with respect to logical requirements imposed on advocates, it does not matter.

Independent Needs or Advantages

So far, we have examined both the traditional and the comparative advantage cases as single units of proof. In each example, the steps follow one another in logical sequence; each step of the argument depends on the steps that precede it. This arrangement is clear and easy to follow, but it has one potentially fatal weakness: the loss of any one step of the argument will lead to the collapse of the entire structure. The analogy is to the old-fashioned Christmas tree lights, in which the failure of a single bulb causes the lights to go out all along the chain. In our example of the traditional case, if the affirmative is unable to win each of the steps—the significant harm of existing health policies, the inherency arguments establishing that the medical care system as currently structured cannot provide adequate care for all, the efficacy of the plan, and the relative freedom of the plan from defects—the entire case will fail. Likewise, the affirmative's failure to sustain any link in the development of the comparative advantage case will doom the entire case.

Sometimes it may not be feasible to assume in advance that every step of the case can be carried by the affirmative, particularly if the arguments are highly controversial and the evidence seems balanced. As a hedge against this possibility and as a way to increase the affirmative's strategic options, teams in recent years have developed cases arguing independent needs or advantages. Basically, such a case offers two or more advantages that can be obtained by the same plan, but independently of one another. Or they contend that the same plan can independently solve two or more different problems. Even if the affirmative loses one of the advantages or needs by failing to establish some critical step in its development, the remaining needs or advantages will still provide good reasons to affirm the resolution.

Below is an example of an affirmative case that claims independent advantages. The resolution is that the United States should significantly change the method of selecting presidential and vice-presidential candidates.

> [Presentation of the Plan: Universal Voter Registration Sponsored and Financed by the Federal Government.]

I. First advantage: The plan will increase citizens' participation in politics.
    A. Many eligible voters do not now vote.
    B. State and local laws prevent many from registering to vote.
    C. If these individuals are registered, many of them will vote.
    D. Increased voting will enhance the legitimacy of the political process.
II. Second advantage: The plan will secure social policies desired by minority groups.
    A. Many nonregistered individuals are members of racial or ethnic minorities.
    B. Politicians are sensitive to the wishes of these groups and want their votes.
    C. Increasing the voting ratio in these groups will increase their value to politicians and thus prompt legislation that is in their interest.
    D. Social policies in the interest of minority groups are desirable for the nation as a whole.

Even if the affirmative is unsuccessful in establishing that overall political participation will increase, it still has an opportunity to win the debate if it can establish that legislation benefiting minority groups will be enhanced. The second advantage does not depend on proof that overall rates of voting will increase. Likewise, the affirmative can lose the second advantage and still be able to win the debate if it can sustain the first.

For needs or advantages to be truly independent, two important conditions must be met. First, each advantage must satisfy all the proof requirements of the affirmative. It is not possible, for instance, to prove significance and inherency on one advantage and efficacy and freedom from disadvantages on another. Each advantage by itself must provide full and complete justification for affirming the resolution, or else the advantages are not really independent.

Second, the advantages should not be linked to the same basic assumptions or processes of reasoning. Otherwise, the negative could attack the foundation of all the needs or advantages without responding to them individually. In the above example, one advantage depends on the response of the general population to universal registration, and the other depends on the reaction of racial and ethnic minorities. To preserve the independence of the advantages, the affirmative should argue that these responses are completely unrelated. On the other hand, if the negative can establish that there is no link for any group between easier registration and increased voting, it will have shown that the advantages are not independent and will have defeated them both by showing that the plan will not meet its need: voting rates will not increase.

Some debaters have developed affirmative cases in which large numbers of advantages can be claimed from a single plan—more, in fact, than the affirmative can present or defend in any single debate. In such a case, the affirmative can choose combinations of advantages to present in each debate, based on its assessment of the strengths and weaknesses of its opponents and the interests and predispositions of its judge. This kind of case, sometimes referred to as a *modular* case, affords maximum flexibility to the affirmative. Of course, each of the modules must meet the two tests mentioned above.

One modification of case structure that sometimes occurs, especially with independent needs or advantages, is the presentation of some arguments that are separate from the structure of the advantages. These arguments, often called *overviews* or *observations*, may contain arguments common to all the advantages or may establish principles that are necessary in order to consider any of the advantages. For instance, for a resolution to reduce the average length of the workweek in order to provide employment opportunities for all, an affirmative case could be structured as follows:

I. First observation: The forty-hour workweek is established by federal law.
II. Second observation: Neither labor nor management will be the first to reduce the workweek voluntarily.

$$\left[\begin{array}{l}\text{Presentation of the Plan: Federally Mandated Work Sharing to}\\\text{Reduce the Unemployment Rate to 4 Percent.}\end{array}\right]$$

I. First advantage: Increased employment will reduce individual death and suffering. (Details omitted.)
II. Second advantage: Increased employment will reduce crime and delinquency. (Details omitted.)
III. Third advantage: Increased employment will reduce mental illness. (Details omitted.)

This example illustrates the benefit to the affirmative of separating the observations from the development of the individual advantages. Were the case not organized in this fashion, the affirmative would need to develop the same two *observation* arguments under the heading of each advantage.

On the other hand, the presence of these observations is often a signal to the negative that the advantages are not completely independent of one another. In this example, all three advantages depend on the common inherency arguments contained in the observations. The defeat of these arguments will doom the entire case, even though the significance of each advantage is established independently of the others. For this reason, the negative errs in assuming that arguments that the affirmative may label observations or overviews are trivial in comparison with the advantages and cannot decide the outcome of the debate.

Although observations are often found in cases that argue independent needs or advantages, they serve other purposes and may be used in other types of cases as well. They may make relatively noncontroversial claims. Placing such a claim into an observation signals that the affirmative may wish to waive it from dispute. Or the observations may state factual claims to which the affirmative seeks either agreement or objection before proceeding to the more "meaty" advantages or needs. Whenever observations are part of the case structure, they tend to be presented as we have described them here — as arguments prior to the affirmative's major contentions.

One additional comment bears mention with respect to the independent needs or advantages case. The affirmative's purpose in arguing such a case is to increase flexibility and strategic options. That purpose is hurt if the affirmative feels compelled to argue all of the advantages throughout the debate, even if it concludes that some of them have been hopelessly lost. We do not believe that the affirmative must sustain *every* individual argument it introduces. The key question is whether those arguments that it *does* sustain, taken together, meet its responsibility to establish the four stock issues discussed in Chapter 9. Obviously, no debater should concede advantages that may be won. But knowing when to abandon a losing need or advantage is part of the strategy of advancing independent arguments in the first place. We shall return to this topic when we consider rebuttals and extensions.

The Criteria or Goals Case

A fourth type of affirmative case, the *criteria* or *goals case,* argues that the resolution should be affirmed because action pursuant to it would approach some desired goal or satisfy valued criteria. In some respects, this case form is similar to the comparative advantage case. Its concern is with the future consequences of the resolution, and the attainment of a desirable goal certainly can be called an advantage. There is, however, an important difference in emphasis between the two case forms. The criteria or goals case begins with an explicit statement of the objective to be sought and a defense of its value. It then proceeds to argue why affirming the resolution is the best way to achieve the objective. Consequently, this case form makes the value judgment much more explicit.

In both the traditional and the comparative advantage cases, the value judgment underlying the significance claim is often left unstated, and the affirmative often seeks as nearly universal a value judgment as possible. By contrast, the criteria or goals case prominently features the value judgment and invites the negative to contest it.

Below is a sample outline of an affirmative criteria case on the resolution that the federal government should control the supply and utilization of energy in the United States:

I. An optimal energy policy should satisfy the following criteria:
    A. It should rely on renewable energy sources.
    B. It should rely on safe energy sources.
    C. It should cause minimum damage to the environment.
    D. It should provide energy at the lowest possible cost.

II. Existing energy sources cannot satisfy these criteria.
    A. Coal and oil are not renewable.
    B. Nuclear power is not safe.
    C. Coal and nuclear power threaten the environment.
    D. All current technologies are expensive.

[Presentation of the Plan: Mandatory Short-term Conservation and a Long-Term Commitment to Develop Solar Energy.]

III. The plan will more nearly satisfy the criteria.
    A. Solar energy is renewable.
    B. Solar energy is safe.
    C. Solar energy will not endanger the environment.
    D. Solar energy will provide low-cost energy once the initial costs are paid.
    E. Conservation is the best short-term approach pending the development of solar energy.

In this example, it is easy to see how the criteria case rearranges but satisfies the basic proof requirements of the affirmative. Part I combines part of the significance proof (justification of criteria) with freedom from disadvantages (since the criteria are claimed to be optimal). Part II represents the proof of inherency—the reasons that the criteria cannot be met in the absence of the resolution. Part III combines part of the significance proof (the degree to which the criteria will be met) with the proof of the resolution's efficacy.

When should debaters choose a criteria or goals case? It may be a wise choice if two conditions are met. First, if the case depends on a value judgment that the affirmative thinks can easily be sustained in argument, the criteria format may be appropriate. In the example above, the affirmative could reason that it would be difficult for any negative to deny that we should use a safe energy source or one that offers minimal risk to the environment. In other words, the affirmative could conclude that the value judgment underlying the case would be easy to establish and hard to dispute.

But the second condition is equally important. The case is a good choice if once the value judgment has been established, the affirmative's success on that argument makes it easy to support the remainder of the case. Once all four criteria are established in the example above, for instance, there would be few sources of energy other than solar power that would satisfy them all. The affirmative in this example would gain mileage by explicitly stating the criteria and then inviting the negative either to accept or contest them.

On the other hand, we can also name the circumstances that are least favorable to the criteria case. If the criteria seem good but would be hard to justify once they were specifically attacked, it probably is better not to feature the value judgment so prominently. For instance, most people intuitively believe that inflation is harmful, and so a case that proposes that the control of inflation be a key criterion of any policy would have a strong surface appeal. But as debaters who have wrestled with this problem know, argument and evidence can be arrayed so as to deny the harms of inflation, and it is harder than one may think to defend the harms in the face of such a challenge.

The second circumstance that is unfavorable to the criteria case is one in which the negative can offer additional criteria of an optimal policy that dwarf those of the affirmative in importance but lead to the opposite conclusion. Obviously, in such a situation, the case form will be the affirmative's undoing.

There is a variation on this case form that we should mention. Sometimes the affirmative chides the present system for failing to live up to its own goals and then suggests that affirming the resolution would provide the means to bring the system in line with its own ideals. A system's goals are often stated in lofty, if vague, terms that are virtually impossible for specific acts to achieve. The Employment Act of 1946 declared the nation's economic goals to be maximum employment, productivity, and purchasing power. Later, President Lyndon B. Johnson called for the abolition of poverty in the United States. There are obvious political benefits in stating goals so broadly, but the very expansiveness of the statement makes the goals difficult to achieve. It may be easy for debaters to conclude that the present system has failed to meet its goals and to imagine that affirming the resolution could enable us to do better. Such a case first identifies the relevant goals, then explains why current policies have failed to meet them, and finally offers a plan that, according to the affirmative, will enable us to do better.

Debaters sometimes find this variation on the case form attractive for the wrong reason. They believe that since the case supports the goals of the present system, those goals can be presumed to be good and do not need explicit defense by the affirmative. But only if the negative chooses to support the goals of the present system will the affirmative enjoy this benefit! The negative has many other available options, as we shall see. It can completely disassociate itself from the present system, or it can support the actual performance of the system while ignoring or repudiating its stated goals. If the negative follows either of these approaches, the burdens on the affirmative will be exactly the same as in any other version of the goals or criteria case. The fact that their criteria are goals of the present system makes no difference.

The Alternative Justification Case

The case forms that we have examined all seek either to justify, in a generic sense, the full scope of the resolution or to argue for the resolution on the basis of a single plan that embodies its central principles. Unlike the other four forms, the alternative justification case seeks to defend the resolution on the basis of any of several plans that may be offered. In some respects, this format resembles the independent needs or advantages case. But there is a crucial difference: in the alternative justification case, the advantages derive from multiple plans, but in the independent advantages case, they derive from a single plan.

The following outline illustrates the structure of the alternative justification case for the resolution that the jury system in the United States be significantly changed:

I. Military justice

[First plan: Transfer military justice to civilian courts.]

   A. Safeguard the constitutional rights of the individual. (Details omitted.)

   B. Reduce command influence over the conduct of a trial. (Details omitted.)

II. Civil cases

[Second plan: Transfer most civil cases to a national system of arbitration.]

   A. Reduce court congestion from auto accident cases. (Details omitted.)

   B. Reduce court time devoted to divorce cases. (Details omitted.)

III. Jury selection

[Third plan: Adopt national standards for jury selection procedures.]

   A. Eliminate racial discrimination in jury selection. (Details omitted.)

   B. Eliminate sex discrimination in jury selection. (Details omitted.)

This example illustrates the strategic purpose of the alternative justification form. Theoretically, the affirmative should be able to win the debate if it sustains its position on any one plan and shows that any one advantage of that plan offsets the disadvantages that the negative may bring against the plan. So if the negative wins a major disadvantage against nationwide jury selection standards, the affirmative can safely abandon that plan and its advantage and carry the debate on either of the other two plans. In the independent advantage case, in contrast, the affirmative can abandon an advantage but is stuck with its plan and must defend it against the disadvantages. The sum of all the advantages is weighed against the sum of all the disadvantages.

It may seem at first that the alternative justification case form offers the greatest strategic options to the affirmative and should be used whenever possible. But there are difficulties. The first, and most obvious, is imposed by time constraints. Each of the plans and each of the advantages must satisfy all the proof requirements discussed in earlier chapters; otherwise the alternative justifications will not independently warrant the resolution. But the affirmative has no more time in which to present three plans and five advantages (or needs) than it does to present one plan and one advantage. Consequently, breadth often is obtained at the expense of depth. It may be easier for the negative to establish that one or more parts of the case should be rejected out of hand because they are incompletely developed. Similarly, in resubstantiating and extending the case, the affirmative must be extremely careful to allocate time properly, covering all the plans and advantages it wishes to carry, or the strategic choices may be foreclosed by running out of time. Few debaters, even those with several years of experience, are able to allocate their time precisely.

The second difficulty with the alternative justification case is that many people believe it to be unfair or illegitimate. They contend that it makes it too easy for the affirmative to win and effectively penalizes the negative for developing winning arguments. On a more theoretical level, they suggest that an affirmative vote is a decision to adopt a policy but that the alternative justification case makes it impossible to know which policy is being adopted. After all, in deciding the outcome of a debate, a judge cannot attach conditions to the decision, for instance, voting affirmative if it is plan number three that is put into effect. So, the argument runs, the affirmative either must defend a single policy (so that it is clear what is being adopted) or else win all of the alternative justifications (so that it does not matter). The first choice brands the alternative justification form as illegitimate, and the second undermines its strategic value for the affirmative. Both argue against using the case form.

We do not agree with these criticisms. The theoretical argument depends on the belief that to vote affirmative is to adopt a policy, whereas we have maintained that an affirmative vote is merely an expression of belief that the resolution is probably true. For that purpose, it is enough that the resolution be shown true on the basis of any single plan, just as we permit a team using any of the other case forms to offer only one plan as an illustration of the resolution. As for the "fairness" challenge to the case form, it fails to consider the opportunities for independent or conditional arguments that also are available to the negative, which will be considered later.

On a theoretical level, then, we find no reason to reject the legitimacy of the alternative justification case. Yet the fact that many people believe otherwise should be a cause for concern. The affirmative using this type of case runs the risk of arbitrary defeat by judges who reject it out of hand. Or, as sometimes happens, the affirmative may convince a judge of its right to use such a case, but only by taking so much time defending the legitimacy of the case that it is unable to sustain any of the alternative justifications. Besides, since the proof requirements for any case format are the same, each element of the alternative justification case must fully satisfy the four basic stock issues. For this reason, as we have said, this case requires talents of word economy, argument selection, and time allocation that surpass those possessed by even the most experienced debaters. So it may not be surprising that the alternative justification case is widely discussed as a theoretical option but is very seldom used in practice.

The Process of Case Writing

Before leaving the subject of affirmative case construction, we shall briefly examine the steps in writing the actual case—the sequence in which the affirmative's choices are made and implemented.

1. Determine the case area — the subject matter on which the case will be based. This decision should be made on the basis of factors discussed at the beginning of this chapter.

2. Decide on the central thesis of the case. The central thesis is a succinct statement of what the case will argue; it is an organizing image around which the case will be constructed. The thesis can usually be cast in the form "X (some condition) characterizes negative land and makes Y (some significant problem or the absence of some significant advantage) inevitable." For example, for the resolution that the federal government nationalize all energy companies, one case thesis could be, "The market system always assures energy shortages." A succinct statement of the thesis is easily understood and remembered by your listeners.

3. Consider what will need to be proved in order to show the truth of the thesis and simultaneously meet the proof requirements of significance and inherency. In our example, the affirmative needs to prove (1) that the control of energy through a market system characterizes negative land, (2) that supply shortages are persistent, and (3) that supply shortages cannot be avoided in the context of a market system. This list of proof requirements can be used as a check list in writing the case. Of course, the affirmative that develops independent arguments will have a more elaborate thesis. For example, step (2) above can refer to both supply shortages and distortions or production decisions, which then can be developed as independent harms.

4. Write the specific affirmative plan if there is to be one. At the same time, be sure to ask whether the plan answers the case thesis. If not, you will have great

difficulty proving the resolution's efficacy. If so, the affirmative should be able to anticipate the arguments to be made regarding efficacy and freedom from disadvantages.

5. Decide which case format to use. As we suggested, this choice has nothing to do with the proof requirements on the affirmative but is determined instead by such factors as the nature of the case thesis, the nature of the available evidence, the question of whether one wishes to highlight the present or the future, the decision about whether to make the value judgment explicit, and the debaters' individual abilities. The affirmative may select any of the case formats listed in this chapter or it may formulate its own, as long as the basic proof requirements are met.

6. Determine the major arguments that must be carried in order to sustain the affirmative case. These major arguments are called *contentions*. They often correspond to the list of what must be proved in order to carry the case thesis, or sometimes to the stock issues. There usually are between two and five contentions, and it is important that they be organizationally clear. Unrelated ideas should not be combined in the same contention, nor should the same basic idea be scattered among several contentions in an excess of substructure. Of course, if the affirmative develops independent needs or advantages, this step will include both deciding what the needs or advantages will be and formulating the major contentions supporting each need or advantage. Sometimes the needs or advantages themselves are called contentions, and the supporting arguments are designated as subpoints, but the process is the same. If the case structure is to include any observations, they should be identified at this time as well.

7. Word the individual contentions. This is an important stage that is often not given enough attention. The way that the contentions are worded may affect the judge's understanding of, and reaction to, the arguments. Contentions should be specific enough that their meaning is clear. "Present energy policies will destroy civilization" does not tell an audience much about the specific harms that the affirmative will claim. In contrast, "Air pollution from fossil fuels will kill millions" specifies both the source and the nature of the harm. Contentions should be stated in simple, declarative sentences so that they will be clear and will facilitate note taking. If possible, they should be worded in parallel structure so that the listeners can anticipate what is coming next and be able easily to remember the basic pattern. Nouns and verbs should be chosen carefully to create the images that the debater intends. And, both to attract the audience's interest and to promote variety, the contentions should be worded in the language of the subject being discussed, rather than in debate theory or jargon. "Significance" or "inherency" does not make a very interesting or compelling title for a contention.

8. Develop the individual contentions. Here, too, many debaters mistakenly assume that developing the contention is merely a matter of reading the specific pieces of evidence that they intend to use in its support. But evidence alone does not make an argument. Developing a contention has four steps: (1) State the contention. (2) Explain it. The explanation will both amplify what the contention

means and indicate what will be offered as support for it. In this way, it previews the evidence and provides the context in which the audience should evaluate the evidence. (3) Present the evidence, and (4) Show the impact of the evidence — how the evidence helps establish the contention. The relationship between evidence and argument should not be left for the audience to discern.

At this point, the affirmative must decide how much evidence to include in its initial presentation. Here there are two somewhat conflicting considerations. On one hand, the first affirmative speech should be able to convince the listeners, in the absence of refutation, of the probable truth of the resolution. This goal argues for including as much, and as strong, evidence as possible. On the other hand, time limits will prevent offering everything in first affirmative. And the affirmative will not want to use all of its "ammunition" in the initial speech and have nothing further to say in later speeches. These considerations lean toward reducing the amount of evidence in the first speech and holding some of the strongest evidence to use to resubstantiate the case in the later speeches.

It is impossible to determine hypothetically how to resolve these cross-pressures; the affirmative will need to do so each time it develops a case. A good way of dealing with the problem is to work backwards. That is, the affirmative first asks what it wants its final position on a given argument to be, and then figures out the steps that are likely to lead to that final outcome, and accordingly decides which pieces of evidence should be read in which speeches.

In recommending this approach, however, we should add two cautions. One is that the first affirmative speech must not be substantially weakened as a result. After all, this speech alone must be sufficient to convince an audience on first hearing it of the probable truth of the resolution. The other caution is that it is unwise to save very many pieces of evidence for later speeches. The time required to answer negative arguments and advance the affirmative position often will make it impossible to read more than a few pieces of new evidence in resubstantiation.

9. Assemble the various contentions, the plan, and any other arguments into a coherent speech. The structure of the speech should follow a sensible pattern, such as that of the examples in this chapter. In particular, the plan should be presented before any arguments that depend on knowledge of its details. Although the first affirmative speech used to be delivered extemporaneously, a prepared manuscript is now the general rule—and for good reason. The manuscript permits the affirmative to use the exact language it wants, to use previews and summaries to link its arguments, and to select words that are both stylistically pleasing and persuasive. Unfortunately, the benefits of a manuscript are often lost when it is assembled hastily or haphazardly. Since this speech will influence the judge's initial impression of the affirmative case and the affirmative debaters, it is certainly worth the time required to write the speech carefully and with sensitivity to its function as persuasive communication.

10. Finally, practice giving the speech. Practice will make the affirmative more familiar with the text; it will enable the debaters to check that the speech falls within the prescribed time limits; it will permit a sample audience to offer reactions

to whether the speech is clear and persuasive; and it will enable the speaker to focus on the best use of voice, gesture, and bodily action in the delivery of the speech.

These ten steps should give the affirmative a case that initially will serve it well as it prepares to contest the case to be offered by the negative.

Summary

Although the affirmative must satisfy numerous requirements in constructing its case, it also is given several important choices. One key choice is the case area — the subject matter of the resolution with which the case will deal. In making this choice, the affirmative selects the arguments on which it will ask concurrence with the resolution. The choice should be guided by wide-ranging research, personal interest in the case area, and an assessment of what the strongest arguments are. The choice may produce a stock case that is featured prominently in the literature on the topic, a squirrel case that initially seems peripheral, or a stock case that has some unconventional arguments.

The affirmative also may select the format in which to present its case, since any format must satisfy the basic proof requirements. The traditional case is organized in a clear progression according to the stock issues and focuses on the current evils that the resolution can remedy. The comparative advantage case addresses the consequences of the resolution — the benefits that will result if it is implemented. The stock issues are addressed, but their organization is often less explicit. The affirmative can also argue independent needs solved by, or advantages accrued from, acting on the resolution, as long as each need or advantage fully warrants the resolution and the development of the arguments does not depend on common logic or assumptions. A fourth case type is the criteria or goals case, in which a value judgment is set forth and explicitly defended and in which affirming the resolution is claimed to enhance the desired value. Finally, the alternative justification case offers both multiple plans to illustrate the resolution and separate advantages for each. Although these five case formats are currently the most common, the affirmative may use any format that will enable it to present its case.

Writing the affirmative case is a ten-step process. The key steps are (1) selecting a case area; (2) formulating the case's central thesis; (3) identifying the proof requirements dictated by the central thesis; (4) framing the affirmative plan if there is to be one; (5) selecting the case format to be used; (6) determining the major arguments, or contentions, of the case; (7) wording the contentions clearly and precisely; (8) developing the contentions with explanation, evidence, and impact; (9) writing the first affirmative speech, and (10) practicing the delivery of the speech.

We have now completed our discussion of affirmative case construction and shall next turn our attention to the negative.

Questions for Discussion

1. Once debaters have researched the resolution, how should they select a specific subject area for their affirmative case?
2. What are the relative merits of stock cases and squirrel cases?
3. If proof requirements remain the same, regardless of case format, why does the format matter?
4. What are the major differences between independent needs and alternative justification?
5. How is the affirmative case hurt by failing to follow each of the ten steps in case writing?

Chapter 12

Negative
Case Construction:
The Position

When defending the negative, many high school and collegiate debaters do nothing more than present several arguments in a "shotgun" fashion. Although many of the arguments presented may be valid and persuasive, they frequently do not achieve their objective: they do not produce a coherent negative position against the affirmative. By this we mean that it is not clear what the arguments add up to, as they do not take an overall substantive stance with respect to the affirmative case.

When debaters fail to make clear their substantive stances, they do not give the judge a clear explanation of the reasons for debating against the resolution. For example, in attacking a proposal for unilateral nuclear disarmament (with the United States beginning to disarm before any Soviet initiative), as a negative you could argue that the Soviet Union desires world communism and that our armaments are a necessary deterrent to that. The negative could also argue that we already have constructive arms control negotiations to deal with problems connected with nuclear weaponry, that these negotiations may be disrupted by the affirmative proposal, and that other U.S.-Soviet agreements in social and economic spheres may mitigate the problem posed by the affirmative. Finally, the negative could argue that the Soviets cannot be trusted in any of their relationships with the United States and that the affirmative proposal should be rejected for that reason alone. But this is hardly a coherent negative position and gives the judge no guidance in rejecting the resolution.

Instead of the fragmented approach described above, the negative could develop the thesis that our relations with the Soviet Union should be conducted in a cautious, incremental fashion, given the Soviets' doctrinal history and lack of trust in them. Although there are steps the United States can take to minimize the risks of nuclear arms, such as gradual arms control, social contacts and economic exchange, the military and political risks of unilateral disarmament are simply too unknown and potentially too dangerous to justify the proposition.

This chapter will examine the development and uses of a negative position as a way of exploring and summarizing the negative case. We shall describe the idea of a negative position; discuss various approaches to the development of a negative position; and finally, suggest various uses of the negative position.

The usefulness of the negative position does not depend on the acceptance of a particular model of debate, such as policy making or hypothesis testing. Furthermore, the negative position can be used against any type of affirmative case structure. To help explain the negative position, we shall work with a single example.

The Idea of a Negative Position

The idea of a negative position starts from the premise that the overriding objective of the negative is to show that the resolution should not be affirmed. The negative then determines what combination of arguments is most likely to attain this objective. The position is a statement of the concepts on which these arguments are based—the negative's general perspective on the affirmative case. Consequently, it is unique to each affirmative case. It is a comprehensive and internally consistent stand to be adhered to by both negative speakers in response to the arguments made by the affirmative.

We shall illustrate the development of a negative position by using the continuing national debate on domestic energy sources. During the 1970s, the country began to have petroleum shortages. Some Americans advocated the removal of all government controls over the price of oil, claiming that government price regulations kept profits at a level that discouraged oil companies from exploring and processing new sources of oil within the United States. Many claimed that the resulting disincentives to domestic production also contributed to oil shortages and made the nation more dependent on foreign oil supplies that continually increase in price. These conditions, they insisted, contributed to the oil shortages.

Those arguing against removing price controls claimed that the concentrated nature of the oil industry required price controls because the industry could exploit its position to raise the prices of domestic oil to a much higher level than a competitive market would produce. They also claimed that the oil industry would not use its increased profits from deregulation to develop new sources of domestic oil but instead would limit supply and reap even greater profits. Therefore, decontrols, they contended, would only add to the consumers' inflationary burden and not increase the oil supply.

These two opposing positions presented each side's view of the problem and the relationships between the oil producers and consumers as well as the best solution to the problem. You should be able to understand how those people opposing change viewed the problem as posited by those favoring change. At the same time, you should see how the negative position on the oil problem strongly suggests the types of policies that the negative was defending in the debate. It was apparent, for instance, that the negative believed that price controls were necessary to attain the affirmative goals; that indeed, the American people would receive the same amount of oil at lower prices with government regulation than without it.

The negative position, then, is a substantive stance against the affirmative, based on how the negative decides that people should and will think and act in regard to a given policy. Its aim is the emergence of a cohesive, consistent thesis statement on the policy under consideration. When clearly defined, the negative position should take into account both what the affirmative has proposed and its own analysis of that proposal. In essence, the negative position is its view of the whole question addressed by the debate resolution.

As noted above, this larger view of the negative stance is often neglected in academic debating. Instead, the listeners may be presented with assertions that are sometimes referred to as negative positions but that fall short of a comprehensive stance in response to the affirmative. The negative, for example, does not develop a negative position just by presenting a list of random observations regarding the affirmative case. A case in point is, "Observation 1: The affirmative did not prove that oil companies need more money to develop more production" or "Observation 2: The affirmative did not prove that we need more oil." Neither of these claims commits the negative to an overall position on the topic.

A negative position is also not established simply by listing the negative stances on the stock issues. The statement, "The negative will prove that the affirmative case has no inherency, that its plan will not meet the need, and that the affirmative plan will result in numerous disadvantages" does not express a negative position.

Finally, the negative has not established a position just by taking a stance on the affirmative's need issue. The comprehensive position must encompass the negative's stance on both the need and the plan. The second negative, even if confining the speech to plan attacks, should make its strategy choices based on the same overall stance as that offered by the first negative.

In contrast with these forms of unconnected argument, an overall negative position takes into account all the aspects of the affirmative case and arranges these parts into a negative framework. The negative, in effect, takes a broad look at the facts, values, and policies pertaining to the affirmative issues and arranges them within its own units of proof. The negative then uses its synthesis to conclude that it is more rational to reject the affirmative's proposal than it is to risk affirming it. The extended debate on the oil controversy presented above illustrates how the negative looked at the affirmative goal and decided why the affirmative solution would not meet its need.

Benefits of a Negative Position

There are a number of benefits in developing a negative position or comprehensive stance in response to the affirmative's proposal, and we shall describe several of them.

Maximizes Impact. The development of a negative position should help you gain the greatest possible impact from your arguments. You should be able to relate to this overall position each of your arguments against specific parts of the affirmative case. A random selection of arguments should be avoided, and the audience should be able to understand how individual arguments fit into a coherent explanation of why the resolution should be rejected. Each argument will hold greater weight in deciding the debate if you can convince the judge that your claims justify a decision in your favor. Arguments often must be assessed in the context of relative impacts — weighing issue x against issue y — and a clear negative position gives the judge a framework in which to weigh and understand competing claims. If the negative offers price inflation (issue x) as a reason to reject oil price decontrol, it should do so in a conceptual manner that will defeat the affirmative's claim (y) that bureaucratic regulation should be avoided at all costs. Such ambiguous claims will be difficult for even the most experienced judge to resolve (for the negative) without the development of a negative position.

Improves Time Allocation. In academic debate, each side has from sixteen to twenty minutes to present its constructive arguments. From the standpoint of time alone, it is crucial for you, as the negative, to focus on those issues that hold the most promise of defeating the resolution. Otherwise, you may waste time on arguments that will do you little good even if you win them. A general view of the affirmative case will help you focus on the most important issues. It is strategically advantageous, for example, to concentrate on inherency arguments, as opposed to harm arguments, if your overall stance suggests that this approach is more likely to defeat the resolution.

Avoids Contradictions. The negative position should help you and your partner plan your arguments toward a common goal. This coordinated effort also should help you, as a team, avoid contradictions. If part of your position on the deregulation of oil prices is that price regulation is best for the consumer, then both of you should plan arguments consistent with this view. The first negative should not argue, for example, that the United States is now moving toward deregulation if the second negative is to argue that deregulation will result in great harms for the American people. An overall position used by both speakers should help you keep your agruments consistent.

Directs Research. The negative position also helps you target your research against particular affirmative cases. The number of different approaches that can be used to attack an affirmative case and the variety of research materials both far exceed the time for research available to the negative. The early development of a negative position allows you to begin your research with a clear notion of what you are researching and to be selective in your review, rather than requiring you to sift through many irrelevant documents in the hope of uncovering some usable arguments. One word of caution is needed here, though. The development of a negative position to direct your research assumes that you have already investigated the topic; otherwise, your knowledge of the topic may be too limited to decide on the best negative position.

Risks of Point-by-Point Debating

The coherent universal approach also should help you avoid the pitfalls of the most widely used alternative to a negative position — the point-by-point approach. Debaters who use this kind of attack usually have no organized view of the case; instead, they usually arrange a group of arguments around whatever evidence they have and hope for the best. They may decide, for example, to defend the present system on one harm, use a minor repair on another, and perhaps, in the first negative, run a counterplan on another. Second negatives may quickly decide which of their stock disadvantages they can present and use them in the hope that one or more will apply to the affirmative case. Although those using this approach may stumble into a consistent position, the odds are much higher that there will be a random attack. The point-by-point method has several inherent risks.

Risk of Contradictions. The first, and perhaps the greatest, risk is the possibility of contradictory arguments between the first and second negative. If you use a point-by-point approach, you could try to deny everything that the affirmative argues. On the oil deregulation topic, for example, the affirmative may argue that the nation is running out of oil and that removing the price ceilings will encourage industries to increase the prices of the present oil and use the increased profits to develop new resources. Further, the affirmative may argue that the failure to seek out these new resources will result in overdependence on foreign sources, as well as dangers from unemployment at home. In the absence of a well-developed position on price ceilings, you, as a first negative, may claim that overdependence on foreign markets is acceptable, and your partner, as a second negative, may try to prove that removing price ceilings will result in greater dependence on foreign sources. But an alert affirmative will point out that one of you is claiming that dependence on foreign sources is acceptable and that the other is asserting that it is not. This contradiction will put you in an awkward position and strengthen the affirmative position.

Difficulty of Assessing Argument Strength.   The second risk of the argument-by-argument approach is that it usually makes it hard for both the debaters and the listeners to determine the relative importance of the arguments. When arguments are presented randomly, without a close relationship to a general position, there may be no guidelines by which the listeners can distinguish those arguments crucial to deciding whether to adopt or reject the resolution.

In regard to the price ceiling example, the opponents can offer many objections to removing price restraints. They can argue that there is no harm in lower automobile usage because of the oil shortage, that price ceilings are essential to low-priced oil, that Americans should encourage more foreign consumption, and that removing the ceilings would merely deplete domestic sources that could be valuable in the future. If the negative's main position is that the consumer would be helped by regulation, then it will be easy for the listeners to discern that the second objection is the most important. But without this negative position, neither the debaters nor the listeners may see the relative importance of that argument. The major argument may be lost in the attack, and the result may be that none of the arguments seems overwhelmingly important. The negative's chances of obtaining a decision in its favor are greated reduced if the judge concludes that the arguments are not compelling.

Emphasis on Affirmative Strengths.   A final risk of the argument-by-argument approach is that it tends to emphasize the affirmative rather than the negative strengths. The affirmative usually develops a coherent position on the resolution by the very process of developing its case. If you, as the negative, merely respond point by point to the affirmative case, you will keep yourself within the affirmative position. Even if you present persuasive individual arguments, you will surrender to the affirmative perception of the broader issues and philosophies underlying the resolution. You will be responding to a point of view that the affirmative presumably chose because it was to its advantage. A developed negative position, on the other hand, gives you your own territory and permits you to distinguish the most important arguments given by both sides and not risk spending all of your time talking about the affirmative strengths. In addition, by developing your own position, you are better able to explore the different philosophies of policy which, in many cases, may contain your strengths. But if you use the point-by-point approach, you may preclude the examination of these alternatives because your claims will arise only from the specific arguments against the affirmative case.

Construction of the Position

Constructing a negative position requires several steps. Your effectiveness in developing an imaginative consistent position will depend on your ability to analyze, ask relevant questions about the resolution, and recognize the essential features of debate theory and technique. Although our suggested steps in developing the position are not usually followed as separate parts, we are dividing them here for the sake of convenience.

Use of Cognitive Skills

Our first recommendation is that you try to make maximum use of your skills for imaginatively obtaining and processing information. To devise unique negative positions, you must be able to deal with the affirmative case according to your knowledge of the topic and your critical and creative powers. Your effectiveness will hinge largely on your willingness to reorganize previous experiences in dealing with new situations argued by the affirmative. Obviously, you will need to search for information on the resolution. But it is equally important that you apply this knowledge to the affirmative case. You should look for variety and unconventionality in examining your information. Your aim should be to find unusual applications of your data in deciding on your negative position. In attacking a proposal guaranteeing national health insurance for all United States citizens, a conventional negative may argue that medical care will do little to decrease morbidity and mortality, since they are more a function of social considerations (for example, housing, sanitation, food) than of access to medical assistance. The conventional position may also argue that the proposal is too costly and would cut into other governmental expenditures. A marginally clever affirmative could defeat this position by proving that a significant number of deaths and illnesses could be eliminated under medical care and that the loss of other governmental programs would be outweighed by the lives saved. A more innovative and insightful negative, however, could prove that the government programs eliminated under national health insurance would be those devoted to improving social conditions and that the affirmative, though saving some lives with medical care, would cause a net increase in death and disability. By tying ideas and strategies to a central position that anticipates affirmative responses and incorporates answers to them, the negative can build a strong, consistent, and strategically defensible attack.

Steps in Constructing the Position

The development of the negative position has several cognitive stages, each of which is necessary in order to build the strongest negative attack possible. In a logical and recommended order, they are identifying the affirmative's central thesis, identifying the affirmative's unstated assumptions, identifying the affirmative's minimal proof requirements, identifying possible negative replies, and selecting arguments.

Identifying Affirmative's Central Thesis.   Your first step in developing a negative position is taking a comprehensive, analytic stance on the affirmative case and reducing the affirmative case to its central thesis so that you can explain in a few sentences its overall position. As in the negative position, the affirmative's central thesis will not be a mere listing of affirmative arguments. Rather, it will be a succinct statement of the affirmative's general frame of reference with respect to the resolution.

In regard to the oil price deregulation example, you could ask, "Is the affirmative claiming that there is a shortage of oil? What are the harms flowing from this shortage, and how are they related to price ceilings?" In regard to the plan, you could ask, "Is the plan to remove price ceilings within the resolution? How does the plan relate to the problem, the harms, and the inherency? What does the plan do?" In other words, you could raise questions that give you an overall view of the logic of the affirmative case.

Identifying Unstated Assumptions.   The next step is to identify the affirmative case's unstated assumptions. In almost every instance, the affirmative will construct its harms, inherency, and solution on assumptions that it expects its audience to accept without identification or critical examination. In the oil price controls debate, for example, those who called for removing all price ceilings usually assumed that it was generally harmful for the country to have less oil, that the effects of oil shortages on employment would be bad, or that there were no alternatives to increased oil production. In regard to inherency, most of those calling for removing all price ceilings assumed that price regulations always keep prices below market levels. They also usually assumed that profits and the profitability of oil production were the same, even though many analysts argue that the critical factor is not the total amount of profits made but the size of the investment required to generate a particular profit. In regard to the plan, those calling for removing price ceilings often assumed that the removal of price constraints would encourage the oil industry to find and market new sources of oil. The opponents of oil price decontrol had to identify and answer these kinds of unstated assumptions in formulating their position.

Identifying Affirmative's Minimum Proof Requirements.   The third step in establishing a negative position is deciding what arguments the affirmative must win in order to justify the resolution. These may include asserted arguments, unstated assumptions, and what is proved explicitly. One way to do this is to ask what the affirmative must win under each stock issue. Again, in the controversy over oil price controls, the affirmative had to be granted that the regulation of prices would improve the availability of gasoline. At the same time, the affirmative had to be granted that there were alternative sources of gasoline. In regard to the plan to remove controls, the affirmative had to be granted the argument that industry actually would use increased profits to explore for oil and produce more gasoline; otherwise, the American people would be left with the same problem that the affirmative proposal was designed to correct. In short, the negative should ask which arguments the affirmative must win on its case in order to win the round and then incorporate them into the construction of its negative position. At the same time, the negative should identify arguments that the affirmative does not need to win in order to win its position on the resolution. Generally, it is a waste of time to develop a negative position against arguments that the affirmative can yield without losing the debate.

Identifying Possible Negative Replies.   The fourth step is for you, as a negative, to identify the arguments that can serve as counterproofs to what the affirmative is arguing, what the affirmative is assuming, and what the affirmative is ignoring. You should identify as many arguments as possible under each key area that the affirmative must win in order to prove that the resolution should be adopted. You should then present those arguments that you think have the best chance of convincing the audience to reject the topic. For example, in the oil price control debate, those arguing for removing price restraints had to convince their audience that this would lead to more gasoline. Against this claim, many people argued that such action was not necessary because other actions would produce more exploration for oil and marketing of gasoline and that alternatives to gasoline, conservation, and rationing could be used. Once you have listed all of these kinds of arguments, you can choose which will enable you to defeat a particular issue that the affirmative must win in order to gain the decision. The most practical approach is to list under each argument the unstated assumptions that you can contest and all of your possible counterarguments. You should also consider how the affirmative is likely to respond to your position and what you will say next.

Selecting Arguments.   Finally, you must choose your arguments and synthesize them into a coherent statement of how you propose to attack the affirmative case. On any given case knowledgeable and imaginative debaters will have hundreds of arguments that they can advance as units of proof. Both time and psychological restraints will force you to be selective. You should consider several criteria in choosing your arguments.

   1. Select arguments consistent with your personal beliefs whenever possible. You need not avoid all arguments whose preponderance of evidence is on the other side. If this position were carried to the extreme, many significant issues would never be debated. Responsible advocates would be irresponsible if they presented only arguments they liked, even though other arguments may actually determine the truth of the resolution. Nonetheless, you will probably be more comfortable with those arguments to whose values you are committed.

2. Select arguments that enhance your position. You should keep in mind at least two major considerations in making this decision. The first is to choose claims that the affirmative evidence actually supports. When you can show the listeners that the affirmative evidence actually supports a negative claim, you will need to do less work and be more able to convince them of the negative position's validity. The second consideration is to choose claims supported by the most credible and complete evidence and the most logical warrants.

3. Whenever possible, choose arguments that are consistent with your judge's perception of reality. Some claims are harder to prove than others because they do not relate to the world as the listeners perceive it. There is considerable evidence that suggests that we expect new information to fit our past experiences. Whenever possible, keep your arguments within the listeners' frame of reference and do not present arguments that they will dismiss as unrealistic. This principle applies especially to arguments that are complicated and difficult to explain. The time restraints imposed by most debate formats limit the extent to which arguments involving long chains of reasoning can be used. When faced with a choice, you probably should choose the more readily believable and easily explainable arguments.

4. Choose arguments that you think best fit your judge's value system. People are more receptive to new ideas if they fulfill a known want or need and do not conflict with their values. In many cases, judges may be forced to choose between two values, both of which they respect. The debater who has chosen the value that the judge ranks more highly has distinct advantages.

5. Choose arguments on which you will get the benefit of the doubt if the results are uncertain. For example, a negative position that there are no harms to cigarette smoking is probably unwise. If the evidence is in dispute, the affirmative will get the benefit of the doubt since there is a reasonable risk of harm.

6. Finally, choose arguments that do not conflict with those of your partner. In regard to the oil price controls debate, even if the country were moving toward deregulation, the negative in the long run could lose psychological ground by making this argument in the first constructive speech and then arguing a disadvantage of deregulation in the second constructive speech.

After you have considered these guidelines, you must put the position into a coherent statement that will enable you to advance and sustain a consistent point of view. Your aim is to give the listeners a readily identifiable reason for rejecting the resolution. This outcome is possible only if the negative makes this position clear, carries it through the defense, and wins most of the units of proof supporting that position.

Uses of a Negative Position

As previously stated, the negative position evolves from the debaters' choices. When using this position, you should capitalize on both your own strengths and your opposition's weaknesses.

Introducing the Case

The first use of the negative position is usually the introduction to or overview of the negative case. Sometimes this is one simple statement. For instance, in the oil price controls example, you could say, "The affirmative calls for the abolition of all price ceilings on oil. The negative will defend the position that price ceilings on oil should be maintained as presently constituted." You could then outline the present system and contrast it with the affirmative proposal so that the judge can clearly distinguish between the two positions. Or, the negative position statement may be considerably longer and require more explanation. In the oil price controls case, you could claim at the outset that price ceilings are not only justified but also minimize harm to the consumer because regulation keeps production stable and prices low.

These examples should not imply that all negative position statements must commit the negative to defending a policy option. You may choose to use straight refutation and still present a position statement. Again, in the oil price example, you could say, "The affirmative calls for removing all price controls on oil. The negative position is that the affirmative proof does not verify their claims on their position." You then should show which claims lack either the evidence or the logic or both to sustain the affirmative position.

If you support a counterresolution — a policy option different from the present system or anything envisioned by the resolution — your position should follow logically from the affirmative claims (of need) but oppose the affirmative proposal. You should briefly review the affirmative policy and then state the alternative policy that you will defend. It is essential that you point out the key differences in the two proposals. In all instances, your aim in an opening statement is to secure a clear position before the listeners so that they can see the connection and importance of all arguments posited by the negative.

Your selection of a policy option, a straight refutation, or a counterresolution will depend on the affirmative claims offered and their relative strengths and weaknesses. The negative position may be any one or a combination of the above, depending on the negative's strategic assessments and analytical developments.

Linkage to Other Arguments

The second major use of the negative position is to use it to connect all the subsequent arguments made by the negative. As each argument is presented, you should refer back to the negative position. In the case of oil price controls, if the negative claims that price ceilings protect consumers from inflationary demands, you should remind the judge that this argument is consistent with the negative position that price regulation is not harmful and also is helpful to the general economy.

The connection of the negative position with all major arguments should also be carried into the second negative. Its use may become more specialized for the second negative, but it is just as relevant. Above all, the negative position should not be argued by the first negative and then dropped by the second negative. In the oil price controls debate, an example of a connected negative position is for the first negative to argue that price regulation does not harm consumers because such controls protect them from higher oil prices. The second negative may argue a disadvantage that claims that eliminating price restraints will cause inflation and eventually lead to a recession. In both cases the two speakers can show that both arguments connect with the general negative position that price restraints will be helpful to the economy.

Uses in Rebuttals

Finally, it is important that the negative position be carried into rebuttals. To do so, you must show the judge how each major argument relates to the negative position. This will also protect you from making unwise choices and keep before the judge the choice that he or she is asked to make. Otherwise, many good negative arguments may be lost in rebuttal because the judge misses the connection with the negative's overall position. An effective use of the negative position in rebuttal is to make a very brief statement of its salient parts after each major argument.

This does not mean that the negative has to repeat and reexplain each of its points. Such a strategy would waste time better spent on other issues and lower the credibility of the arguments. But it is important for the negative to emphasize and clarify the arguments that it hopes to win in rebuttals.

Summary

The concept of a position is the negative's general perspective on the affirmative proposal. In other words, it is the negative's overall stance on the resolution. The goal is to enhance both the debaters' and the judges' understanding of the different positions on the resolution taken by the affirmative and the negative.

The major benefits in using a negative position are in helping you maximize the impact of your arguments, allocate your speaking time, coordinate team efforts, target your research efforts, and, finally, avoid the pitfalls of point-by-point debating.

The best uses of a negative position are in helping you make strategic decisions about where to attack, how to attack, and what to argue through in rebuttals. The maximum use of the position approach comes through preround planning, extensive research, imaginative decisions, and coordination of effort during the debate.

Questions for Discussion

1. What are the difficulties of a point-by-point approach to refutation? How can the negative position overcome these difficulties?

2. What are the implications of developing a negative position that is inconsistent with the judge's value system?

3. Does the usefulness of the negative position depend on the paradigm of debate to which one subscribes? Why or why not?

4. Using the oil deregulation example discussed in the text, what are several possible negative positions? What are the strengths and drawbacks of each?

5. How does the negative position help the negative maximize its benefits and minimize its burdens?

6. Why should contradictory arguments be avoided? How can the negative position help avoid them?

Chapter 13

Negative Case Construction: Requirements

The affirmative must present, defend, and win four major issues on resolutions of policy in order to justify the adoption of the resolution. These issues are (1) does a significant problem exist that justifies a new policy? (2) is the resolution necessary to correct the problem? (3) does the affirmative proposal effectively deal with the problem? and (4) do the benefits of the affirmative proposal outweigh the disadvantages? These are often called stock issues because they are generally regarded as essential to the resolution.

If challenged, the affirmative must also prove that its solution of arguments in defense of the resolution really lies in affirmative land. Thus, in addition to the four stock issues, the affirmative often faces a jurisdictional question: do the affirmative arguments actually lie within their resolutional territory?

As we said in Chapter 2, issues are questions vital to the resolution. The negative, therefore, must win the greater probability of truth on only one of them in order to justify the rejection of the resolution. If you prove, for example, that the affirmative proposal is not necessary to correct the alleged problem, then all other stock questions are moot. A no answer to this one question proves the resolution is not true and, thus, should be rejected.

In this chapter, we shall discuss several techniques to aid you in constructing a negative case. Our suggestions are designed to help you prove that the affirmative has failed to meet its burdens on one or more of the issues.

We assume that at this point in your preparation you will have arrived at a negative position around which you will construct all your arguments against the stock issues. Furthermore, we assume that your goal is to test the probable truth of a resolution offered by the affirmative as a hypothesis for solving a problem. Many of our suggested techniques, however, apply equally to situations in which you may be trying to persuade judges who believe that your job is to present a

191

single alternative policy to be compared with the affirmative proposal. Many of these techniques are also appropriate for the stock issues judge who is primarily concerned with determining which side did the better debating.

Jurisdiction

In debating the substantive issues of a resolution, it is first sometimes necessary for you, as a negative, to settle jurisdictional disputes. As we saw in Chapter 8, a major purpose of framing a resolution's specific wording is to help determine which arguments lie in affirmative land and which in negative land. Arguments on one side are closed off to the other. Disputes often arise over the jurisdiction of certain arguments. When you, as a negative, feel that the affirmative has presented arguments outside its jurisdiction, you should challenge the legitimacy of the affirmative position. You should issue this challenge early in the debate, as you will waste time arguing substantive matters with the affirmative if they are not resolutional. And to do so will not test the probable truth of the resolution, since the affirmative will be using arguments that do not support the resolution at hand.

In academic debate, three distinct jurisdictional disputes are common: topicality, extratopicality, and justification. A much less common jurisdictional dispute is the question of counterwarrants.

Topicality

Topicality centers on whether the affirmative actually defends the resolution. As we explained in Chapter 8, there are three circumstances in which the affirmative may fail to be topical. First, the affirmative will occasionally be factually inaccurate. For example, if the resolution calls for the federal government to reduce the powers of labor unions, the affirmative will not be topical if it calls for the reduction of a power that the labor unions do not already possess. Simply by its carelessness in handling factual information, the affirmative in this case is not testing the resolution. As a negative, you should question, at your first opportunity, this affirmative mistake.

Second, topicality disputes often arise over the meaning of words in the resolution. This is perhaps the most common topicality dispute, chiefly because the key words in many resolutions have many meanings. Consider the resolution that the United States should strengthen its foreign military commitments. One possible definition of a foreign military commitment is a situation in which the United States committed more military support to other countries. But it could be argued that a U.S. commitment to American troops stationed abroad is also a foreign military commitment. Likewise, *strengthen* could mean "to increase resources" or "to prune away excess." In these situations, there is more likely to be a topicality challenge over the second definition. You are warned, however, that alternative definitions do not necessarily discredit the affirmative's definition. The outcome of a clash over definitions will depend on the supporting claims advanced by both sides in defense of their positions. For the negative to win its point of view, it usually must present its own standards for topicality and win the supporting arguments on their behalf. Below are listed some possible options for the negative in establishing standards.

Most Reasonable Definition.   One standard you can set is to claim that the affirmative should advance the most reasonable definition. When you argue this position, you try to win the claim that *a* reasonable definition is not enough. Instead, you argue that the affirmative is obligated to advance the *most* reasonable definition. Usually, debaters making this claim argue that the best definition grows out of the resolution's context. On the foreign military commitment resolution, for example, you could argue that when students of international relations, as well as those directly involved in foreign policy making, discuss U.S. foreign policy commitments, they usually mean that the United States is making a commitment to a foreign country. You could claim that they would almost never interpret the word *commitment* to apply to Americans stationed abroad.

Negative debaters who argue against the reasonableness standard and demand that the judge resolve topicality on the basis of the best definition should be aware of several possible objections. Affirmative abuse of the term *reasonable* is usually argued on the grounds that reasonable is too subjective or ambiguous; however, that places a burden on the negative to find a clear and objective interpretation of the best definition. The negative must be prepared to offer an example that meets its criteria of best. Otherwise, many negative debaters would establish standards that are difficult, unfair, or impossible for any affirmative to meet. For example, suppose that the debate resolution calls for the federal government to take regulatory measures to enhance environmental quality. The negative could argue that since *quality* is an ambiguous term, the affirmative must use the best definition of quality. Further, the negative could insist that the best definition of quality is one that receives the unanimous endorsement of experts in the field of environmental studies. Obviously, it is unlikely that the affirmative will find a definition of quality unanimously accepted by scholars in the field. Hence, what first appears to be an unreasonable affirmative is quickly overshadowed by a highly unreasonable topicality demand.

Limiting the Scope of Debate.   You could also argue that a major function of the resolution is to limit the scope of the debate. From this position, you could argue that just any possible definition is unacceptable. If the affirmative assumes this position, it may well lead to a situation in which anything it wishes to propose will be topical. The resolution then will not limit the relevant subjects for discussion. One example of this kind of standard is a resolution calling for greater control of land use in the United States. If the affirmative defines *land* as "anything under, on, or above the earth," then it can propose any conceivable action; the scope of the debate is unlimited.

Such broad definitions may make it impossible for a negative to be prepared to debate unles it has extensive warning of the example of land use that the affirmative may offer. Furthermore, it may be impossible to test the truth of any resolution. If a term means too many things, then it may have no meaning or life of its own. In this circumstance, you could argue that the affirmative is obligated to present a definition that narrows the scope of the debate, in order for meaningful discussion to emerge.

Common Man Standard.   Another standard you can use in challenging definitions is to argue that the common-knowledge definition is best. Under this standard, you insist that the topic be defined in accordance with those definitions that the average intelligent person would propose if he or she were exposed to the topic without any discussion. Again, consider the topic calling for increased federal control of labor unions. If the affirmative presents a case calling the American Bar Association a labor union, you could challenge this definition on the grounds that such associations are rarely perceived as labor unions by most educated people.

Parameter.   In recent years, the committee drafting the topics for intercollegiate debating has submitted, along with the resolution, a statement detailing their opinions of the topic's meanings. Although the committee readily admits that their interpretation is not binding, many debaters argue that it should be. Likewise, at the high school level, the committee that words the resolution also frames a statement of the problem area, in the form of a question to which the resolution is one answer. Like the parameter statement at the college level, the statement of the problem area is intended to place the resolution in context. Some argue that the parameter statement sets a reasonable limitation on the topic which enhances the possibility for an intelligent debate. It is often claimed that the committee's statement is free from the restraints on meanings of words that often result from a competitive bias during a debate. For this reason, many claim that if all debaters stay within the parameter, jurisdictional disputes will be minimal, and the debate can focus on more substantive issues.

Judicial Standard.   Another possible standard is the *judicial* definition, or that drawn from court decisions. In applying this standard, you should argue that the courts are in the business of defining words. Furthermore, in interpreting the meanings of words, courts rarely use dictionary definitions but instead consider the legislation surrounding the context of words. For a resolution dealing with federal control of labor unions, for example, you could argue that it is unreasonable to refer to the American Bar Association as a labor union, since the courts define such groups as associations or professions. Instead, the courts often define labor unions in much the same way as do legislative bodies. Legislation referring to labor unions usually refers to organizations in which employees bargain collectively with employers on such matters as wages, working conditions, and fringe benefits.

Defending All Terms.   Finally, you should challenge the affirmative on topicality when its example of the resolution does not encompass all of the key words of the resolution. Your chief standard for making this challenge should be based on the grounds that each word has a special meaning. Therefore, the resolution will not get a true test unless the affirmative defends all of the key terms. For example, suppose that the affirmative advances a resolution calling for the federal government to place stricter controls on the gathering and use of information in the United States. In its case supporting this resolution, the affirmative plan deals only with controls on the use of information. You should argue that the affirmative is not topical because its case does not consider both the gathering and the use of information.

Extratopicality

Topicality concerns whether the affirmative actually supports the resolution with arguments that lie within its territory. Extratopicality is whether the affirmative's advantage or the solution of its problem actually accrues from the resolution or from some other source. An affirmative advantage, for example, is said to be extratopical if it does not stem from the resolution.

One challenge to extratopicality may grow out of elements in the affirmative plan, not required by the resolution, that actually become the bases of the affirmative benefit. For example, suppose that the resolution calls for significantly increasing the energy independence of the United States. The affirmative claims an advantage of increasing foreign food aid as a result of its proposal. The affirmative has a plank in its plan calling for an increase in gasoline taxes as a means of securing funds for the food aid. You could argue that the advantage is extratopical because it stems from the transferral of money gained from the gasoline tax and not from the increase in energy independence. In fact, you could even use a counterresolution to eliminate the affirmative advantage. You could propose to tax cigarettes (or any other commodity) and give the revenues to food aid, proving that there is no specific need to increase energy independence.

A second extratopical dispute often arises when the resolution offers a necessary, but not a sufficient, condition for the advantage claimed by the affirmative. Suppose that the affirmative calls for decreasing the power of teachers' unions in the public schools on the grounds that the unions oppose instruction on cardiac pulmonary resuscitation (CPR). The affirmative claims that this instruction is needed. As the negative you could argue that overcoming the power of the teachers' unions may be necessary to obtain this instruction if, indeed, their opposition is a major force in blocking it now but that instituting CPR instruction also would require many other actions unrelated to the labor unions. The affirmative will also include provisions for training qualified personnel, equipment for CPR education, and money for the program (something that the school board, rather than the teachers' union, had probably objected to). A decrease in the power of the teachers' unions becomes an incidental effect in the massive CPR program.

Therefore, the resolution is a necessary, but not a sufficient, condition to ensure the affirmative benefit.

Justification

Justification arguments assume that it is the burden of the affirmative to endorse, and also to give reasons for endorsing, all key terms in the resolution. Your main standard for making justification arguments is simply that every word has both a distinct meaning and a distinct reason for being in the resolution. Therefore, if the specific wording of the resolution has not been defended, that resolution should be defeated. The affirmative will have failed to establish the probable truth of the hypothesis that it was assigned to defend. For example, if the resolution calls for the federal government to initiate and enforce safety guarantees on consumer goods and you, as the negative, can prove that it is unnecessary to enforce safety guarantees, you can claim that the resolution should be rejected.

You are also urged to keep an eye on nonresolutional alternatives. For example, a key question on inherency is the relationship between the resolution and the problem. Without the resolution, will the problem be solved? If the resolution in its entirety is not required to solve the problem, then the question is answered to the negative's benefit, and the resolution is unjustified. For example, a resolution calling for the federal government to mandate self-extinguishing cigarettes may involve several justification questions: (1) Is it necessary for the federal government to do the job? Perhaps the states could adopt the affirmative proposal. (2) Is the term *enforce* justified? Perhaps the federal government is not needed to enforce the use of the self-extinguishing cigarettes. (3) Are consumer goods necessary? It could be argued that one could simply ban cigarettes, making the resolution totally unwarranted. Of course, each of these possibilities must have a fully-developed negative argument in order for the justification challenge to carry weight.

Counterwarrants

There has been a recent development in jurisdictional disputes in the use of counterwarrants. Though few critics espouse this approach, the technique is being used by a few debaters. Counterwarrants are examples of the resolution, presented by the negative, that allegedly warrant the resolution's rejection. Essentially, those who use counterwarrants as jurisdiction attacks argue that the affirmative has selected an unrepresentative example of the resolution for its test. Testing a truly representative example, such as the negative introduces, makes it clear that the resolution should be rejected. The underlying logic here is that although the resolution may be supported by reference to an example, it is ultimately the resolution, rather than the example, that will be endorsed. Even if one atypical example supports the resolution, a representative example does not. For example, the affirmative defends the resolution calling for increased military commitments abroad by urging that more funds be spent to improve the recreational facilities for

American soldiers in Europe. The counterwarrants proponent contends that increasing the number of nuclear weapons in Europe is a far more representative example of the resolution and that on the basis of this better example, the resolution should be defeated.

The affirmative's major response to counterwarrants is to argue that the negative is imposing an unreasonable standard on the nature of the topic. The essence of this answer is that using broad resolutions calling for change does not mean that the affirmative must justify every change. For example, rarely does the resolution call for all possible increases or decreases in any course of action. In the foreign military commitment example, it is reasonable to assume that it may be true that we should make some additional commitments but equally true that we probably should not adopt every conceivable increased military commitment. Thus, counterwarrants may place an unreasonable interpretation on the meaning of the term *should adopt*. We can opt for a major change in a given policy without opting for all possible changes.

A simple example further exposes the logical fallacies of a negative arguing counterwarrants. Suppose that you are considering a resolution that advocates going to the store to buy fruit. You (as an affirmative debater) have selected oranges as your example of the resolution, since you like oranges, need them, and can afford them. The negative argues that you should reject going to the store to buy fruit, since you are allergic to apples, cannot afford grapes, and hate plums. These examples do nothing to deny the desirability of going to the store for oranges, and since oranges fall within the jurisdiction of buying fruit, do nothing to disprove the original resolution.

Finally, the pragmatic implications of a counterwarrants strategy may degrade the quality of analysis in a debate, turning the resolutional test into an academic nightmare. Given the broad nature of many debate propositions, the testing of a resolution by the use of all, the best, the most topical, or simply the most, examples may make the debate a simple listing of examples and disadvantages, avoiding substantive discussion on any policy issues that may be incidentally involved. Although other strategies, such as the misuse of conditional counterplans, jurisdictional disputes, or even the straight refutation approach, may result in similar faults, the counterwarrants approach appears especially to encourage this sort of shallow debate. The argument that such a strategy is merely a function of, or necessitated by, broad-based topics, is of little comfort to a judge who must resolve this morass of competing claims. The affirmative who effectively advances this criticism of the counterwarrants approach may find much agreement among many critics.

Significance of the Problem

In attempting to justify its need for a change in policy, most affirmatives will describe a problem in which an alleged fundamental flaw is claimed to be producing significant harms to society or at least is denying society significant benefits in the absence of the resolution. Usually the affirmative will attempt to demonstrate this significance in either qualitative or quantitative terms or both. Quantitative significance involves tangible harms to individuals that can be measured or estimated by the number of people affected and by the degree of harm in loss of life, money, health, and other physical items. Qualitative significance establishes a threat to intangible aspects of human life, such as loss of freedom, virtue, or other qualities valued by individuals or society as a whole.

Alternative Value Judgments

As a negative speaker, you may often wish to try to minimize the significance of the affirmative harm or benefits. One approach is to establish a different value judgment as being of higher importance. Establishing countervailing values hinges on demonstrating that the affirmative's harms are based on value judgments that should play a secondary role to other values. Often, the affirmative significance will grow out of threats to life, property, or human rights. Suppose that the affirmative's plan, for example, is based on a case in which invasion of privacy through the use of wiretapping is needed to save lives. You can argue that the right to privacy should take precedence and that this competing value would be injured by the affirmative plan.

You can also sometimes challenge affirmative values on the grounds that they should be discounted because they involve harms that the individual voluntarily chooses to endure. Suppose that the affirmative calls for a ban on cigarettes on the grounds that smoking is harmful to health. You could argue that although health is important, the right to make one's own choices is a more important value than life itself.

You may also choose to minimize the importance of qualitative significance by attacking its subjective nature and establishing quantitative significance as being the only true objective standard. The negative may claim, for example, that only a serious threat to many lives can justify change, not the possibility that some individuals will gain a greater freedom to act. Your emphasis is on the fact that you can observe the number of people saved from death, but you may never know how much increased freedom would have resulted from a given act.

Logical Issues.   Causal argument should not be confused with the claim that a change in A is followed by, or in some way connects with, a change in B. The latter is a correlation illustrating that the presence of A tends to be associated with the presence of B. Suppose, for example, that the affirmative claims that smoking causes heart attacks. You could challenge this causal link by showing that many people who smoke do not have heart attacks. To claim a direct causal link between the two, the affirmative must show that all other factors that can cause heart attacks have been controlled for in studies or that the effects of other factors are negligible. Therefore, if you can show that hypertension, heredity, and other factors also correlate with a high incidence of heart attacks, you have set causality aside and may even have cast doubt on the correlation between smoking and heart attacks.

Methodological Issues.   Sometimes you will also wish to take a careful look at the researcher's methods in studies that find a causal relationship between harms and present problems. One area of overstatement is one in which your opponent takes a conclusion derived from a small sample and generalizes it to a broader population. You should be alert to the twofold nature of the inference that your opponent is making: first, that the smaller population is a representative sample of the large one and, second, that the relationships and conditions in the experimental and natural environments are the same. You should examine the methodology and make sure that these inferences are justified.

You should also be alert to possible sample errors when the affirmative cites studies in which its conclusions have been made in situations in which two or more "independent" variables are correlated. An example is an instance in which the affirmative claims that achievement tests are an accurate predictor of academic success. Such variables as family income and ambition can also affect the outcome; yet it may be virtually impossible to control one of these factors because they are closely correlated. Social scientists claim that this type of correlation is spurious because the chance for sampling errors is infinite. Even when the best methods for selecting the sample have been used, events that happened long before the sample was taken can affect the outcome.

You should also carefully examine the controls on experimental findings used as studies to justify significance. Sometimes adequate controls do not exist. Sometimes the relationship between certain variables cannot be tested in an uncontrolled environment. Yet often the environment cannot be properly controlled. Many studies, for example, are conducted over a period of time. If a group of people are being tested over a period of years for the effects of alcohol on their bodies, it cannot be assumed that each will have the same experiences each day in all respects. People will be exposed to different sets of environmental conditions that may have an influence on their emotional behavior that cannot be attributed to alcohol.

In objecting to the type of uncontrolled studies described above, you can strengthen your objection by using two other types of arguments. First, you can suggest that other causes may work jointly with the affirmative's asserted cause to create the harm and that we cannot be certain that these other causes will not still cause the harm, even in the absence of the affirmative's cause. We usually refer to these other causes as *multiple causalities*. An example of the multiple causalities argument arose when debaters considered a resolution calling for a guaranteed annual income. The negative teams argued that affirmative studies that asserted a link between malnutrition and inadequate income did not control for dietary ignorance among the poor and that such ignorance perpetuated poor nutrition even after the affirmative plan was adopted.

Second, you can argue that some factor other than the affirmative's cause is the real cause of the problem. In this situation, your factor is an alternate causality because it excludes the affirmative cause from any relationship with the harm. An example is a claim by the affirmative that oil companies are not exploring for more gas because low profits do not permit such expenditures. You can discount this causal relationship if you can show that the companies have invested profits during the same period in other enterprises. Then you can argue that the real reason for the lack of investment is the incentive to withhold gas, provided by the economics of industries that control the market. If you can explain away the affirmative's empirical relationship as being the result of some other event, then the cause-and-effect claim usually falls.

General Tests.   When the affirmative claims that one event causes another, the negative should ask at least five questions: (1) Is the relationship between the two events one of causation or merely statistical correlation? (2) Are the researcher's methods adequate to support the existence in the real world of a causal relationship between the two events? (3) Does the first event involve factors that coexist in all situations in a way that makes impossible adequate controls for one or the other factors? (4) Does the existence of a causal relationship between the two events depend on outdated evidence? (5) Can events other than those argued by the affirmative either be working with or working to the exclusion of the affirmative events in causing a second outcome? If the answer to one or more of these questions is yes, then the causal link in the affirmative claim is dubious.

Outdated Evidence

A third challenge to the affirmative's claims based on the relationship between harm and present policies is the use of outdated evidence. You can introduce new evidence that would have negated the argument of the affirmative's findings had the newer evidence been considered. For example, if the affirmative claims that the nation will be out of oil by a given time but fails to include evidence that proves there are significant new findings of oil, then you will have a valid challenge to the conclusion. Of course, on some topics — such as fundamental social values — evidence never is outdated. On the other hand, when a description or forecast of empirical conditions is involved, evidence can very quickly become obsolete.

Inherency of the Problem

The affirmative will have to demonstrate that there is a fundamental flaw in negative land that calls for action stated in the resolution to solve the problem. In addition to disputing this claim by minimizing the harms, you may attempt to show that the problem is not inherent. A pattern of analysis similar to the one we urged on the affirmative in Chapter 9 can be used here.

Analyzing the Affirmative Inherency

Before you can launch any meaningful attack on the affirmative inherency, you must first answer two important questions: (1) what are the essential features of the negative territory? and (2) what is the causal link, if any, between the negative territory and the affirmative alleged problem?

Identifying Essential Features.   The first step is to identify the essential features of your own negative land. The next step is to see if a barrier exists between the negative land and the solution of the affirmative problem. If the affirmative calls for the legalization of marijuana, then you will probably find that your argumentative territory consists of present policies that make such sales illegal. Then the question is whether the affirmative's advantages can be gained while marijuana sales remain illegal. It may be possible to solve the affirmative's problem by means other than the affirmation of the resolution.

Assessing the Causal Relationship.   The next step in answering the basic inherency question is to see if the affirmative has indeed established a causal relationship between the core of negative land and the problem. It may not be necessary to change the core of negative land to correct the problem. For example, if the federal government cannot or will not act, perhaps the state governments can. Or, if the federal government is not acting in an affirmative direction under present policy, perhaps it can act through another nonresolutional policy. Finally, if administrative agencies cannot surmount the bureaucracy, then perhaps the courts can solve the problem. All of these arguments are aimed at showing that forces outside the resolution have the motives and/or means to solve the problem isolated by the affirmative.

Challenging the Affirmative Inherency

Once you have identified the alleged relationship between the negative land and the affirmative problem, you should be ready to consider possible challenges to the validity of the affirmative inherency claims. In developing your attacks, you should consider one or more of the options below.

Minor Changes.   One way to show that the agents or motives are not sufficient to perpetuate the problem is to demonstrate that minor changes that will eliminate the problem can be made within negative land. If this argument is true, you will have proved that the affirmative's proposal need not be adopted in order to solve the problem. Of course, such minor repairs should be nontopical, or they would lie outside negative land. Many theorists argue that these can be presented conditionally. If the affirmative can stipulate by fiat that its proposal should be considered as if it were adopted, then the negative may make a similar stipulation with regard to its minor repairs. In our view, fiat simply means that neither the affirmative nor the negative has to prove that the changes will be adopted; only that they should be. These conditional counterarguments are not proposed as policy options, but merely as a device to show that the affirmative's resolution is not needed and that the affirmative's agents cannot prohibit nonresolutional changes. All such minor repairs, of course, depend on the scope of the resolution. Many such repairs simply call for more money, personnel, minor changes in enforcement procedures, or increased action through another agency other than the one offered by the affirmative. If the affirmative calls for greater support from the federal government for medical care, the negative could attempt to show that the increased use of private and state money can solve the problem, assuming, of course, that the repairs are nonresolutional.

A word of caution is necessary. It is not always easy to distinguish between a minor repair and an inherent change in policy. Suppose, for example, that the affirmative argues for a resolution requiring that the United States change its foreign trade policies. The affirmative argues for the removal of American trade barriers on domestic manufacturing industries on the grounds that this policy is needed to improve the economies of the less-developed countries as a means of supplying them with export markets. The negative argues that such drastic changes in trade policy are unnecessary and that the economies of the less-developed countries can be helped by extending their debts or by simply giving them more foreign aid. In this context, the negative proposes these changes as minor repairs and argues that they are nontopical extensions of current programs that can alleviate the affirmative harm. Although such changes may or may not be effective and although the minor versus major nature of the dispute may vary with annual congressional appropriations or political attitudes, the repairs can be reasonably defended as minor. The negative offers nonresolutional alternatives that do not conflict with the structure or attitudes of the present system.

Using the above example, suppose that the negative suggests that the United States grant massive subsidy incentives to private industries to export raw materials to less-developed countries at a lower cost. The goal is to improve the less-developed countries' export capacities and economies. Such a change is topical because it proposes an enormous revision in American foreign trade policy. If the affirmative can win this, the repair will be rejected as illegitimate.

Other Motives.   Another option in your challenge to inherency is to question the affirmative's indictment of present agents. The negative can show other motives by the indicted agents that point to an opposite direction. If the affirmative's proposal calls for the elimination of all price restraints on oil, based on the argument that present policies discourage exploration, you can point to the exploration efforts currently under way. Or, you can argue that agents not isolated by the affirmative have countervailing motives and mechanisms that can solve the problem. In the oil example above, you could argue that the oil company's fear of nationalization encourages them to keep oil production high. Finally, you can argue that other agents outside the control of the resolution are causing the problem. Again, in the case of the oil price decontrol resolution, the negative could argue that the real problem lies with foreign governments that the affirmative proposal would not affect.

False Inherencies.   You should also be careful of false inherencies. Occasionally the affirmative will argue an existential inherency in which it merely argues that a harm exists whose fundamental cause cannot be determined but that can be solved by the plan. Your obvious response is that the affirmative cannot guarantee a solution, since it cannot identify who is causing the problem. On other occasions, the affirmative may offer plans that rely on the same agents whose motives now block nonresolutional solutions. Such advocates usually rely on a "magic wand" concept of fiat power to get their proposals adopted. This view of fiat ignores our admonition that fiat is but a convention and that the program would be adopted through normal persuasive channels. You should certainly question whether a change in attitudes will actually occur once this concept of fiat is effected and day-to-day operation under the plan provisions commence.

Strategic Choices

You should watch for several limitations of negative inherency argumentation. The foremost, perhaps, is the existence of an inevitable strategic choice. You should evaluate the inherency arguments and compare them with plan attacks that could defeat the resolution. It is extremely easy to get caught in an awkward dilemma. For example, if you argue that the present system is correcting the problem, you should not at the same time claim disadvantages to correcting the problem. (You may, of course, allege unique disadvantages to the particular method by which the affirmative tries to solve the problem.) Another pitfall to guard against is the overuse of repair mechanisms that are offered with little or no evidence. Overdoing them may place you in another dilemma. The judge is left to choose between a mechanism without evidence to solve the problem in negative land and actual documented plan-meet-need evidence offered by the affirmative. You should also be certain that your minor repairs are not resolutional under a reasonable definition of the resolution — particularly under an effect-oriented resolution that specifies only the final outcome. For example, if the resolution calls for the federal government to adopt policies to increase energy independence, many advocates may claim that any mechanism that achieves such energy independence is topical.

Ultimately, the negative's success in defeating inherency arguments depends on its development and use of a consistent theory of inherency. This book stresses the hypothesis-testing theory as a desirable and coherent explanation. It emphasizes the negative search for causality and in so doing tries to force the affirmative to show why the resolution is necessary to correct the problem. Those listeners who subscribe to the stock-issues system paradigm will certainly view inherency arguments as an absolute voting issue, but only if the negative can show that the present system cannot solve the problem. Those who adhere to the policy-making paradigm will probably, at most, view inherency as a factor affecting the relative risks in the policies being discussed. The policy maker, with a focus on plan provisions and relative policy benefits, will consider inherency in the context of systems comparisons and may downplay the emphasis on causality and core motives.

Adequacy of the Solution

As argued in Chapter 9, the affirmative must demonstrate that taking the action suggested by the resolution will solve the problem or accrue the advantage offered as a rationale for change. This task is normally attempted by detailing a plan that attempts to remove or circumvent the core barriers in negative land and that then demonstrates how these resolutional changes will solve the problem. These changes are varied — legalistic action, jurisdictional shifts, and changes in institutional roles, to name a few. The negative has a number of options in disputing the affirmative claim that its proposal will solve the problem. One option is to argue that the affirmative's suggested resolutional change is actually nontopical, as we discussed above. In essence, the listener is asked to reject the resolution because the affirmative failed to present the resolution that is supposed to be debated on that particular occasion. The two major types of argument against the adequacy of a solution are, however, plan-meet-need arguments and disadvantages. The remainder of this section will examine each of these basic approaches.

Plan-Meet-Need Arguments

You can argue that the affirmative proposal will not meet the need. Usually this type of attack is directed toward the plan's structure.

Types of Plan-Meet-Need Arguments.   One type of attack relies on the absence of something necessary for the plan's successful operation. You will usually present the affirmative proposal as dependent on a chain of circumstances and then show that a missing link in the plan will permanently prevent the entire plan from working. For example, suppose that the affirmative is calling for a federal program that will convert the nation's energy production to nuclear power. You could argue that this energy program depends on a specific amount of uranium, which you will attempt to show does not exist in sufficient supplies. You then will argue that such chronic material shortages will prevent the plan from working. Or you may be able to show that some other cause of the problem will not be affected by the plan.

   Another form of plan-meet-need argumentation involves agents whose motives and means are to be changed or used in the plan. You can sometimes argue that the plan will not solve the problem because it will be circumvented by those whom the plan hopes to affect. This argument is particularly effective when the negative can show that those opposed to a course of action have been left with a means of getting around the proposal. For example, if the affirmative claims that under the law, labor unions do not want to report accidents on the job, they will find ways of not reporting under other laws as well.

Closely akin to the circumvention type of argument is the *cooptation* argument. The negative attempts to show that even if the proposal is adopted, the designated agents will not enforce it faithfully. In both instances, the negative points to a reemergence, under the plan, of agents with bad motives and means identified by the affirmative inherency. The plan's effect on various actors may or may not be obvious but should not be overlooked. The affirmative will, or should be forced to, clarify the intent of certain relevant plan provisions. You should examine such statements for factors that will block the plan's intent — an agent's motive and a means for expressing it. Sometimes you can show that the attempted failure will produce conditions actually worse than any alleged affirmative harm.

Constructing the Argument.   In constructing a plan-meet-need argument, you must be sure to explain the barrier that will prevent the affirmative plan from solving the problem. Your obligation here is similar to the affirmative's obligation in demonstrating inherency when a human agent is involved. You should show both the motive and means for the agent to block the solution of the need, after first indicating what the affirmative proposal attempts. One such plan-meet-need argument against a plan that prohibits the sale of alcohol on Sunday so as to reduce drinking could be presented as follows:

I. Plan-Meet-Need: The affirmative proposal will not reduce alcohol consumption.
   A. The proposal attempts to decrease consumption by curtailing Sunday sales.
   B. Drinkers will circumvent the sales restriction.
      1. Their motive rests on their psychological or physiological addiction to alcohol.
      2. They can circumvent the proposal by buying alcohol in another state, buying illegally produced alcohol, or buying more on other days.
   C. As a result, the proposal will not decrease alcohol consumption but will merely shift sales.

The ideal plan-meet-need argument is the plan's total failure to solve the problem. Few plans, however, are completely without efficacy. Realizing this however, should not discourage plan-meet-need attacks. Those that demonstrate that a plan does not meet a substantial part of its need may effectively reduce the level of significance that the affirmative may claim. This reduced level may be outweighed by your disadvantages, thereby enabling you to defeat the resolution. For example, if the affirmative calls for a plan that creates jobs for 100,000 people, it is possible that the first negative will show that only 50,000 jobs are needed. The second negative may show that the plan can create only 20,000 jobs as well as present a disadvantage whose effect is to eliminate 30,000 jobs, thereby removing any affirmative advantage. The negative should defend the desired impact of the plan-meet-need and its relationship to other arguments presented in the debate.

Plan Specifics.   Attacks on the deficiencies of the plan's specific provisions, apart from those that implement specific actions contemplated by, and the general philosophy embodied in, the resolution, are important to some listeners but are inconsequential to others. We view incidental problems with affirmative plans as minor shortcomings and not worthy of the time spent for negative attack. If the proposal is otherwise desirable, the plan can always be amended later if it is found to be defective or to create other problems. In other words, a plan's crucial provisions are those that implement the resolution and its underlying principles. Plans may do more than that, of course. But just as the extra features of a plan cannot offer valid reasons to favor a resolution (since those features are not essential to the resolution), by the same token they cannot offer valid reasons to reject a resolution, either. This perspective eliminates many problems of extratopical plan provisions, because the advantages or shortcomings of plan planks that are not part of the program implied by the resolution are not relevant to the ultimate acceptance or rejection of the resolution. A specific financing method, for example, is important only to the extent that it is an essential part of the resolution itself.

We hasten to note that many judges do not agree with the above interpretation of the plan. Many initially view the plan as defining the resolution and regard any deficiency in the plan as grounds for rejecting the resolution. Although we view problems with the plan as insignificant unless they apply intrinsically to the resolution, the policy maker is likely to see any deficiencies in the plan as offsetting its benefits. The reason is largely that the policy-making judge must choose between the affirmative and negative plans rather than judging the probable truth or falsity of the resolution.

Disadvantages

Disadvantages are a second major form of argument against the adequacy of the affirmative's solution. Disadvantages are an effort to maximize the importance of the potential costs of any attempt to solve the problem through the mechanism offered by the affirmative.

One view of a disadvantage is to view it as an affirmative advantage flipped on its side. The disadvantage must be inherent in the resolution (or in the plan if one believes in that point of view). In other words, there is no way to have the resolution and avoid the harm. Moreover, the disadvantages must be unique. It is not a disadvantage to adopt the resolution if the harm is going to result under any system. Finally, the disadvantage must truly result in a significant harm. Like the affirmative advantages, the harm can grow out of a number of sources, such as a lack of cost effectiveness, program effectiveness, or distorted priorities. In short, it must offer a greater threat to the values that the affirmative seeks to protect or threaten the alternative values that the negative claims should be given a higher priority. Disadvantages are constructed and presented in a manner analogous to that for affirmative advantages.

Types of Disadvantages.   The hypothesis-testing judge seeks disadvantages that are intrinsic to the resolution. They are called *generic disadvantages* because they apply generally to any plan that the affirmative may devise for setting up its program. These disadvantages are often a trade-off within the resolution. The judge is often asked to choose between effectiveness in fighting crime and increased invasion of privacy or to choose between increased unemployment and increased inflation.

Other types of disadvantages apply only to the particular affirmative plan presented in the round. Often the debater will argue as a disadvantage that the plan creates an unforeseen harm. An example of this type of harm is one in which the affirmative calls for a federal program to feed starving people in the Third World. The negative argues that feeding people now will merely lead to overpopulation, thus producing ten times more people to starve in the future.

The negative also often argues disadvantages that allege that the harm will simply be shifted from one area to another. For example, if the affirmative calls for a program to eliminate barbituates, the negative may argue that people will simply shift to alcohol or cigarettes, thus causing greater harm than the significance claimed by the affirmative. Another example is a case in which the affirmative argues for the release of prisoners and the negative argues that such a policy will result in a greater harm to the community, by releasing criminals.

Finally, you may claim disadvantage from the plan's antagonizing effects on powerful agents. Proposed government interference in the economy, through increased regulation, for example, allegedly will result in a loss of business confidence, leading to decreased production, a loss of jobs, and ultimately more death and suffering than the condition described by the affirmative will.

Constructing Disadvantages.   In setting up your disadvantage, you should give attention to both the source of the harm and the structure of the argument. The source of the harm, for example, should be clear, and the effect of the disadvantage should be unmistakably a harm. Such arguments as "The affirmative proposal costs money" are examples of what many judges consider to be an insignificant harm. But such arguments as "The affirmative proposal substantially increases the risk of nuclear war" are examples of disadvantages that sound like harms. The complete structure of such a disadvantage could be as follows:

I. Disadvantage: The affirmative proposal runs a substantial risk of nuclear war.
   A. Affirmative significance increases unemployment.
   B. Increased unemployment will increase the military personnel shortage.
   C. An increased military personnel shortage will increase the risk of war.
   D. War kills more people than the affirmative saves.
   E. Present employment policies do not run the affirmative risks.

Summary

The negative's principal objective is to show that the resolution is untrue and should be rejected. The negative has several options in constructing arguments against one or all of the major stock issues, as well as in launching jurisdictional attacks. The usual division of labor is for the first negative to attack the need and the second negative to attack the plan and present disadvantages. This division is by no means mandatory. It is most important to plan a division of labor with consistent arguments developed from a well-conceived negative position.

If you, as the negative, elect to make jurisdictional attacks, you may choose topicality, extratopicality, justification, or counterwarrants. Should you succeed in showing that the affirmative lacks jurisdiction and really derives its arguments from negative land, then all other issues become moot.

You have a number of options available in attacking significance. You can dispute the affirmative's value judgments or suggest other values that are more important. You can also challenge the existence of causal relationships between the harm and present policy, whether such relationships are based on analytical or empirical studies.

In arguing inherency, your main question will always be, without the resolution, can the problem still be solved? If you can show that it can, you will have demonstrated that the problem is not inherent in negative land and hence that the affirmative proposal is not needed to solve the problem.

Finally, you may try to defeat the resolution by showing that the affirmative's proposal will not effectively deal with the problem or that the disadvantages outweigh the benefits derived from the resolution.

Questions for Discussion

1. How does the negative position influence whether to use topicality arguments and if they are used, what kind?

2. What are the relative strengths and weaknesses of the five standards of topicality presented in this chapter?
3. Is it appropriate to require the affirmative to justify all of the key terms in the resolution?
4. How appropriate is the use of counterwarrants as a type of jurisdictional argument?
5. What determines whether a minor repair is legitimate? How can minor repairs function in a viable attack on inherency?
6. What is the relationship, if any, between justification and inherency burdens?

Chapter 14

Negative
Case Construction:
Structures

As previously stated, the overriding objective of the negative is to show that the resolution is not probably true and hence should be rejected. At least three general structures of argument may be used to show that the resolution should not be affirmed. These alternatives are (1) straight refutation, (2) defense of the present system as constituted or with minor repairs, and (3) the counterresolution. In this chapter, we shall explore these approaches and the opinions about their use.

Straight Refutation

The negative using straight refutation offers no constructive claims of its own. Rather, straight refutation consists exclusively of attacks on the affirmative claims. The affirmative has the responsibility of supporting the major issues inherent in the resolution. If the negative succeeds with straight refutation in casting sufficient doubt on the validity of the affirmative claims, the judge usually will reject the resolution because the affirmative has failed to establish its probable truth.

Uses of Straight Refutation

One way to use straight refutation is to demonstrate that the affirmative has used spurious logic to support a major claim. In Chapter 4, we explained the four general tests that you can apply to any inference: (1) Does the claim relate directly to the evidence? (2) Does the claim say something different from what the evidence says? (3) Does the claim ignore the question? (4) Does the language of the claim equivocate? If the affirmative fails to satisfy any of these four tests on a major claim, you should argue that your opponent has not proved the truth of the resolution.

You could, for example, show that the inherency of the affirmative is based on an untrue assertion that a causal link exists between negative land and the problem. In the debate over the removal of price controls from natural gas, you could dispute the link between gas shortages and price controls by arguing that the Department of Energy allows gas companies an adequate rate of return on domestic production and that the concentrated nature of the industry encourages companies to withhold oil supplies at competitive market prices.

Another form of straight refutation is an attack on the affirmative evidence. Various objections can be lodged against the evidence. One is an attack on the source's credibility, showing that the source is incompetent to make the claim, that the source has a bias or vested interest, or that an individual has an ax to grind. In the debate on expanding the sale of handguns, the affirmative could read evidence from the National Rifle Association to support their argument that the availability of handguns does not result in more homicides. As a negative, you could dispute this evidence by offering proof that the National Rifle Association is an organization controlled by the major manufacturers of handguns and, therefore, that it cannot be trusted to render a reliable opinion on the subject of handgun control.

Another objection you can make against the evidence is to question its context. On the handgun control topic, for example, the affirmative may read evidence from a statement by Senator Edward M. Kennedy, including his paraphrase of an argument in favor of the sale of handguns, in a way that might suggest that Senator Kennedy agreed with the argument. Actually, he opposed it. In response, you should dispute the affirmative interpretation of the evidence by noting that Senator Kennedy's statement goes on to refute the paraphrased argument and then concludes that the sale of handguns is undesirable.

Problems with Straight Refutation

Even though straight refutation may be sufficient to show that the resolution should not be adopted, it is rarely adequate by itself unless the affirmative makes gross errors in case construction. Also, many judges who view debate as an instrument of decision making, as a device to help audiences decide what to do about important problems, feel that all debaters have an obligation to share with their audience their thinking about the full range of assumptions and alternatives that should be recognized in choosing wisely. Otherwise, debaters may minimize the complexity of the topic and may sacrifice an enlightened judgment of the audience for the sake of victory. To ensure against such an adverse reaction, you probably should introduce and analyze a position as thoroughly as time and circumstances permit. Some listeners feel that straight refutation falls short of these objectives and allows you to shirk your responsibility because you can merely deny your opponent's claims without offering any constructive alternatives. They argue that the audience has nothing with which to compare the affirmative proposal and may have chosen a weak policy simply because it knew no other.

Finally, some judges object, on ethical grounds, to using straight refutation as the sole form of negative argument. Some critics believe that it is highly presumptuous for a debater to assume the ability to discredit every point that the affirmative makes. To ignore the problematical nature of serious debate and to assume that the absolute truth lies in negative land is to reduce the act of debate from an intellectual dispute over an important matter of policy to a game played only for its own sake. Hence, the insights that the audience gathers from a debate are negligible, for the debate degenerates into a contest of juggling words. From some educators' point of view, this verbal play is not ethically defensible because it ignores the debater's responsibility to the audience from whom he or she is seeking a response.

In our view, straight refutation skillfully executed is sufficient to cast doubt on the probable truth of the resolution. But we seldom advise debaters to pursue an exclusive strategy of straight refutation, both because many people react adversely to it and because it seldom is the negative's strongest option.

Defense of the Present System

Most policy resolutions are worded so as to call for a change from the approaches currently in use. Therefore, another method that the negative can use to cast doubt on the resolution's probable truth is to defend the present system. If the present system is working well and is capable of taking care of the problem, then by implication there is no reason to change. If the resolution calls for change, but there is no need to change, then the resolution is not probably true.

If you elect to defend the present system, you probably should begin by establishing a general frame of reference that justifies established policy—if not as an ideal course of action, then certainly as a better one than the alternative proposed by the opponent. For example, if the affirmative calls for a limitation on the present freedom of speech, you could argue that freedom of speech, even with risks, is a better course of action than are restrictions on a constitutional right and that any restriction on freedom of speech is a more serious risk than is any problem described by the affirmative.

In this way you utilize your knowledge of human psychology. Most people cling to what they have until they see something better. When you, as a negative debater, take this initiative in the debate, it forces the affirmative to show that its proposal is more satisfactory than the present system. What you are suggesting is that society is entitled to know, before affirming new policies, whether it is possible to correct the stated evils and still maintain the present system. It is entitled to know whether the status quo is worth retaining.

Status Quo or Repairs?

In defending the present system, you have a number of options. The present system may be superior to the affirmative plan without any alterations. Or perhaps the present system can evolve without changing its inherent characteristics.

Claiming that the present system currently has the administrative authority to make new procedures, that the judicial power already exists to deal with the problem, or that other governmental agencies can act exemplify this approach. In the terms we used earlier, you can show either that negative land already includes the means to overcome the problem or that it is capable of developing such means without changing its major character.

But you may find that the present system cannot combat the problem without any changes. You do not have to defend the present system as a static phenomenon, however. If you choose, you can defend it by keeping its essential features but still proposing alterations. These alterations in the present system are sometimes referred to as *minor repairs*. This approach is especially effective when the changes do not alter the basic structure of the present system's operational features. The approach typically advocates the use of more money or labor or resources already available. For example, if the affirmative calls for more imports of oil to meet domestic demands, you could advocate the substitution of fuel sources, other than petroleum, for oil by users who can switch easily as a means of freeing oil for automobile consumption. This method is especially effective when the affirmative inherency does not indict the motives and means of those administering the present policy. It is reasonable to assume, therefore, that the administrators can modify an existing policy without altering its essential features.

Problems with Minor Repairs

If you use minor repairs, you must be careful to avoid certain pitfalls. For some people an important question is how minor the repairs really are. The excessive advocacy of minor repairs may subject the negative debater to the charge that he or she has drastically changed the nature of the present system, to the point that it is not really the system being defended. The basic assumption behind such a concern is that the negative debater assumes different or larger burdens by departing from the present system.

Frankly, we do not believe it matters whether the repairs are minor or major. The reason takes us back to fundamentals. The most essential task of the negative is not to defend the present system but to oppose the resolution. Hence negative land represents all the ways in which the resolution can be opposed. It may be changed in ways small or great, but as long as it necessarily negates the resolution, its function is the same. From this point of view, the important question is not how major or minor the repairs are, but whether they maintain negative land, as distinct from affirmative land. If the boundaries blur, then the negative is in trouble.

Another pitfall to avoid is the advocacy of minor repairs that can be encompassed within a reasonable interpretation of the resolution. If the resolution, for example, calls for the federal government to place greater controls on oil companies and the affirmative plan proposes allocation of oil at the wellhead, a negative minor repair that has the present system using the federal government tax on windfall profits to accomplish the affirmative proposal can be called resolutional. Hence the negative is actually supporting an argument that properly belongs to affirmative land. This error usually results when debaters forget the basic principles of inherency. The negative does not defeat inherency by advocating the resolution in any of its forms. Rather, the task is to show that the affirmative's problem can be solved without affirming the resolution.

Finally, you should consider minor repairs in light of the disadvantages you plan to argue. One negative speaker may repair the present system to the point that the negative is left with virtually no disadvantages to adopting the affirmative proposal. If the repair is indistinct from the affirmative plan, then any disadvantages to the plan will also occur in the repaired present system. If the first negative, for example, "repairs" the oil allocation topic by using the state government as its agency, then any second negative disadvantages from oil redistribution become irrelevant, since the disadvantages are no longer unique to the affirmative proposal. They will occur whether the federal government or the state has the job of allocation.

A Combination Strategy

In most instances, your most effective strategy in using straight refutation and a defense of the present system is probably a combination of the two. On the resolution that all American citizens be guaranteed a job, you could use straight refutation against some of the arguments. You could then defend the system of supply and demand by showing that the affirmative has exaggerated its evils. Finally, you could show that the evils are not inherent in the system of supply and demand and can be corrected by making a few minor changes in the present system. This practice obviously enables you, if you wish, to compare the evils under an alternative system with the evils that you think will result under the affirmative proposal. If you use this method, you could even choose to admit that some of the evils complained of in the status quo do exist but at the same time stress that society does not want a proposal worse than the one now in effect.

The Counterresolution

Finally, the negative can deny the resolution by offering an alternative resolution — supporting an action different from the one offered by the affirmative or from existing policy. For example, suppose that the affirmative resolution calls for the American people to elect their president by the means of direct vote. As a negative, you may choose to prove the resolution untrue by showing that the present electoral college method of choosing the president is superior to direct election. But you could instead try to prove the affirmative proposal untrue by arguing that having the Congress elect the president would be better than the direct vote method. The latter is a *counterresolution*, sometimes called a *counterplan* or a *counterproposition*. Debate theorists generally agree that the counterresolution is a legitimate technique for showing that the affirmative resolution should not be adopted. There are, however, many opinions about the functions, requirements, and legitimacy of certain types of counterresolutions.

Functions of the Counterresolution

In our view, the counterresolution is a technique for arguing by example that the affirmative has failed to prove that the action stated in the resolution is necessary and sufficient to resolve the problem. In other words, the counterresolution is merely a rhetorical example of nonresolutional policy that would be at least as advantageous as the affirmative proposal. Its function is to cast doubt on the resolution by offering an equally valuable alternative.

Furthermore, a counterresolution need not preclude attacks against the need or a defense of the present system, because counterresolutions do not commit the negative to a particular policy. They merely show that the affirmative proposal is not the most appropriate way to correct the affirmative problem or that the adoption of the affirmative's proposal will preclude the resolution of a greater problem. In either case, the affirmative resolution is untrue.

Neither do counterresolutions claim to be better than all other policies. In a sense, the counterresolution serves the same function as straight refutation. It argues that the affirmative has not proved a need for its proposal, since the counterresolution is at least equally desirable. Finally, in our view, the negative does not forfeit presumption by presenting a counterresolution. Presumption does not lie with any side or system; instead it is always against the resolution.

We readily admit that many theorists do not share our view of the counterresolution's functions. From the policy-making viewpoint, the counterresolution is a statement of a negative policy position that differs from whatever policy is being pursued by the present system. Under this model, the negative often concedes that there is a need for change but argues that the counterresolution offers a more desirable policy. This position usually means that the negative is blocked from defending the present system. In the policy-making view, presenting a counterresolution and also defending the present system could clutter the debate with these options, making it unclear which option the judge would choose should the negative be awarded the decision. (The negative could still argue, however, that the affirmative proof does not truly demonstrate a need for a change in those instances in which the affirmative resolution and the counterresolution do not overlap. This latter argument is used only if the counterresolution does not cover some aspect of the affirmative need.) Finally, policy makers see presumption with whichever system offers the least risk of change. They will, therefore, usually emphasize a comparison of the degree of change, the possible reversibility of policy, the degrees of decentralization, and the reliability of the evidence supporting the policies.

Requirements of the Counterresolution

Theorists also disagree about the necessary requirements for the counterresolution. This diversity can probably best be illustrated in the context of the most widely accepted counterresolution: the policy change that either (1) moves in a direction different from the affirmative's to accomplish the same goal, (2) suggests a different agent for change, or (3) both. For example, if the affirmative advocates a proposal for the federal government to regulate oil supplies to meet an energy shortage, you could propose that the federal government implement a program for the increased use of coal to meet the same problem. The above example is a counter-resolution using a change in direction. Another example is one in which the affir-mative uses the federal government as an agent for change and the negative uses the state and local governments for the same purpose. In any case, the traditional counterresolution presents a well-defined alternative to the affirmative plan.

Much of the disagreement over the use of the traditional counterresolution is either in terms of the criteria that the counterresolution must meet or in the nature of the criteria. These are:

The Nonresolutional Criterion. The counterresolution must be nonresolutional. It must move in a direction or use an agent for change other than that specified in the resolution. In our opinion, if the negative's counterresolution is topical, it has actually upheld the resolution and thereby defaulted on its primary obligation. If the negative wins its counterresolution, the resolution still has been proved true, although by the negative. An affirmative decision therefore is justified, even if the affirmative loses the desirability of its example of the resolution.

Some theorists disagree with our position. Many argue that if the affirmative offers its plan as a definition of the resolution, then the negative will be free to offer any new policy as nonresolutional as long as it is not the affirmative plan. If the affirmative, for example, calls for the federal government to exert greater controls on labor unions through regulations on collective bargaining and claims that this plan is the definition of the resolution, some theorists argue that it is acceptable for the negative to offer a counterresolution in which the federal government would exert greater controls on labor unions by any means other than the affirmative ex-ample. We disagree. As we stated in Chapter 9, even though it may often be desirable to limit the scope of the debate by focusing on a specific example of the resolution, this example or plan is nothing more than one facet of a broad topic. The affirmative operationally calling such examples the resolution does not make it so, and neither does such labeling make negative counterresolution examples of the topic any less topical. Suppose that the affirmative defends a resolution calling for the increased control of labor unions by operationally referring to controls of union elections as the resolution. Such affirmative claims do not lessen the fact that a negative counterplan calling for the removal of the right to strike is equally topical.

Still fewer critics argue that any counterresolution other than the affirmative's example of the resolution should be acceptable, because the debate is staged to gain skills in the art of advocacy and it really does not matter whether the counter-resolutions are topical as long as something is disputed. Again, we reject this point of view. We strongly feel that although all debate skills are important, it is equally important to develop the skill of proving a resolution to be probably true or false. This goal cannot be achieved if both sides defend the resolution.

The Competitiveness Criterion.   A widely accepted requirement is that the counterresolution be competitive with the affirmative plan. Since the purpose of the counterresolution is to deny the probable truth of the resolution, then it must be impossible to affirm both. This statement generally explains what the concept of competitiveness means. But more precisely, how do we know when a counterresolution is competitive? Three different standards have been proposed.

First, some theorists have suggested that the counterresolution is competitive if it corrects the affirmative problem. For example, if the affirmative proposal calls for the federal government to increase aid to education, a counterresolution that achieves the same goal through state action will demonstrate that the affirmative's proposal is untrue, that is, that the federal government is not needed to correct the alleged problem. Of course, this standard implies that duplicative actions are always undesirable. Sometimes, though, it may make sense to pursue simultaneously several paths to the same goal. In the area of civil rights, for example, it may be the wisest policy to empower both federal and state governments to prosecute alleged violations. Because duplicative action may sometimes be in order, we do not think the counterresolution will necessarily be competitive just because it meets the affirmative problem. The negative must show why duplication is inappropriate in the particular case.

Second, the counterresolution may be thought competitive if it is mutually exclusive with the affirmative proposal. For example, if the affirmative proposal calls for the deregulation of oil prices in order to remedy an energy shortage, the counterresolution must propose some action incompatible with oil price deregulation in order to be competitive. Certainly, few theorists would accept as competitive a counterresolution on the above topic to provide increased federal aid to education, unless the negative can show that both plans cannot be adopted simultaneously. The argument here is simply that the adoption of one does not preclude the adoption of the other, and so there is no reason not to have the benefits of both.

The above example illustrates a counterresolution that is not mutually exclusive with the affirmative proposal. A mutually exclusive counterresolution can be illustrated by the following example: If the affirmative calls for a proposal deregulating the air industry, and the negative offers a counterresolution intensifying a regulatory system, then the two proposals are mutually exclusive. Both cannot be adopted at the same time. The counterresolution can be incompatible with the resolution, even though it does not solve the affirmative's problem. Suppose that the affirmative proposal calls for increased American initiatives throughout the world as a means of increasing American independence from foreign countries. You, as a negative, counter with federal world government, using the argument that Americans, along with the rest of the world, will be better served by more American interdependence on foreign powers. In this case, you could admit that the counterproposal will decrease our independence but at the same time argue that interdependence will be beneficial for more people. You could then show that the affirmative proposal moves us away from a more important goal, and even though you do not solve the same harm by adopting the negative's proposal, you provide a greater advantage.

Third, a counterresolution is competitive if, even though not inconsistent with the resolution, it is better to affirm only the counterresolution rather than to affirm both. For example, the affirmative proposes to increase public funding for abortions. The counterresolution may outlaw abortions. Strictly, we could do both. But as a matter of policy, it makes far more sense to do one or the other, but not both. Hence, in this example the counterresolution would be judged competitive.

Of the three standards we have discussed, the first seems to us to be an inadequate assurance of competitiveness, because duplication sometimes is a wise approach. But either the second or the third standard, in our judgment, represents a sufficient condition for competitiveness.

The Added Advantage.   Some theorists argue that the negative forfeits presumption when it offers a counterresolution; therefore, it must have some advantage over and above those advantages offered by the affirmative. The policy maker generally believes that the counterplan must offer some advantage over the affirmative plan, even if it is only a reduction in risk. We do not believe that a counterresolution must satisfy this requirement. As we stated, we believe that presumption rests against the resolution—not with the present system. Moreover, if you succeed in proving that the counterresolution is equal in value to the affirmative proposal, you have demonstrated that it is not necessary to adopt the affirmative resolution to achieve the advantage.

Nontraditional Counterresolutions

Thus far, our discussion of the counterresolution has centered on the traditional approach in which the negative advocates another course of action in the hopes that the listener will perceive his or her proposal as superior to the affirmative resolution. Other types are more controversial.

The Conditional Counterresolution.   A conditional counterresolution states, in effect, "Here is one possible way of dealing with this problem without adopting the resolution; therefore, the affirmative has not proved a need to adopt the resolution." With this approach, the counterresolution is not being offered as an option for approval; rather, it is an argument by example that the original resolution has not been adequately defended. Put another way, the rejection of the resolution does not automatically result in the acceptance of the conditional counterresolution. Instead, the resolution is defeated on its own merits (or lack of them).

Some debaters will claim that they are offering a conditional counterresolution. But in our view, as a practical matter, any counterresolution is conditional. This position is based on the assumption of the hypothesis-testing supporter that the debate is not necessarily being staged to select a policy option. Accordingly, no action is taken. Instead, the debate attempts to establish the probable truth of the resolution.

An example of this type of counterresolution was used by the negative in the final round of the 1973 National Collegiate Debate Tournament. In this round, the affirmative offered a broad program of federalized medical care. The negative offered a conditional counterresolution for one portion of the total program, asking the audience to reject the remainder on other grounds.

Arguments against the legitimacy of the conditional counterresolution are varied. A major objection is the time factor. Many insist that it is just not possible within time constraints to defend a resolution properly against a number of conditional arguments. Another objection is that conditional counterresolutions, when presented in large numbers during the debate round, lack sufficient detail for an adequate evaluation of their ability to solve the problem and their possible advantages and disadvantages. Some critics believe that the debate should be centered on the best policy system and that no well-defined policy emerges when conditional counterresolutions are presented by the negative.

We feel that the critics' objections are unfounded. First, we do not advocate the mere mentioning of a number of counterresolutions. Certainly, the conditional counterresolution should meet the same criteria as the traditional counterresolution does. Second, we do not think any counterresolution is presented as a policy for adoption. All counterresolutions are designed to test the truth of the resolution and not to implement policy. Third, the question of whether to present a few or many arguments is a strategic choice. The apparent gains to the negative from presenting multiple counterresolutions may be offset by shallowness of the coverage or the failure to attack other aspects of the affirmative proposal. As a practical matter, these strategic considerations limit the number of options actually discussed.

The Study Counterresolution.   A more recent approach is the *study counterresolution*. Debaters using the study counterresolution usually feel that not enough is known about the affirmative's problem for any specific action to be undertaken. At the same time, they believe that they must present a policy option in order for the judge to vote negative. They assume that unless they defend a policy, an affirmative ballot is assured. Therefore, they offer a specific counterresolution calling for further investigation of the affirmative's problem. Usually this call is accompanied by a plan to publicize the findings of the study after a period of time.

The study counterresolution is usually offered in situations in which the negative alleges that it is too early to make a policy decision because planners lack the necessary information. Usually the negative claims that the evidence presented by both sides is inconclusive, and therefore what is needed is not an immediate decision but more study. Advocates using this approach usually claim that they are not quarreling with current decision-making processes but instead are merely trying to give decision makers more information before they adopt policy.

Many judges object to the study counterresolution. Some argue that because decision makers in the real world must always act on the basis of imperfect information, judges likewise should make their decisions based on the policy arguments in the debate. They view the requirement that the affirmative prove that additional study will not yield useful results as an unrealistic and excessive burden to predict the future.

Many of these same critics argue that the study counterresolution is based on the false assumption that more information is an asset to the policy maker when, in fact, many policy makers cannot digest an overload of data. They also argue that perhaps we should act and study at the same time, changing policy later if desirable.

Although we share many of the objections stated above, our major quarrel with the study counterresolution is simply that it is not really a counterresolution. Instead, it is just a way of arguing that the affirmative has not met its burden of proof, that in fact the affirmative evidence does not warrant a need to change. Actually, those who use it probably have no real policy option to present. Yet they are unwilling to stake the outcome of the round on the argument that the affirmative has not proved its case. They may possibly fear that policy-making judges will feel that they must adopt something and that without a counterresolution of some sort, they will have no option except to vote affirmative. From our perspective, if the affirmative data truly are inadequate, this argument should be sufficient to show that the resolution is probably untrue and a negative ballot is justified.

Summary

The negative has at least three options in structuring its case. It may use straight refutation, a defense of the present system as constituted or with minor repairs, or the counterresolution. Depending on one's view of each of these approaches, the debaters also have the option of combining these within the same case.

Straight refutation consists of arguments designed to show that the affirmative proofs do not warrant adoption of the resolution. Such arguments make no explicit defense of any alternative system. Instead, they focus on the affirmative's deficiencies in developing its case. We recognize this approach as legitimate because the affirmative's main obligation is to show that the resolution is probably true. The affirmative has failed in this task if its claims do not warrant adoption of the resolution.

Defense of the present system can be a means of showing that the resolution is untrue because the present policy is superior. You may defend the present system as it currently stands or with minor alterations.

The counterresolution is another means of showing that the resolution is untrue. In our view, the functions of straight refutation, defense of the present system, and the counterresolution are the same. Though critics differ on the functions, requirements, and the legitimacy of certain types of counterresolutions, virtually all recognize the approach as a worthwhile method of proving that the affirmative proposal should be rejected.

Questions for Discussion

1. What are the risks, if any, of limiting negative attacks to straight refutation?
2. Should a counterresolution be rejected because it is topical, even if it meets the three standards for competitiveness advanced in this chapter?
3. How can the traditional counterresolution indict the affirmative and demonstrate its failure to meet its burdens?
4. Is an added advantage necessary for a counterresolution? Why or why not?
5. Besides the civil rights example discussed in this chapter, in what other circumstances are redundant actions by topical and nontopical agents of change desirable?
6. In what circumstances, if any, can the study counterresolution be offered as a legitimate negative strategy?
7. What are the similarities and differences between the traditional and the conditional counterresolution?

Chapter 15

Attacking and Defending Arguments

Although the development of constructive positions is fundamental to effective debating, the dynamic quality of the debate results from the ongoing process of attacking and defending arguments. It is the direct confrontation and the progressive development of different stances on the major issues that change the format from a series of isolated argumentative speeches to direct clashes of ideas on specific arguments. The ultimate objective of probing opposing positions is to refute or reestablish arguments that either diminish or strengthen the probable truth of the resolution.

This chapter focuses on techniques useful in attacking and defending arguments in debate. The general principles of refuting and rebuilding a case, which we discussed in Chapter 6, apply here. In addition, there is a more specialized process of attack and defense in debates. In exploring this process, we shall examine (1) the use of the flow sheet as a means of keeping up with the progression of arguments, (2) the techniques for attack and defense that follow the first affirmative, and (3) strategic considerations in attacking and defending arguments.

The Role of the Flow Sheet

Properly identifying the arguments in dispute is necessary for effective debating. This process requires skill in analyzing others' arguments and in constructing one's own arguments. To aid in such analysis, most debaters, as well as most judges, need an instrument for the accurate recording of arguments during the debate. The most common instrument is the flow sheet, which consists of an outline of particular speeches as they are presented in the debate.

Outlining a Debate Speech

Essentially, the outline of a debate speech corresponds to the basic form you use in your other courses of study. The outline uses a notational system to indicate the relationship of arguments in a speech. The notational system normally includes roman numerals, capital letters, arabic numbers, and the like. Whatever system is used, the symbols and their ordering principle should show *coordination* and *subordination*. For example, all of the assertions of an outline in which roman numerals are used for the major arguments should be of the same importance, thus coordinating the major ideas. If you assert that oil prices should be deregulated, you can argue that this policy results in shortages, forces us to depend on foreign products, and harms our international relations. The roman numerals would be:

I. Regulated prices cause oil shortages.
II. Regulated prices force an overdependence on foreign markets.
III. Regulated prices are harmful to our international relations.

The major coordinate arguments are, in turn, supported by subordinate arguments. In fact, the bases for the major arguments are found in the subordinate arguments. In the first argument above, for example, it might look as follows:

I. Regulated prices cause oil shortages.
   A. Oil companies have no incentives to explore.
   B. Oil companies import costly foreign oil.

Most outlines will further break down the subordinate arguments into subdivisions, usually with arabic numbers. It is often at this level that you outline the evidence used to support the claims. In the example above, the outline of the point would be as follows:

I. Regulated prices cause oil shortages.
   A. Oil companies have no incentives to explore.
      1. Twelve companies have decreased exploration since regulation began.
      2. Professor Robert Doe says regulation of prices is the major reason for a lack of exploration.
   B. Oil companies import costly foreign oil.
      1. Foreign oil is more expensive.
      2. Oil companies have consistently increased imports of oil since regulation.
      3. Professor Robert Doe says regulation of prices is the major reason why imports of oil have consistently increased.

The flow sheet is a natural progression from the outline. The outline enables you to record the structure of the arguments within a particular speech, and the flow sheet enables you to follow particular arguments across all of the speeches in the debate.

Merits of the Flow Sheet

The advantages of the flow sheet are numerous. For example, it enables you to trace the development of an argument throughout the debate. It is a chart not only of what is said in each speech but also of how arguments develop over the course of the debate. The resulting diagram often helps in the construction of your responses, as you can tell at a glance what each debater has said on each argument.

The flow sheet also helps you decide quickly which arguments to emphasize. Because in rebuttals the speaking time is cut, the effective debater often must drop some arguments. The flow sheet enables you to locate important arguments quickly and to reject arguments that should be dropped in the organization of rebuttals.

One of the flow sheet's most valuable qualities is that you can quickly spot contradictions and inconsistencies, both your own and those of your opponent. For example, the affirmative debater can glance at the negative's inherency arguments on the flow sheet and compare them with the outline of the argument on the disadvantages to see if the negative is claiming that the present system is moving toward the affirmative position while at the same time arguing that disadvantages will result from adopting the affirmative proposal.

The flow sheet can also help debaters recall arguments in the round. Some debates may contain over a hundred arguments. Few people can recall them all, particularly when there may be multiple responses to each argument. Recording all the arguments aids memory and also encourages the debater to reduce personal bias toward the importance of arguments, thereby avoiding the risk of omitting an argument that may appear to be unimportant early in the round but that may turn into a major argument by the end of the debate.

Finally, the flow sheet provides feedback for analysis after the debate. By studying the flow sheet after the debate, you can often quickly identify where your mistakes were made. This study enables you to plan new responses and approaches to your opponent's positions, as well as to plan new strategies for your own case in future debates. The flow sheet often enables you to make more constructive use of the judge's reasons for decisions. In other words, it should enable you to see which responses to an argument the judge considered to be dispositive or persuasive.

Procedures for the Flow Sheet

The major rule for the use of the flow sheet is to outline the speeches vertically and the responses to individual arguments horizontally. To do this, you should use large sheets of paper, either legal tablets or art pads, turning the sheets sideways. If the legal size is used, several sheets will be needed to preserve legibility. If the art pad is used, one or two sheets for case and plan will suffice.

1. The first step is to divide the sheets into columns, using separate sheets for the case and the plan. Case speeches should be allotted seven columns. Make the columns for the constructive speeches slightly larger than those for the rebuttal speeches. Figure 15.1 illustrates a legal-size sheet for the case side in a typical debate. (Some debates, of course, will depart from this pattern.)

Figure 15.1

14″

First Affirmative Constructive Speech	First Negative Constructive Speech	Second Affirmative Constructive Speech	First Negative Rebuttal	First Affirmative Rebuttal	Second Negative Rebuttal	Second Affirmative Rebuttal

8½″

Divide the sheets on which the plan arguments will be recorded as follows: If legal-size sheets are used, position pages widthwise and draw four columns down the page, one for the second negative constructive and one for each of the four rebuttals. On the first page draw a line across the page about three to four inches from the top. This provides space for the plan. If the art pad is used, hold it lengthwise and draw five columns, one for the plan, one for the second negative constructive, and three for each of the rebuttal speeches that ordinarily cover plan attacks. Figure 15.2 illustrates the art pad flow sheet.

Figure 15.2

14″

Affirmative Plan	Second Negative Constructive Speech	First Affirmative Rebuttal	Second Negative Rebuttal	Second Affirmative Rebuttal

8½″

2. In the far left column of the case and plan sheets, outline the affirmative case and plan as presented in the first affirmative's constructive speech. Use the suggested numbering and lettering system as a guide in organizing the outline. Write large and legibly enough so that your partner can read the flow. When legal-size sheets are used, you may wish to record major contentions or small groups of plan attacks on separate pages.

3. Subsequent speeches should be outlined in the next adjacent column, with entries parallel to the arguments in the preceding speech to which they correspond. Hence the order of the outline for subsequent speeches will correspond to that of the first affirmative, not necessarily to the order in which the arguments are discussed in a later speech. If a major new argument is delivered that does not directly correspond to a preceding argument, such as an overview or a counterresolution, it should be outlined on separate sheets of paper, drawing enough columns on the pages so that every speech in which the argument will be touched on has a space. The overall objective is to develop both a vertical outline that enables the debater to determine which arguments have been used in the debate and horizontal lines of argument across the speeches that enable the debater to determine how each argument was developed.

4. You may also find several other techniques helpful. You may, for example, want to use abbreviations to speed your recording of arguments. For example, *Sig* could stand for significance, *DA* for disadvantage, and *In* for inherency. You can also use stars or different colors for important arguments; draw brackets around arguments that are being grouped; use arrows for contradictions; make special notations for dropped, illogical, or nonevidence arguments; record different speeches with multicolored pens so that affirmative and negative arguments can be easily distinguished; and whenever possible write your own constructive arguments in advance as a time-saving device and an organizational aid.

Above all, you should not understate the importance of the flow sheet. Many errors among debaters come from faults in making a flow sheet. Practice in this technique is important. You should practice both when participating in debates and when listening to others debate. Flow all speeches in the debate, even those that occur after your final speech is finished, so that you will have a complete record. You should remember that faster flowing usually means more preparation time for your own speeches during the round and more time to help your colleague. This time cushion is particularly important when planning the rebuttals.

The First Negative Constructive

In Chapter 6, we examined the major methods of attacking and defending arguments. In this and the following section, we shall be mainly concerned with the adaptation of these methods to the first negative and second affirmative constructive speeches, both of which tend to concentrate on attack and defense.

Establishing a negative position, as we noted in Chapter 12, is the first step in the attack on affirmative arguments. Once this position is established, all other arguments against particular affirmative assertions are planned and executed within the framework that the position defines.

If you are doing the first negative attack, you generally should follow the affirmative outline when using either straight refutation or a defense of the present system. The negative refutation in this situation should be directed against the specific arguments of the affirmative. This has two major advantages. It makes it easier for the debaters and judge to flow the negative arguments and also helps ensure that a direct clash on the affirmative contentions will take place. Of course, following the affirmative order does not mean attacking every affirmative argument. As we found in Chapter 6, there are several types of arguments that it may not make sense to attack — those that are obvious, incidental, functionally duplicative, or multilevel. Arguments of these types can be granted or ignored as the negative debater proceeds through the affirmative case structure.

An example of this approach follows. Suppose that the first affirmative outline offers as its first contention the following:

I. Lack of occupational safety kills and maims thousands.
   A. Thousands are needlessly murdered in America's work place.
      1. Statistics from the National Safety Council reveal that over 14,000 Americans die annually on the job.
      2. Further data show that an additional 2.2 million are injured yearly due to occupational hazards.
   B. Worker injuries extend beyond the employment setting.
      1. Morbidity is no less important than occupational mortality. Often the loss of a limb is just as devastating as the loss of life.
      2. Death and injuries cause needless grief and torment to family members.
   C. The workers have a right to safe and healthful working conditions.

The negative could construct the following outline against such a contention:

I. Advantage (contention 1): Jobs are unsafe. Negative position: Present safety measures are adequate.
   A. Refutation: (1) Affirmative statistics are flawed. (2) Deaths are actually decreasing. (3) Current safety regulations solve occupational dangers. (4) Statistically significant decreases in death are possible with new technology.
   B. Refutation: (1) The affirmative should quantify the impact; no real advantage is offered here. (2) Safety regulations described above mean that there will be no significant harm in the future. (3) The affirmative does not offer empirical study, just opinion in the first affirmative. (4) Workmen's compensation compensates injured employees.
   C. Refutation: (1) The negative evidence above applies here: if working conditions are becoming safer, then there is no real harm. (2) Not a

constitutional right; no court has ruled on this. (3) The affirmative does not quantify the impact of this argument on the round; if we lose it, what is the effect? (4) The affirmative has not offered a legal source, only some person who thinks safety is important; certainly not a source on which to base policy.

The negative usually retains the above structure unless one of two circumstances requires a change. When the negative produces a counterresolution, it usually presents at least a partially independent structure of its own. The negative may also deviate from the affirmative structure when strategic considerations so dictate. An example of such considerations occurs when the first negative decides to attack only the underlying assumptions of the case, believing that if those are refuted, then all of the individual affirmative contentions will automatically fall with them. For example, if the affirmative case has built its entire need for a change on the assumption that full employment is a goal of the present system that can be enhanced by the affirmative plan, the first negative may ignore the affirmative structure and spend its entire time refuting the underlying assumption that full employment is a desirable goal.

As a first negative, you should strive for independent responses to affirmative contentions that can be extended in rebuttals. Whenever possible, you should avoid limiting your refutation to the proofs offered by the affirmative; rather, you should add your own counterarguments. For example, in attacking an oil import case, if you simply expose the insufficiency of evidence indicating U.S. dependence on foreign oil in the affirmative argument, it is possible that the second affirmative will supply the additional evidence, leaving you little to add in your rebuttal. But by offering counterarguments, such as the maintenance of our own oil reserve, you will usually have extensions on your own arguments. Having extensions is a fundamental consideration in helping you decide in advance how you want a chain of arguments to evolve by the conclusion of the debate.

Finally, as a first negative you should check both the negative position and your own chain of arguments with your partner's arguments before your presentation. This check offers the best assurance that case arguments will not contradict plan attacks.

The Second Affirmative Constructive

A well-conceived affirmative case is usually constructed around a central thesis that stresses the inadequacies of the present policy, while at the same time showing why nothing short of the action implied by the resolution can solve the problem. You should normally begin with a comparison and contrast between this original position and the one defended by the first negative. For example, if you, as an affirmative, condemn capital punishment, offer arguments to prove that capital punishment is unjustified, and show that only the abolition of this practice can solve the problem, you will normally begin the second affirmative with a review of this position. If the negative has countered with a defense of capital punishment, you can show how the positions differ. By reviewing the two positions and showing how they differ, you can often render irrelevant many negative attacks, as well as group related negative attacks and answer them collectively.

When defending the affirmative, you should try to stay within the affirmative case structure in refuting attacks on it. A good example of this practice occurred in the final round of the 1961 National Collegiate Debate Tournament. The topic called for a federal program of comprehensive National Health Insurance. The second affirmative began his defense of the case by repeating his basic contentions: (1) Americans suffer and die because of the neglect of their health care, and (2) the primary reason for the death and suffering is because people do not have the money to secure adequate medical protection. The debater then proceeded to state the negative attacks as responses to those contentions and then to defend the contentions against attack.

If the harm and significance of your case have been attacked in the first negative speech, you may wish to present new examples of harm and significance, possibly even new advantages, as a means of bolstering your case. If inherency has been challenged, you may wish to expand on inherency analysis, usually expanding on the original links between negative land and the cited problem, by further explaining the logic of the claim and offering additional examples. If a counterresolution has been proposed, you should deal with it separately from any case attacks. If time permits (and you should make the time available), you should repeat major aspects of harm, significance, and inherency not refuted by the first negative. Internal summaries of each element in the affirmative case are vital to the clear delineation of each argument as it relates to each major issue considered in the second negative constructive speech.

Strategic Considerations

The attacking and defending of arguments should occur in all speeches following the first affirmative, and even in this speech, certain preemptive attacks are often used as an anticipated defense of one's position. The one exception to this general rule may be in the second negative constructive if you elect to deal with only constructive plan attacks and disadvantages. The process of attack and defense inevitably will involve you in a number of strategic considerations.

Selecting the Argumentative Stance

Selection of an argumentative stance on your opponent's arguments is, perhaps, the first major consideration. Several factors may influence your decision on your argumentative stance. A major goal is to make sure it is consistent with the overall position you are taking with respect to the case, be it affirmative or negative, but considerations of planning, flexibility, audience analysis, and time will help dictate your choices.

Planning.   One strategic consideration in refutation is where your argumentative stance will leave you in rebuttal; that is, will a given stance, if won, help defeat or support the resolution? For example, if you are debating the advisability of world food aid and you are clearly winning an argument that states that food aid will lead to overpopulation, you will want to maximize the impact of this argument, knowing that if you win this argument alone you will win the debate. In the same debate, however, you may also be winning a plan-meet-need that states that feeding people is impossible (or at least that all the people cannot be fed). In this case you may choose not to extend this argument at all in rebuttals, realizing that if you win this argument, the chances are you still will not win the debate independently. Some people will still be fed, and so the affirmative, though having a substantially reduced advantage, will still have an advantage. In addition, the argument, if viewed in respect to other arguments, may cut against a more compelling aspect of your attack of the resolution: the plan-meet-need may reduce the impact of the overpopulation disadvantage and thereby will reduce your chances of victory.

Flexibility.   You will also want to take a stance that maximizes your options and minimizes your burdens. The objective is to permit maximum flexibility. For example, suppose that the affirmative is defending the use of selective private campaign financing for the election of public officials. The following arguments illustrate how you can maximize your flexibility in rebuttal by presenting selected arguments in your constructive speeches. In arguing against the benefits of selective private campaign financing, you could advance a conditional counterresolution that bans all private campaign financing and replaces it with total public financing of elections. Along with this argument, you could argue a disadvantage, asserting that the affirmative program could conceivably place the government in the control of only one political ideology. For example, you could claim that its use of selective financing will allow the New Right to run politics in Washington. In the disadvantage, you could also claim that the counterresolution will stop the New Right from coming to power. However, it is important to note that the disadvantage could occur merely as a result of the affirmative proposal, even if the counterresolution does not affect the New Right.

The above example will give you flexibility in rebuttal because it leaves you at least two options. First, if you are losing the counterresolution, you may still be able to win the fact that the plan allows the New Right to run the government. Second, if you are winning the counterresolution, this issue just places more credence in your argument, assuming that you are losing the position that the New Right will not come to power. Thus, by leaving yourself an out, you are able to be more flexible in rebuttal and have a greater chance of winning the argument(s) and, thus, the debate.

The type of flexibility exemplified above capitalizes on the hidden strengths of your position and allows you to adapt to the judge's philosophy on how the decisions should be made. Flexibility in a policy system is important to the judge who views himself or herself as a policy maker because it allows the proposed policy to shift in directions necessary to match changing social conditions. For the hypothesis tester, flexibility can demonstrate that you have not limited yourself in the pursuit of truth. Inflexible decisions on the types of arguments to extend can doom an advocate faced with a judge having an opposite view. For example, for policy makers it may be fallacy to argue that the judges are not adopting any policy if they vote negative, whereas it may be equally foolish to insist that if hypothesis-testing judges vote negative, they are adopting a policy system.

Audience Analysis. Your argumentative stance should also reflect as much as possible the judge's value system. No matter how objective judges may try to be, they will be bothered by voting for arguments that they find morally repugnant. For example, some debaters have been known to claim that saving an American's life is more important than saving the lives of people in other countries. Many judges find this belief offensive. Likewise, your stance should also take into account the judge's philosophical perspective. For example, if you know you are debating for a judge who is a strong supporter of government regulation and you have choices among disadvantages, you should probably avoid arguments based on the theory that the affirmative proposal will lead to increased government controls. It is unlikely that this argument will convince the judge that more government controls in themselves constitute a harm. Often, of course, you will not know the value system of your judge. In those circumstances you must make inferences based on the value systems shared by most people.

Time Factor. First, choose arguments that can be explained well within the debate's time limits. Some economic theories, for example, involve such complicated mathematical models that it can take hours to explain the stance and even longer if the explanation alone is not sufficient to persuade the audience.

Second, spend more time on arguments that received the least substantive refutation and initially on arguments that cannot be easily refuted by a direct response. In this way, you are more likely to gain argumentative ground. An important factor is the amount of time necessary for the proper assessment of the argument's impact. You gain no argumentative credit unless your defense or attack affects a major issue. It is extremely important that time be allotted for you to explain how your attack or defense makes a real difference to the debate's outcome. Usually you will want to combine such an explanation with internal summaries of your coordinate arguments. To ensure their successful assessment and summation, a wise choice is to avoid spending too much time trying to salvage any particular argument, even if it is potentially a winner. For example, little is accomplished if as an affirmative, you resurrect a portion of your harm if in so doing, you fail to refute a plan attack that takes out all of your harm. A good approach is to study the judge's reaction both to your speeches and to those of your opponent. This observation will often tell you whether more or less time should be spent on particular arguments, especially in rebuttals. You should always be prepared to adjust your attacks if your initial assessment turns out to be wrong.

Logical Structure.   Finally, keep in mind that arguments should be internally coherent. If your subordinate claims in support of a claim are not consistent with the claim, you have probably weakened your chances of advancing the argument in your favor. For example, suppose that the negative advances an argument that the free market should regulate hazardous products and defends the government's current regulation of the free market. At first, this argument may appear to support the advanced claim. When scrutinized, however, you will see that the claim on government regulation denies the first claim of a free market existing at all. The affirmative need only say that its plan will operate as a further government check, thus easily winning the argument.

Conditional Versus Explicit Arguments

Another important argumentative consideration is using the conditional rather than the explicit argument. The conditional argument is one developed hypothetically, so the debater need not be committed to it. When the conditional argument is used, it should exploit unstated assumptions in either team's position but should not go so far as to produce an internal contradiction.

In general, conditional arguments against inherency create fewer problems than between the need and plan, because the inherency structure is, to some extent, a single causative factor, the absence of a resolutional action. The negative, for example, could argue several mechanisms short of the resolution that could be used to solve the affirmative problem or that agents not isolated by the affirmative have countervailing motives or mechanisms that could solve the problem.

These kinds of responses demand no consistency because the negative is not offering them as a policy but merely as examples of why the affirmative proposal is not needed; each response is conditioned on its ability to demonstrate that the need for the resolution is untrue, not that the conditional policies add up to a consistent option.

At the same time, the conditional arguments must not contradict the disadvantages, because any disadvantages must grow out of the affirmative proposal. If the affirmative is calling for a federal program for more jobs, for example, it would be contradictory to read evidence in first negative to create more jobs conditionally on the state level and therefore insist that the affirmative proposal is not needed, while at the same time arguing that there are disadvantages to the creation of more jobs. When you find yourself in this situation, a good strategic choice is to try to salvage one leg of the conditional argument found to be inconsistent. Although you should avoid presenting contradictory evidence, when it happens, it is best to admit error and surrender one or the other of the arguments. Some judges simply throw out both sides of the argument, but many will permit you to give up one or the other.

Use of a Central Thesis

Another strategic choice is using a central thesis. Chapter 12 considered the development of a central thesis for the negative. The development of a similar position also is necessary for the affirmative. In both cases, a central thesis provides a reference point from which whole groups of attacks can be easily answered or rendered irrelevant. Furthermore, it enables a more rapid appraisal of arguments by both sides in rebuttal and implants in the judge's mind a clear reason for decision.

Examples of central theses for the affirmative are the positions that the present system lodges discretion in officials, whereas the affirmative plan mandates action; the present system relies on inefficient regulation, whereas the affirmative plan allows the market to work; and the present system relies on postaction checks on abuses, whereas the affirmative plan detects abuses before they occur.

Consider a central thesis associated with favoring oil price deregulation. The central thesis may be that the present system of price regulation is inefficient in that it fails to promote more exploration, whereas the removal of regulation will allow the market to offer increased profits to oil companies that, in turn, will use them to explore and develop more petroleum resources. If you are arguing this position, you should develop the central thesis in rebuttals to the final affirmative position that it demonstrates a higher probability of increased exploration than the negative minor repairs do, because it mandates deregulation as a means of increasing profits for the oil companies.

You should also make maximum use of the central thesis in plans. This is an especially good technique for the first affirmative rebuttalist to use to neutralize certain types of attacks. The central thesis can be simply that the affirmative plan separates conflicting roles in the present system. For example, if you propose that the powers of the Central Intelligence Agency (CIA) be decreased, you could preempt a negative attack that the president will coopt the agency, by showing that under the affirmative proposal, the CIA would be directly responsible to Congress.

Another example of a plan central thesis is the claim that the plan shifts jurisdiction over a problem from one level to another. For example, if you are arguing for the decreased use of coal as an energy source because of its environmental problems, you could incorporate a plan that would shift all regulatory responsibility for strip mining from state agencies to the Environmental Protection Agency. This plan provision would presumably defeat a cooptation argument that employment and industry pressures would be a foremost concern of any state agency.

Another plan thesis could be based on forced compliance provisions. If you are calling for the increased use of coal to solve the nation's energy problems, you could award triple damages to miners injured as a result of safety violations of this plan. This plan's provisions could be used to defeat an argument that increased coal production will increase occupational injuries among miners because of the economic disincentives to the improved enforcement of penalties of mine safety laws.

In some plans, you may wish to use a thesis that offers incentives for compliance. On the coal topic, rather than changing the penalty structure, you could use a plan that offers tax incentives to industry to upgrade safety standards. You could also use this plan to turn around any safety argument, because the plan gives industry a reason to make coal mines safer than they are now.

Several other examples of central theses in plans may be useful to you as an affirmative. You may, for example, choose to build your plan around the position that education results in attitude change, thus preventing circumvention and business confidence disadvantages. In calling for the increased use of coal, for another example, the negative could argue circumvention of safety standards on the grounds that industry will not comply because of the additional costs. To protect against this argument on the affirmative, you may wish to provide all necessary staff, training, and funds for nationwide implementation of coal-mining safety standards. This plan could help defeat an argument alleging that industry will remain convinced that it is economically unwise to upgrade safety standards, by providing education and implementation of an economically productive industrial safety program.

Another plan central thesis could use the idea that the plan offers a favorable cost-benefit ratio and thus will save money over a period of time. If you, on the affirmative, call for a program to increase the nation's use of coal, the negative could allege that the plan will not work because there is no means for transporting the coal and because transportation would offset any affirmative gains. To prevent this problem, you as an affirmative, could argue for upgrading existing railroad systems as a means of guaranteeing coal transports. This plan provision could defeat a social cost argument because the secondary economic benefits of increased rail transport may far exceed the initial cost of implementation.

Finally, you may want to use the thesis that the plan mandates administrative action and provides sanctions for disobedience. In the coal example, the negative may object to your claim that increased use of coal is the best energy policy on the grounds that coal companies will ignore with impunity the plan provisions strengthening mine safety standards. You could include in the plan a provision for the Department of Labor to conduct periodic spot checks on mines with provisions for penalties for safety standards violations. This provision could defeat an argument that inspections will be coopted, because the plan mandates that the inspections be unannounced and provides sanctions for any disobedience of that plan provision.

Grouping and Dividing Arguments

Grouping arguments is also a useful technique for attack and defense. In grouping arguments, it is wise to look for arguments that rely on the same central thesis, even though they are applied against different parts of the case or plan. On the deregulation of oil prices debate, for example, the negative may argue that oil companies will not use increased profits for exploration but instead will invest the profits in other enterprises. The negative may also argue, elsewhere, that the oil companies will not use the increased profits for more exploration but instead will pass them on to the stockholders. On the affirmative you could answer both arguments with a plan provision that mandates the reinvestment of profits in exploration for new reserves. Since the plan provision defeats both arguments, you may want to call attention to it, explain it in responding to one argument, and then cross-apply it to the other one. When doing so, you will need to identify the provision (in attacking the second argument) and explain its applicability.

You should also be alert to multiple arguments used by the other side against the same issue that may be answered by the same response. A good example is the application of a single inherency response to a group of negative minor repairs. If the affirmative is arguing for a new federal energy policy that switches the nation to nuclear energy, it is possible that the negative may offer a number of minor repairs according to which the country would rely more on coal and solar energy and the greater exploration of fossil fuels. If you read affirmative evidence claiming that even if all of these sources of energy are used, the country will still be short of energy by a given period, then you can group all of the minor repairs and refute the negative argument by applying its original evidence, which proves that even the most efficient use of all such additional sources will still result in major shortages.

In grouping arguments, nevertheless, you should examine all grouped attacks to make sure they are not subject to an interpretation that would render one or more of them independent. If your opponent can establish that one of his or her arguments has force apart from the others that you have grouped together, he or she may be able to ignore your grouped response and extend the one individual argument on its own merits. In the example above, it is conceivable that a different kind of exploration of the nation's coal reserves may not have been incorporated in the evidence. A good technique for avoiding this problem is to bracket the arguments on the outline that are to be answered collectively and then examine each one to make sure the one answer applies to all.

Dividing arguments is another effective technique for saving refutation time. The key is to find hidden assumptions in the opponent's position that should be dealt with independently from the position itself. An example is instances in which the affirmative calls for an increased program of jobs for Americans and claims unemployment as its major harm. A close look at this argument reveals that the affirmative is assuming that unemployment really is harmful. The negative could challenge this implied assertion and deal with it independently, according to the other argument that the nation faces chronic unemployment problems. Another technique for dividing arguments is the negative's developing independent or conditional arguments against affirmative contentions. For example, the negative could argue that the affirmative is exaggerating the harms of unemployment in calling for a federal program to increase employment but at the same time offer a conditional counterresolution that would increase jobs through some method other than the one contemplated by the resolution. The policy maker, of course, may have theoretical objections to such a strategy, but we feel that it is perfectly acceptable.

Exposing Inconsistencies

Finally, you should expose inconsistencies whenever possible. One obvious place to look for contradictions is between the structures of the need and the plan arguments. The affirmative should look for contradictions between the first negative's advocacy of minor repairs of the present system and the second negative's plan attacks that apply to both those repairs and the affirmative plan. If the affirmative argues for the deregulation of oil prices, the first negative could argue for minor repairs to encourage deregulation, and the second negative could claim a disadvantage from deregulation. The disadvantage becomes irrelevant if the first negative's minor repairs are expanded. The negative should look for contradictions between the affirmative inherency and the mechanics of the affirmative plan. For example, the affirmative may claim that the present system does not work because of the perverse nature of a particular agency and, at the same time, empower a similar bureaucratic, governmental agency in its plan.

Another way to expose inconsistencies is to find flaws in the team members' responses to related arguments. An example is a case in which one debater indicts the actions of one group of actors before the plan is adopted and the other speaker uses that same group of actors to implement his or her plan. Draw arrows on your flow sheet to indicate contradictory arguments; otherwise you may overlook them.

You should also look for contradictions in the use of evidence, especially when conditional arguments are used. For example, if the affirmative is arguing for a proposal to increase consumer product safety, it may use as its primary example the compulsory installation of air bags in automobiles as a means of saving lives. The first negative may choose to counterpropose methods for increasing seat belt usage instead of requiring air bags as a means of saving lives and to reinforce the counterresolution with evidence on the effectiveness of seat belt usage in reducing overall traffic fatalities. In the same debate, the second negative may argue that the increased use of safety devices encourages additional risk taking by drivers because the devices engender a false sense of security and may offer proof by example that other countries have tried such devices and found that overall traffic fatalities actually increased. In support of these two positions, one negative speaker reads evidence claiming that safety devices reduce traffic fatalities, and the other speaker reads evidence claiming that safety devices will increase traffic fatalities. Here is an obvious inconsistency, necessitating the loss of at least one of the two positions.

Finally, you should be aware of several other instruments for exposing inconsistencies. Cross-examination is a good means for exposing inconsistencies. Furthermore, whenever possible, the debater should exploit inconsistencies as reflecting on the credibility of the opponent's entire position. You should emphasize inconsistencies in rebuttals and encourage the judge to reject both sides of the opponent's arguments as being unreliable. Judges who view themselves as policy makers will be more likely to reject both of the inconsistent arguments, contending that the debater has given them no coherent approach for which to vote. Other judges will allow the debater either side of an inconsistency, so long as each is sufficient to defeat the opponent's argument. Even for the latter group of judges, however, there is merit in identifying inconsistencies, because you will make it clear that the opposition cannot win both of its original arguments. From our perspective, the judge's resolution of inconsistent positions must be determined on the bases of the evidence presented, the framework of issues, and the debater's analysis in a given round.

Summary

The process of attacking and defending arguments is the major distinguishing feature between individual argumentative speeches and a clash of ideas, which is the essence of debate. Effectiveness in attack and defense often depends on your use of the outline of arguments, your consideration of the requirements of each particular speech in the debate, and your ability to make good strategic choices.

Proper identification of arguments is necessary for effective debating. We recommend using a flow sheet to record the progression of arguments across all the speeches in the debate.

In developing the first negative, you should first establish a negative position and then plan and execute all other arguments against affirmative assertions. In developing the second affirmative, you should compare and contrast your original affirmative thesis with the one advanced by the negative and relate all arguments to this difference in positions.

Finally, we suggest using a number of strategic considerations in planning and executing your refutation. These include selecting an argumentative stance that is consistent with your overall negative position and watching where it will leave you in rebuttal. We further advise that your argumentative stance provide you with maximum flexibility, be selected in accordance with time constraints, be chosen with a view of what different judges are willing to accept as plausible, and make maximum use of a central thesis. We also recommend grouping and dividing arguments as an effective rebuttal technique and exposing contradictions and inconsistencies in your opponent's arguments.

Questions for Discussion

1. How can a flow sheet increase understanding of the arguments and positions in a debate?
2. What special problems does the presentation of a counterresolution have for flowing a debate?

3. What factors should be considered in making strategic choices for refutation?
4. What are the strengths and weaknesses of grouping, dividing, and spreading arguments?
5. How does the negative position guide the planning and execution of all arguments against affirmative claims?
6. Throughout the debate, how can the original affirmative thesis and the one advanced by the negative be contrasted?

Chapter 16

The Rebuttal Speeches

As discussed in the last chapter, the conscious and careful crafting of attack and defense is critical and should begin after the first affirmative speech. Following the first affirmative, you are free to use as much or as little of each constructive speech as you choose for refutation. Only four speeches in academic debate are set aside strictly for refutation, and these are referred to as the *rebuttals*. It is in these speeches that the ideas about the resolution offered by each team are brought into confrontation so that the resulting clash may test the probable truth of the resolution.

It is extremely important for the outcome of the debate that you effectively use the rebuttals. You should utilize these speeches to respond to your opponent's positions and arguments, rather than merely to repeat what you have previously said or to add new constructive arguments. It is during this period of the debate that constructive positions should be compared and examined in a competitive setting. Unquestionably, without the proper use of rebuttals, effective choices cannot be made or proper conclusions reached.

The rebuttals are also important strategically. They are the last and resolving speeches in the debate. Therefore, unless the rebuttal time is used effectively, you can give solid constructive speeches and still lose the decision. The outcome of the debate often will hinge on your use of strategic choices, including the correct decisions in each rebuttal position, the nature and types of extensions, and the balancing of arguments.

Major Considerations of Rebuttal Strategy

Rebuttals are usually the speeches that make or break the course of argumentation in a debate round, and since they are the last presentations, time, advance planning, and the opponent's choices must be taken into account.

The Last Presentations

As you shape your rebuttal speeches, you should keep in mind several considerations. One is that the rebuttals are the last presentations in the debate. This means that they are your last opportunities to coordinate the arguments supporting your position and to extend in defending your assigned position or launching attacks on your opponent's position. This choice includes even more, however, than merely extending on previous arguments. All rebuttalists, particularly the last two, must try to resolve the issues by emphasizing the arguments the team hopes to win. In this manner you attempt to make your final impression on the judge regarding the strength of your position. This means, for example, that you cannot just show the judge that a piece of evidence destroys a claim of your opponent; you must also show why the argument should be awarded to your side.

Time Restrictions

As you choose arguments for rebuttal, you must also be aware of the increased time restrictions. In most academic debate formats the time allotted for rebuttals is usually about half that allocated for the constructive speeches. Your response to this increased time pressure may be critical to the outcome of the round. First, it means that you must carefully select the arguments that you will discuss in rebuttals. You should not go into rebuttal believing that you will be able to advance the same number of arguments, the same amount of explanation of arguments, or the same amount of evidence used to defend arguments that you can present in the constructive speeches. The prime consideration thus must be the number, depth, and combinations of arguments. Your choice will be helped by the careful preparation of constructive arguments before the round, which will reveal the range of arguments that your opposition can use against you.

Advance Planning

Generally, you should not introduce new arguments but should choose arguments that are closely related to existing argument structures in the round, both your own and your adversary's structures. You must plan your arguments ahead of time and decide before the rebuttals the arguments on which you want the debate to be resolved. Moreover, you must not only plan your own arguments but also predict what the opposition will say about each argument and what extensions your opponents will make in rebuttal. There simply is not time to develop new positions; rather, every spare second must be spent extending the lines of reasoning that have already been developed.

The outcome probably will hinge first on the quality of your original arguments; if they were weak initially, they are not likely to become strong in rebuttal. It is too late in the rebuttals to resurrect poor constructive arguments. The outcome may also hinge on the extent to which each speaker plans a rebuttal with the partner's rebuttal in mind. The first affirmative rebuttal, for example, must choose which arguments to extend on the case. It is rare indeed that he or she can cover in depth all those points raised in the first negative rebuttal. In choosing, the first affirmative rebuttalist must deal with those arguments that cannot wait until the last affirmative speech. All critical issues — those on which the debate may be won or lost in the minds of the affirmative — must be identified and extended by the first affirmative rebuttalist. Otherwise, this speaker will put an impossible burden on the second affirmative rebuttalist.

Utilize Your Opponent's Choices

Finally, as a rebuttalist you should always remember that many of your burdens are based on your opponent's decisions and arguments in the rebuttals. A good strategy to use in making these decisions is to try to capitalize on what the opposition does not cover. If the first affirmative rebuttalist, for example, drops a critical inherency argument, the second negative may wish to give great import to this point in rebuttal. Or if the second affirmative argues a turnaround on a negative disadvantage and the second negative rebuttalist drops the argument, it seems logical that the second affirmative rebuttalist quickly attempt to add the impact of the turnaround to that of the affirmative harm.

The Use of Extensions in Rebuttals

If debate is to serve properly as a truth-testing or decision-making instrument, constructive arguments must be subjected to the strongest possible tests. It is highly unlikely that positions and strengths will emerge at random through the mere repetition of the constructive speeches. The goal of the debater should be to extend the arguments made in each previous speech, thus probing deeper into the argument's logic and validity. Extension is not accomplished merely by repeating previous claims or shifting to new arguments. Instead, it is accomplished by showing, through a progression or advance of the existing analysis, that your opponent's arguments are less true than yours, that they do not diminish your claim, or that they actually help your position.

Types of Extensions

In Chapter 6 we described three different approaches to extensions, and it may be useful to review them here. You may choose among types of extensions, using one or all three in any given case.

The Use of Evidence. You may extend through the use of evidence. This technique can be overdone, especially if you overuse the technique by saying, "My opponent's expert says this, but mine says this," and leaving it at that. The judge may be left with nothing on which to base his or her decision, other than a group of experts who state different claims on the same subject. This rarely leads to an analytical determination of the resolution's probable truth. Instead, you should attempt to show not only that the evidence reaches different conclusions but also why your own evidence on the argument is superior to that of your opponent. For example, you can question the source of evidence your opponents have used or you can point to the lack of qualifications for their authorities, likewise reducing the argument's cogency.

Counterarguments.   A second type of extension offers counterarguments or exposes the logic of the opponent's claims. In this instance, you reveal the inherent weaknesses of your opponent's arguments by demonstrating that other proofs show that the opponent's claims lack the force they need to win the issue. For example, you show that other claims can be made about the same position and that the truth of one argument does not exclude the truth of another. Or you may apply the tests of logic to your opponent's argument to see if it is valid or irrelevant. You could raise the question of whether the claim follows from the premises on which it is based. You actually look to see if the argument is fallacious when considered according to the accepted patterns of inference.

Turning the Evidence.   The third type of extension is to try to show that your chain of reasoning actually refutes the opponent's position or that it, in effect, supports your position. When used properly, this is perhaps the most effective extension because you rely on the claim and evidence that your opponent already has accepted as true. One way to show that your opposition's evidence refutes its own position is to demonstrate that the opponent's arguments are contradictory. An example is in a debate in which the affirmative calls on the United States to ship food to foreign countries to prevent starvation. The first negative could argue that existing programs are shipping the food abroad to solve the problem. The second negative, however, could argue a disadvantage to shipping the food abroad, thus putting the negative in a contradictory position. Had they selected their extensions carefully so that they knew the nature of the alleged problem, they could have decided in advance whether the negative's need or plan arguments put them in a better position and used only the preferable argument in the round.

Another way to use the opponent's arguments against it is often called a *turnaround.* You take the entire unit of proof offered by your opponent and try to show that, in effect, it proves your case rather than the case of your opponent. This technique is often used by the affirmative in responding to negative disadvantages. The first affirmative rebuttal speaker tries to show that the disadvantage actually proves a need for the affirmative propositions and usually tries to claim it as further evidence that the resolution is true. An example of this type of argument was used in the final round of the 1979 National Collegiate Debate Tournament. The affirmative advocated a reduction in the standard workweek by the adoption of work sharing. The second negative argued that the unions would respond by striking and would ultimately hurt the economy, and it read evidence to that effect. The first affirmative rebuttal speaker attempted to turn around the argument by showing that labor on previous occasions had actually gone out on strike to obtain work sharing and that the affirmative proposal would decrease labor unrest.

A third way of using the opposition's arguments against it is to try to place it in a dilemma. A typical source of dilemma is the conflict between inherency and efficacy arguments. For example, if the affirmative claims that present attitudes prevent a resolution of the problem, you may be able to show that those same attitudes will ultimately keep the affirmative proposal from meeting the need. Frequently you will set up this argument by asking for an inherency motive, if it has not yet been provided, in the first cross-examination period. After the second affirmative gives the motive in its constructive speech, you will often be able to show why the presence of that motive will keep the affirmative proposal from meeting the need. Then you will prove that the affirmative loses either inherency or efficacy, in any case showing that it neglected one of the three stock issues.

Planning Extensions

Ultimately, the outcome of the debate will turn on the impact of the extensions. Several considerations must be kept in mind in planning extensions. It is important that all extensions be planned realizing that the burden of proof rests with the affirmative by the theory of presumption. Should the judge conclude that the teams have equalized their positions, he or she probably will vote negative because the presumption rests against the resolution. Therefore, the affirmative must have the preponderance of the evidence and proof. At the same time, you, as the affirmative, should initiate arguments that will have the balance of proofs on your side. This often means that you must examine all extensions. For example, in using disadvantages, the second negative may see all extensions except one and that one response could be sufficient to defeat the disadvantage. For example, if the first affirmative argues nonuniqueness against an unemployment disadvantage, meaning that the disadvantage will occur under the present system, then there is no net disadvantage in adopting the affirmative proposal, and it will not matter if the second negative rebuttalist wins on all other extensions, because the unemployment will occur whether or not the resolution is adopted. Thus, the nonuniqueness argument is sufficient to defeat the disadvantage.

Finally, the judge's theory of debate may influence the impact of an extension. For example, for the hypothesis-testing paradigm judge, an affirmative calling for the rejection of a counterresolution merely because of the absence of an added advantage, is probably wasting its time because the hypothesis tester is likely to believe that an added advantage is unnecessary if the negative can show that the problem can be solved better by a counterresolution. Policy-making judges, however, are likely to insist on an added advantage, since they are likely to view the two policies as equally risky.

As previously stated, new arguments are usually not considered to be acceptable in rebuttals. A new argument can be thought of as a new aspect of the logic of one's position, rather than as a logical progression of that established position. For example, if the affirmative claims that we need federal support for medical care on the ground that many people cannot get adequate medical attention because of the cost, and as a negative you show that the care is available through private and state resources, most judges will regard the affirmative response as a shift that claims that people are attitudinally disposed against private and state sources.

There are valid reasons for insisting on a logical progression from an original position, rather than permitting a shift to a new argument in rebuttal. The most important, perhaps, is that such a rule increases the depth of clash and, therefore, improves the chances that the truth of an argument will be discovered. The practice also helps the debater acquire one of the dialectical skills that debate offers. Without experience in responding directly to challenges, the debater probably gains little from debate beyond the development of constructive speeches. Finally, if the debate is being used as a decision-making instrument, it is unlikely that the audience will gain insights that come from the give and take on a position unless the extensions are directly applied to the previous responses. In fact, the audience may become confused on the issues, because the arguments will have become so muddled that many will be unable to follow the lines of reasoning.

You should also be aware that judges disagree on what should happen in a round in which arguments are dropped at various points in the debate. Some believe that if you drop an argument — cease to mention it — and your opponent does not reestablish it, then that argument should be dropped from the round. The judge will ignore even a potentially winning argument if it is made only once in the round and if the one who makes it lets it fall out of the debate. Other theorists believe that this position gives an unfair advantage to the second affirmative rebuttalist, by allowing the first affirmative rebuttalist to drop even the entire case and still win the round. There are those who believe that if both teams drop an argument, then the argument lies dormant only until one of the debaters makes an extension on it. For example, the second affirmative rebuttalist may still win an extension on an argument raised in the first negative rebuttal, even if the second negative rebuttalist did not mention the argument. Finally, there are some judges who think that an argument once introduced in the round should never be dropped out of consideration as a voting issue, even if no one else brings up the argument again. Some theorists think that this practice is unfair to all of the debaters because the arguments are extended by the judge rather than by the debaters. After all, debaters may intentionally drop arguments, and furthermore, debaters cannot refute the judge's extensions on the arguments. The judge, in effect, does the debating for the debaters rather than letting them provide the reasons for the decisions. Generally, the burden is on the debaters to extend the issues that they (the debaters) view as critical in deciding the debate. However, such decision rules must be determined in the course and context of the arguments presented.

Making Choices in Rebuttal

Many of the most essential and difficult strategic decisions that a debater must make are in regard to choices, and a number of factors should be considered in focusing the conclusion of the debate on these choices.

Time Constraints.   As you plan rebuttals, you must face up to your choices. You must first remember the time constraints and the range of arguments. The best guiding principle is to make sure that the time spent on each argument is justified by maximizing the strength of your position. You should always be concerned, as the close choices are made, that you do not lose more than you gain.

You should waste as little time as possible. Prune useless words and phrases, dispose of wasted arguments or those that do little to advance your position, and ascertain the minimum that must be said on an argument to carry it. Label concisely and organize simply.

Issue Constraints.   You should also make conscious choices within each issue you want to win. This decision should be based on the relative strengths you discover in the arguments and issues raised by both teams. For example, you may have an excellent attack on the studies that your opponents are using, but it may take so long to explain that you would sacrifice some disadvantage responses that make victory far more likely. You should ask two questions: What does my position gain if I win this argument? What happens to my position if I lose this argument? If the answer to the first question is "My side gets the decision," then the argument merits considerable attention. In the second instance, if the answer is "Very little that makes a difference," then the argument should probably be dropped from further consideration.

Relative Strengths of Arguments.   The problem of making choices becomes much more difficult when many arguments are about equal in strength. Often you will face several arguments that can either win or lose the debate for you. This situation may become a matter of choosing between the depth and the number of responses or between the power lost per argument and the strength of each argument. The advantage of in-depth coverage is that the analysis is strengthened and the argument is more sharply focused, but the risk is that the judge may not accept the argument, no matter how much time is spent on it, and you may have very little else left on which the judge could vote for your position. The advantage of extending many arguments is that it maximizes the options for both judge and debaters. But a spread of arguments runs the risk of encouraging shallow analysis and bad choices in rebuttal. Perhaps the safest strategy is a mixture of breadth and depth in rebuttal arguments. In an argument that you feel you can win through a lengthy development, you probably should use in-depth analysis. But in an argument that you must win or else lose the debate and whose resolution is in doubt, you may wish to make several brief responses in the hope that their number and weight will ensure their survival. This approach will increase the demands on your opponents to respond to several arguments in rebuttal.

Speaker Limitations.   The ability of the speaker to present clearly a certain number of issues and extensions in the rebuttal speech should not be forgotten. Although some advocates can give many answers and extensions clearly, others cannot. Hence, the number of answers that you can effectively present should form a part of your strategy.

Judge Preferences.   You should know the judge's preferences. If you know that the judge objects to a spread of arguments, then you should probably choose more in-depth analysis. But you should always tell the judge why you have chosen a particular argument and what difference it makes to the final outcome. Otherwise, the judge may interpret an argument quite differently than does the debater who presents the argument. You must always connect the impact of the argument with the thesis of your case. For example, if you are arguing a disadvantage that undercuts the affirmative significance, you should explain this to the judge. Take time to show that more benefits are lost through the disadvantage than are gained by the affirmative advantage.

Extension Strategies.   Your strategy in making extensions on arguments may well determine their effectiveness. Although the best rebuttals ultimately grow out of intensive topic research, sound flowing techniques, and extensive practice of past rebuttals, in any given round they must come from the realistic assessment of the competitive situation. The objective, of course, is to try to make your choices defeat those of your opponents. The best approach is to emphasize your strengths and minimize your burdens, based on your opponent's predicted and actual argument. The goal can best be reached by maximizing the certainty of arguments and preempting impossible replies whenever possible in early rebuttals.

Argument Placement.   Another important consideration for developing strong rebuttal positions is making sound decisions on the initial placement of arguments. If extensions will make an issue more compelling, introduce the arguments earlier in the debate. But a strong extension that runs the risk of being muddled if presented early in the debate should be saved until later. This strategy could apply to the placement of a negative argument that takes a long time for the affirmative to explain. If it is placed in the second negative constructive speech, the affirmative will be forced to use valuable time to explain its position in the first affirmative rebuttal when time pressures are greater. Raising the argument in the first negative constructive, on the other hand, gives the second affirmative time to explain it.

Maximizing Your Opponent's Burden.   You can also impose analytical burdens on your opponent. You increase your chance of a favorable decision by exposing contradictions in your opponent's positions, insisting on proof when it is missing, and attacking weak evidence. The presentation of counterevidence in the face of an incomplete analysis also strengthens your options. Finally, the use of the turn-around places a tough analytical burden on your opponents. They must defeat your claim that the argument works for your benefit, a claim that they may never have considered and one whose impact may greatly influence the judge's decision and the debate's resolution.

Minimizing Your Burdens.   Likewise, you can minimize your burdens in rebuttals with careful planning and wise choices. One way to minimize burdens is to use generic inherency responses that logically subsume other alternatives to prove that only the resolution can solve the problem. Suppose, for example, that the resolution calls for the federal government to control all elementary and secondary education. In response to your affirmative case, the negative has suggested numerous state, local, and private means to obtain your advantage. If you are able to reply that the uniformity of a solution is needed, then you do not have to reply to each of the negative's suggestions individually. Since only federal control is capable of achieving uniformity, you will have shown generically that the resolution is necessary in order to gain the advantage.

You should also move quickly to recognize your opponents' arguments that neutralize one another. But avoid making a spread of arguments — usually just questions—that can easily be answered with one or two words. Whenever possible, group arguments whenever they can be answered with one single response.

You should, of course, adapt all of these strategies to each particular debate round. The logical demands often change from round to round, and you should respond to these changes. Do not allow yourself to be talked into a few standard forms of attack. For example, if your opponent makes one argument the major issue, then concentrate on it extensively, but do not permit it to monopolize your time to the detriment of your own constructive arguments. In other rounds, a spread of arguments by your opponent may require you to reduce the number of your arguments.

Teamwork in Rebuttals

You should use techniques that allow you to work for and with your partner. Teamwork is absolutely essential. The stance that partners take on all issues and arguments supporting the major thesis or position must be coordinated to increase its effectiveness. Rarely will a team be successful if each team member plans his or her own strategies without coordinating them. For example, if a second negative ignores the case and, therefore, ignores preemptions of the plan attacks that may be offered in the case or the first negative's inherency attacks that prompted answers that now set up plan-meet-needs, this speaker sets the stage for tragedy. The negative, like the affirmative, should treat its case as one unit rather than as a series of fragmented arguments. This position calls for coordination between partners, continuity in planning arguments, and constant attention to what arguments and strategies all debaters used during the round. The team members must work for a common resolution of the arguments rather than no resolution at all.

Each debater should work for his or her partner. Usually a good aid for both team members is the use of a simple structure. For example, as a second affirmative constructive, you should fit your arguments into the general case outline so that the first affirmative rebuttalist does not have to work through a long list of subordinate arguments in order to reach the main argument. It is equally important for you, as the first negative rebuttalist, to crystallize the arguments under issues, explaining the impact of the argument on the issue and then stressing the importance of that impact to the debate's outcome. In a debate on the merits of providing governmental public service announcements on the harms of smoking, suppose that the first negative rebuttalist has extended a minor repair to increase smoking education in the schools, a conditional counterresolution advocating private sector public service announcements, and a solvency attack denying the benefits of smoking education. If the second negative rebuttalist is left with a flow sheet of forty arguments and pieces of evidence to extend, the speech will be difficult, at best. The first negative rebuttalist should condense the arguments into several conceptually distinct and impacted issues. These steps should make it easier for the second negative rebuttalist to move through those arguments to be extended without having to worry about a complicated structure. Of course, every effort should be made to avoid contradictions between partners.

In addition, each team member should be conscious of the proper use of preparation time. If the team is allotted a total of ten minutes for preparation between speeches, rarely should the first negative take more than four or five minutes before his or her constructive. As a rule, this speaker should use little or no time before the first negative rebuttal. The second affirmative constructive also should take very little preparation time. If you have done your planning, you should have your structure in mind and be able to answer most of the first negative's attacks. This practice leaves considerable preparation time for the two affirmative rebuttals.

Working with your partner also means preparing appropriate cross-examination questions that help your partner. For example, if the second negative cross-examines the first affirmative, he or she should ask questions that help the first negative constructive plan the arguments. For example, determine what answers the first negative needs in order to develop the negative position. Likewise, the second affirmative can help the first affirmative rebuttalist construct his or her arguments by anticipating certain plan attacks and asking questions to elicit answers that the first affirmative rebuttalist can exploit later. The second affirmative should make a list of questions as the plan attacks are being presented, in order not to overlook any of them in the cross-examination period. You also should remember to ask about causal links, evidence, and the like.

Regarding the affirmative, partners should work together on both case and plan. For example, both affirmative partners should know what plan attack preemptions will be used in the first affirmative constructive so that the second affirmative will know what extensions to plan for in the last affirmative rebuttal. Regarding the negative, both team members should discuss, before the debate, possible strategies for both the plan and the case. This discussion enables them to suggest ideas to each and to anticipate likely affirmative attempts to preempt the plan attacks. By suggesting possible affirmative answers, the first negative rebuttalist can also assist the second negative rebuttalist in planning rebuttal responses. When both members record both case and plan, it is easier for them to review extensions with each other to ensure that key arguments are not lost in the shuffle. This suggestion also applies to the affirmative. The aim is a coordinated effort that leads to a strong position.

Communication Strategies

Finally, strategies of communication in rebuttals may also influence the effectiveness of one's arguments. You must make your arguments clear to the judge. Helpful techniques include statements that tell the judge where you are in a chain of arguments, reiteration of answers obtained in cross-examination periods in later speeches, maximum use of fundamental positions by referring arguments back to them, transitions, internal summmaries, and balancing arguments. The alert debater will watch the judge and adjust speech patterns, transitions, and even arguments to the feedback he or she is receiving. Any technique that stresses the importance of an argument, including the use of varied language and pitch, will help the argument stand out in the debate.

The Four Rebuttal Roles

Each rebuttal has a unique function in the debate process and thus places a unique responsibility on each speaker. These responsibilities arise out of the strengths and problems that are allotted to the affirmative or the negative.

The First Two Rebuttals

Relative affirmative and negative advantages and duties must be remembered, calculated, and used in the first two rebuttal speeches.

Negative's Advantages.   In planning its argument selection in rebuttal, the negative should not lose sight of its advantages. These are (1) the negative need win only one stock issue, but the affirmative must win all of them; (2) the negative has selectivity of arguments within stock issues, with the possible exceptions of certain inherencies, minor repairs, or turnarounds on disadvantages, but in contrast, the affirmative may be in a position in which a loss on any argument under any issue could cost it the decision; (3) the negative has a twelve- or fifteen-minute block of argumentation between the second negative constructive and the first negative rebuttal that is hard for the affirmative to overcome psychologically. Each negative speaker should keep these advantages in mind as his or her speeches are planned.

First Negative Rebuttal.   The major chore of the first negative rebuttalist is to recast the debate into the negative light. This chore requires that arguments be condensed into issues that combine to prove the negative position. To do so, the first negative rebuttalist must advance his or her arguments against the second affirmative constructive responses and also provide a structure of arguments on the case that the second negative speaker can use in the final rebuttal. Moreover, the first negative must select arguments that avoid those, such as contradictions, that put the second negative into an untenable position.

As a first negative rebuttalist you should use several techniques toward these ends. In selecting arguments, stress the arguments that you are winning. Whenever possible, focus on arguments that the affirmative will have to overcome in order to win the round. At the same time, do not ignore the arguments you are losing if you can or must salvage them. Pay special attention to added advantages that come in the second affirmative constructive. These are new advantages, not part of the original affirmative case, that represent independent reasons to affirm the resolution. These must be answered in the first negative rebuttal so that the affirmative will have a chance to extend the arguments. Likewise, you should watch for inconsistencies in negative arguments that must be dealt with before the second negative rebuttal. Finally, you should always dwell on arguments that the affirmative must answer or run the risk of losing the round, such as a strong topicality extension that the first affirmative rebuttalist ignores at his or her peril.

In executing the speech, you should first identify the issue that you are extending and the second affirmative's constructive position on it and then give the answer. In so doing, you should be careful to read good evidence. Although all speakers should always be selective with evidence, the first negative rebuttal is an especially important place for which to reserve some of the best evidence.

A second important technique is in the careful use of preparation time. Since the first negative has about fourteen minutes during the previous speeches in which to prepare, rarely should you use any of the ten minutes of the team's preparation time. You should still be able to study the flow sheet to make sure that you avoid possible affirmative traps. You should watch for any affirmative attempts to "sandbag," or hold back, its best positions or evidence for the later rebuttals. Remembering that no new arguments should be introduced during the rebuttals, you may wish to ask the judge to hold the affirmative to its second affirmative constructive positions. Finally, you should stress the importance of your answers to your overall position; always keeping in mind that the objective is to win issues and not just arguments.

Affirmative's Advantages.   As the affirmative plans its rebuttals, it too should be especially attentive to its strategic advantages. These are (1) the affirmative has the advantage of recovery because the affirmative has the last speech in the debate; (2) the affirmative can be selective in its responses in the second rebuttal; (3) the affirmative can use independent harms, inherencies, and advantages to its benefit in the last rebuttal; and (4) the affirmative has the cohesive structure of its case for its advantage, which should increase the clarity of its position.

First Affirmative Rebuttal.   The first affirmative must cover the plan attacks and, with careful selection, return to portions of the case structure, acknowledging the first negative extensions and then giving extensions to those arguments extended by the first negative rebuttalist. As a first affirmative, this role will often require you to sustain the affirmative position in the face of massive negative attacks; to execute brief, but often multiple, responses to negative plan attacks; and to cover and advance the affirmative argument in a manner that provides a structure for the second affirmative rebuttal. Since you must cover twelve to fifteen minutes of negative claims, you should not attempt to resolve the debate, but you should be sure to keep the affirmative position viable. This chore requires a carefully conceived and executed plan of defense. In conceiving the attack, you should anticipate second negative responses on all of your answers.

For the disadvantages, you should identify the causal links and press hard when they are shaky or missing. You should look for the threshold of the attack and try to reduce the impact of the attack by showing that remaining in negative land produces the same effects, thereby demonstrating that the argument is not a net or unique disadvantage. As a first affirmative rebuttalist, whenever possible, you should use your plan planks carefully but quickly if the plan itself contains the mechanism by which to anticipate and respond to the attack. Whenever possible, you should turn around the plan attack, showing that the alleged attack really is an additional advantage for the affirmative. You may wish to review our discussion of turnarounds in Chapter 11. If possible, you should try to neutralize the impact of the attack, usually by using the countervailing causes. Or, if the impact works in your favor in the plan attack, let the harm stand and try to remove the link to the affirmative proposal that makes it a harm and change it into your advantage. In the absence of a turnaround, you should try either to show the absence of a link or to establish that the negative fails to offer links between the plan and the alleged objection. On the case, the first affirmative usually must drop some first negative extensions. You should, therefore, go to the affirmative's weakest areas, always getting to those that will lose the round if not covered and keeping a constant watch for preemptions.

You should strive for economy or brevity of language. This technique can best be achieved by practicing rebuttals. You should use labels that tell the judge where you are. You can also use your voice and nonverbal symbols in ways that help hold the judge's attention and alert him or her to significant arguments.

The Final Rebuttals

The second and final affirmative and negative rebuttals must establish decision rules for the judge to consider and, in so doing, focus the debate on the key issues and answers that should determine the end of the dispute.

Decision Rules.   As the debate moves into the last two rebuttals, each speaker must concentrate on decision rules in order to establish the superiority of his or her own analysis. A *decision rule* is a principle that establishes the criteria by which the judge must decide inconclusive arguments. The rule states or implies what arguments are to take precedence over others. These rules are critical. For some arguments, the date of the evidence may be the crucial factor. If the argument concerns the employment rate, for example, recent figures will be more persuasive than those of the previous year. Another critical factor is arguments that have been dropped in previous speeches. This is especially true for the negative when the first affirmative rebuttalist drops extremely damaging attacks in the case or for the affirmative when the second negative rebuttalist drops a disadvantage that has been turned around. Another possible decision rule may relate to who gets the benefit of the doubt. Finally, some extensions can be identified as being unreasonable. For example, the affirmative may be calling for a plan to increase employment, and the negative may extend by claiming that the affirmative position is invalid because the affirmative cannot give an exact count of the number of jobs. The negative's proposed decision rule should be rejected as long as the affirmative can account for an important increase in jobs.

Your opponents may overclaim impacts and argue decision rules that have little foundation in reality. Against a food case that argues for greater American assistance to the chronically hungry or malnourished, the negative may advance a plan-meet-need argument that certain leaders in less-developed countries may prevent the food aid from reaching the people, and they may claim that this absolutely denies the affirmative advantage. Such an assertion may be preposterous, given the enormous and varied number of people who would benefit from the proposal. In addition to attacking the negative's decision rule of claiming the meet-need as absolute, you may want to establish a decision rule in the judge's mind as to the lack of credibility in all negative claims, given the absurdity of the above argument.

Second Negative Rebuttal.   The objective of the second negative rebuttalist is to resolve one or more of the issues in terms of the negative position. At the same time, you, as the negative, should try to preempt the second affirmative rebuttalist. These twin goals demand that as a second negative rebuttalist, you resolve the arguments only in your format; you must preempt the second affirmative rebuttalist extensions.

It is important that the second negative avoid certain pitfalls. These include attempting to extend on all arguments in the debate, identifying all previous extensions speech by speech, ignoring all structure, and trying to reexplain all affirmative arguments. Instead, you should, on the plan side, carefully cover all attacks on any plan attack that you hope to win, pointing out the impact of the answers. You should not hesitate to drop plan attacks that your side is going to lose anyway, as long as they have not been turned around. Answering turnarounds may be the most important plan responsibility of the second negative rebuttal, since these arguments otherwise would give added strength to the affirmative. Quickly drop a plan attack if it sacrifices essential areas you may win on the case side. Whenever possible, you should group arguments. Often one answer will weaken several attacks. On the case side, try to show where the affirmative extensions either ignore or miss the point of the negative position. You may wish to divide your time nearly in half between responses to the plan and to the need.

At a minimum, you, as the second negative rebuttalist, must advance arguments that tie directly into the latest affirmative arguments, showing the impact on the major issue and emphasizing why the negative response justifies the rejection of the resolution. You should avoid presenting isolated arguments without serious impact on the issues. Another chore is to stress those arguments that you feel have the best chance of winning and to de-emphasize those that you are least likely to win. For example, if it appears that spending even three or four minutes on one disadvantage may defeat the resolution, this is a much better strategy than taking portions of this time to defend inherency arguments that you will probably lose in any case: there is no time to spare.

Other important considerations for the second negative rebuttalist are the use of multiple, independent extensions, including those that take the least time but carry the greatest impact. This obviously puts a much greater burden on the second affirmative, a strategy that should work to the negative's advantage. As the second negative, you are also encouraged to read new evidence if necessary to carry the issue. Finally, a negative summary is vital. It is important that the second negative rebuttalist leave neither the judge nor the second affirmative too much discretion in how the issues should be resolved.

Second Affirmative Rebuttal.   The objective of the second affirmative rebuttalist is to demonstrate the failure of the negative position by filtering it through the affirmative case structure, logic, and evidence. The usual approach is to cover the vital plan attacks and then to return to the case structure, identifying the second negative extensions and then giving the second affirmative responses.

In dealing with the plan attacks, you, as the second affirmative rebuttalist, must not overlook any second negative response that independently wins the attack. You should be especially alert to disadvantages dropped by the second negative rebuttalist that the first affirmative rebuttalist has attempted to turn around. The last affirmative speaker should seize on this failure as a means of adding to the significance of the affirmative case. If the negative has made headway on some of the plan attacks, you should balance its gain against your own significance, showing how your advantages outweigh the plan attacks. For example, if you are dealing with a plan-meet-need that, at best, takes out only a portion of the advantage, be sure to remind the judge that the attack, even if true, is not absolute in its impact. If the disadvantage deals with the same value as the affirmative does, you should try to show that the disadvantage will not occur but that even if the disadvantage is given to the negative, the affirmative still has more significance to reduce through the adoption of the resolution. If the negative plan attack deals with another value, you should try to convince the judge that the attack is not true or that even if it is true, the affirmative harm carries a higher-priority value. For example, millions are saved from suffering through the adoption of the affirmative proposal, whereas the fundamental rights of only a handful are in jeopardy through the disadvantage.

For the case, you, as the last affirmative, should follow the structure of the first affirmative constructive speech. You should be especially alert to two areas of argument. First, you must get to the most damaging extensions offered by the second negative rebuttalist. Second, you should respond to any damaging arguments made in the first negative rebuttal that the first affirmative rebuttalist has failed to answer.

Finally, as the second affirmative rebuttalist, you must identify for the judge exactly why the affirmative carries the preponderance of evidence and arguments on each of the three major issues. You need not claim to have won all the arguments. But you must balance the negative attacks against the affirmative arguments in a manner that gives the judge a reason to accept the resolution.

Summary

Rebuttals are fundamental to debate. They help the debater generate and test ideas about the resolution, without which the constructive positions would fail to receive the proper comparison and contrast necessary for deciding the resolution's probable truth. The main approach to fulfilling the rebuttal function is for each rebuttalist to plan his or her attacks and defense in a way that minimizes burdens and maximizes options.

The rebuttal functions can best be performed through proper use of the rebuttal strategies, argumentative extensions, and the four rebuttal periods. The final impact of these functions usually hinges on the outcome of the argumentative extensions, a process that does not merely repeat the original position but actually advances the arguments made in each speech by probing deeper into the argument's logic and validity.

Questions for Discussion

1. How accurate is the statement that debates are won or lost in the rebuttal speeches?
2. Why should rebuttal speeches be planned before a round of debate begins? How can advance planning be done?
3. Should you turn your opponent's argument whenever possible?
4. What is the difference in rebuttals between the extension of arguments and the presentation of new arguments?
5. Why are decision rules important? How can they be established in the final two rebuttal speeches?

Chapter 17

Cross-examination

For most of the debate, only one side presents its arguments at a time. The only way to match affirmative and negative arguments is for the audience to make mental comparisons. In contrast, cross-examination allows arguments to be developed through direct interaction between the debaters who are asking and answering questions. This method is as old as the Platonic dialogues, in which Socrates developed arguments for his readers by questioning various other characters and allowing the constructive position to emerge from the interchange. As a component of academic debate, however, cross-examination is relatively new. It was first proposed in 1926, won wide acceptance in high school contests following its adoption in 1952 by the National Forensic League, and came into widespread use at the collegiate level after its introduction in 1976 at the National Debate Tournament.

There are many possible formats for cross-examination. As we noted in Chapter 7, the most common pattern is for a cross-examination period to follow each constructive speech. Each of the four debaters serves once as questioner and once as respondent, in addition to delivering a constructive and a rebuttal speech. Cross-examination periods usually are three minutes in length.

Cross-examination is an integral part of the debate. It is a time when positions may be clarified and important gains can be made for use in later speeches. Accordingly, it must not be treated simply as entertainment or as a diversion to keep the audience attentive while the debaters prepare for later speeches. The maximum value of cross-examination can be obtained through a clear understanding of its goals, the necessary preparation, the conduct of the examination itself, and the follow-through later in the debate.

Goals of Cross-examination

From the standpoint of the questioner, cross-examination serves several important goals, which we shall consider in this section.

Clarifying the Opponent's Position

Perhaps the most significant goal is to clarify and define the opponents' position and to force them to commit themselves. Sometimes clarification is necessary because the questioner did not listen carefully or misunderstood what was said in the constructive speech. When questions of this type are needed, they should be asked clearly, directly, and quickly.

More often, however, clarification will be necessary because the opponents' original position is not clear. It may be deliberately ambiguous so that the opponents can move in different directions depending on what refutation they encounter. It may be vague because the opponents want to avoid having to take a stand. Or it may depend on assumptions that have not been stated or developed. Obviously, it is difficult to refute an argument that is not adequately specified, and it may be futile to take time to refute it if the opponents have left themselves so many outs that they can always say, "Oh, we really didn't mean that." Cross-examination can force the opponents to take a stand, reveal their underlying assumptions, and indicate the stance that they are preparing to defend.

Eliminating Ambiguity. The following example illustrates the use of cross-examination to define the opponent's position. In a debate on air pollution controls, the affirmative argues that ambient standards—standards that regulate the amount of pollution in the atmosphere without identifying its source—are ineffective. Such an argument is vague — it is unknown what ineffective means. The negative will have difficulty defending ambient standards without knowing more specifically why these standards were attacked. So the following cross-examination sequence is used to define the affirmative position:

Q. *First of all, why aren't ambient standards effective?*

A. They aren't effective because they merely take a sampling of the air and tell how bad the pollution is. That doesn't tell who is polluting. It doesn't tell — what about, if the weather is going the wrong way, it will give a wrong reading. And because of these two things it doesn't help at all in enforcement, which is what we need.

Q. *Okay, so it's the weather and you can't define the extent, right?*

A. No. Not that you can't define extent. You can't tell who is doing it. You can't define responsibility.

Q. *Okay, fine.*

Now the affirmative position has been clarified: the cause of the trouble is that ambient standards do not permit enforcement agencies to identify who is polluting.

With this knowledge, the negative can determine its method of refutation. It may choose to argue that ambient standards do permit identifying the polluters, that some other means of identifying specific polluters is available, or that it is not necessary to identify specific polluters in order to control pollution. But whichever of these responses is chosen, the negative can be confident that it will truly answer the affirmative's argument.

Eliminating Vagueness.   In much the same way, cross-examination can be used to eliminate vagueness resulting from a desire to evade choices. Suppose, for example, that an affirmative plan proposes to apportion new electrical power plants on a cost-benefit basis. Since this phrase may encompass a multiple of virtues and sins, it is understandable that the negative may desire a more specific set of criteria. Cross-examination may be used for this purpose:

Q. *You've said you'll use cost-benefit analysis, right?*

A. Yes.

Q. *What factors will be considered as costs?*

A. Adverse effects on the environment, risks of accident, things like that.

Q. *How much weight will you give to the risk of accident?*

A. I don't know; our board will decide.

In this example the questioner did not succeed in obtaining a substantially more specific version of the plan. But the statement "I don't know; our board will decide" may be just as useful. It clearly states that the affirmative will take no position, deferring judgment to the agency established in the plan. That knowledge may be just as valuable to the negative — suggesting the uncertainty built into the plan and leading to an argument about the board's power.

Identifying Unstated Assumptions.   Another way to clarify the opponent's position is to identify unstated assumptions or undefined terms, as the following example illustrates: The affirmative has proposed a world food reserve that would be used to supply needed food in the event of disasters. However, the first affirmative speech has not defined what a disaster is for the purposes of the plan. Clearly, the affirmative case rests on assumptions — for example, that disasters are unpredictable, that they are irregular, that they cannot be controlled, and so on. These assumptions need to be identified so that the negative can determine whether the definition of disaster in the affirmative plan relies on the same assumptions. For this purpose the questioner proceeds as follows:

Q. *What is your definition of disaster?*

A. Disaster is anything—well, we define natural disasters as anything climatic.

Q. *Well, say in Bangladesh only 10 percent or 20 percent of the crop planted actually comes up; is that a disaster?*

A. Yes, because it is a reduction in the total predicted supply.

Q. *What if it's only a 10 percent reduction?*

A. Yes, this is what triggers our plan, a 10 percent crop reduction.

In this example, the respondent risks difficulties by using a very broad definition of disaster. Subsequent questions, however, clarify the meaning, and the negative is now able to examine whether the plan and the affirmative case arguments rely on the same assumptions.

Defining Stasis in Controversy

The second purpose of cross-examination is closely related to the first: defining precisely what is at issue. All of us have been in arguments that proceed in so many different directions that we lose track of just what the dispute is about. We are likely to pause and ask someone to restate just what the disagreement is. When we make such a request, we are inquiring about what the controversy's focal point, or *stasis*, is.

For any given argument, there are many possible stases. If one side supports and the other opposes community-based treatment programs as an alternative to prisons, the dispute could turn on the question of whether community-based programs are sound in theory, are effective, are affordable, introduce additional problems, require special efforts to create them, and so on. Each of these possibilities reflects a different stasis.

Unless the participants in the dispute can determine just what is at issue, their arguments are unlikely to clash directly. Rather, they will repeat their positions, neither side directly engaging in or responding to the argument of the other. In contrast, when stasis is identified, everyone can focus on what is in dispute.

Cross-examination can be useful in establishing stasis. In the air pollution example above, such an exchange could proceed as follows:

Q. *Are you aware that we support ambient air standards?*

A. Yes, I am.

Q. *You realize that we think they are sufficient to enforce pollution standards?*

A. Yes, but we don't agree.

Q. *I know. You think they are ineffective?*

A. That's right.

Q. *Why are they ineffective?*

A. Because they don't permit you to identify the specific polluter.

Q. *And it's necessary to do that?*

A. Yes, it is.

Q. *So our disagreement is about whether you have to identify the specific polluter in order for pollution standards to be effective?*

A. I suppose so.

In this example, the question in dispute has now been framed. Arguments that pertain to unrelated questions can be omitted by both teams, and the audience can focus on the specific disagreement. Determination of stasis in cross-examination, then, aids in selecting the arguments to be used in later speeches. Arguments that are pertinent to the stasis should be featured prominently; those that are not can probably be omitted.

Although the determination of stasis is intended as a method to identify precisely where the disagreement lies between the two teams, significant agreements may also be discovered. Locating stasis may require excluding possible controversies because they are not in dispute. In the air pollution example, the questioner could show that the witness has not contested the technical ability to establish ambient standards or monitor the air and has not disputed whether ambient standards — if enforced — could be effective. Cross-examination could determine that questioner and respondent agree on those points. This agreement would signify that these questions could be waived from further dispute, as continued argument on agreed matters would be a waste of time. Identifying agreements, as well as disagreements, is an important function of cross-examination.

Establishing the Decision Rules

Cross-examination also may establish the appropriate decision rules for resolving a dispute. A *decision rule,* discussed in Chapter 16, is a statement that if certain conditions are met, the dispute will be resolved in favor of one side. To use a simple example, the statement "A man is innocent until proven guilty" functions as a decision rule. It answers the question "Who gets the benefit of the doubt?" by stating that if a jury is in doubt as to guilt or innocence, they must vote to acquit, since the prosecution has not proved guilt.

When audiences are asked to evaluate the probable truth of policy resolutions, they will frequently be undecided. Seldom will arguments be resolved unequivocally. More likely, the listeners will have partial confidence in each of the competing judgments. The audience will need to know how to resolve their doubts, regarding both particular arguments and the probable truth of the resolution as a whole. If the debaters do not provide the relevant decision rules, the judges must improvise them. In a contest involving evidence, one judge might decide that the most recent evidence is preferable. In a dispute about the effectiveness of a given policy, another judge might decide that the burden of proof rests on the party who initiated the argument. In a choice between alternatives, yet another judge might feel that the less risky alternative is best. Still another might hold that a position that can be tested empirically is preferable to one that cannot.

In regard to all of these examples, two points are worth noting. First, the judges must invoke some sort of decision rule to resolve disputes. Even if they are unable to articulate what their decision rule is, they must still have recourse to one. Second, the judges have no choice but to impose a personal decision rule if the debate fails to supply one. The use of highly personal decision rules is likely to make judging more erratic, simply because the debaters never know the grounds of judgment.

This is when cross-examination can be useful. The interchange can clarify the decision rules and give the judge a clear standard for decision. Sometimes the respondent may suggest a decision rule in the course of the answer, or sometimes the questioner may propose one and seek agreement with it. To return to the air pollution example, an interchange such as the following could help establish a decision rule:

Q. *Why do you have to identify the specific polluter?*

A. So you can press charges for violation of the act.

Q. *Does the act itself have any deterrent value?*

A. Not much if the violaters know they can't be caught.

Q. *How could we tell if the act served as a deterrent?*

A. I suppose if people who had polluted the air prior to the act quit doing so.

Q. *Even though the polluters couldn't be identified, if people quit polluting after the act, could we conclude it had had a deterrent effect?*

A. I suppose so, unless there was some other cause for the decline.

Of course, the questioner cannot always expect the respondent to be so cooperative! Nevertheless, in this example, a clear decision rule emerges. The audience trying to weigh the competing claims about ambient standards will decide that they are enforceable if former polluters can be shown to have stopped polluting the air, in the absence of another explanation for this result. This decision rule supersedes whatever personal notions the audience may otherwise have used. Knowing the relevant decision rule, the debaters can direct their energies toward showing whether or not the conditions of the rule have been satisfied.

Identifying Deficiencies in Proof

A fourth purpose of cross-examination is to identify deficiencies in proof.

Internal Deficiencies.   Sometimes these deficiencies are *internal* — for example, a piece of evidence is out of date, or the evidence does not say what the opposition claims that it does. In these circumstances, the questioner could ask about the specific passages in the evidence that are at issue. In the following example, the affirmative has claimed that state and local governments will not enforce regulations against industries because they fear that the industry will relocate to another city or state.

Q. *Let's examine your evidence for a moment. You told us about relocation, correct?*

A. Yes.

Q. *You quoted Congressman James Symington. Could you please repeat what he said?*

A. "Local enforcement officials hesitate to enforce standards, since industries have the option to relocate their facilities in areas with less stringent regulations."

Q. *Okay. Now that says they hesitate. Does it say that they don't enforce the laws, in the end?*

A. Well, we can read other evidence that says that.

Q. *Symington says that industry has the option to relocate. Do industries actually relocate on the basis of these sorts of regulations?*

A. Yes, they do.

Q. *You haven't proved that yet, have you?*

A. Well, we can read the evidence.

Q. *But neither of these two points is established in the Symington quotation, right?*

A. Not in that quotation, no.

The deficiencies in the evidence have been identified — in this case, the affirmative's unwarranted extrapolation from the literal language of the evidence. Moreover, remedying these deficiencies becomes an additional proof burden on the affirmative, as later in the debate it must read the additional evidence to which it referred during the cross-examination.

Challenges to evidence should not be made lightly or frivolously. As the previous example illustrates, they often take quite a bit of the cross-examination time, which is then not available to achieve the other purposes of cross-examination. Moreover, making routine challenges to evidence may strike listeners as "playing wolf." For these reasons, evidence challenges should be reserved for situations in which there is some serious problem with the evidence that, if not noticed, will cause the evidence to be given much greater weight than it deserves. When such challenges are introduced, the questioner should be precise about what piece of evidence is involved and what words in the evidence are the focus of the question. The questions should not be asked in an accusatory manner, but in a direct way that will elicit either recognition or denial of the alleged deficiencies.

External Deficiencies.   At other times, the deficiencies in proof may result from *external* considerations. For example, the opposition may have developed a generalization by referring to a number of examples but failed to consider an important counterexample. Cross-examination can be used to pose the counterexample, inviting the opposition to resolve the discrepancy between it and its generalization or else exposing its inability to do so. In arguing for a single six-year presidential term, for instance, the affirmative could claim that the powers of the modern presidency are so great that an incumbent is virtually assured of reelection, thereby denying the electorate a true contest. The cross-examination could be used to confront the opposition with an embarrassing counterexample:

Q. *You say that incumbent presidents are almost always reelected, right?*

A. Yes, that's right.

Q. *Then why weren't Gerald Ford and Jimmy Carter?*

Another type of external deficiency in evidence may be a discrepancy between the evidence and other conditions that are known by both teams to be true. Again the confrontation type of question may be useful. If, for example, the negative asserts that the economy is rapidly improving, the affirmative could ask such questions as "Are you aware that the unemployment rate is currently in excess of 7 percent?" or "How come inflation remains in double digits?" The respondent will need either to modify the original claim or be able to explain the seemingly contradictory empirical facts.

Advancing One's Own Position

The first four purposes we discussed all relate to the use of cross-examination to probe your opposition's arguments. But questioning also can be used to advance your own position. If only certain portions of your argument have been attacked, it may be useful for you to identify areas that were not touched. Doing so in cross-examination may lay the groundwork for a constructive argument built on the undisputed claim. This purpose usually can be accomplished quickly and with simple questions:

> **Q.** *You didn't dispute our claim that the demand for energy is dropping, did you?*

The function of such a question is to narrow the area of controversy, by indicating arguments that have been waived from consideration.

An illustration of the value of such questioning can be found in the following example. The first negative speaker has presented a number of mechanisms by which the state and local governments can control pollution and prevent industrial relocation. Rather than respond to the specific mechanisms, the second affirmative has chosen to discuss the general problem of industrial relocation. By exposing areas that were not challenged, the questioner can point to deficiencies in the second affirmative's resubstantiation.

> **Q.** *Did you ever disagree with my initial analysis that industrial location is a regional choice?*
>
> **A.** It doesn't matter; interstate compacts won't work.
>
> **Q.** *That doesn't answer my question. Did you deny that industrial location is a regional choice?*
>
> **A.** No, we didn't.
>
> **Q.** *In regard to tax incentives, did you ever talk specifically about tax incentives for not relocating?*
>
> **A.** Yes, we did.
>
> **Q.** *Didn't your quotation say that any industry that didn't want to control pollution wouldn't do it even with the tax incentive?*
>
> **A.** It was saying that an industry that couldn't afford to do it, couldn't do it with a tax incentive.
>
> **Q.** *Was it talking specifically about incentives for not relocating?*
>
> **A.** No, but that doesn't matter.

In this interchange, the questioner establishes that affirmative refutation is not specifically applicable to the mechanisms defended in the first negative speech. Now the responsibility is clearly on the affirmative either to show that the general arguments are applicable to the specific negative mechanisms or to substantiate the claim that "it doesn't matter."

Cross-examination can also identify areas in which your opposition has implicitly, though not overtly, agreed with your basic assumptions. The opposition may choose not to speak to those assumptions but to develop arguments that clearly imply agreement. Cross-examination can be used to make that agreement explicit, thereby tying the opposition to a definite position. Suppose, for example, that the affirmative has described the harms of inflation. The negative, without taking any position on the harms, has concentrated its attention on methods by which the present system is trying to combat inflation. An interchange similar to the following could be used to identify the latent agreement:

Q. *Now, we've said that inflation is a serious problem. Do you agree with that?*

A. Our position is that the present system can solve it.

Q. *But is it a serious problem?*

A. We haven't said.

Q. *You said the present system can solve it. Is it actually trying to do so?*

A. Yes. All the mechanisms we talked about prove that.

Q. *Why would the present system be so concerned about solving inflation if it isn't a serious problem?*

A. Okay, we'll give you that it is a serious problem.

It now becomes unnecessary for the affirmative to present additional arguments and evidence to establish that inflation is harmful, since this position has been accepted by both teams. Instead, the affirmative can concentrate on points that remain in dispute. Likewise, should the negative proceed to offer plan objections to the evils of controlling inflation, then the underlying assumption of those objections — that it is a mistake to control inflation — will need to be reconciled with the negative's own admission that inflation is a serious problem.

Goals for the Respondent

Our discussion so far has focused on the questioner's goals of cross-examination, since the questioner has primary control of the time. But the interchange is not without benefits for the respondent, too. For example, your, the respondent's, position may be advanced by clarification and explanation. A question may reveal that there is an important point in your argument that your opponents truly do not understand (and that the audience may have missed as well). A question about that point should be taken as an opportunity to amplify the original remarks, to introduce an illustration or example, or to state the original position more clearly. Such explanations should not be attempted indiscriminately in response to all questions, for then the impression would be created that the respondent is stalling and deliberately wasting time. But in the right circumstances, when the respondent has a strong argument, the cross-examination period can help make the original set of arguments clearer and hence more compelling to the audience.

Perhaps the greatest benefit of cross-examination for the respondent is the opportunity it provides to enhance his or her own credibility and hence the credence that will be given to the respondent's arguments. The respondent who appears cooperative, interested in sharing information, and concerned for the needs of the audience will convey the impression that he or she has nothing to hide, is genuinely interested in determining the probable truth of the resolution, and regards cross-examination as an educational rather than a game-playing exercise. The personal credibility of such a witness inevitably will affect the credibility of the arguments he or she has advanced.

Preparing for Cross-examination

The seemingly spontaneous nature of the cross-examination interchanges is misleading. Skilled questioners and witnesses prepare for cross-examination just as thoroughly as they do for any other phase of the debate. One of the most important steps in improving proficiency in cross-examination is using advance preparation effectively.

Preliminaries

Preparation begins with the analysis of your own case and the cases you are likely to encounter when debating on the negative side. Thinking about the arguments in the case should lead you to find places for questioning: places where the opposition needs to be committed to a stance and instances in which the stasis will be unclear if not defined in cross-examination, decision rules will be crucial to establish, deficiencies in proof should be pointed out, and so on. The central thesis of the affirmative case and the negative position should be especially helpful in suggesting places for questioning. With your own affirmative case, you should be the most hostile critic. Try to anticipate potential negative arguments by imagining what you would ask if you were forced to debate on the negative side against your own case. Since you should be more familiar than anyone else is with the vulnerable spots in your case, if you follow this procedure conscientiously you should be led to important questions.

Once you have identified the places where cross-examination might be beneficial, the next step is to try to imagine the kinds of questions that would be most likely to accomplish your goals. It is often useful to consider the specific wording of your questions. Try to imagine the response of the opposition to the questions, and decide what your next step will be for each of the various answers that you can imagine.

One form of question that may be particularly helpful in this respect is the dilemma. A *dilemma* is an argument that specifies a limited number of possible options and an undesirable consequence for each. A simple dilemma might be "If a Republican is elected, prices will rise, but if a Democrat is chosen there will be a war; and those are the only two parties that have a chance to win." To the questioner, the value of the dilemma is that the number of alternatives is limited. For this reason, the questioner will be prepared to follow them up, regardless of which option is chosen. Of course, the effectiveness of the dilemma depends on its truly being a dilemma. But if there are additional alternatives besides those specified or if one of the specified alternatives leads to a consequence that is not really so bad, then the power of the dilemma is lessened considerably.

Practice Drills

Once you have identified places where cross-examination would be beneficial and have imagined the types of questions that might be asked, try out the questioning by asking another member of your team to play the part of the opposition. Work through the interchanges, perhaps tape-recording them so that you will know exactly what you asked and what responses you received. On the basis of these practice drills you may be able to modify the questions to make them more precise or to devise a more efficient approach so that you can accomplish your goals with fewer questions.

This type of drill work should be done on a regular basis with other debaters, in "reliving" past debate rounds — while using the flow sheets from these rounds — and anticipating future debates. A surprising amount of what is learned through such drills will stay with you and be remembered during the actual rounds.

Preparation During the Debate

Advance preparation, however, cannot substitute for careful preparation during the round itself, since no situation will present itself in exactly the form that you have anticipated. The most important steps in in-round preparation are (1) identifying the areas to question, (2) selecting among the potential areas, and (3) arranging the question sequences.

Identifying Areas. As you take notes on the opponent's speech, indicate on the flow sheet the arguments about which questions may be helpful to you. Do not identify the points at which you could ask a question but whose response would make little difference. Instead, identify those at which one or more of the goals of cross-examination could be enhanced, and devise a distinctive symbol to identify these questions on your flow sheet.

Immediately before it is time to question, look over your flow sheet and see how many areas of potential questioning you have identified. If there are not enough, you may need to inspect your notes again and add more questions. More likely, however, you will have identified more areas for questioning than you can develop in a three-minute period, and then the problem will be how to determine priorities.

But what is enough? To answer that, look back at the examples of cross-examination sequences that were presented earlier in this chapter. If you read them aloud, you will see that the complete interchange lasts anywhere from about ten to forty-five seconds. Very short sequences are the rule when the question is a simple one, its purpose is clear, and a lengthy answer is unlikely. Longer question sequences are necessary when a chain of questions must be developed, when the respondent can make a lengthy or evasive answer, or when the answers are not clearly predictable and you need to be prepared to follow up in several different directions. Obviously, each debate is different, and no general statement will always apply. But on the whole, questions about the details of evidence, questions to clarify what a position is, and questions to locate agreements take less time. Questions to force a commitment, to identify the dispute's stasis, and to establish decision rules are likely to require more time.

Determining whether you have enough to ask, then, is a simple matter of multiplying the lines of questioning that you may wish to develop by the time you think that each sequence will take. If you assume that short sequences will last between ten and fifteen seconds and that long sequences will take from thirty to forty-five seconds, you will quickly see whether you have enough material to occupy three minutes of time. If you do not, you are never obligated to use the full three minutes. But before relinquishing time that may be valuable to you, check over your notes again to see if there are areas that you overlooked.

Selecting Areas.   If you have too much material, then the next step is to determine priorities. To do this, weigh the value of accomplishing your goals in the cross-examination period against the value of developing the argument later in your own speeches. For example, if a brief series of cross-examination questions will make it unnecessary for you to develop a five-minute argument in your subsequent speech, then you obviously should ask the cross-examination questions, because they will free your time to develop other arguments in your speech. At the other extreme, if deficiencies in proof can be identified equally well through questions and answers or through an argument in a later speech, then there is no strong reason to ask this sequence of questions in cross-examination if choices among areas must be made.

Arranging the Question Sequences.   Once an appropriate number of short and long question areas have been identified, the final step in preparation is to determine the order in which you wish to ask the questions. Often it is simplest just to follow the order of the opponent's arguments or the order of your own case. Unless there is a good reason to do otherwise, questioning about the arguments in order will be easiest for listeners to follow. Sometimes, however, it may be useful to vary the order if the response to an early question will affect later questions during the same cross-examination period. An easy way to remember the order of the questions you wish to ask is to number the various symbols you have made on your flow sheet, beginning with 1 for the first question you plan to raise and continuing for whatever number of questions you wish to ask.

We have discussed the various steps in preparation as if they were isolated. Approached in this way, several minutes would be required to make each of the decisions and be prepared to cross-examine. Yet questioners typically are expected to begin almost immediately after the completion of the respondent's constructive speech. The only way to be prepared so quickly, of course, is for the various steps to be practiced so much that they become automatic. It may be best to begin in practice situations, in which there is no time pressure, so that you can carefully go through each of the steps. Then, progressively reduce the amount of time that you allow yourself to make the key decisions in preparation. Soon you will be able to prepare for cross-examination almost instinctively.

Conduct of Cross-examination

So far we have considered the purposes of cross-examination and how to prepare for it both in advance and during the actual debate. In this section we shall examine the conduct of the cross-examination sequences themselves.

The Questioner

Decisions must be made about the order in which the debater will question; sequences or chains of questions must be developed and worded; the questioner must know when it is futile to continue an exchange; demeanor must be appropriate; and a proper record must be kept of the results of the cross-examination exchange. Each of these matters will be discussed in turn.

Determining Which Speaker Will Question.   Most cross-examination formats allow either member of the opposing team to question the person who has just finished speaking, as long as each speaker questions only once. It is important to decide, therefore, at which time each speaker will question.

One approach is for the person who will deliver the next constructive speech to question. For example, the first negative speaker questions the first affirmative. This approach has both benefits and drawbacks. The person who is about to speak will be familiar with his or her own arguments and consequently with the objectives to be gained in cross-examination. It is easier to apply the results of the cross-examination in the next speech if the same person handles both tasks. But questioning immediately before one speaks reduces the amount of time available for preparation, and it suggests that the two opposing speakers are operating independently of each other rather than as a team.

A second approach is for the person speaking next not to be the one to question. In this view, the second negative should question the first affirmative, the first affirmative should question the first negative, and so on. The advantages and drawbacks of this approach are the mirror images of the first. It gives more preparation time to the person about to speak, and it suggests a team effort, since the debaters question knowledgeably about arguments that are not their own. But it reduces the chance that just the right questions will be asked, and it makes it harder to follow through on cross-examination in the next constructive speech. This latter problem is aggravated, of course, if the next speaker pays little or no attention to the cross-examination but uses the three minutes to prepare for the upcoming speech.

A third approach is to vary who will question from round to round, based on the nature of the case, the special strengths and weaknesses of each questioner, the need for preparation time, and similar considerations. This approach has the obvious benefit of maximum flexibility, but it requires careful coordination between the debaters on a team. If each person believes that the partner is preparing for cross-examination, the result may be that neither one does so! Then the choice of who asks the questions will be a last-minute decision, and neither will have had the opportunity to prepare. The net result may be to waste the cross-examination period altogether. For this reason, relatively few debaters leave the choice of who should question to be decided anew in each debate.

Developing Question Sequences.   The questioner should practice developing questions in *sequences,* or *chains.* The logic behind this suggestion is that few witnesses can be expected to make major admissions or concessions. Cross-examination may indeed produce major gains, but it is likely that they will be obtained through a series of small questions that are followed through in the constructive speeches. A question such as "Now you really don't have any inherency in your case, do you?" is unlikely to produce a satisfactory response. Worse, it is an invitation for the respondent to repeat and amplify the points in the original case, thereby using valuable time that could have been spent asking additional questions.

The following example illustrates the need for asking a series of small questions rather than one big one. The affirmative has constructed methods by which eyewitnesses can identify suspected criminals in a police line-up, and the affirmative case has enumerated many possible factors that can distort accurate identification. The cross-examination period begins as follows:

Q. *All right, why won't the witness change his mind if we tell him that the investigative methods are all wrong? Why won't he change his mind?*

A. Okay, there are two reasons. The first is that once he has seen the suspect and identified him, he has a psychological image of that guy and believes that he is the criminal. And secondly, if six months ago you were very nervous in a line-up and you identified someone, you are not going to recall those suggestive influences.

In this example the questioner is trying to confront the respondent with a contradiction in his or her case. Knowledge of the deficiencies of eyewitness identification should make eyewitnesses more reluctant to identify criminal suspects. But there is no way that a respondent will answer a broad question by admitting a major inconsistency in his or her own case. Rather, as in this example, the respondent will use the question as an opportunity to amplify the original presentation and perhaps, as here, to add additional arguments and motives that were not claimed originally but assist in answering the questions.

To prevent this position, questioners should develop questions in a sequence, beginning with questions on which agreement can be readily gained and proceeding gradually to the questions that might pose the problem for the respondent. In the above example, suppose that the questioner had developed a sequence similar to the following:

Q. *You've claimed that eyewitness testimony is unreliable, right?*

A. That's right.

Q. *Because suggestive influences distort the witness's identificationn?*

A. Yes.

Q. *Is the evidence sure that these suggestive influences are widespread?*

A. Oh, yes.

Q. *Did you have much trouble finding evidence on this point?*

A. Oh, no, we have six or seven good studies here that we found right away.

Q. *I'm sure you do. This information could be available to others, too?*

A. Sure, just go to the library.

Q. *Now, one last question. Are people likely to make statements that they know to be inaccurate or unreliable?*

A. Well, not usually.

In comparing this example to the previous one, several points should be noted. First, the questions do form a sequence, each one building on what has gone before.

Second, the chain begins with a question to establish the position of the opposing team. This initial question alerts the audience to the specific argument that is being discussed so that they can follow the dispute on their flow sheets. And it is a harmless question that is likely to elicit agreement, providing the information on which the questioner then can build in order to explore disagreements.

Third, the questioner does not ask the "killer" question, "Aren't you being inconsistent?" — which was essentially the opening question in the first example. Even at the end of a sequence, the questioner cannot expect the respondent to make a major admission that will damage his or her case. It is more likely that the respondent will evade or give an irrelevant answer. For this reason, the cross-examination should provide the materials necessary to make the argument but stop just short of the killer question. Then, in the next constructive speech, the speaker can build on the results of the cross-examination. He or she can observe that since the identification procedure is widely known to be unreliable and since the affirmative has granted that people do not generally make statements that they know to be unreliable, there should be an easy solution. Confronting eyewitnesses with the knowledge that suggestive influences are distorting their perception should lead them to be more cautious, thereby reducing the likelihood of faulty identifications. Now the argument is complete: the combination of what was obtained in the cross-examination and what was developed in the subsequent speech produces a fully developed argument.

The general procedure for cross-examination sequences, then, is to begin with a question identifying the subject matter in dispute and the opponent's position, then to pose questions that are likely to elicit agreement, and to proceed in steps until all the necessary information has been obtained and all that remains is the final response, the ultimate implication of the argument. This final step, however, should not be developed in the cross-examination, but in the subsequent speeches.

Wording of Questions.   Questions should be worded simply, with a single idea per question. If the question has several complex clauses and must be divided in order to be answered, the questioner has wasted time. Questions should be phrased in neutral language; if the wording is loaded, it will be difficult for the respondent to offer any meaningful answer. Wordy questions should be pared down in order to save time. A question such as "Is it the belief of you and your partner that prices are rising?" can be pared down to "Are prices rising?" A good rule of thumb is to limit each question to a single independent clause and to begin with the verb phrase.

Knowing When to Stop.   Just as important as initiating questions in sequences and wording them carefully is knowing when to abandon a line of questioning, either because the respondent already has said as much as can be expected (so that further questioning is unproductive) or because the respondent is having difficulty understanding the questions (so that continuing on the same lines may be an inefficient use of time). In either situation, the questioner is likely to feel frustrated. The temptation is great to continue, hoping that one more reformulation will clarify the meaning or elicit the intended answer. But the chances of success in such situations are minimal, and there is little gain in pursuing the matter. If the witness really is being evasive, the audience should be able to recognize that. If the questioner really is having difficulty being understood, further thinking later when not under the time pressure of the cross-examination may be the answer.

The following exchange from a debate on establishing a world food reserve illustrates why it is unproductive to pursue a point when no satisfactory answer is likely:

Q. *Everything you argue on the case side of the flow is dependent on capital?*

A. That is the first response.

Q. *That is the first response?*

A. We have two negative positions here: Number one, grain reserves are not necessary; but number two, to the extent they are, they are adequate.

Q. *If grain reserves are not necessary, why is the present system trying so hard to have them?*

A. If the present system is trying so hard to have them, then what's the inherency?

Q. *Let me ask the question again. Grain reserves are so undesirable, why are we trying to have them?*

A. I never said that grain reserves are undesirable; I only said they are not needed to gain your advantage.

Q. *If they are not needed, why are we trying to get them?*

A. I repeat . . .

Q. *Don't ask me a question, just answer the question.*

A. Would you repeat the question and try to explain it?

Q. *If grain reserves are not needed, why are we trying to have them with the present system?*

A. Oh, I don't know. They might be a nice thing to have.

The questioner is no better off at the end of this exchange than if the sequence had stopped four questions earlier before "Let me ask the question again." Faced with the retort, "What's the inherency?" it would have been better for the questioner to make some offhand response and then shift the focus of questioning elsewhere.

It is difficult to abandon a line of questioning when one appears to be in a "one-down" position; the temptation is great to keep at it in order to shift the situation to one's own advantage. But it is just such efforts that produce the waste of time that the above exchange illustrates.

Demeanor. The questioner's demeanor should convey the impression of cooperativeness, congeniality, and sincere interest in the exchange. The questioner should be careful not to appear superior to the respondent and not to browbeat the respondent into submission. Televised versions of courtroom dramas are not the best model for cross-examination in academic debate. If the witness is uncooperative, tries to filibuster, denies the obvious, or refuses to be pinned down to a position, the questioner should be sure not to allow frustration to interfere with the careful selection of questions or the conduct of the exchange. The questioner's facial response could indicate that both the questioner and audience are aware of what is happening and are humoring an obviously uncooperative witness. But the questioner should retain a friendly and congenial attitude, should stop when no more gains are possible, and should then develop later an argument about the implications of the respondent's silence or evasiveness.

Note Taking.   The questioner's final concern should be to note the results of the cross-examination so that they can be followed up later. Pledges by the respondent to produce evidence should be noted in the appropriate place on the flow sheet; important admissions should be similarly annotated; and relevant statements regarding the dispute's stasis or decision rules should also be indicated. Although the bulk of the note taking will be done by the two debaters who are not involved in the cross-examination, the questioner should note important gains for later reference.

The Respondent

The respondent's primary goals in cross-examination, it must be remembered, are the enhancement of personal credibility and the opportunity to clarify or advance arguments. The first of these goals depends largely on attitude and demeanor. The respondent should be attentive to the questions and clear and direct in replying to them, suggesting interest in the cross-examination and a genuine desire to cooperate with the questioner.

Answering Questions Directly.   If a question is clear, there is no point in attempting to evade it; such tactics usually are immediately recognizable and bring the respondent's credibility into question. The following interchange illustrates this problem. The first affirmative has discussed the problems of poverty, referring to the evidence that describes the "barren lifestyles" of the poor. During the cross-examination, the questioner attempts to probe this ambiguous statement to commit the affirmative to a position:

Q. *You talk about the barren lifestyles of the poor. What makes them barren?*

A. Just because they don't have enough money.

Q. *But what specifically happens to the poor when they lack enough money? Where do they cut back in whatever they have to buy?*

A. It's often been called a dismal choice.

Q. *Sure, but can you tell me where, specifically? Where do they cut back?*

A. First comes the idea that they have to get enough of one thing, spend all their money in one area, and cut back in everything else. You can't say specifically for each family, because it's different among each group and each style.

Q. *Can you indicate where poor people generally cut back so that we can identify where the problem lies?*

A. The problem is that they just don't have enough money.

Q. *Well, wait a minute now. Where do they cut back? Can you tell me where they cut back?*

A. Well, if they're going to spend all their money in one area, they're going to have to cut back in all other areas.

Q. *Fine, but where is the tendency to cut back?*

A. Where?

Q. *Right.*

A. It all depends on which group of people you have.

Q. *But overall, where's the tendency? Can you tell me where the harm of poverty lies?*

A. It lies in the lack of money.

Of course, in this example the questioner pursued the point far beyond any reasonable expectation of gains. But the respondent's evasion of a fairly direct question is apparent to the listeners. Rather than directing attention away from the question, evasion only suggests to the audience that the respondent "has something to hide." If anything, the audience's interest is further aroused, and psychologically, the respondent is placed on the defensive. When a question is clear and direct, the best strategy is to answer it clearly and directly.

The questioner controls the cross-examination time, in that he or she determines what questions to ask. Sometimes the questioner may wish to proceed to a point via an indirect route and will ask questions that do not seem to bear directly on the point at hand. But it is not the role of the respondent to determine whether a question is relevant. An answer such as "that's not important," "it doesn't matter," or "it doesn't pertain to the case" is not acceptable. Either the question has a relevance that the respondent does not immediately perceive, in which case the questioner is entitled to continue to develop the point; or else the question turns out really not to be pertinent, in which case it will do no damage.

If the question demands knowledge that the respondent cannot necessarily be expected to have, there is no harm in admitting ignorance. In fact, it is far better to say directly, "I don't know," than to attempt to conceal ignorance by inventing an answer on the spur of the moment which then commits the respondent to an untenable position. Hasty answers given in cross-examination may haunt a team in rebuttals by creating proof burdens that it is not possible to satisfy.

Demeanor.   Just as a questioner sometimes will encounter a hostile respondent, so the respondent may have to deal with an uncooperative questioner. Here, too, the witness has great opportunities to enhance his or her own credibility simply in contrast with the questioner's demeanor. Should the questioner make frequent interruptions, attempt to browbeat the respondent, or ask unfair or loaded questions, the respondent has everything to gain by remaining calm and pleasant. The audience quickly will notice the contrast in attitudes.

To say that the witness should remain positive in demeanor, is not to say that affronts from the questioner must be ignored. If the questioner persists in interrupting, it may be appropriate to ask, "May I please finish my answer?" If the question is truly unfair, it may be perfectly in order to say, "That's an unfair question; may I explain why?" If the questioner inappropriately demands a yes-or-no answer, the respondent should feel free to say, "That can't be answered by yes or no." The key point, however, is that the respondent make such statements matter of factly and without becoming hostile.

Clarifying and Advancing Arguments.   Besides enhancing personal credibility, the respondent's other major objective is to clarify and advance arguments. Some of the important considerations here are defensive in nature, intended to ensure that the respondent does not take on unnecessary burdens. For example, some questions require qualified answers. They cannot be answered unequivocally one way or another because the answer depends on other factors. The respondent who replies to such a question with a "yes, but . . . " or "yes, provided that . . . " may be cut off by the questioner before having a chance to provide the necessary qualifying phrases. For this reason, any necessary qualifying statements should be placed at the beginning of the answer, prior to the yes or no. For example:

Q. *Do you believe in free elections?*

A. For people educated and trained in the values of democracy, yes.

If the qualifying phrase had not been placed at the beginning of the answer, this sequence might have gone something like this:

Q. *Do you believe in free elections?*

A. Yes, for . . .

Q. *Then why don't you demand them in the Soviet Union?*

Just because the respondent has not had a chance to qualify the answer, the impression is created that an overextended generalization has been confronted with a significant counterexample, when in fact the respondent's true position was limited in the first place by the nature of the situation.

Avoiding Impossible Burdens. The witness also should be careful to avoid taking on too great a burden. Particularly under the pressure of a relentless questioner, respondents sometimes try to display bravado by committing themselves to absolute positions that are impossible to prove and may invite massive dangers later. In the semifinal round of a national debate tournament, the affirmative case proposed testing new products for possible toxic effects before allowing them on the market. In the face of needling by a questioner who wanted to know what tests would be performed and what would not, the witness tried to stop the line of questioning by declaring that the affirmative would test all chemicals for all possible combinations of effects.

The respondent may have thought that the matter had been put to rest, but the questioner was able to calculate that this proposal would require an almost infinite number of tests to be conducted, at a cost that would exceed by several times the gross national product of the world. On the basis of this admission, which had been obtained during the cross-examination, the questioner was able later to claim that the affirmative plan was absolutely unworkable. A more careful witness would have avoided making such an absolute statement (which was not required by the nature of the case arguments), because it assumed a burden that could not be fulfilled. Likewise, if the respondent should assert that something always or never is the case, the questioner need find only one counterexample to discredit the position.

The witness also should be careful that cross-examination questions are not used to shift the burden of proof from where it properly belongs. In a debate over medical care costs, for example, suppose that the affirmative argument is that the expenses of medical care are so astronomical that national health insurance is required. The negative position is that a number of funding sources are available, from private health insurance to free care, to ensure that people who need care are able to receive it. In response to a question such as "Now can you prove that all these different funding mechanisms are actually working?" one might feel justified to answer, "Well, to prove inherency, it is your responsibility to show that they aren't."

This sort of response should be used sparingly, however, If it is easy to prove what is asked for, and particularly if it helps the respondent's position to do so, it is better to forget the technicalities of where the responsibility lies and supply the needed information, thereby enhancing one's credibility. The time to be sure that the proof responsibility is not shifted is when the answer is not clear-cut and when it matters greatly who gets the benefit of the doubt.

Sometimes the respondent will have the opportunity to do more than avoid taking on extra burdens; that is, the answers will not be only defensive in nature. Every respondent's dream is an open-ended question such as "I didn't understand your first contention; could you please explain it?" In such a case the respondent should take advantage of the invitation. Without stalling, being verbose, or obviously wasting time, the witness should restate the argument at issue, explain the argument in other terms, offer an example or illustration if appropriate, and finish by explaining the importance or impact of the argument on which clarification was sought. Of course, the questioner may interrupt and move on to other questions before this process is completed, but each few seconds that the respondent is able to spend clarifying the argument for the audience as well as for the questioner is additional time beyond that available in the constructive and rebuttal speeches to establish the arguments and their importance.

The Partners

During each cross-examination exchange, one member of each team will not be actively participating. These debaters also have important roles to play, however, in recording the results of the cross-examination.

Although the questioner and witness will take brief notes as they proceed, the major job of note taking should be done by the nonparticipating partners. At their desks, they should note important admissions (being as precise as possible about what was admitted), pledges to prove arguments that are in dispute, unfair questions, and so on. They may wish to make these notes directly on their flow sheets or else on a separate note pad.

In practice, relatively few partners cooperate with the cross-examination by taking careful notes. Instead, they tend toward one of two extremes. Some use the cross-examination period as additional preparation time for their own speeches. Hence they do not listen carefully to the cross-examination and are not aware of its results. It is not surprising, then, that they are unable to follow through on what was obtained. Since they do not listen and since no one took good notes, the sequence is forgotten.

The other extreme is displayed by nonparticipants who appear to lack confidence in their partners' ability to ask the right questions or answer them in the right way. Such persons are so attentive to the cross-examination that they become participants themselves, whispering questions or coaching the respondents on the possible answers, gesturing wildly to some point on the flow sheet that they wish to have questioned, or shaking their heads furiously in disagreement when the respondent offers some answer. Behavior of this sort will almost inevitably call into question the credibility of both the members of the team and will suggest that they are unable to work together as part of a team effort. Even if only on a subconscious level, such a perception will affect an audience's evaluation of the debaters' performance.

Follow-through

Largely because of faulty note taking, many of the gains obtained in the cross-examination often remain undeveloped throughout the debate. For many judges, cross-examination sequences will have value only if they are used in later speeches.

But with proper listening during the cross-examination period and careful note taking, a good job of follow-through ought not to be difficult.

Follow-through does not come during the cross-examination itself, but during subsequent speeches, either immediately following the cross-examination or later in the debate. (Some sorts of follow-through, such as commenting on the failure to produce evidence that was pledged, may be deliberately saved for the final rebuttal speeches.)

The nature of the follow-through varies with the cross-examination results obtained. It may use any of these approaches:

1. Reminding the audience of the proof burdens accepted by the respondent and examining the record to see whether those burdens have been fulfilled. Debaters who neglect this sort of follow-through are implicitly permitting an answer such as "My partner will prove that in the next speech" to stand as a euphemism for "We can't prove that, and we know you will forget about it and not ask us to."

2. Identifying admissions gained ("Now, you remember that in cross-examination they admitted that government policy was the most significant determinant of inflation") and explaining the significance of the admission ("This means that the private sector is not the place where controls are most needed to stop inflation; nor is it likely that wage and price controls will work without government spending ceilings").

3. Pointing to the opponent's inability to answer a question ("Now, they never could tell you whether the earth is gradually warming, cooling, or staying the same") and the implications of this failure ("Now, how can their board make all the adjustments for climate effects when we don't even know what these are?").

4. Making explicit a decision rule that emerged during the cross-examination and pointing out why it works to your benefit and why your opponent has failed to satisfy the terms of the decision-rule ("In cross-examination we established that the most recent evidence should prevail. They never disputed that claim, and their evidence is older than ours is").

Follow-through might be thought of as the final step in a process of cross-examination that begins with an understanding of fundamental goals, includes advance preparation, and requires careful attention to the questioning interchange itself. The process is not complete until its results are used to illuminate the argument subsequently in the debate.

Summary

Cross-examination is usually the three-minute questioning period at the end of each of the constructive speeches. For the questioner, the cross-examination has several goals. (1) It can be used to define the opponent's position, by eliminating vagueness or forcing a choice among alternatives. (2) It can be used to determine the argument's stasis, or focal point. (3) It can establish decision rules that specify how a disagreement is to be resolved. (4) It can identify deficiencies in proof and determine whether or not the opponents are able to provide the needed proof. (5) Finally, it can be used to advance one's own position, by identifying areas that have not been attacked or by waiving certain claims from dispute. For the respondent, the cross-examination (1) makes it possible to clarify or explain arguments and (2) offers the opportunity to enhance one's personal credibility.

Preparing for the cross-examination begins well in advance of a debate, by examining fruitful areas for questioning in the cases being debated on the topic as well as probing one's own case for likely trouble spots. Then questions should be imagined that may be helpful in accomplishing the specific goals. In-round preparation involves marking on the flow sheet the places where one wishes to question, selecting the question sequences, and determining the order in which to ask them.

Questions should be formed in sequences, beginning with a question that identifies the argument in dispute, proceeding through the questions likely to elicit agreement, and then moving on to the disagreement. The questioner should stop just short of the ultimate impact of the exchange, leaving that to be developed subsequently in a constructive speech. Questions should be worded simply and directly, with a single idea in each question. The questioner should be able to determine when further questioning is unlikely to be productive. The questioner's general attitude and demeanor should suggest cooperativeness, sincerity, and congeniality.

The respondent should answer questions simply and directly, without attempting to determine their relevance. If a question demands obscure information, the respondent may be justified in admitting ignorance. Like the questioner, the respondent should be certain that his or her demeanor suggests a positive attitude toward the interchange. In addition to enhancing credibility, the witness may advance or clarify arguments. Sometimes this process is defensive, as when the witness avoids taking on needless burdens, takes care to place qualifying phrases at the beginning of the answer, and resists questions that shift the burden of proof. Sometimes it is offensive when an open-ended question gives the witness a chance to amplify arguments.

Partners of the questioner and respondent should not ignore the cross-examination, nor should they coach the participants. All debaters should remember that the process of cross-examination is not complete until the follow-through on the results occurs in subsequent speeches.

Questions for Discussion

1. What will happen to a cross-examination period if the questioner and the witness do not have clear goals in mind?
2. How can one's affirmative case thesis or negative position be used to develop sequences of cross-examination questions?

3. Why are questions framed in chains or sequences more desirable than a large number of individual questions?
4. Why should the final step in a cross-examination sequence often be held back for the next constructive speech?
5. How can the witness use the cross-examination period to best advantage?
6. What is the best means to ensure that the gains of the cross-examination are followed through in later speeches?

Chapter 18

Communication Skills in Debate

In our previous chapters, we emphasized the view of argumentation as a method of problem solving. Our aim has been to help you gain insights and skills in developing reasons designed to influence others' attitudes toward such problems. Such a view requires you, as the arguer, to communicate with others and to attend to the quality of your communication as part of your persuasive efforts. By communication we mean the generation, in another person, of intended meaning. This process requires a number of skills, including the invention, development, and presentation of reasons that the receiver should believe the message.

Thus far, we have focused on the invention and development of arguments. This chapter will concentrate on communication skills related to the presentation of arguments. We shall discuss the adaptation of debate speeches to the critic judge, various styles of presentation for the debate speech, some aspects of the use of language in debate, and some special concerns in the delivery of the message.

Audience Analysis and Adaptation

As you plan your speeches in debate, you must make rhetorical choices involving the selection and placement of arguments. To maximize your effectiveness, you should preface such choices with a careful analysis of your audience, since your goal is the adaptation of ideas to people so as to influence their behavior. If done properly, this approach also will reward your audience, as it should yield clearer messages, thereby helping your audience decide whether to accept or reject your claims.

The General Audience

The first sources of information you should consult in planning your message are those theories of audience analysis that explore the audience's characteristics and the appropriate techniques of selecting, planning, and managing messages and responding to the audience's reactions. These theories are described in most texts on public speaking. Theorists recognize that successful speakers make message decisions that benefit their audiences by reaching out to the listeners' concerns rather than simply gratifying the speakers' own egos. In any speaking situation, you should be aware of your audience's interests and prejudices and their relationships to the message, the limitations of the human ability to listen to and comprehend any message, the likely effects of your message on the audience, and the proper methods of tempering or enhancing such effects.

Certain problems relevant to the debater's message also arise from the presence of a collection of individuals. The size of the audience can influence their response to the message. For example, intimacy, which may invoke favorable responses in small groups, may have little or no effect on large groups. Another determinant of the audience's response to a message is the degree of the group's homogeneity. Large homogeneous audiences may have common interests and higher expectations that the speaker must address. A large group will also be influenced in their response to a message by the degree of the group's solidarity. If the listeners are strongly committed to the group, they are more likely to respond intensely to a message directed to the group than they would as individuals.

Finally, you should find out the role your audience will play during your speech itself. An audience that intends to sit passively while you speak is less likely to pay close attention to your words than is one that is actively interested in your speech. You may wish to adjust the length or complexity of your message to account for this.

We urge you to use audience analysis as a rhetorical strategy, a means of gaining the desired response from listeners. An effective strategy will often demand that you consider many factors, including your own perception of the rhetorical situation; the message, including its ideas, language, and organization; the listeners and their expectations; the situation, including the time and place in which the communications will occur; the medium for presenting the message; the conditions under which the debate will be presented; and the likely effects of the message on the audience. Careful planning for each of these factors is essential to almost any speech. Communication strategies incorporating these factors can be used for many audiences, speakers, speeches, and purposes.

The Critic Judge

Because the typical academic debate involves a single critic judge, we now shall explore techniques of analysis that apply specifically to such critics. One major rhetorical strategy is being aware of the characteristics of different judges. For example, the debater needs to know whether a particular judge is especially concerned with issues, debate skills, or both when evaluating the debate. The issues judge will probably demand attention to the breadth and quality of constructive arguments and to genuine extensions in rebuttals. The debate skills judge is more likely to be concerned with an emphasis on clarity, conciseness, and oral persuasiveness, particularly in rebuttals. Some judges, even though they appear to adapt for the individual debate, will harbor certain unconscious biases that will surface in their evaluations. You should therefore plan your arguments and positions in accordance with the qualities that your judge finds most desirable.

Although we respect and encourage the development of the skills required to analyze information, we also encourage the rhetorical goal, which is designed to train the advocate who can influence behavior in a public arena. Even if a critic judge can accept the sloppy use of linguistic, vocal, and bodily skills or delivery, the communication aspects of debate training are likely to be neglected. Audiences in the real world do not present an undifferentiated forum. Some may be knowledgeable on technical issues and respect in-depth argumentation, whereas others may be non-specialists who need more extensive explanation and persuasive appeals. As long as you know in advance what kind of presentation the critic desires or even requires in order to understand the issues, your adaptation to different types of judging can be an opportunity to practice speaking to all types of audiences. We believe that the goals of academic debate are better served if the debater learns to communicate various forms of arguments in a variety of contexts to a variety of audiences.

You often have several opportunities to find out information about your judge before a debate. If the same group of people judges repeatedly, usually information about the judge's predispositions can be obtained from other debaters and debate coaches. Examining the judges' past evaluations, including ballots and oral comments made after rounds, is sometimes helpful. Whenever possible, you should read the judges' statements of their philosophy of their role as critic and talk with as many judges as possible about what they look for when judging a debate. Although some may not like this kind of interaction, most will be happy to answer general questions.

You can also find out much information during a round. Watch the judge's reaction to arguments. If a judge looks puzzled, then slow down and explain the argument more carefully. Also, watch the judge's flowing capability and adjust the delivery rate and repeat arguments when necessary to accommodate the judge's difficulties. One helpful device is to label arguments clearly and to allow the judge time to write down the labels. Although interpreting the judge's responses during the debate may be difficult, it usually will improve your communication.

The Judge and Speaker Credibility

Your communication effectiveness can be enhanced by your credibility to the judge as a sender of messages as well as by your behavior during the debate. Credibility is directly tied to the judge's evaluation of the debater's believability and trustworthiness. To enhance this credibility, you can project the image of one who is trying to carry on a straightforward discussion. You can strengthen this image by being completely honest in the presentation of your position and the evidence for your arguments. Your credibility is also helped by correctly interpreting your opponents' arguments and being courteous to them. Finally, your credibility is reinforced when you maintain a serious but composed attitude toward the presentation of issues in the round. Most judges recognize competition in the confrontation of ideas, but many reject excessive personal competition — expressed in rude and obnoxious behavior — because they believe it distorts the search for the resolution's probable truth. You can enhance your credibility by showing creativity and rigor in testing your ideas without using personal innuendo or histrionics.

In competitive debate, source credibility will often go beyond the control of any particular debater because one team will be more familiar to the judge or because other conditions will grant one side higher credibility. In these situations, if you are a member of the lower-credibility team, you should strive to overwhelm your opponents on the quality of your performance. The most effective compensation is to present superior arguments and evidence.

The following presentational behaviors should especially be avoided:

1. Loud and aggressive delivery. Judges are often made to feel uncomfortable and even offended when listening to a shouting match in a broom closet. It is easy to make yourself look like a clown if you are speaking in a room that calls for the volume of a phone booth, even though your voice could be heard in an auditorium. Belligerent or overly aggressive delivery may have the same effect on a judge. In these situations, many judges undoubtedly ask, "What is the speaker so upset about?" Such delivery may lead the judge to feel that you are, argumentatively, in a drowning position and are calling for help.

2. Arguments based on the illogical twisting of your opponent's position. Suppose that you claim that your opponent's position stating that inflation is not harmful (because debtors and some producers are helped by it) will encourage hyperinflation and a quadrupling of prices. An intelligent judge will recognize this as an attempt to skirt the argument. Nor will it help your credibility to set a red herring for your opponent.

3. Using illogical positions on losing issues in the hope of confusing the judge. Few critics will reward advocates for their skill in argumentative confusion.

4. Spurious and frequent accusations of wrongdoing by your opponent. Such practices will usually create sympathy for your opponent. Many judges will view seriously false accusation that your opponent misused evidence.

5. Finally, the misuse of evidence, particularly using selective reporting or fabricating evidence. This is the most likely way to reduce credibility in the eyes of judges, and most judges do, and in our opinion should, find such practices inexcusable.

Adjusting to Judges

You also must be able to adjust for biases and incompetencies in judging. Unfortunately, every debater on some occasions will be faced with a judge who is biased against him or her or is not qualified to judge.

In dealing with a biased judge, it is good to remember that bias is usually constrained by the judge's desire to avoid the appearance of impropriety if the opponent clearly loses. Thus, you can improve your chances for victory by making every effort to increase the margin of superiority of your arguments over your opponent's.

Incompetence is a judgment that is usually relative to one's preferred style of debate. If you like to speak very rapidly and provide minimal depth in arguments, then you may consider many judges to be incompetent to understand all your arguments. In these situations, if you hope to increase your chances for carrying the issues, you have no alternative but to adapt your presentations to avoid the perceived shortcomings of a particular judge. When there is a single judge, this adjustment should not create serious problems if you take the time to discover the judge's predispositions before the round.

When there are many judges, you may decide not to alter your style for a particular judge if you feel confident that another style will win the ballots of the majority. If a judge's reasons for a decision are unpredictable, you may be able to adjust your presentation by spending extra time establishing a clear rule for that judge to follow in the round. Above all, you should deal with bias and incompetence in the round through rhetorical adjustments rather than continuing in your usual style and then crying foul play after the fact. You should remember that the receiver is as fundamental to the process of communication as is the source and may necessitate as much careful analysis as does the content of your arguments.

You must also often adapt to the judges' theoretical variations. As noted in previous chapters, some judges have strong theoretical preferences that must be considered in order to win a favorable decision. We believe that this condition is sound educationally because it gives you an opportunity to test your positions before a variety of audiences who have different views about what constitute good reasons in the evaluation of assorted proofs. To be effective, you must often reconcile your own theoretical positions with those of the judge. You therefore must try, before the debate, to understand the judge's theoretical position and all of its implications and make the necessary adjustments in your presentation. Often the theoretical beliefs accompanying a particular view can, with some imagination, be translated into the terms of a different point of view, without any sacrifice of the arguments' merits.

Ultimately, you will have to decide what theory to follow in a given round. Once you have made that choice, it is better to stay with it than to experiment. Impromptu experiments with a theory almost always alienate even a theoretically neutral judge. It is also important that you and the judge understand all of a theory's implications. Above all, you must be prepared to defend the theory if challenged to do so by your opponent. Even if judges do not agree with your theory in principle, they will often grant you the argument because the defense of your position was better than your opponent's attack on it. In other situations, the judge may have no theoretical preferences, and then it is often desirable to establish a decision rule. If such a strategy is followed, however, you must observe the same precautions noted above.

Personalization of the Speech

Another way of adapting your arguments to the judge is through the personalization of your speech. To do this, you must attempt to gain acceptance of your position on the resolution by adapting to the judge's frame of reference. Instead of engaging in tactics that alienate the judge, such as combative threats and the like, you should try to establish shared values.

In addition, you must sustain an atmosphere of rationality and reasonableness. Finally, you should appear eager to engage in an open and free discussion on all issues. You are trying, by means of logical analysis, to convince an impartial and rational person to accept your claim. It therefore seems unlikely that you can badger such a person into acceptance.

In academic debate, you should attempt to break down barriers by drawing the judge into a close or confidential relationship with you. Techniques to achieve this result include: (1) addressing the judge by name; (2) whenever possible, using an informal presentation — using humor with caution, especially being careful that it is in good taste and avoiding humor at your opponent's expense; (3) positioning yourself in the room in order to maintain close eye contact with the judge; and (4) using vocal variations that tell the judge when something important is being conveyed and when a subject is inconsequential; and finally, (5) conveying an impression of reasonableness simply by being willing to make concessions that do not seriously injury your case. This act not only puts you in a good light, but it also should enhance the quality of the debate by weeding out the irrelevant issues. These techniques will often establish a closer link with the judge. You must be careful, however, not to destroy your effect by overdoing them or engaging in any credibility-reducing behavior, such as described above. In a competitive situation, these interpersonal links are always tenuous and must be protected.

Finally, maintaining a confident, competitive posture is important. Your competitive posture is closely linked to your credibility or the judge's disposition toward you. In debate rounds, many judges are undoubtedly influenced by their perceptions of which team appears to be winning the debate, even if the arguments are found logically deficient when carefully examined.

You should project as much self-confidence as possible when you face an objectively superior opponent. Voice projection becomes important. You must assert your independence and not allow yourself to be bullied into damaging positions. You must display faith in your position and be reluctant to make concessions. Your opponent's mistakes and contradictions in earlier speeches should be emphasized in rebuttals.

When faced with an evenly matched opponent, you should moderate your projection of self-confidence to avoid the appearance of stridency. You can be less concerned about concessions and the balance of authority during the cross-examination. You should pay greater attention to thorough extensions and exploration of the argument's content in the rebuttals.

When faced with a clearly inferior opponent, you must try to avoid the appearance of haughtiness. Generosity becomes the order of the day. You should not ridicule inadequate arguments. You should watch the judge for signals that indicate coverage of a weak argument, and you should avoid overkill. Excessive preparation time should not be taken if the judge shows signs of impatience. All of the foregoing, nevertheless, does not supersede the importance of winning the arguments that are necessary to win the debate. Superior debaters should not allow their concern for the feelings of an inferior opponent to draw them into a loss on a technicality or blunder.

Different Communication Styles

Traditionally, style has been included as one of the several aspects of the art of public speaking. Style is distinguished from the creation, arrangement, and presentation of arguments by its preoccupation with propriety. As we use the term *style,* our preoccupation is also with language, but we, perhaps, are less concerned with its virtues and more with its uses to aid understanding of how words work in debate to affect behavior

It is not our purpose to present a treatise on all the dimensions of style. Rather, we shall focus on selected aspects that can reduce ambiguity and enhance understanding. Although all debaters must develop their own characteristics of speech, effective communicators seem to share certain features. These features usually are not inborn, but, rather, require practice and preparation.

Clarity

One stylistic quality desirable in debate is clarity of argument. Part of a natural, comprehensible style is the functional labeling of arguments. In other words, the label should explain the essence of the argument, since that may be the only thing the judge will remember. You are also encouraged to avoid using debate jargon such as conditional counterresolution, inherency, minor repairs, and the like. Such terms usually confuse the issue at hand. Clarity is often greatest when the sentence structure is simple, especially when you want the judge to record your arguments on paper.

When you are familiar with the thesis of the affirmative case and the generic negative arguments on a particular topic, a rapid, succinct explanation of standard points becomes automatic, and the adaptation to new arguments becomes easier. Practicing constructive speeches is helpful. Material that requires a complex explanation may need additional advance work, which could necessitate writing it out and practicing presentation. In this way, you can be sure that your explanations of and introductions to crucial arguments say precisely what you intend. Finally, you should eliminate personal speech idiosyncrasies that detract from the impact of your arguments. For example, many debaters overuse such phrases as "you know what I mean," "I would argue," "going on," "O.K.," "in terms of," "most importantly," and other such meaningless phrases and thereby lose the important ideas. Recording your speeches will often reveal these annoying verbal mannerisms.

Force

You should use techniques that will reinforce the initial impression of your arguments on the judge's mind. Your arguments can often be strengthened by varying your speaking rate and pitch for different portions of the speech. When everything is spoken at the same rate or volume, most of the argumentative impact will be lost. You should slow down on words that are essential to an argument and speed up on superfluous words in reading the evidence. You can use phrases and other traditional devices to highlight for the judge important parts of your argument. You can use analogies and other exploratory devices to emphasize arguments whose meaning is not obvious. Of course, you should use these techniques sparingly; not every argument is crucial. Finally, summarizing the preceding arguments and assessing the impact of the arguments on the progress of the debate also will help the judge.

Certain techniques are particularly helpful in reinforcing the impression of an argument. If possible, use the momentum of your arguments to strengthen the transition between constructive argument and refutation. For example, the second affirmative speaker should summarize the major contentions and the evidence supporting them before proceeding to the first negative arguments. You should also have a good working knowledge of words that have continued rhetorical appeal in the mind of the critic and that can de-emphasize shortcomings in the proof package for particular arguments. For example, a short response that a policy is "repugnant" often convinces judges to reject arguments that, because of their nature, the advocate may be unable to fully refute with evidence and reasoning. Literary devices such as metaphors, similes, analogies, and the like can also be used to flavor dull arguments. Such devices, of course, should be incorporated into the speech in a manner that makes their use seem natural.

Finally, you should always be aware that the force of your arguments is often determined by the strategic choices you make in rebuttals. You must be willing to summarize the debate in the last two rebuttals and make necessary concessions to buy extra time for explanation. This device helps give judges decision rules — something they usually like and that often works in your favor.

Economy of Expression

Economy of expression refers to the ability to convey the maximum possible amount of content in the minimum number of words. It is not speaking more rapidly but eliminating excess verbiage. This skill requires advance preparation and practice. In your practice, you should rewrite your constructive speeches, making arguments that you wish you had thought of earlier but did not, explaining evidence that you thought spoke for itself in the debate but apparently did not, and finally, experimenting with different assessments of argument impacts. You also should revise your rebuttal speeches until you have said exactly what you wish you had said in the round. This practice should help you refine your expressions and prepare for responses from your next challenger. In addition, you should keep in mind the techniques described below.

Short Labels

First, you should reduce the number of words in labels on arguments to the shortest phrase that conveys the full intended meaning. For example, the statement that "unemployment harms people by causing them to commit suicide" can better be expressed by "unemployment encourages suicide." Try to eliminate meaningless words such as "in today's debate," "the fact that," "in terms of," and so forth. Whenever possible, memorize and use short signal words for refutation, such as "wrong," "but," or "no," as a means of paring down transitions, particularly in rebuttals.

Use of Case Thesis

A second way to economize on language is to rely on the core thesis of the affirmative case or negative position to answer many attacks rather than to attempt to explain unnecessary new arguments. You also can cross-reference your arguments in constructives. If your opponent has twice presented the same argument, you can answer it once and then refer back to your previous answer. But cross-referencing should be used sparingly in rebuttals so as to reduce the judge's confusion at the higher rates of speed that usually prevail in the early rebuttals. Another device is to record evidence in full but to bracket the portion of the evidence to be read in rounds and to eliminate words that do not affect the context or meaning of the evidence. It also helps to remember the principles of strategic choice in rebuttals.

Sense of Timing

Finally, economy of language is aided by developing a *time sense* for arguments that allows you to pace the speech and make necessary adjustments while speaking. For example, commonly used constructive arguments should be timed so that your material is commensurate with the amount of time available for its development. You should become familiar with the number of short rebuttal arguments that you can give per minute so that you can make more informal choices and avoid overkill or undercoverage during the speech. It also helps to be aware of elapsing time during the speech. Assuming that the judge has no objections, you may wish to have your partner give vocal countdowns of minutes during rebuttals to ensure that your attention to the remaining time will not be distracted by your concentration on the arguments. You may also want to devise general guidelines for dividing your time between plan and case in rebuttals.

Delivery

The physical requirements for good speaking in debate are essentially the same as they are in any form of public address. A good speaking voice will depend on controlling your breathing, releasing tension in your throat and neck, and using speech modifiers, especially your tongue and lips. You should develop a pleasing voice that responds to the sentiments being expressed and does not detract from the message.

Physical Behavior

Nonverbal physical behavior is important to communication. Judges are sometimes influenced by the visual impressions of your sincerity. Therefore, you should use body movements that improve comprehensibility rather than detract from it. An important physical consideration is visual directness or direct eye contact with the judge. Another aspect is posture. Although many debaters ignore it, there is evidence that a speaker's stance does have an impact on how the message is received. Movement can also be helpful in conveying thought and symbolizing transitions, and debaters should be aware that certain body movements can help explain arguments. Finally, gestures with the arms and hands can aid communication, both the conventional gesture, which can be used to emphasize a point, and the descriptive gesture, which is used to explain.

Vocal Variety

Variation in voice is especially important in debate, both for emphasis and to maintain the listeners' interest. The variable attributes of the human voice are its rate or speed of utterance; its pitch or melody pattern; its quality or mood; and its force, or amount of volume and stress. The requirement of speed in modern debating necessitates certain techniques of voice manipulation to ensure that comprehensibility is not sacrificed.

Rate Variation

Debaters should also vary their rate of speaking. You must be aware that the rate can become so rapid that many judges will not be able to follow you. Nonetheless, many arguments often must be presented. Rate variations enhance comprehension in such circumstances. Labels on arguments should be read much more slowly than evidence is, and important points, particularly in rebuttals, should be covered slowly. Inflection of tone is also crucial. Changes in quality and pitch can indicate importance when speed is necessary. Reading in a different tone the parts of an evidence card that are critical to an argument can highlight them without reducing speed. A change in volume, such as louder or softer transitions, can be used for persuasive effects. Tone variations can also be used to add humor.

Clear enunciation is vital in high-speed debate. Fast debate is not necessarily bad, but when it cannot be understood, all analysis, logic, and communication are lost. Judges at both the high school and college levels are becoming increasingly wary of this practice. Practice your delivery. Find vocal drills in basic speech books and recite them. Many of these drills will help you learn to scan evidence so that reading takes place in phrases, a pattern that makes the evidence more readily understood.

Summary

The study of the theory and practice of argumentation includes both analytical and communication skills, including audience analysis and adaptation, communication styles in debate, economy in the use of language, and the vocal and bodily techniques of oral presentation.

To understand and use the listeners' values and perceptions as a basis for influencing belief, you should determine the qualities that the judge looks for in debaters; adapt to the judge's preferences, including traditional variations, before and during the debate; be aware of the importance of source credibility and use it to your advantage if possible in dealing with the judge's biases and incompetencies; and finally, personalize your speech and develop a confident and competitive posture.

You should concentrate on enhancing the clarity and the force of your argument. To be effective, your style must be individualized through practice, and our recommended techniques can help.

Develop economy of expression through advance preparation of arguments, and practice your speeches. Economy in language includes using labels, short sentences, cross-referencing, and a time sense for arguments.

In presenting your speech, use both nonverbal and verbal communication and vary the rate, pitch, quality, and volume of your voice.

Questions for Discussion

1. How do communication skills contribute to effective debating?
2. When arguing before a critic or judge trained in debate, what special audience adaptations are necessary?

3. What are the major elements of an effective speaking style?
4. What language problems do time constraints and other features of current academic debate formats create?
5. What factors influence the effective use of the body and voice in presenting a debate speech?
6. What are the advantages and disadvantages of using the spread in academic debate?

Chapter 19

The Evaluation of Academic Debate

In discussing the conventions of academic debate in Chapter 7, we observed that evaluation is made by a third party, not by the participants in the controversy. We also mentioned that the evaluation is based not directly on the merits of the resolutions but on the comparative abilities of the debaters who argue for and against the resolution. These conventions make the evaluation of debate a specialized activity. The aim of this chapter is to help debaters understand the evaluation process. Without such an understanding, they cannot adapt to their listeners' expectations or benefit from the evaluation.

Two Roles of the Evaluator

Two different types of evaluation are performed simultaneously, usually by the same person. First, the evaluator acts as a *judge*. The responsibility of the judge is to determine which side, affirmative or negative, did the better debating. In making this decision, the judge in effect is determining whether the resolution is probably true, based only on the arguments presented during the debate. The judge does not vote for a team because of his or her personal belief that its position is correct. Rather, the standards of judgment are the decision rules that emerge during the debate, supplemented by the judge's own understanding of the principles of argumentation and debate.

At the same time, the evaluator plays the role of *critic*. In this capacity, he or she is asked to examine each team's performance against ideal standards toward which the team ought to aspire. The critic not only determines how far the team is from this standard (usually by awarding points on a scale reflecting gradations from excellent to poor) but also makes specific comments, orally or in writing, on how the debaters can improve their performance.

Expectations Regarding Judges

Certain minimum expectations can legitimately be made regarding all judges, but other expectations will depend on the debate paradigm to which the judge subscribes. In any case, however, there are certain things that debaters cannot reasonably expect of their judges.

Minimum Expectations

Debaters are entitled to make certain basic assumptions about their judges. First, they may assume that the judge is interested in and attentive to the debate. Although all debaters will occasionally encounter a judge whose mind is elsewhere, they can usually expect that the judge cares about the debate and wants to pay attention to it.

The second assumption is that the judge is unbiased toward the subject being discussed. The judge may care deeply about the subject and may come to the debate with strong personal feelings about it. But you can assume that most judges try to set aside their personal beliefs and preferences and evaluate the merits of the resolution only on the basis of the debaters' arguments and not on their own preconceived notions.

Finally, it is reasonable to assume that the judge is intelligent and capable of listening carefully to arguments and evidence, drawing reasonable inferences, and applying common sense to the debaters' ideas.

These three assumptions are the minimal expectations that debaters safely can make regarding their judges. Depending on the conventions of a specific region or area, additional expectations may be appropriate. For example, in some regions only teachers and coaches of debate are used as judges. In this case, you can assume that they are familiar with argumentation and debate theories such as those presented in this book, and you can refer to theoretical concepts in the debate. Likewise, you can assume that the judges will take careful notes, usually in the form of a flow sheet. Consequently, you need not be so concerned with repeating and emphasizing your main points as you otherwise would, as the judge will have recorded them. You also can assume that the judges will have heard many debates on the same topic, especially as the year proceeds. Therefore, it may be appropriate to discuss fairly technical issues, to abbreviate common terms, and to omit basic explanations.

In contrast, other regions scrupulously avoid using debate teachers and coaches as judges, in the belief that they are an overly specialized and atypical audience. Sometimes judges are business and professional men and women, members of civic clubs, or intelligent citizens — who have no specialized training in argumentation and debate and who have previously heard few, if any, debates. With such judges, it is reasonable to assume that they will not take copious notes, and so it is important to limit the number of your arguments and to emphasize their main points. You should assume that these judges are not familiar with argumentation and debate theory and thus avoid abstract theoretical discussions and discuss the necessary points of theory in ordinary rather than technical language. It is reasonable to assume that these judges' familiarity with the topic is limited to what one would encounter in the newspapers, magazines, radio, and television, and so explanations of technical arguments will be necessary, and jargon should be avoided.

There also are regions that use a variety of types of judges. In such circumstances, debaters must find out as much as they can about the orientation of specific judges so that they will know what assumptions are appropriate. If you debate in a region that uses many types of judges and you do not know the orientation of a specific judge, the safest plan may be to make no assumptions beyond the three basic ones described above and then to watch for clues to the judge's behavior as the debate progresses.

Judging and Paradigms

Many judges do not think of themselves in terms of the debate paradigms that we sketched in Chapter 7. Judges who are not debate specialists are particularly unlikely to think of themselves as hypothesis testers, policy makers, critics of public speaking, or trial judges. For nonspecialist judges it is necessary to use principles of argument on which all paradigms will be likely to agree and to discuss disagreements in general rather than paradigmatic terms. Other judges, however, do think of themselves as fulfilling a certain role, and it will be easier for debaters to select and use arguments if they know the judge's particular role definition.

Hypothesis Testing.   For example, the judge as hypothesis tester — the role we recommend in this book — will try to answer the basic question of whether the resolution is probably true. He or she will be less concerned about the specific action that may be taken to implement the statement of the resolution, except as any discussion of such action applies to the more fundamental question. Accordingly, such a judge will look to the negative to raise sufficient doubt as to justify rejection of the resolution and will look to the affirmative to establish that the resolution is probably true. The hypothesis tester's quest is not for certainty, because no statement about values or policy can be definitively determined to be true. Rather, the decision turns on whether enough reason has been given to justify the judge's commitment to its probable truth.

In a debate conducted according to the hypothesis-testing paradigm, therefore, the specific statement of the resolution is important. As we established in Chapter 8, the resolution does not only stake out the general territory for discussion but also determines the boundary between affirmative land and negative land; statements even slightly different from the stated resolution can serve as alternative hypotheses. The details of the plan that the affirmative may propose are considerably less important because the judge believes that no plan will be implemented, regardless of whether the decision is affirmative or negative. Indeed, all discussion of possible plans (or counterplans) lies in the realm of the hypothetical. Moreover, the negative in a hypothesis-testing debate need not commit itself to support an alternative resolution (though it may be strategically desirable to do so), since rejecting the resolution does not entail accepting any other alternative. Decision makers who determine that they have not been convinced of the resolution's truth do not automatically conclude that the resolution is false, much less that some other resolution is true.

Policy Making.   Judges who play the role of policy maker, as described in Chapter 7, will make very different assumptions. These judges seek to determine the best available policy for responding to a problem. According to this view, it is impossible not to act; the decision not to support the affirmative policy automatically commits the judge to support the policy that the negative defends. A negative stance of straight refutation — attacking the individual arguments of the affirmative without necessarily supporting any policy alternative—is not acceptable, because the negative that does not support a policy forces the judge to favor the affirmative.

In a debate conducted according to the policy-making paradigm, the exact wording of the resolution is less important than it is in the hypothesis-testing paradigm. The resolution does identify the boundary between affirmative land and negative land, but the purpose of this boundary is only to identify the range of policies among which each team can choose. The actual decision in the debate is between the specific policies that each team selects from among the available alternatives. Therefore, the details of the plans (and the counterplans) become particularly important. The discussion of plans is not hypothetical; an affirmative or negative vote is a statement that the policy advocated by the favored team ought to be adopted. Furthermore, in a policy-making debate, the negative gains nothing by suggesting, but not committing itself to support, possible alternatives to the affirmative. For example, if the affirmative proposal calls for mandatory gasoline rationing, the negative will not be helped by observing that a hefty increase in the gasoline tax could limit consumption of gasoline just as well. Unless the negative actually supports an increase in the gasoline tax, the judge will be unable to choose that option. For this reason, the negative must be very clear about what policy option it wants to defend. Arguments not cast in the context of a comparison between the affirmative's and negative's policy options are essentially irrelevant. They do not contribute to the debate because they do not help answer the question of whether the affirmative's or the negative's policy should be endorsed.

Public Speaking.   If the judge acts as a critic of public speaking, you must have an even different set of assumptions. According to this view, the merits of the resolution — either as a statement of probable truth or as a policy to be implemented—are not the primary considerations in the debate. Rather, the discussion of a specific resolution is only a convenient way to permit the judge to evaluate the two teams' public-speaking abilities. A judge who is a public-speaking critic will attempt to discern which team better displays the attributes of skilled speaking as they are described in textbooks and practiced by accomplished speakers. Such a judge will determine which team used the evidence more effectively, which used more incisive analysis, which was more gifted at refutation, which had better delivery, and so on. The final judgment will not speak to the merits of the resolution as discussed in the debate but will be a summary of each team's performance according to the stated criteria. Many debate ballots include spaces for judges to rank each speaker on skills such as analysis, evidence, refutation, and delivery. The hypothesis-testing or policy-making judge will be likely to interpret these items as requests for criticism, not judgment. These items are determined only after the decision is made. In contrast, the judge who is a public-speaking critic is likely to use such evaluations as a way to arrive at the decision. In a debate conducted according to this paradigm, it is important for the debaters to be conscious of the skills being evaluated and to demonstrate their proficiency at these skills. The selection of the best policy, or the determination of the probable truth of the resolution, is secondary. As in many other public-speaking occasions, the speaker who best adapts to the situation will succeed.

Other Paradigms.   Some judges may think themselves as analogous to trial judges, imposing on the advocates stated proof burdens and rules of evidence and procedure. Judges in this role probably are less likely to respond positively to theoretical innovation. Other judges may conceive of themselves as political theorists, concerned with selecting the best process for policy formulation rather than the policies themselves. Still others may think of themselves as evaluators of public argument, judging the debaters according to the degree to which the arguments presented in the debate corresponded to the arguments on the same topic presented in the public forum. Some judges view themselves as referees whose job is to ensure that each side has a theoretically equal chance to win. And yet others believe that they represent a *tabula rasa*, or "blank slate," and must decide debates without being influenced by any prior predispositions. There is an infinite number of roles in which judges might imagine themselves, and each will affect the assumptions about how the judge decides which team did the better debating.

Implications.   How should the debater react to the different judging paradigms? If the judge's paradigm is well known, both teams may choose to conduct their arguments within its framework. But the judging paradigm is not a set of blinders. A hypothesis-testing judge will not automatically discount arguments about the consequences of a specific plan if both teams choose to focus the debate on such arguments. Likewise, a policy-making judge will not automatically reject hypothetical arguments if both teams in the debate have shown their willingness to accept them. Most judges work within whatever paradigm emerges in the debate itself, and what emerges often is not a pure form of any of these paradigms but, rather, a hybrid of several. Judges who proclaim that they are a *tabula rasa* are not saying that they have no beliefs or predispositions but are expressing the common belief of all judges that the orientation of the judge should be subordinated to the experience of the debate.

But sometimes the two teams appear to use different paradigms, without giving the judge any basis for selecting one of them as a guide to judgment. Or sometimes no clear paradigm emerges from the debate, and the judge must impose one. In situations such as these, the debaters must be aware of the differences among the paradigms, thus enabling them to formulate their arguments within the framework of different paradigms. Often, changes in terminology and emphasis will make it possible to transfer arguments from one paradigm to another. For example, a conditional counterplan can be reformulated as a counterplan providing for studies and action contingent on the study results. In this way, a hypothesis-testing argument is transferred into the policy-making paradigm. Similar transfers may be made between other paradigms, making it unnecessary for the debaters to determine which paradigm is best before considering the substantive issues. Rather, the issues can be put into language applicable to all paradigms. Although they may view it from the perspective of different paradigms, the debaters can address the same issue.

What Debaters Cannot Expect

Finally, there are certain things that debaters cannot realistically expect of their judges. Some judges may indeed be willing to act as described here, but the debater who expects it as a matter of course is likely to be disappointed.

Cross-application.   First, judges cannot be expected to cross-apply arguments. Often, an argument in one part of the debate will have important implications for another part of the debate. For an example of cross-applying arguments, suppose that the affirmative plan calls for the registration of all draft-eligible youths. The negative argues that draft registration will not work because many youths will not comply and then suggests that draft registration is disadvantageous because it will create a national data bank that threatens invasion of privacy. Clearly, the disadvantage depends on the effectiveness of registration, and the efficacy argument establishes the ineffectiveness of registration. Logically, if the negative prevails on the efficacy argument, then the disadvantage is defeated. If people do not comply with registration, then the damaging personal data will not be amassed. The effective registration that would trigger the disadvantage will not occur. The affirmative may choose to call attention to this relationship between the negative arguments, in order to avoid answering the disadvantage. The affirmative may concede the efficacy argument regarding that particular provision of the plan (thereby undermining the disadvantage), while attempting to defend the plan on the basis of its other elements.

Whose responsibility is it to make such cross-application? Some judges choose to do it on their own initiative, but most believe that for them to cross-apply arguments is to intrude unjustifiably into the debate itself. They believe that it is the debater's responsibility to make the cross-application. In the example above, if the affirmative failed to notice the linkage between negative arguments, each of the negative arguments would have to be evaluated independently on its own merits. If the affirmative failed to note the linkage, the negative might win on the disadvantage, even though it lost the efficacy argument.

Resolution of Stalemates.   Second, judges cannot be expected to resolve doubts or conflicting claims that are left unresolved by the debate itself. Again, some judges try to break the deadlock on stalemated issues, but many others believe that they must treat the issues in exactly the same way they emerged in the debate — in this case, as a stalemate. Judges who hold to this latter belief will tend either to waive unresolved matters, giving them no role in the final decision, or to determine which team should have the benefit of the doubt, and they will award the contested argument accordingly. Again, the responsibility for bringing disputes to a clear resolution rests with the debaters rather than the judge.

Examination of Evidence.   Third, judges cannot be expected to examine the evidence used by the debaters. When controversies involve the text or implications of evidence, it is tempting for debaters not to resolve the matter but simply to invite the judge to examine the evidence—especially if they are convinced of the correctness of their interpretation. Some judges willingly inspect evidence and regard doing so as an important part of their role, but others believe that doing so undermines the oral quality of the debate. The latter believe that the decision must be based on the speeches delivered by the two teams. If these speeches fail to make clear the meaning or value of a piece of evidence, the judge has no grounds for inspecting the evidence. If the details of a piece of evidence are important enough to provoke controversy, then they are important enough to be discussed by the debaters during regulation time. According to this view, the only circumstance in which a judge is justified in inspecting evidence at the conclusion of the debate is one in which his or her own failure in note taking is responsible for the insufficient detail.

Assessment of the Incomprehensible.   Finally, judges cannot be expected to evaluate arguments that they are unable to understand. As we stated in the last chapter, debate is a specialized form of communication with many unique conventions. Judges, whether specialists or not, are usually willing to accept these conventions. But no one can be expected to evaluate arguments that are incomprehensible. It is the debater's responsibility to make the argument clear and capable of being understood.

Expectations Regarding Critics

As we have said, the same person will usually function as both judge and critic. As judge, the evaluator attempts to make a comparative assessment, determining the relative strength of the two teams. But as critic, the evaluator makes an absolute judgment, evaluating each team against the ideal standards for performance.

The Critic's Role

The critic is an educator, concerned with improving the quality of each speaker's debating. There always is room for improvement, and the critic suggests possible improvements by examining each team's performance in the light of what could have been achieved.

We have described the ideal view of the critic's role, but it should be recognized that all critics deviate somewhat from this ideal. Although the educational motive of contributing to the quality of debate should be the only influence on the critic, there sometimes are other motives. Debaters should recognize that these other motives may work against the educational objective.

For example, many critics are former debaters and enjoy imagining how much more effective the debate would be if they were participating in it. So the suggestions for improvement become "here's how I would have done it better." Sometimes these suggestions are useful, but sometimes they are impractical, invite greater problems, or depend on perfect hindsight. Critiques which are a form of vicarious participation should be scrutinized carefully; some of the suggestions may not be practical.

Another motive of critics is concern over changes in the debate activity. Like any other process, debate changes over the years. Critics are likely to find debates conducted much differently from the way they were ten, five, or even three years ago. It is natural to see in the past a "golden age," and so it is understandable that some critics see these changes as signs of decline. Motivated by a desire to restore debate to its perceived former greatness, such critics believe that the offending debater must be brought to account. Their duty, therefore, is to mete out punishment in the form of low speaker points and unfavorable, even harsh, criticism. Just as it is important to take constructive criticism seriously, it also is important to recognize that not all criticism is constructive. Unduly harsh criticism should not provoke anger or withdrawal if it is tempered by the debater's understanding of the critic's possible motives.

The Critic's Standards

Even if the critic's evaluation is not distorted by these pressures, different critics will have different notions of the ideal against which they measure debaters' performance. Sometimes their ideal standards are derived from a particular paradigm of debate. For example, the hypothesis-testing critic's objective is to test the hypothesis, and their criticisms and suggestions will be based on that. In contrast, the policy-making critic's main objective is to improve the debaters' ability to choose intelligently among alternatives. Advocates of other paradigms will derive their standards of criticism from them.

Sometimes ideal standards do not come from a particular paradigm but from the consensus of the community. For example, the misrepresentation of evidence is a universally condemned practice. The critic may suggest a more careful use of evidence quite apart from the paradigm to which he or she subscribes. These universal norms should be taken seriously by debaters, since virtually all critics will impose similar standards.

Finally, some notions of the ideal are personal. For one critic, the use of direct quotations without paraphrases is ideal behavior; for another critic, it may be unimportant. One critic may favor parallel structure in organization; another may not care. When dealing with criticism that reflects personal standards, the debater needs to be especially careful. Obviously, it is important to incorporate the critic's suggestions if one is going to debate for the same critic in the future. It is less certain, however, that changes should be made as a general proposition, because other critics might find them more distasteful than helpful. The key question in such circumstances is whether the suggestion of one critic makes sense. If it does, the changes ought to be made, and it is likely that other critics will be similarly influenced. If not, it may be wiser to ignore the suggestions except when debating in front of that critic again.

Critics do not always make clear the relative weight to be given to their comments. Sometimes debaters give critiques of particular details more weight than they deserve; sometimes they treat a critic's offhand suggestions too seriously; and sometimes, conversely, they dismiss a truly substantial critique because it appears to be an afterthought. It is important not to assume that the first critical suggestion is always the most important or that the comments that appear on the ballot are necessarily the critic's fundamental views. If it seems to you that a critic is obsessed with trivial detail, that perception is probably a good sign that you have misperceived the relative weight of the various critical suggestions.

Learning from Evaluation

In some regions it is common for judges to announce their decisions at the end of the debate; in others, debaters learn their judge's decisions and critiques when they receive the written ballots. In either case, the frame of mind in which debaters receive and react to evaluation has much to do with their deriving the maximum educational benefit from the debate.

Learning from Judgment

Whether they do so orally, in writing, or both, judges can be expected to identify the basis for their decision and to explain the decision by referring to what occurred during the debate. Debaters cannot learn from decisions or improve their performance if they are unaware of the bases for the decisions.

All decisions are inherently subjective. By its nature, debate deals with questions for which there are no clear-cut answers; hence, the test of an argument's strength is its ability to withstand attack and be perceived as acceptable by the audience. It is quite possible for there to be disagreements about the outcome. Debaters may think that they lost a debate in which they received the decision (though it is more likely to occur the other way around!). When there are panels of judges, individual judges do not always agree. The subjectivity of decisions is a fact of life that debaters must accept. Nothing is gained by becoming upset over a decision with which one does not agree. Over the long run, injustices and misjudgments may even out.

By the same token, debaters need to remember that judges are human and, hence, capable of error. Every debater occasionally will receive a faulty decision because the judge was not paying attention to the debate, was confused, or simply made a mistake. Particularly unnerving is the situation in which the judge decides ten minutes too late that the decision should have been reversed! Occasional errors by judges have to be tolerated; no good is accomplished by criticizing a judge on the grounds that he or she makes an occasional mistake.

It is also necessary to remember that debaters are responsible for their own choices. For instance, if you choose not to contest the topicality of an affirmative case, you cannot fault the judge for voting for the case, even though he or she does not believe it to be topical.

Finally, all judges are entitled to common courtesy. When a judge chooses to discuss a decision, it is inappropriate for the debaters to dispute the grounds for the decision or to browbeat the judge into admitting error. The decision has been made, and it will not be changed. The judge performed the task conscientiously and made what he or she thought to be the best decision on the basis of the arguments in the debate. Carrying on the debate beyond the allotted time will not change matters. It is one thing to ask questions of a judge in order to clarify ambiguous points in the explanation of a decision, to be able to understand the judge's reasoning, or to ask for suggestions about what should be done differently next time. But it is quite another thing to vent one's frustration at an unfavorable decision by being discourteous to the judge. Such behavior, analogous to killing the messenger who brings bad news, should be avoided.

Learning from Criticism

As with judgment, criticism may be offered orally at the end of the debate, in written comments on the ballot, or both. Oral critiques are relatively common, although they seldom are put to good use by the debaters. Interested mostly in combing the critique for hints to the decision, debaters frequently do not pay attention to the substance of the critique and may quickly forget valuable suggestions.

To avoid this problem, we recommend that you take brief written notes on the critique's main points. These notes can then be consulted later, away from the tension of the immediate situation. Particularly when a critic makes suggestions for the reorganization of arguments, a more effective choice of rebuttal extensions, strategic possibilities unrecognized by the debaters, or other similarly complex changes, written notes can preserve the suggestions that otherwise may be forgotten as soon as the critic has left the room.

Cumulative Learning

Many debaters make the mistake of believing that once they have determined why they won or lost individual rounds, the usefulness of written ballots is at an end. This is a serious mistake. There is great value in keeping ballots, rereading and studying them carefully.

First, you should inspect them to see if there are consistencies in the bases for judgment or in the suggestions for improvement. For example, if you lost two of four affirmative rounds because you failed to demonstrate inherency and one other judge noted that inherency was weak, although the negative failed to make it a basis for decision, you should strengthen the inherency of your case! One ballot may be the result of fluke or personal idiosyncrasy, but when there are patterns, they are worth attending to.

Second, you may get ideas for possible cross-applications of arguments — either because the judges themselves chose to cross-apply them or because reading the ballot suggests a possible cross-application not apparent during the debate.

Third, the ballots may indicate arguments that were not important to the final outcome and on which you were wasting your time. Fourth, the judges' explanations may indicate that there were arguments or explanations that were consistently misunderstood; this should suggest to you the importance of modification. Fifth, if you repeatedly have the same judge, you may be able to spot patterns indicating that judge's standards for judgment and criticism.

Summary

In this chapter we investigated debate evaluation. The same evaluator usually fulfills two quite different roles, as judge and critic. The first role involves assessing the performance of the two debate teams and determining which did the better debating. In reaching that decision, judges will be guided by the debate paradigm to which they subscribe. Regardless of the paradigm, however, debaters are entitled to assume that judges are attentive, disinterested, and conscientious. Debaters are not entitled, however, to expect that judges will resolve issues left ambiguous in the debate, that they will apply arguments that the debaters failed to examine, or that they will inspect evidence that is in dispute.

In their role as critics, evaluators attempt to improve the overall quality of performance. They evaluate debaters according to ideal standards and make suggestions for improvement. These ideal standards are, in part, dictated by their paradigm of debate but are also affected by both universal norms of the debate community and the critic's personal standards.

Judgment and criticism can be beneficial to the debater if they are approached in the proper frame of mind. Debaters must remember that both judgment and criticism are subjective processes, that there is no "right" answer. Accordingly, debaters may disagree with their judges or critics. Rather than berate the evaluator or ignore the evaluation, it is important to understand how such disagreements develop and to be prepared to modify one's behavior to make the disagreements less likely. Evaluators are human and do make mistakes, but the ultimate responsibility to make arguments clear and comprehensible to the evaluator rests with the debaters. Under all circumstances, judges are entitled to common courtesy and respect.

Both judgment and criticism may be expressed in oral comments, in written comments on the debate ballot, or both. Debaters should take notes on oral comments so that they can be preserved for later reflection and discussion. Written comments should be analyzed carefully, usually under circumstances removed from the tension of the debate situation itself. Properly used, ballots and critiques can be important to a debater's education, supplementing the training received from one's own teacher or coach.

Questions for Discussion

1. Judge and critic are two separate roles performed by the same person. On what grounds could you argue that the roles are not distinct?
2. How is a debate affected if the debaters' expectations regarding the judge differ from those we described?
3. In what ways can debaters, during a round, help to shape the judge's decision-making process?
4. What should a debater do when a critic offers suggestions for improvement with which the debater disagrees?
5. Ballots and critiques can supplement the training received from one's own teacher or coach. How?

Unit Three

The Context of Argumentation and Debate

Chapter 20

The Larger Picture

In Unit One we examined the theory and practice of argumentation as applicable to general settings, both formal and informal. In Unit Two we explored the principles of argumentation as applicable to the specialized area of academic debate. In both cases we were concerned with learning a set of thought patterns, skills, and techniques. In this final unit, we shall consider how these skills and habits of thought contribute to our development as individuals and to the effectiveness of a free society. We shall conclude our discussion of argumentation by viewing it in its larger context as an academic discipline and as related to other disciplines. We shall examine argument as an agent for understanding ourselves and as a social instrument for making critical decisions.

Argumentation as a Critical Instrument

Suppose that you are sharing an apartment with two friends and a controversy arises over whose turn it is to go to the store for groceries. In trying to resolve this problem, you and your friends can proceed in a critical or noncritical manner. First, you can decide by chance, perhaps by flipping a coin. Second, you can decide by desire or impulse. Third, if there is a heated dispute, you can fight over the matter until the stronger one establishes the superiority of his or her position by overpowering the weaker one. Fourth, you can appoint a friend or outsider to decide the issue for you. Fifth, you can argue the matter in an attempt to persuade the other to choose a given course of action.

As rational people, we tend to reject the first three methods because such methods do not apply thought to the decision. In that sense they are noncritical. Decisions by chance and impulse ignore the pertinent evidence and values and thus omit the elements necessary for rational decision making. Furthermore, chance precludes any valid attempt to predict the best course of action; those who decide by chance are clearly gambling against the odds that the best option will emerge. Force is rejected because it, too, is regarded as an irrational mode of decision making. Forced behavior violates cherished principles of personal autonomy and often undermines the very goals sought by the imposition of force. Free people reject the notion that justice should be the exclusive possession of those who wield the most power. The authoritarian method also is often rejected, not necessarily because the decision is not thoughtful, but rather because it runs contrary to many people's desire to decide for themselves. People tend to prefer an environment in which all those involved participate in the decision-making process. The authoritarian method denies this opportunity to all but a few. Group decision, after deliberation on the available alternatives, is generally the most acceptable method because it offers people a chance to proceed rationally and collectively in deciding the issues that govern their lives. So, the most acceptable means for deciding who shall go to the store is to discuss the matter until a resolution is reached.

Argumentation as a Critical Tool

The chief tool available to us to make reasoned decisions about issues contingent upon values, policies, and facts is argumentation. Suppose that you must choose a major subject. If you elect to use the critical approach, you will not decide by rolling dice or consulting an astrologist. Instead, you will inquire into the facts, motives, and values regarding the various subjects open for study, hoping to be able to identify, verify, and weigh the arguments that support your choices.

Such contingent questions may also necessitate public decisions. In late December 1979, for example, the Soviet Union sent troops into Afghanistan. President Jimmy Carter first selected moral suasion as one means of effecting a Soviet withdrawal. His second proposal was that the United States sponsor an international boycott of the Olympics scheduled to be held in Moscow in the summer of 1980. President Carter offered many reasons to support his belief that the boycott was desirable. Immediately following the release of Carter's proposal, millions of other Americans continued arguing the merits of the boycott as a way of curbing illegal Soviet aggression. Many defended the president's position by suggesting that the boycott would demonstrate to the world that America would not honor an aggressor nation by sending its athletes to compete on the offender's soil. Others contended that the boycott would create a poor precedent by subjecting the world's sporting events to political exigencies, an effect that the creation of the Olympics sought to remove. Others decried the proposed course as unfair to the many athletes who had trained for years for the opportunity to compete and who should not have to sacrifice such efforts for political ends. Those engaged in the debate used argument to measure the worth of President Carter's proposal and, thereby, to influence the course of events.

The uses of argument in the public debate over the Olympic boycott exemplify the role and nature of argument as an instrument for resolving social and political problems. When properly employed, this argumentative process produces reasoned decisions built on sound analysis and the logical demonstration of validity. Admittedly, argument is not always founded on reason. Yet, we shall consider here the relationship between arguments and decisions because we believe that a dedication to argument eventually compels the application of reason to the solution of collective problems and the resolution of conflict in a free society.

Assumptions About Argumentation as a Critical Device

The view of argumentation as a critical device depends on certain assumptions. The premises that actions should be reasonable, that decisions should be justified through critical inquiry and persuasive explanation of ideas, and that a clash of ideas helps arrive at the probable truth are fundamental to such a view.

Actions Should Be Reasonable.   The statement that argument is critical to decisions depends on certain assumptions. Basic is the belief that although social change induced through our collective efforts is often desirable, such efforts should be guided by a sense of order and regularity. This assumption seems plausible for a number of reasons. Experience demonstrates that change is best approached through careful planning. Moreover, underlying social and cultural problems continually reappear in new circumstances and forms requiring that objectives and policies be redefined. Finally, although change may upset some individuals, it is more likely to be beneficial if there is some consensus in its favor.

The rationale for consensus building in making social change is twofold: first, people generally are reasonable and therefore are inclined to act rationally in changing their behavior and, second, people accept change best when they help formulate it. The second rationale embodies the values of free choice, the idea that change is best received when we are free to select among alternative courses of action. Argumentation promotes free choice because it enables us to respond to problems in more than one way. It also serves to legitimize the social control necessary to induce desirable social change. All parties in a dispute may agree to accept the judge's decision after argument, thus at least temporarily resolving a controversy. Consensus building through argument enables change to take place in an orderly manner.

Decisions Should Be Justified Through Critical Inquiry and Persuasive Explanation of Ideas.   The primary purpose of argument is to demonstrate the probable truth of a claim. Conclusions purporting to justify rational decisions can be validated only through a careful examination of the relevant facts, motives, and values in the problem situations. Such deliberative decisions, in turn, are presumed to be superior to those made by impulse, prejudice, desire, or trial and error, precisely because they are critical in nature. This line of reasoning does not mean to exclude emotional appeals from decision making. Emotional appeals can be both reasoned and critical. But it does insist that rational decision making begin with an analysis of the arguments. And at its best, the argumentation process does not permit noncritical methods to circumvent the rational elements of persuasion.

A Clash of Ideas Helps Determine Probable Truth.   Through intellectual conflict, ideas are tested, and their emerging strengths and weaknesses are forced out into the open. The competition among ideas is enhanced because the objects of argument are innately uncertain and subjective in nature. The usual arena is in the realm of uncertainties. Usually, argument revolves around such matters as war and peace, justice and injustice, and wisdom and folly. These are subjects on which the truth cannot be determined by empirical inspection. Argumentation may serve the same function, however, of producing results that people will regard as reliable. If a claim withstands rigorous testing and criticism, we can act with greater confidence that the claim is probably true, though, of course, we can never be certain. The best we can do is to say that claims derived through argumentation have a high probability of being true. But the probability is higher than would be the case if the claims were derived by means of a noncritical method.

President John F. Kennedy recognized the invaluable benefits derived from a clash of ideas in reaching a decision that continues to affect our global future. Faced with the Cuban missile crisis, Kennedy rejected the decision-making methods of chance, impulse, or authoritarian action. Instead, he insisted on a high-level debate among experts before making a final decision about the action to take. Perhaps no greater crisis has confronted the nations of the world in this nuclear age, and an open exchange of ideas was utilized to arrive at the best possible decision, the closest thing to a probable truth in the ever uncertain political context.

The probable nature of truth raises several important questions about the competition of ideas through argument. For example, what constitutes the proof of a particular claim? Argumentation theorists differ on the nature of proof. Some see it merely as a process of gaining adherence to a position by relating it to a prior belief of the listener. Others see it as statements that can be verified through observation or formal reasoning. In their present forms, these two philosophies are often mutually exclusive. For example, if proof is anything that a listener will believe, verification often will be unnecessary, for people often will accept a statement as true just because they want it to be true. On the other hand, if proof is totally divorced from the audience's beliefs, then argumentation may be useless as a decision-making instrument, because it ignores the concerns of the real world. We can argue, for example, that people have landed on the moon, but if our listeners believe that this is impossible, then our claim will have little or no impact.

From a historical perspective, conflicts over proof between secular and sectarian factions in society have tested the human condition. Centuries after the heavenly discoveries and theories of Copernicus, Galileo faced mental and physical persecution for his claim that the earth was not the center of the universe. Given the inflexible beliefs of his sectarian audience, Galileo's attempts to prove his arguments met with staunch opposition. To view the critics of Galileo as critical thinkers, however, would be incorrect, for the divergence of real-world concerns from the probable truth may be too great a chasm to close with rational argumentation. Time, however, provides a means for even the most controversial proof to find a critically thinking audience and an accepted place in the historical texts of probable truths.

As we are using the term, proof has elements of both of the definitions that we indicated earlier, proof as gaining adherence to a position related to prior belief and as statements verified through observation or formal reasoning. In our view, the arguers' aim is to verify their assertions to the satisfaction of their critical listeners. Proof is what convinces the reflective thinker. The purpose of argument is not merely to influence others but also to influence others by meeting the proof requirements of the critical mind. The mixture of fact and value arguments that will meet the expectations of a critical mind must, by nature, vary according to the subject of controversy and the mind to which the arguments are addressed. Therefore, the predominance of probability statements in argumentation makes proof of a claim dependent on the advocates' skill in analyzing the issues and the audience.

Argumentation and the Self

The study of argument benefits both the individual and society. For the individual, the benefits are similar to those claimed for a liberal education. The study of argumentation, like that of all the humanities, offers the potential for human development through growth and interaction with the environment.

Argumentation Contributes to the Self

Like other parts of the humanities, argumentation helps us in several ways gain control over our lives and establish our identities and satisfying relationships with others.

Critical Thinking.   First, the study and use of argument helps us in our quest to acquire the accoutrements of intellectual freedom. One of these is critical thinking. Argumentation as a discipline demands attention to the laws of valid inference and warranted claims. It requires that conclusions be drawn from substantial premises, either as general truths extracted from particular cases or as particular propositions inferred from general laws. Argumentation is largely based on the cognitive skills required in these mental processes. The development of arguments, for example, encourages critical thinking because it consistently demands the questioning, examining, and restructuring of knowledge according to the laws of validity and warrant.

Systematic Investigation.   Argumentation also encourages a systematic mode of problem solving. Conclusions must be supported by findings gathered through research. Every question in the argument is open to research and investigation. As arguers, we must know the methods of gathering information as well as its analysis. We must observe, classify, hypothesize, analyze, experiment, sample, and generalize. We must then apply these methods to all of the available evidence that our research and investigation can produce and examine the motives and values held by ourselves and society that are involved in reaching a decision on the basis of such evidence.

Communicative Skills.   A third tool developed by using argumentation is communicative skills. As advocates, we attempt to interpret complex ideas for our listeners in order to persuade them to accept our position. In doing so, we must connect messages with purposes and audiences. Argumentation thus offers the kind of intellectual stimulation that results from the ability to handle complicated ideas and to communicate more successfully with others. One means to this end is a mastery of the variables in the communication process. The study of argument contributes to our understanding of communication through its emphasis on the generation and arrangement of persuasive appeals, the critical functions of audience analysis, and the adaptation of ideas to audiences.

The failures and successes of communicating ideas to audiences are exemplified by twentieth-century efforts to establish global organizations. In attempting to persuade listeners to accept their positions, Presidents Woodrow Wilson and Franklin Delano Roosevelt faced the classical communicative challenges of connecting messages with purposes and audiences. In trying to persuade America and the world of the necessity for a League of Nations, Wilson apparently failed to communicate the wisdom of his ideas to a partisan opposition. By ignoring that opposition and the implications it held for his dream, Wilson's message was lost, and its purpose was overshadowed by the nationalistic emotions of his domestic and foreign opponents. Roosevelt, on the other hand, communicated the need for a global organization, a United Nations, to bipartisan actors in the relevant political sphere. Albeit, the development of nuclear weaponry and the proliferation of new nations, as well as the casualties and devastation of World War II, gave added credibility to the messages that Roosevelt delivered. President Roosevelt, however, realized the necessity of relating ideas to audiences in order to gain acquiescence to his position.

Critical Choices.   A fourth way in which argumentation promotes the self is by encouraging the development in both arguer and listener of the skills needed to make critical judgments. As advocates, we must judge which arguments to employ, which evidence to use, and which values to include in our presentations. The outcome of a dispute may, in fact, often hinge on our ability to bring the whole range of our ideas about topic and audience into this judgment.

Argumentation also helps the audience make enlightened choices. As we have said, a major reason for debate is that contrasting beliefs enter into full and fair competition. In this competition, the audience, relatively free of inborn prejudices and other similar beliefs, judges the best course of action. In this manner, argumentation protects our liberties and contributes to human dignity by encouraging enlightened choices. We believe that as we increase our capacity to choose for ourselves, we increase both our freedom and our dignity.

Improving Values.   The enhancement of critical judgment through advocacy also improves our values. By nature, choices reached through argument are grounded partly in values and partly in facts. Argumentation encourages a consideration of both before decisions are made. Consider the political controversy over public referenda versus decisions by popular representatives in the context of a vote on tax structures. Facts, such as the predictions of popular opinion polls based on examinations of similar situations in the past, may establish what the effect of a public referendum may be on local tax structures. But if the objective of considering such a plan is to improve the lot of the people, then their values must eventually be considered in deciding whether or not such an outcome is desirable. Both the advocates and the audience must choose among schemes of values as their positions are defended and their decisions are reached. Discrimination in values is improved as judgments are made about which policies are good or evil and which policies succeed or fail. Neither the advocates nor the judges can escape those value considerations and still reach a decision through argumentation.

Testing Ideas.   Finally, argumentation promotes intellectual freedom by allowing us to align our ideas with our common knowledge. We learn by testing our thoughts and emotions on others, observing their intellectual or physical reaction, and then adjusting our ideas or behavior in response. Argumentation gives us an excellent opportunity to use this testing. It is an inherently social activity and requires audiences—or at the very least, arguers serve as audiences for one another. The audience is equipped with social knowledge, including normative judgments, implicit premises, and rules and norms and facts, all of which can be conducive to action.

When we argue, we draw on this knowledge in our arguments and at the same time generate new social knowledge. In interacting with others through argument, we develop "self" to the extent that the self is a composite of what we know. At the same time, argument leads to a consensual validation, in that the members of a given audience are led to regard certain of our ideas as knowledge. Argumentation thus becomes a means for both the arguer and the listener to acquire social knowledge. In this sense, truth is related to quality of the argument and depends on the evaluation of others. The more rigorous the test of argument and the facts used to support it are, the greater is the contribution to the development of social knowledge.

Argumentation Discloses the Self

Another advantage of argument is that when we use argument, we must make choices that disclose our nature. Argument occurs when disagreements exist and people are seeking to resolve the disagreement. As arguers, we choose among the relevant facts, values, and beliefs as we attempt to secure this consensus. The choices we make tell us something about our value structure and our perception of our audience's value structure. If we attempt, for example, to gain a consensus on an issue involving a conflict between human life and civil rights, the choices we make between the two reveal something about our hierarchy of values and make us more conscious of what we treasure most.

At the same time, our resolution of the conflict in values also reveals information about our perception of the culture of which our message is a part, since we are attempting to persuade other people to approve our choices. Since our persuasions recognize prevailing opinions, they indicate the social thought of our audience. In arguing, if we place a high priority on human life, we may also be saying that we believe that our listeners share this value. Certainly, if our arguments do not mirror to some extent our audience's social tone, our messages will probably have minimal social utility. Thus, argumentation effectively used reveals the social thought of both the arguer and the audience.

Risks in Arguing

Although in arguing we may benefit from the experience of self-discovery, we also risk rejection and injury to our self-image. When we argue, we deliberately enter our ideas into competition. We also consent implicitly to a public probing and critical examination of our values and beliefs. Each arguer must recognize the right of others to be heard and to refute opposing views. In so doing, we risk having our positions proved wrong in the eyes of the other parties involved in the dispute. We also risk having to change our own beliefs in the face of new arguments that we had previously not considered or accepted. We accept these risks by the very nature of the means we use to achieve our ends. We deliberately choose a method of critical judgment that brings contrasting beliefs into full and fair competition. In this competition, the rational alternative has a chance to emerge.

Often the differences on a given issue are so balanced that a decision is difficult to reach. As more arguments are presented, we, as rational arguers, may decide that the choices have come to warrant a course of action other than the one we originally advanced. Moreover, even if we do not come to a conclusion different from the one we started with, our listeners may. As arguers, we must thus accept as the price of obtaining the many benefits of argument the risk of seeing our ends defeated.

Argumentation and Society

The study and practice of argumentation also contributes to society's well-being. Its principal contribution to a free society is its use as an instrument for resolving controversy and making decisions. In this respect, it offers three major benefits.

Public Decision Making

Argumentation enables large groups of people to resolve differences on contingent issues. By agreeing to submit differences to argumentative adjudication, we increase the probability that a sound decision will be reached. This method also reconciles the need for expert opinion in a government with majority rule. The American people make, either directly or indirectly, the basic decisions about their policies.

One role of argumentative discourse is that it helps all of us develop the attitudes and understanding essential to intelligent decisions and actions. If properly used, argumentation permits those whose job it is to choose among rival claims to benefit from a critical examination of these issues. The decision is made after contrasting beliefs have been argumentatively examined. It is not necessary that complete agreement be reached, but there must be a sufficient consensus for public decisions to be made and action to be taken. In this manner, argumentative discourse helps resolve social controversy by encouraging the expression of reflective judgment after the consideration of conflicting views.

In the realm of public policy in the American constitutional system, much argumentative discussion surrounds the public decision-making process involved in ratifying a constitutional amendment. Particularly when the amendment is of great social and political import, as was the case with Prohibition, the Equal Rights Amendment, and others, the media, relevant political experts, concerned social organizations, and vocal citizens play an essential argumentative role before the decision maker, in this case the American public, can reach a conclusion. Obviously, this results in the resolution of a public controversy, provided that those who opposed the decision are willing to accept the described process and outcome and those who originally supported the decision are content to maintain their commitment.

Airing Opposing Views

Argumentative discourse, in addition, permits opposing views to be considered before decisions are made. No matter how strong a position may appear to be, considering the opposing views gives us a better picture of its merits. In this way, argument helps society guard against erroneous assumptions of infallibility and allows one body of opinion to operate as a corrective and a restraint on another. When opposing views are not aired, society will not reexamine its assumptions and beliefs. The danger is increased that these beliefs will be applied to a situation that they do not fit, simply because they never have been questioned. If society's decision makers engage in argumentation, this danger is reduced, since the opposing views are aired.

Through the airing of differences, argumentative discourse also serves society by encouraging groups to reach compromises. The legal community recognizes that free speech often invites disagreement and unrest. Similarly, argumentative discourse encourages dissatisfaction with policies based on untenable postulates.

The First Amendment of the United States Constitution may protect the right of free speech, but argumentative discourse provides society with an instrument to exercise and appreciate this right. The process of argumentation encourages the presentation of unpopular ideas and opinions and probes the strengths and weaknesses of conventional views. The activity also guards against the silencing of minority opinion, either by intimidation or legal restraint, and encourages criticism and differing positions to emerge.

Quality of Social Decisions

A third value of argument for society is its contribution to the quality of social decisions. As a decision-making device, argumentation is a unique form of persuasion. It employs both inquiry and advocacy. Through inquiry into the facts, motives, and values involved, the arguer identifies, defines, and verifies the existence of a problem. The issues in a conflict may vary from the American role in foreign policy to the merits of intercollegiate athletics. In the investigative stage of advocacy, we try to uncover the truths surrounding a problem. We use the search for arguments as a means of discovering and formulating what we think is the essence of the situation. Once we attempt to persuade others to accept the truth that we have uncovered, we use argumentation to influence their beliefs and behaviors. We may strengthen, modify, or abandon our belief in what we thought was true on the basis of this interchange. When all advocates are committed to reach the highest-quality decisions, the process of argumentation will winnow out the less tenable decisions and permit the stronger ones to survive.

Uses of Argumentation in Society

Argumentation thus offers numerous benefits to society. Likewise, society may choose how to use argumentation as an instrument for decision making. As advocates, we should be aware of the significance of variations in the methods of decision making and the assumptions underlying each method.

Methods of Public Advocacy

In the social context, advocates use public discussion and public debate to arrive at socially beneficial decisions.

Public Discussion.   Those who argue often also do the deciding. We refer to this method as *public discussion*. It differs from public debate, described below, in that the interaction between advocate and audience is limited to the participants themselves. Whether through a consensus, compromise, or capitulation, the same people who argue also make the decision.

Public Debate. Another way of using argument to reach decisions is for the advocates to call on a third party to choose among their opposing claims and positions. We call this method *public debate*. The arbiters may be the American people, in a national election; a jury, in a trial; or a critic judge, in a collegiate debate. The arbiter may be elected or appointed. In any case, the decision is made by persons outside the group of advocates. The advocates argue but do not vote.

Purposes of Arguing

Argumentation as a decision-making instrument can be used by different members of society for a variety of purposes. Sometimes argument is used by candidates for national office addressing the body politic; at other times it is used by a family trying to decide when to go on vacation. Sometimes the decision-making agency requires a highly structured setting, such as legislative debates, courts of law, and debate tournaments; other contexts may be more casual, such as a group of debaters en route home from one tournament trying to convince the coach where the next tournament should be, two students trying to convince the rest of their class of the merits of their respective positions on the legalization of marijuana, or a spirited family discussion around the dinner table. The dialogue may be spoken or written. In certain situations, such as debate tournaments, the discourse may have rigid time limitations. In other contexts, the argumentation may extend over many months, such as a national election. In many debate settings, the procedures and codes may be formalized, as in college debate tournaments, Congress, and courts of law. In other situations, rules may be open-ended, as in a campuswide student debate over official university policies regarding dormitory visitation and recreation practices. In this instance, disputes will occur in various settings, from group discussions to *ad hoc* student conversations to bulletin boards and the student press.

Society's use of argumentation to help resolve problems in these various contexts rests on the notion that a clash of ideas helps uncover the best solutions. People who hold contrasting positions agree to a public probing and critical examination of their arguments. Thus, the odds are reduced that one position will win by default because its positions were not exposed or that one position will win because one party tricked the audience into thinking that there was only one side to an issue. As a result of this competition of ideas, public opinion is molded on various issues. In such give and take, both the false and the true have an opportunity to be exposed. From this process, the public in a free society eventually takes its stand.

Ethical Assumptions

The effectiveness of argument in problem-solving situations also rests on the assumption that as arguers we have certain ethical obligations in our deliberations.

If argumentation is to be used to help audiences decide the contingent questions of life, the responsibility lies with us as advocates to share with our audiences our own awareness of the facts surrounding a problem.

Further, we should share our assessment of the assumptions and alternatives implicit in the subject matter itself. In part, at least, our ethical stature also depends on an attitude of open-mindedness, at least to the point of recognizing that not all truth lies on our side. This does not mean that we are not competing for favorable responses from our audience but, instead, that we are helping them toward an enlightened decision by making the best arguments we can in terms of the available evidence, logic, and assumptions. We should set forth each position in its own right along with the strongest arguments that support it, and we should attack and defend each position in an intelligent and rigorous manner.

In meeting the above responsibilities through argumentative discourse, we as advocates are both cooperating and competing with others. By engaging in argumentation, we are cooperating with our adversary as a means of helping the listener understand the issues. Likewise, in trying to convince the listener that we have the strongest position, we are also competing for the listener's vote. The cooperative act ensures that opposing views will not be suppressed. The competitive act ensures that a public challenge to different points of view will take place. Even if all the arguers desire victory, they nonetheless have subjected their means of victory to a reflective, critical, and internal check that gives greater promise for truth to emerge. Those who judge make their decision after a more complete exposure to the examination and criticism of the arguments on both sides of the question. Although it is undeniably true that advocates sometimes win decisions without meeting these responsibilities, an advocate who fails to assume these greater responsibilities reduces the possibility that argumentation will facilitate sound decisions.

Only Contingent Questions Require Argumentation

Finally, argumentation better serves society as a decision-making instrument when its use is confined to questions whose answers are uncertain or lie in the realm of contingencies. Admittedly, argumentation can be used to make any collective decision. But it is not always the best instrument for resolving certain types of differences. For example, if a group differs in its opinions on who won the World Series in 1939, they can argue the matter. They can even call in a third party to serve as judge. They can marshal their best arguments to support their respective positions and present their cases. But such an exercise would be foolhardy. There is only one answer to this problem, and it can be found in an almanac. There is no reason to debate a matter that can be settled by empirical investigations. An almanac is obviously more reliable, because its empirical findings resolve the matter with a much higher degree of probability than can personal evaluations and interpretations.

But many collective problems cannot be resolved by empirical means. Consider a question that continuously faces the American people: what should the purposes of education be? The answer is obviously important because the accepted purposes of education will influence the development and destiny of us all. For example, if the emphasis is on conformity to existing mores, the results of education will be quite different from those produced by an educational system that emphasizes practices that guide people into recognizing and solving their own problems. But there is no almanac, laboratory, or textbook that can resolve these differences. The decision calls for personal judgments as well as facts. Hence inferences must be drawn and judgments must be made. Argumentation is a means by which society can infer and judge such issues. In advocacy, positions can be logically developed, presented rationally, and challenged through attack and defense before the choices are made. Argumentation thus functions to solve problems that must be resolved in this manner. It does not substitute for empirical procedures, but it is a valuable tool when empirical means do not yield answers.

Argumentation, Philosophy, and Rhetoric

We explained argumentation as a study of the art of devising good reasons to justify actions and beliefs. We showed particular interest in debate as one form of argumentation, a means of helping people use arguments in an adversary setting to communicate their ideas effectively to others. This process of communicating various forms of argument in many different contexts draws on a number of universal tools, including analysis, research, communication, and criticism. Thus, the study of argument necessarily integrates subject matter from a number of academic fields. We hope that you will be interested in pursuing further the study of argumentation and that doing so will require you to become familiar with the academic fields that contribute to argumentation theory and practice. In this section, we shall conclude our study of argumentation by examining its special relationship to philosophy and rhetoric. Our objectives are to explain these relationships and to show how you can increase your understanding of argumentation by studying them.

Argumentation and Philosophy

Argumentation has a logical structure and a rhetorical content, aligning itself with philosophy in its logical structure. Philosophy is concerned with searching for truth through reasoning. One means of searching for truth is to look for meanings that can often be found in questions of fact, value, and policy. One branch of philosophy — logic — is concerned with the reliability of statements as instruments of knowledge. The logician's primary tool is language. Philosophers invariably use language in their search for consistency and significance in reasoning, and their words and phrases must be precise if they are to discover meanings or truths.

Although the philosophers' method is concerned with the form of argument, their main goal is to test and demonstrate the logic of their conclusions to others. They examine the structure or form of the reasoning that leads from some data to a conclusion. For example, in the argument "all air is colorless; the sky is composed of air; therefore, the sky is colorless," the philosopher is not concerned with the content of the statements but with their form. The goal is that the parts of the premise are distributed so as to produce a valid conclusion if the data underlying the premise are correct. The philosopher uses argument to test the internal consistency of a position or, as some may claim, a consistent truth. For the logician, internal consistency is an end in itself. To obtain this end, the philosopher must use argument. Philosophers fit their reasons into the framework of argumentation. Their conclusions from the argument gain credibility among nonprofessionals by means of the facts that support them. The philosophers' desired outcome is a consistent and comprehensive conclusion. Therefore, the validity of philosophical arguments is relative to the proofs used to establish them, and the philosopher, like the debater, must select from the available proofs. Philosophy and argumentation, then, share the goals of the search for truth and the discovery of self.

Argumentation and Rhetoric

Argumentation also contributes to and uses the art of rhetoric. In contrast with the philosopher's goal of logical validity in using argument, the goal of the rhetorician in using argument is persuasion. Traditionally, rhetoric has been concerned with informative and persuasive discourse. Its primary function comes from the audience-speaker relationship. It seeks to influence actions, attitudes, and beliefs by exploring complex ideas.

A central concern of rhetoric is argumentation. Although persuasion includes attention to style and delivery, the principles and techniques of discerning and communicating sound reasons also are important.

Instead of the logician's concern for the form of argument, rhetoricians look for the argumentative position that will most easily persuade their audience to accept their ideas. They want to know the effect that certain arguments will have on their audience. Rhetoricians do value an internally consistent position in the structure of their arguments, but they must also consider the relationship of their reasons to reality because they are attempting to influence a world that measures value by means of social utility.

Rhetoricians convince others of the truth by means of persuasion. In our example about the color of the sky, rhetoricians would be concerned with both the internal consistency of their premises and their acceptability to an audience. They probably would reject the conclusion that the sky is colorless because it cannot be proved by observation. Rhetoricians seek action and, therefore, use argumentation to explain the relationships between their reasons and the goals, values, and motives of their audience. Advanced study in argumentation leads naturally to a concern with the principles and theories of rhetoric.

The Common Dimension

Philosophers and rhetoricians use argumentation for different purposes, but rhetoricians depend on the logicians' rules for logical validity when they choose their argumentative position. And logicians also provide rhetoricians with a method for defending their positions from attacks that are logically unsound. For example, logicians prepare rhetoricians to refute the attack that a politician wept in public and is, therefore, unfit to be president. The logician's tools can help the rhetorician detect the fallacious thinking behind this argument.

At the same time, the logician also uses the rhetorician's techniques. The logician often turns to rhetoric in order to give meanings to argumentative forms. The concept of the plausibility or force of an argument also comes from the rhetorician. Just because an argument does not contradict itself is no guarantee that anyone will take it seriously. The question of what arguments will be forceful to an audience, and under what circumstances, is the concern of the rhetorical theorist. The content of logical forms must have some real-world basis, or their use will be of little practical value.

A strong case can be made that the uses of argument by the philosopher and rhetorician are nearly identical. Both are trying to demonstrate validity, and both have equal concern for the strength of proofs. Although there is truth in this position, it can be said that their mutual concerns differ. The logician uses logical reasoning to decide what is probably true. Although rhetoricians likewise seek the truth, they are concerned mainly with practical action. They join the logician in coming as close to validity as possible, but they also seek to persuade. Logicians may succeed by merely explaining their position; rhetoricians must change attitudes. Philosophers openly display their techniques as they demonstrate validity; rhetoricians may often fail if their techniques become too obvious.

But philosophy and rhetoric often do coincide in their use of argument to demonstrate logical validity and establish rhetorical proofs. The distinction between the two disciplines also becomes blurred as one views rhetoric less as a search for the available means of persuasion and more as a search for the deeper philosophical basis of probable truth. It is in its application to the audience that rhetoric assumes its practical role. But in its relationship to dialectical discussion and reasoning by dialogue, rhetoric acquires its theoretical foundation. The dialectical aspects of inquiry and the discovery of ideas by determining what questions to ask in any given case bring rhetoric very close to philosophy.

Both rhetoric and philosophy develop the individual personality, but through different techniques. Rhetoricians expose the self by accepting the risks of confronting audiences with their ideas. Philosophers, however, expose the self by inviting criticism of the soundness of their premises.

Argumentation thus has implications for both rhetoric and philosophy. It is at the center of the activity for rhetoric—the provision of good reasons as an instrument of persuasion. Argumentation shares with philosophy the goal of searching for the truth and the discovery of self. But philosophy differs somewhat from argumentation in its introverted perspective. Both fields depend on argument as the major instrument to sustain their search for truth and discovery of self.

Summary

In Units One and Two we described the nature of argumentation and the specific application of argumentation to academic debate. In this unit, we focused on the relationship of argumentation to liberal education, particularly as a means of better understanding ourselves and others and of serving society as an instrument of decision making. We emphasized the relationships among argumentation, philosophy, and rhetoric.

Arguments can be developed in a rational manner that can serve society in rational decision making. Argumentation has many benefits for both the individual and society. The study of argumentation can help individuals develop their critical thinking; encourage systematic problem solving; assist in the growth of communication skills; nourish the skills with which to make critical judgments, including the practice of choosing among values; and allow self-discovery.

For society, the study and practice of argumentation offers two methods of problem solving, public discussion and public debate. Both rely on the critical examination of the issues, including the consideration of opposing views in various social contexts and in problem areas in which empirical modes of decision making would be ineffective.

Argumentation has a close kinship with both philosophy and rhetoric. From philosophy, argumentation draws its style of inquiry, while at the same time providing philosophy with an epistemological instrument for establishing validity in philosophical argumentation. From rhetoric, argumentation draws its concern for substance and persuasion, while at the same time offering rhetoric the techniques for communicating sound reasons for the acceptance of a position.

Questions for Discussion

1. What are the advantages and disadvantages of the different methods for group decision making discussed in this chapter?
2. We have made several assumptions about the uses of argumentation as a critical instrument. To what degree are they correct?
3. What are the major potential benefits to society and the individual of using argumentation? Besides the examples we mentioned, what are some other social uses of argumentation?
4. What are the main disadvantages to using argumentation as a method of decision making? What types of questions can be answered best through other methods?

5. How is argument used differently in public discussion and in public debate?
6. What problems are there in treating philosophy, rhetoric, and argumentation as distinct fields?
7. What is the relationship between argumentation and critical thinking?

Suggested Readings

Books

Anderson, Jerry M., and Paul J. Dovre, Eds. *Readings on Argumentation.* Boston: Allyn and Bacon, 1968.

> This volume contains thirty-three articles on various fundamental concepts of argumentation and debate. Included are traditional treatment of such aspects as inherency, burden of proof, presumption, evidence, logic and reasoning and ethics in debate. The authors range from ancient speech philosophers to present-day scholars of argumentation.

Barry, Vincent E. *Practical Logic.* New York: Holt, Rinehart and Winston, Inc., 1976.

> A study of the basic elements of logic. The debater should find the sections on sources of information and the nature of probability especially useful.

Branham, Robert J., ed. *The New Debate: Readings in Contemporary Debate Theory.* Washington: Information Research Associates, 1975.

> Seven essays exploring dimensions of the policy-making paradigm of debate.

Brock, Bernard L., James W. Chesbro, John F. Cragon, and James F. Klumpp. *Public Policy Decision Making: Systems Analysis and Comparative Advantages Cases.* New York: Harper and Row, 1973.

> The authors develop the thesis that the practice of contemporary debate is separated from contemporary public policy decision-making theories. The work is designed to illustrate how debaters can bridge that gap.

Campbell, Cole C. *Competitive Debate.* Chapel Hill, N.C.: Information Research Associates, 1974.

> A guide to practical skills involved in intermediate and advanced debate.

Campbell, Stephen K. *Flaws and Fallacies in Statistical Thinking.* Englewood Cliffs, N.J.: Prentice-Hall, Inc., 1974.

> An elementary treatment of the use and misuse of statistics. The book is well illustrated to guide the beginning student of debate in the proper use of statistics.

Clevenger, Theodore, Jr. *Audience Analysis.* Indianapolis: Bobbs-Merrill, 1966.

> A treatise on the role of the audience in effective communication. The volume offers the debater helpful suggestions on adapting ideas to judges.

Crable, Richard E. *Argumentation as Communication: Reasoning with Receivers.* Columbus, Ohio: Charles E. Merrill, 1976.

> This work is a descriptive approach on how argument functions as opposed to an emphasis on argument forms. Several case studies are analyzed.

Crossley, David J., and Peter A. Wilson. *How to Argue: An Introduction to Logical Thinking.* New York: Random House, 1979.

> The work is a traditional approach to the study of argumentation. Deduction is given a lengthy treatment.

Enhinger, Douglas. *Influence, Belief, and Argument.* Glenview, Illinois: Scott, Foresman and Company, 1974.

> A study of argument as a persuasive instrument. The work develops a defense for the use of argument over alternative methods for influencing belief and behavior.

Ehninger, Douglas, and Wayne Brockriede. *Decision by Debate*. 2nd Ed. New York: Dodd, Mead and Co., 1978.
> A basic text for students interested in the study of argument as a method for making collective critical decisions. Emphasis is placed on a person-centered methodology in the art of debating.

Eisenberg, Abne M., and Joseph A. Ilardo. *Argument*. Englewood Cliffs, N.J.: Prentice-Hall, Inc., 1980.
> A descriptive guide to formal and informal debate with a strong emphasis on applied argumentation.

Fogelin, Robert J. *Understanding Arguments: An Introduction to Informal Logic*. New York: Harcourt Brace Jovanovitch, 1978.
> This volume is a textbook for students studying introductory logic. The work includes an analysis of argument as well as examples of argument for analysis.

Freeley, Austin J. *Argumentation and Debate: Reasoned Decision-Making,* 5th Ed. Belmont, Calif.: Wadsworth Publishing Company, Inc., 1976.
> A basic text for undergraduate courses in Argumentation. While the book treats basic principles of argumentative decision making in different contexts, it is basically a textbook for academic debaters.

Geach, P. T. *Reason and Argument*. Berkeley: University of California Press, 1976.
> This work is an introduction to philosophy text. The debater should find its application of logic to various situations useful in understanding the role of reason in argument.

Hospers, John. *An Introduction to Philosophical Analysis,* 2nd Ed. Englewood Cliffs, N.J.: Prentice-Hall, Inc., 1967.
> A study of the meaning and nature of philosophy. Especially useful for the study of argumentation and debate are the sections treating principles of logic and causal reasoning principles.

Jensen, J. Vernon. *Argumentation: Reasoning in Communication*. New York: D. Van Nostrand Company, 1981.
> An elementary textbook which treats the theory and practice of arguing and debating.

Johannesen, Richard L., Ed. *Contemporary Theories of Rhetoric: Selected Readings*. New York: Harper and Row, 1971.
> A collection of essays, many of which deal with the relationship of argumentation to rhetoric.

Johannesen, Richard L. *Ethics in Human Communication*. Wayne, N. J.: Avery Publishing Group, 1978.
> A basic description of perspectives on ethics in communication. Four case studies illustrate the author's points of view.

Katz, William A. *Introduction to Reference Work, Vol. I*. New York: McGraw-Hill Book Co., 1978.
> A description of basic reference works, including such guides as bibliographies, indexing and abstracting sources, government documents, and other reference materials.

Keefe, Carolyn, Thomas B. Harte, and Lawrence E. Norton, Eds. *Introduction to Debate*. New York: The Macmillan Company, 1982.
> A basic textbook in the theory and practice of academic debate. Eleven different authors contribute chapters to the book.

Kraus, Sidney, Ed. *The Great Debates*. Bloomington: Indiana University Press, 1962.
> A series of essays describing the background, perspective and effects of the 1960 presidential debates between John F. Kennedy and Richard Nixon.

Kraus, Sidney, Ed. *The Great Debates: Carter vs. Ford*. Bloomington: Indiana University Press, 1979.
> An analysis of the presidential debates in 1976 between Jimmy Carter and Gerald Ford. The book contains the complete transcripts of the debates.

Lambert, Karl, and William Ulrich. *The Nature of Argument*. New York: The Macmillan Company, 1980.

A textbook for the introductory philosophy course which is applicable to the uses of argument in debate contexts.

McBath, James H., Ed. *Forensics as Communication: The Argumentative Perspective.* Skokie, Ill.: National Textbook Association, 1975.

This collection of essays is the report of the National Developmental Conference on Forensics held in 1974. The volume contains essays by a large number of teachers of debate. The portion of particular concern for the academic debater is the section on "Theory and Practice in Forensics."

McDonald, Daniel. *The Language of Argument,* 3rd Ed. New York: Harper and Row, 1980.

Although structured for courses in English composition, the work should be useful to the student or oral argument. It includes analysis of several argumentative essays.

Mill, John Stuart. *Philosophy of Scientific Method.* New York: Hafner Press, 1950.

Although the examples are somewhat dated, this work remains a very useful treatment of the nature of logic. The debater should find the discussion on causal argument especially useful.

Mill, John Stuart. *Utilitarianism, Liberty and Representative Government.* London: J. M. Dent, 1914.

The classic defense for freedom of speech as a fundamental essential of a free society. Mill also explains how discussion and debate enhance the potential of freedom of speech.

Miller, Gerald R., and Thomas A. Nilsen, Eds. *Perspectives on Argumentation.* Chicago: Scott, Foresman and Company, 1966.

A series of descriptive essays on argumentation covering such aspects as evidence, reasoning, language, and ethics as applied to argument.

Monroe, Alan H. *Principles and Types of Speech,* 8th Ed. Chicago: Scott, Foresman and Company, 1978.

This work is a basic text on the theory and practice of public speaking. Debaters should find the chapters on speech delivery particularly useful in developing vocal variety and effective use of non-verbal communication.

Moore, W. Edgar. *Creative and Critical Thinking.* Boston: Houghton Mifflin Company (1967 edition).

A descriptive study of approaches to effective thinking. The book emphasizes the interaction between creative and critical thinking in problem solving.

Muller, John H., Karl F. Schuessler, and Herbert L. Costner. *Statistical Reasoning in Sociology,* 2nd Ed. Boston: Houghton Mifflin Company, 1977.

A basic book designed for a first course in statistics as especially applied to the social sciences. Students of arguments should find the work useful in helping them understand and use statistical reasoning and methodology.

Munson, Ronald. *The Way of Words: An Informal Logic.* Boston: Houghton Mifflin Company, 1976.

An elementary study of informal logic. Especially useful for the student of debate are the sections dealing with the nature and uses of language, deductive and inductive arguments, fallacies, and uses of the analogy and examples as means of proof.

Natanson, Maurice, and Henry W. Johnstone, Jr., Eds. *Philosophy, Rhetoric and Argumentation.* University Park, Pa.: Pennsylvania State University Press, 1965.

A series of essays describing the interrelationship among philosophy, rhetoric and arguments. Both the similarities and differences in the three disciplines are explored.

Newman, Robert P., and Dale R. Newman. *Evidence.* Boston: Houghton Mifflin Company, 1969.

A well-illustrated treatise on the uses of evidence. Debaters should find it very helpful in understanding the role of evidence in proof, the credibility of evidence, the uses of statistical evidence, evidence sources, and problems and means of establishing the credibility of evidence.

Nilsen, Thomas R. *Ethics of Speech Communication,* 2nd Ed. Indianapolis: Bobbs-Merrill, 1974.

> The author discusses most of the major ethical concerns of the communicator. The student of debate will find much that is applicable to persuasive tactics of debate.

Perelman, Chaim, and L. Olbrechts-Tyteca. *The New Rhetoric: A Treatise on Argumentation.* Notre Dame: University of Notre Dame Press, 1969.

> An extensive, systematic treatise on the role of argumentation in rhetorical activities. The work emphasizes the connection between the ancient tradition of Greek rhetoric and dialectic and argumentation.

Rhodes, Jack, and Sara Newell, Eds. *Proceedings of the Summer Conference on Argumentation.* Falls Church, Va.: Speech Communication Association, 1980.

> This volume consists of twenty-four essays on the general topic of argumentation and the law; argumentation theory and criticism; and argumentation and forensics. The work should be especially useful for the advanced studies in argumentation.

Rieke, Richard D., and Malcolm D. Sillars. *Argumentation and the Decision Making Process.* New York: John Wiley and Sons, Inc., 1975.

> A descriptive undergraduate text for courses dealing with the processes of decision making through the use of argumentation. The work is audience-centered.

Selltiz, Claire, Lawrence S. Wrightsman, and Stuart W. Cook. *Research Methods in Social Relations,* 3rd Ed. New York: Holt, Rinehart and Winston, 1976.

> An elementary study of the processes of information-gathering in the social sciences. The work is especially helpful for the student of debate in helping understand descriptive studies, "causal relationships," problems of measurement, observational methods, questionnaires and interviews and sampling.

Sheehy, Eugene P. *Guide to Reference Books,* 9th Ed. Chicago: American Library Association, 1976.

> An annotated work of reference sources with listings by subject, author and title. Especially helpful in locating sources in foreign countries as well as those in the United States.

Sproule, J. Michael. *Argument Language and Its Influence.* New York: McGraw-Hill Book Co., 1980.

> A textbook for advanced studies in theories of argument.

Thomas, David A., Ed. *Readings in Advanced Debate.* Skokie, Ill.: National Textbook Company, 1975.

> Fifty-three descriptive essays on the theory, practice and teaching of debate. The collection includes a number of in-depth treatments of such concepts as topicality, inherency, significance and decision models.

Toulmin, Stephen. *The Uses of Argument.* New York: Cambridge University Press, 1958.

> A description of a unique model of argument which emphasizes the ways in which people actually process information. The model eliminates the Aristotelian dichotomy between induction and deduction, and emphasizes a guided progression from premises to conclusions.

Toulmin, Stephen, Richard Rieke, and Allan Janik. *An Introduction to Reasoning.* New York: The Macmillan Company, 1979.

> The volume analyzes the Toulmin model for describing argument and applies the model to the criticism of arguments.

Weaver, Richard. *The Ethics of Rhetoric.* Chicago: Henry Regnery, 1953.

> This book addresses the ethical dimensions of all forms of rhetorical discourse. The ethical problems discussed are often present in debating situations.

Wood, Roy V., and Lynn Goodnight. *Strategic Debate.* Skokie, Ill.: National Textbook Company, 1982.

> An elementary textbook on the basic principles of debate as an activity. The authors have a strong emphasis on the strategies and tactics often employed by high school and college debaters.

Ziegelmueller, George W., and Charles A. Dause. *Argumentation, Inquiry and Advocacy.* Englewood Cliffs, N.J.: Prentice-Hall, Inc., 1975.

> An elementary text for students preparing for academic debating. Considerable treatment is also given to the use of argument in other rhetorical situations.

Ziegelmueller, George, and Jack Rhodes, Eds. *Dimensions of Argument: Proceedings of the Second Summer Conference on Argumentation.* Annandale, Va.: Speech Communication Association, 1981.

> Over sixty essays concerning philosophy of argumentation, argument fields, argument in interpersonal communication, and forensics. Some of the essays report recent research and others outline controversial theoretical positions.

Journal Articles

Branham, Robert J. "The Counterplan as Disadvantage." *Speaker and Gavel.* 16 (Summer 1979), 61-66.

> Argues that the ultimate impact of a counterresolution is the same as that of a disadvantage, since the counterresolution argues that affirming the resolution precludes a more desirable choice.

Brockriede, Wayne. "Arguing about Human Understanding." *Communication Monographs.* 49 (September 1982), 137-147.

> A philosophical analysis of the relationship between arguing and the development of understanding.

Brockriede, Wayne. "Characteristics of Arguments and Arguing." *Journal of the American Forensic Association.* 13 (Winter 1977), 129-130.

> A description of the distinctions between arguments and the process of arguing. Argument is described as an activity which proceeds the act of arguing.

Brockriede, Wayne, and Douglas Ehninger. "Toulmin on Argument: An Interpretation and Application." *The Quarterly Journal of Speech.* 46 (February 1960), 44-53.

> A descriptive interpretation of Stephen Toulmin's model of argument as presented in Toulmin's book, *The Uses of Argument.*

Bryant, Donald C. "Rhetoric: Its Functions and Its Scope." *The Quarterly Journal of Speech.* 39 (December 1953), 410-424.

> A restatement of the classical concept of the relationship of argumentation, persuasion and rhetoric.

Burleson, Brant R. "On the Analysis and Criticism of Arguments: Some Theoretical and Methodological Considerations." *Journal of the American Forensic Association.* 15 (Winter 1979), 137-147.

> An examination of distinctions and assumptions underlying methods of argument analysis and criticism. Much emphasis is placed on the characteristics of arguments and pre-suppositions of argument analysis.

Cherwitz, Richard, and James W. Hikins. "Inherency as a Multidimensional Construct: A Rhetorical Approach to the Proof of Causation." *Journal of the American Forensic Association.* 14 (Fall 1977), 82-90.

> The authors treat inherency as the aggregate, or sum total of antecedent causal conditions: motive, institution, implementation, and means. They argue against a unidimensional treatment of inherency.

Chesebro, James W. "Beyond the Orthodox: The Criteria Case." *Journal of the American Forensic Association.* 7 (Winter 1971), 208-215.

> The author describes a theoretical defense of the criteria case as an affirmative case structure. He argues for its increased use in academic debate.

Cox, J. Robert. "Attitudinal Inherency: Implications for Policy Debate." *The Southern Communication Journal.* 40 (Winter 1975), 158-168.

> The author argues that attitudinal inherency imposes a greater burden on an affirmative debater than does structural inherency in demonstrating the adoption, implementation and enforcement of a proposed policy change. These increased burdens are described in detail.

Cox, J. Robert. "A Study of Judging Philosophies of Participants in the National Debate Tournament." *Journal of the American Forensic Association.* 11 (Fall 1974), 61-71.

The author analyzes the judging philosophies of the critics for the 1974 National Collegiate Debate Tournament. The essay gives some helpful hints for debaters in the framing of questions for judge analysis.

Cronkhite, Gary. "The Locus of Presumption." *Central States Speech Journal.* 17 (November 1966), 270-276.

The author argues that presumption should be defined so that the burden of proof always rests with the person who offers an assertion.

Dudczak, Craig A. "Direct Refutation in Propositions of Policy: A Viable Alternative." *Journal of the American Forensic Association.* 16 (Spring 1980), 232-235.

The author argues that direct refutation is an acceptable negative strategy in gaining the rejection of the affirmative resolution. In essence, he argues that a consideration of policy options is impractical when the affirmative has offered inadequate proof for its case.

Ehninger, Douglas. "Argument As Method: Its Nature, Its Limitations and Its Uses." *Speech Monographs.* 37 (June 1970), 101-110.

An essay describing the uses and limitations of argument as an instrument for rational decision making.

Fisher, Walter R. "Toward A Logic of Good Reasons." *The Quarterly Journal of Speech.* 64 (1978), 376-384.

The author argues for a greater emphasis on values as ingredients of arguments. He further seeks to clarify the relationship between logic and "good reasons."

Flaningam, Carl D. "Concomitant vs. Comparative Advantages: Sufficient vs. Necessary Conditions." *Journal of the American Forensic Association.* 18 (Summer 1981), 1-8.

This essay identifies a species of advantage which accompanies the affirmative plan but for which the plan is not necessary, and argues that such advantages do not warrant affirmation of the resolution.

Goodnight, Tom, Bill Balthrop, and Donn W. Parson. "The Problem of Inherency: Strategy and Substance." *Journal of the American Forensic Association.* 10 (Spring 1974), 229-240.

A descriptive essay on the nature and function of inherency. Essentially the authors describe the relationships among the elements of inherency.

Hample, Dale. "The Toulmin Model and the Syllogism." *Journal of the American Forensic Association.* 14 (Summer 1977), 1-8.

A basic criticism of both the values and limitations of the Stephen Toulmin model on the uses of argument. The author questions Toulmin's description of how arguments function in the arguing process.

Henderson, Bill. "A System of Teaching Cross-Examination Techniques." *Communication Education.* 27 (March 1978), 112-118.

The theory and practice of cross-examination are reviewed, and several useful means for teaching and learning cross-examination are presented.

Hynes, Thomas J. "Study: Hope or False Promise?" *Journal of the American Forensic Association.* 16 (Winter 1980), 192-198.

The author discusses the basic assumptions of the study counterresolution, a strategy which calls for further study of a policy before choosing between alternatives. In general, the writer rejects the assumptions behind the approach.

Isaacson, Thomas, and Robert Branham. "Policy Fiat: Theoretical Battleground of the Eighties." *Speaker and Gavel.* 17 (Winter 1980), 84-91.

A thorough examination of the nature of fiat from the perspective of the policy-making paradigm of debate.

Kaplow, Louis. "Rethinking Counterplans: A Reconciliation with Debate Theory." *Journal of the American Forensic Association.* 17 (Spring 1981), 215-226.

The author's thesis is that the counterplan and other negative approaches against the affirmative resolution are theoretically the same approach. He claims that all debates are counterplan debates, and to treat counterplans otherwise results in a distortion of many major concepts in debate, including inherency, solvency, topicality and extra-topicality.

Keeshan, Marjorie, and Walter Ulrich. "A Critique of the Counter-Warrant As A Negative Strategy." *Journal of the American Forensic Association.* 16 (Winter 1980), 199-203.
    This essay is a reply to the negative argument that the adoption of the resolution would also mean the adoption of undesirable examples. The writers describe the theoretical and practical objections to this negative approach.

Kellermann, Kathy. "The Concept of Evidence: A Critical Review." *Journal of the American Forensic Association.* 17 (Winter 1980), 159-172.
    A review of current uses of empirical studies, including a description of methodological faults. The author offers a number of suggestions for improving the methods of gathering and using information.

Lewinski, John D., Bruce R. Metzler, and Peter L. Settle. "The Goal Case Affirmative: An Alternative Approach to Academic Debate." *Journal of the American Forensic Association.* 9 (Spring 1973), 458-463.
    The essay discusses the nature of the goals case as an affirmative option. Approaches are also suggested for the negative for attacking the goals case.

Lichtman, Allan J., Charles Garvin, and Jerry Corsi. "The Alternative-Justification Affirmative: A New Case Form." *Journal of the American Forensic Association.* 10 (Fall 1973), 60-61.
    A defense of the legitimacy of presenting more than one example of a debate resolution as an affirmative case. The authors argue that the affirmative should be permitted to present several examples if they wish, along with alternative plans, and, should they win even one of the examples, it should be sufficient proof that the resolution is probably true.

Lichtman, Allan J., and Daniel M. Rohrer. "A General Theory of the Counterplan." *Journal of the American Forensic Association.* 12 (Fall 1975), 70-79.
    This essay argues for a broader view of the counterplan by the negative in policy debate, particulary in the area of competitiveness.

_____, "The Logic of Policy Dispute." *Journal of the American Forensic Association.* 16 (Spring 1980), 236-247.
    The authors propose an alternative to the traditional view of the counterplan. Their view is based on a policy analysis model as opposed to the problem-solution model.

Matlon, Ronald J. "Debating Propositions of Value." *Journal of the American Forensic Association.* 14 (Spring 1978), 194-204.
    This article explores ways to analyze and to debate nonpolicy resolutions.

Minnick, Wayne. "A New Look at the Ethics of Persuasion." *Southern Speech Communication Journal.* 45 (Summer 1980), 332-362.
    The author presents a perspective for evaluating the ethical dimensions of all types of discourse. He closely aligns ethical concerns with values.

Patterson, J. W. "The Obligations of the Negative in a Policy Debate." *Speech Teacher.* 11 (September 1962), 202-207.
    While admitting that "straight refutation" is a legitimate means of proving the resolution unacceptable, the author argues that a stronger position for the negative is also to defend an option. He claims that it is psychologically more persuasive and offers more enlightenment for audience decision making.

Paulsen, James W., and Jack Rhodes. "The Counter-Warrant As a Negative Strategy: A Modest Proposal." *Journal of the American Forensic Association.* 15 (Spring 1979), 205-210.
    The essay argues that the one-example affirmative, even if desirable, on broad topics ignores the fact that adoption of the resolution also means the acceptance of undesirable examples of the same resolution. The authors claim that such counter-warrants may often justify the rejection of the resolution.

Pfau, Michael. "The Present System Revisited: Part One: Incremental Change." *Journal of the American Forensic Association.* 17 (Fall 1980), 80–84.

    The author argues that traditional defenses of the present system in policy debates are outdated and calls for new approaches in defending existing policy.

————, "The Present System Revisited: Part Two: Policy Interrelationships." *Journal of the American Forensic Association.* 17 (Winter 1981), 146–154.

    This essay explores how changes in one policy may unintentionally affect other, seemingly unrelated policies. It suggests opportunities for disadvantages which the negative might argue.

Rowland, Robert C. "Standards for Paradigm Evaluation." *Journal of the American Forensic Association.* 18 (Winter 1982), 133–144.

    The author criticizes three current paradigms in debate practice: hypothesis testing, policy systems analysis, and the tabula rasa stance. He also presents a set of standards for the evaluation of all paradigms. In the same issue three responses are presented to Rowland's position. These are offered by David Zarefsky, "The Perils of Assessing Paradigms," 141–144; Allan J. Lichtman and Daniel M. Rohrer, "Policy Dispute and Paradigm Evaluations: A Response to Rowland," 145–150; and Walter Ulrich, "Flexibility in Paradigm Evaluation," 151–153. Following the responses, Rowland offers a rejoinder entitled "The Primacy of Standards for Paradigm Evaluation: A Rejoinder," 154–160.

Schunk, John F. "Affirmative Fiat, Plan Communication, and The Process Disadvantage: The Further Ramifications of Pseudo-Inherency." *Speaker and Gavel.* 18 (Spring 1981), 83–91.

    The author argues against the use of several negative strategies which he claims results in a "pseudo-inherency." These strategies are tested in the above title.

Schunk, John F. "A Farewell to Structural Change: The Cure for Pseudo-Inherency." *Journal of the American Forensic Association.* 14 (Winter 1978), 147.

    The author argues that the affirmative defines inherency by reference to the resolution whereas the negative defines inherency by reference to "structural change." Schunk urges that inherency be defined by reference to the resolution, since not all resolutions call for fundamental change in the policy or decision-making process.

Seltzer, Robert V. "The Alternative-Justification Affirmative: Practical and Theoretical Implications." *Journal of the American Forensic Association.* 11 (Winter 1975), 131–156.

    This essay argues against the use of the alternative justification case. The author claims that it introduces too many options for the advocate to treat adequately and for the listener to absorb.

Willard, Charles Arthur. "The Epistemic Functions of Argument: Reasoning and Decision-Making From a Constructionist/Interactionist Point of View." *Journal of the American Forensic Association.* 15 (Winter 1979), 169–191.

    A study of the interactional approach to argument through an explanation of the concepts of "reasoning" and "decision-making."

Zarefsky, David. "The Role of Causal Argument in Policy Controversies." *Journal of the American Forensic Association.* 13 (Spring 1977), 179–191.

    A description of the role of causal argument in policy claims. The essay should help advocates understand the difficulties in establishing links between such concepts as problems in the present system and a proposed change in policy. A thorough description of the types, proof, and reasons for causal claims is explored.

Zarefsky, David. "The Traditional Case-Comparative Advantage Case Dichotomy: Another Look." *Journal of the American Forensic Association.* 6 (Winter 1969), 12–20.

    The author argues that the distinction between the traditional affirmative case and the comparative advantage case is a false dichotomy, and clearly illustrates how the proof requirements for both are the same. He claims that the two approaches differ only in structure, but not in substance.

Index